The 1812
Aponte Rebellion
in Cuba and
the Struggle
against Atlantic
Slavery

# The 1812 Aponte Rebellion in Cuba

Envisioning Cuba
LOUIS A. PÉREZ JR., EDITOR

Matt D. Childs

# and the Struggle against against
# Atlantic Slavery

THE UNIVERSITY OF NORTH CAROLINA PRESS
CHAPEL HILL

© 2006 The University
of North Carolina Press
All rights reserved
Manufactured in the United
States of America

Set in Monotype Dante by
Keystone Typesetting, Inc.

The paper in this book meets the
guidelines for permanence and durability
of the Committee on Production
Guidelines for Book Longevity of the
Council on Library Resources.

Library of Congress Cataloging-in-
Publication Data
Childs, Matt D., 1970–
The 1812 Aponte Rebellion in Cuba and the struggle
against Atlantic slavery / Matt D. Childs.
p. cm. — (Envisioning Cuba)
Includes bibliographical references and index.
ISBN-13: 978-0-8078-3058-1 (cloth: alk. paper)
ISBN-10: 0-8078-3058-5 (cloth: alk. paper)
ISBN-13: 978-0-8078-5772-4 (pbk.: alk. paper)
ISBN-10: 0-8078-5772-6 (pbk.: alk. paper)
1. Slavery—Cuba. 2. Slave insurrections—Cuba.
3. Slavery—America—History. I. Title. II. Title:
Eighteen-twelve Aponte Rebellion in Cuba and the
struggle against Atlantic slavery. III. Series.
HT1076.C55 2006
306.3′62097291—dc22      2006014641

cloth   10 09 08 07 06   5 4 3 2 1
paper   10 09 08 07 06   5 4 3 2 1

THIS BOOK WAS DIGITALLY PRINTED

For my *compañeros*
and *compañeras*
in this world and
the next

For Jamee and my
little buddy for
keeping me whole
and honest

The ultimate mark
of power may be
its invisibility; the
ultimate challenge, the
exposition of its roots.

—MICHEL-ROLPH TROUILLOT,
*Silencing the Past*

People find it difficult
to act on what they
know. To act is to be
committed, and to
be committed is to
be in danger.

—JAMES BALDWIN,
*The Fire Next Time*

To talk revolutions, to
imagine revolutions,
to place oneself
mentally in the midst
of a revolution, is in
some small degree
to become master of
the world. Those who
talk of revolution find
themselves driven to
making them.

—ALEJO CARPENTIER,
*Explosion in the Cathedral*

Memory is a way
of reviving the past,
the dead.

—CHE GUEVARA,
*Reminiscences of the Cuban
Revolutionary War*

# Contents

# Figures and Tables

# Acknowledgments

A first book for any author accumulates many debts. Regrettably, I can only recognize a small portion of all the people who helped me over many years. First and foremost, special thanks go to my parents, Dotty and Tim Childs, who raised me with the important values of hard work and respect for humanity. My only regret is that my mom did not see the publication of my second book. My second probation officer, Steve Doaks, deserves special recognition for stressing (unlike my first probation officer) that I did have some potential and for encouraging me to go to college.

Aline Helg guided and nurtured this study at the University of Texas. The greatest pleasure in working with Aline was the respect and confidence she expressed in my work, all the while, however, encouraging a level of scholarly rigor, thoroughness, and familiarity with the sources.

Numerous faculty members at UT shaped my formation as a historian during my graduate studies. In particular, I would like to recognize Dave Bowman, Bob Olwell, Jim Sidbury, Toyin Falola, Sandra Lauderdale-Graham, Richard Graham, Jonathan Brown, Mauricio Tenorio, and Sonia Labrador-Rodríguez. Equally important to completing my studies were the solidarity and fellowship with graduate students Marc McLeod, Joanna Swanger, John-Marshall Klein, Michele Reid, Alexandra Brown, Hal Langfur, Mike Snodgrass, Sean Kelley, Michele McAtee, Kevin Roberts, Jason Lowery, Saheed Adejumobi, Joel Tishken, Dan Haworth, Russ Lohse, Patrick Timmons, Robert Smale, and Ken Aslakson.

I would also like to thank scholars who shaped this study through interactions at conferences, archives, and e-mail correspondence: João José Reis, Paul Lovejoy, David Eltis, Jane Landers, Rosemary Brana-Shute, Laurent Dubois, Ada Ferrer, David Brion Davis, Seymour Drescher, Mary Karasch,

Stuart Schwartz, Frank Guridy, Jay Kinsbruner, Luz Meña, Ben Vinson, Robert Slenes, Mariana Dantas, Robert Paquette, David Geggus, Philip Howard, Susan Socolow, Ann Twinam, James Sweet, Kirk Shaffer, and Louis A. Pérez Jr.

I would like to thank my colleagues at Florida State University who read drafts of chapters: Maxine Jones, Joe Richardson, Max Friedman, Michael Creswell, Ed Gray, Albrecht Koschnik, Darrin McMahon, Elna Green, Rod Anderson, Robinson Herrera, Pete Ripley, and Sally Hadden. Dick Greaves and especially Neil Jumonville as department chairs fostered both this book and my development as a young scholar and teacher. A particular thanks goes to my *patron*, Rod Anderson, for making that fateful decision of hiring me. I will continue to offer libations in compensation for the many headaches and sleepless nights, but I am still waiting on my meal at Chez Pierre. Robinson Herrera deserves special recognition for our joint efforts to expand the Latin American history program at FSU. For two years Joan Casanovas was an ideal colleague and fellow Caribbeanist before his *patria* called him back home. Dozens of graduate students at FSU helped me shape this study through working with them in reading seminars and serving on their M.A. and Ph.D. committees. In particular, I need to recognize Andrea Vicente, Matt Harrington, and Lindsey Clark, who read chapter 1. A big thanks goes to Sarah Franklin, who read and re-read the entire manuscript, offered keen suggestions for revising the book, and tutored me in SPSS while supported as a research assistant by the History Department.

This study could not have been completed without the generous financial support of several agencies and foundations. The Lydia Cabrera Award given by the Conference on Latin American History and the Graduate Award offered by the Southwest Council of Latin American Studies funded my four months of research in Spanish archives. A group project with John-Marshall Klein, Marc McLeod, and Joanna Swanger funded by the Ford Foundation's program in Social Science Concepts in Area Studies and an award from the Johns Hopkins University / Ford Foundation Latin American Studies Cuba Research Grant allowed me to begin my initial research in Cuban archives. The generous yearlong support of the Fulbright-Hays Committee and the Social Science Research Council / American Council for Learned Societies International Dissertation Field Research Fellowship provided the financial resources to work in Cuba. The University of Florida Libraries provided a summer research grant to work in their excellent collections. The History Department at Florida State University allowed me to teach an overload for four semesters to bank courses to free up two semesters for preparing the manuscript.

Working with historians, institutions, libraries, archives, and *compañeros* in

Cuba fundamentally shaped my interpretation of the Aponte Rebellion. The Instituto de Historia de Cuba generously provided institutional support to sponsor my research. Amparo Hernández, Fé Iglesias García, Gloria García, Mercedes García, Oilda Hevia Lanier, and Oscar Zanetti oriented my study through the Instituto's vast resources. The generous assistance of José Abreu, Angeles Aguilera, Rebeca Calderón, María del Carmen Barcia, Barbara Danzie, Tomás Fernández Robaina, Mireya Durán, Julio López, Jorge Macle, Nancy Machado, Isabel Marino, José Novoa, Marlene Ortega, Eric Pérez, Olga Portuondo, Yoel Rodríguez, Gustavo Sed, and Eugenio Suárez Castro made my research both productive and enjoyable. Special thanks to Leida Fernández, who went far out of her way to welcome me to Cuba and assist my research. My long and multiple conversations with Manuel Barcia Paz at the "Columnata" about slavery in Cuba and the Americas, which routinely went on for hours as we rudely became oblivious to the others around us, will always be treasured. During my research in Cuba I never had to stay in a hotel because of the generosity of families and friends who opened their homes to me.

A special thanks goes to the editorial skills and patience of Elaine Maisner at the University of North Carolina Press for all of her work on this book. Lou Pérez Jr.'s and the anonymous referee's critiques significantly improved and trimmed the manuscript by encouraging me to reduce the four original social and cultural history chapters into two chapters to maintain a clear focus on the Aponte Rebellion.

During the course of this study, Jamee Mallernee became Jamee Childs. Ever since Jamee tracked me down at the Benson Latin American Library in 1996, only my research in Spain, Cuba, Britain, and long conference weekends have kept us apart. Her decision to marry a historian in the middle of his doctoral studies and then to give up her own job and her beloved Texas homeland to move to Florida powerfully testifies to her love and partnership, but not her sensibilities. As with all my other scholarly writings, Jamee has not read this book, but she helped me finish the project by providing the greatest motivation to leave my work, however briefly, and spend time with her. Just as this project was coming to an end, Gustavito entered our lives and nothing will ever be the same. Every day is better than the last because of him. Someday he will learn how we finished the book together during our morning trips to the Bada-Bean coffee shop in Tallahassee.

July 2005

The 1812
Aponte Rebellion
in Cuba and
the Struggle
against Atlantic
Slavery

# Worse than Aponte

On 24 March 1812 Cuban military officer Vicente de la Huerta and three assistants left the fortress of La Cabaña and headed for the free people of color neighborhood of Guadalupe located just outside Havana's city walls. Cuban judicial official Juan Ignacio Rendón ordered Huerta and his aides to search houses "with the greatest thoroughness" for possible clues to a series of slave revolts that had erupted across the island in Puerto Príncipe, Bayamo, Holguín, and Havana during the last two months.[1] A week earlier, Rendón received a special commission from the captain general of Cuba to find "rapidly and promptly" the leaders of the insurrections and end the terrified panic voiced by the white population throughout the island.[2]

The first revolts occurred near the east-central city of Puerto Príncipe two months earlier. Over the course of two days, beginning on 15 January 1812, slaves and free people of color rose in rebellion on five plantations all located within three miles of Puerto Príncipe. The first insurrection began at the plantation Najasa and immediately involved all the slaves. The rebels burnt the master's house, killed three whites, and then spread the movement to neighboring plantations.[3] Within a matter of hours, slaves revolted at the Daganal plantation where they killed the white overseer, Pedro Cabrajal. Then the uprising moved to the San José sugar estate where the insurrectionaries killed two whites. Later, they spread their movement to the Santa Marta plantation where they killed another white and seriously injured two others. The uprising ended at the Montalban plantation where the rebels killed one white and injured another before the local militia, standing army, and armed citizens finally suppressed the insurrection.[4] By the time the rebellions ended, slaves and free people of color had killed eight whites, injured numerous others, and burnt or partially destroyed several plantations. Colonial officials responded to the bold challenge to their authority by staging a public execution. A crowd of spectators greeted with "enthusiasm" the execution of fourteen slaves and the shipment of sixty-three prisoners to Saint Augustine, Florida.[5]

Shortly after the rebellion's suppression, authorities in Puerto Príncipe reported that several "black bandits" had escaped to the mountains where they planned to spread their "terrible movement" to the eastern cities of Bayamo and Holguín.[6] The governor of Puerto Príncipe warned Lieutenant Governor Felix Corral in Bayamo to patrol the countryside for rebels who had eluded capture. Rumors, stories, and reports circulated that as many as "180 of the revolted blacks from Najasa" were heading toward Bayamo, according to one terrified resident.[7] The planned rebellion in Bayamo came to an end on the night of 7 February 1812 when the slave Antonio José informed his master, Lorenzo Vásquez Tamayo, of the uprising.[8] According to the slave, "many blacks from the town and others from elsewhere were going to unite . . . burn various houses . . . block the entrances [to the city] . . . and attack the military headquarters to seize gunpowder, bullets, and rifles."[9] Bayamo's Lieutenant Governor Corral concluded from the interrogations that "the blacks from the Hacienda Najasa in the jurisdiction of Puerto Príncipe had proceeded in agreement with those of this city" when they began the uprising.[10] The discovery in free black José María Tamayo's house of two rebels who escaped capture in Puerto Príncipe provided the crucial evidence of the link between the two rebellions.[11]

Bayamo authorities extended their search for runaway slaves suspected of participating in the conspiracy to Holguín where they believed the fugitives had found refuge.[12] Colonial officials in Holguín decided to "exhaust all preventive measures" and "brought the women from the countryside to the city until the movement has been pacified."[13] The town council of Holguín adopted measures to suppress any possible rebellion and calm the panic of white residents because "nowhere else is an uprising of blacks more feared than in this city."[14] With the imminent threat of rebellion terrifying the white population, judicial officials began to question vigorously any suspected rebels to get to the bottom of the planned insurrection. The suspicion of possible connections with revolts in other towns only increased when a rural patrol arrested three runaway slaves from Puerto Príncipe near Holguín at the end of February.[15] The questioning of numerous slaves and free people of color finally yielded some results when a female slave denounced the rebellion on 11 March.[16]

Despite Captain General Someruelos's assurance in February that the "rebellions had been suppressed," a month later slaves rose again.[17] This time, however, the revolts erupted not in the interior of the island, but "in the

Introduction

outskirts of the capital."[18] On the night of 15 March an insurrection began at the Peñas-Altas sugar plantation involving slaves and free people of color. In a matter of hours, the insurgents razed the entire estate.[19] During the uprising, the rebels killed the technician in charge of refining sugar, his two children, and two white overseers.[20] The insurgent slaves and free people of color then spread their movement by splitting into three groups to attack three nearby sugar plantations: Trinidad, Rosario, and Santa Ana. At the plantation Trinidad, the slave Amador torched the sugar cane once the group from Peñas-Altas arrived.[21] During the course of the uprising at Trinidad, the revolutionaries killed five whites, including the overseer and his family.[22] Before the insurrection could spread to other plantations, the local militia, standing army, and armed citizens successfully "repelled the . . . attack" on the plantations.[23] Shortly thereafter, the rebels dispersed and took refuge in the countryside. Over the next several months, colonial authorities hunted down most of the rebels. Once caught, the government subjected them to trial, punishment, and execution to calm "the outcry of the public."[24]

Information obtained from the interrogations of several individuals implicated in the Havana plantation uprisings led Huerta and his assistants to the house of the free *moreno* (black) José Antonio Aponte, who had been arrested on 19 March 1812.[25] When officials arrived at Aponte's home, they discovered his door locked. Huerta forced Aponte's son Cayetano to unlock the door for authorities to search the residence. Once inside, Huerta and his assistants ransacked the house for items that could serve as evidence of Aponte's role in the rebellions. Huerta discovered that Aponte's house doubled as a workshop where he earned his living as a sculptor. Many of the free and slave artisans of Havana resided in Aponte's neighborhood, where they dominated several of the skilled trades required of a bustling Atlantic port city in the early nineteenth century. Huerta also found evidence of Aponte's military background as captain of Havana's free black militia, including handwritten copies of three *Real Cédulas* (Royal Decrees) spelling out the rights and benefits for militiamen.[26]

In particular, authorities scoured the house for what several of the arrested conspirators had described as a *libro de pinturas* (book of paintings or drawings). Vicente de la Huerta found a "book of various plans and drawings, hidden with clothes in a dresser."[27] The book of drawings contained maps of streets and military garrisons in Cuba; depictions of black soldiers defeating whites; sketches of Aponte's father, grandfather, and Spanish king Carlos III (1759–88); a drawing of George Washington; portraits of black kings from Abyssinia; and episodes in Aponte's own life. Reports that portraits of the Haitian revolutionary leaders Henri Christophe, Toussaint Louverture, Jean François, and Jean-Jacques Dessalines could be found in Aponte's house terrified Cuban authorities, causing them to question hundreds of people. As Cuban officials investigated the rebellions, they learned that Aponte routinely showed the book to members of the free black militia and numerous others during meetings at his house.

Aponte's book of drawings represents the most important document to emerge from the criminal investigation of the movement. His book attracted the close attention of colonial authorities, fascinated and inspired his followers, and has long been sought after by historians. The book of drawings, unfortunately, has yet to be found by scholars. What does exist, however, is the testimony in which Aponte explained the significance of the book to authorities during several eight-hour interrogation sessions.[28] Colonial officials concluded that Aponte used the book of drawings as a blueprint for revolution to illustrate and explain his plans for the rebellion. Military officer Vicente de la Huerta took Aponte's *libro de pinturas* and the other items recovered from his house back to La Cabaña fortress where they provided the basis for the repeated interrogations of numerous individuals allegedly involved in what would become known to history as the Cuban Aponte Rebellion of 1812.[29]

The book of drawings provided all the evidence Juan Ignacio Rendón and his three assistants required to declare José Antonio Aponte the leader of the islandwide rebellion, with which his name has been henceforth associated. Later, when soliciting a new position in the Spanish colonial bureaucracy, Rendón emphasized that he had "discovered the conspiracy" while working day and night at La Cabaña, "taking the confessions and questioning the prisoners" who planned to rise in revolt, "directed by the rebellious José Antonio Aponte." Rendón then moved with what he described as "speed and promptness" to annihilate the rebellion with an "exemplary punishment."[30] The Cuban captain general, the Marqués de Someruelos, repeated "the urgent necessity of imposing without delay a prompt and exemplary punishment" to restore the "disturbed public tranquility." Someruelos decided, in one of his last official acts as Cuban captain general, that he would "present a horrifying example in the gallows" for those who attempt to rise in rebellion. Only two weeks after the search of his house, authorities ended Aponte's life by hanging. Immediately afterward, they displayed his decapitated head in the "most public and convenient location to offer a warning lesson to his followers."[31]

José Antonio Aponte's name first entered history at the exact moment Spanish colonial officials brutally ended his earthly existence. His book of drawings, the voluminous court records, a detailed examination of his followers, as well as his executioners, and other sources scattered in four countries and over two-dozen archives on both sides of the Atlantic, however,

Entrance to La Cabaña military fortress. José Antonio Aponte and other slaves and free people of color were questioned and imprisoned at La Cabaña for participating in the rebellions near Havana. Photograph by Matt D. Childs.

La Cubaña military fortress. Photograph by Matt D. Childs.

Prison cell at La Cabaña military fortress. Photograph by Matt D. Childs.

reveal that his short-lived rebellion tells a much broader story. When the investigation concluded, notaries recorded over 6,000 pages of testimony. The size of the trial transcript speaks volumes to the Aponte Rebellion's challenge to Spanish rule in Cuba and the numerous people involved. The voluminous testimony from the Aponte Rebellion, recording the normally voiceless and illiterate speaking boldly in their own defense to explain their own actions, provides the core source of documents for my study of the movement.

Criminal and inquisitorial records, described by historian Carlo Ginzburg as "archives of repression," provide one of the few sources available to scholars that record the lives, experiences, thoughts, and transcribed spoken words of people who rarely left their own historical documents.[32] While court testimony provides numerous insights into the consciousness of historical actors, however, they also present several problems. For example, judicial official Juan Ignacio Rendón emphasized that Francisco Javier Pacheco and José del Carmen Peñalver had claimed that free black Hilario Santa Cruz joined the movement in their last confessions before execution. Rendón stressed the validity of their statements testifying to Hilario Santa Cruz's participation in the revolt because the deponents gave them immediately prior to their execution, perhaps with the intention to confess their sins before meeting their maker. Rendón then asked Hilario Santa Cruz if he thought it was "possible for a man to lie knowing his life was going to end?" Hilario craftily responded that Pacheco and Peñalver lied because "it would not be strange if they had been possessed by the devil in those [final] moments" because they had such "evil" thoughts of rebellion. Hilario skillfully denounced all the evidence and testimony against him as unreliable since it came from diabolically inspired insurgents.[33] Likewise, a slave arrested and questioned for participating in the Haitian Revolution also claimed that he was not responsible for rebellious actions because it " 'is the devil who gets inside of this body of mine.' "[34] Strikingly, time and again, slaves and free people of color asserted themselves in responding to questions in ways that clearly reveal judicial officials did not always succeed in soliciting the information they desired.

The answers to questions by lawyers had multiple points of inspiration reflecting fear, honesty, and deception. Trial testimony—especially from an insurrection by slaves and free people of color with the goal of ending slavery and Spanish colonialism—was always taken under duress.[35] Few people involved in the Aponte Rebellion would have been at ease in front of a judge providing answers to questions that would determine whether they would live or die. Actual physical force, threat of force, or the fear of the possible use of force had to inform the answers to some, if not all, of the questions put to the suspected rebels. The degree of separation and mediation from the actual response to the trial record is revealed by the testimony that is recorded not in the first person, "I said," but the third person, "he or she said." I share historian Richard Boyer's belief that trial testimony should not be "transposed back to direct speech, but nevertheless remain confident that just below the surface of notarial convention (possibly with some elisions at times) lie the individual voices."[36]

The brutal execution of the leaders and the physically damaging punishments meted out to slaves on a regular basis provide every reason to believe judicial officials employed torture as a coercive technique in their questioning of the rebels. The trial testimony, however, does not record the cries of pain or the pleas of mercy by the deponents. Having consulted only a small portion of the published trial transcript of the Aponte Rebellion, and none of the archival sources, Stephan Palmié somewhat naively suggests by deduction that "a quest for truths" by his interrogators may have resulted in them concluding that the facts "could only be gained from the man [Aponte] if they preserved his bodily and psychological integrity."[37]

The coercive power of the state rarely leaves evidence of its own abuses, whether under Spanish colonial control in Havana or twenty-first-century American imperial power in Guantánamo Bay in the name of the so-called war on terror. Beyond the court record, however, evidence exists which likely indicates the use of torture. Correspondence between military prisons and hospitals authorizing the transfer of rebels for medical treatment after being questioned almost certainly attests to extreme physical coercion.[38] Puerto Príncipe governor Francisco Sedano was forced to replace one lawyer in charge of interrogating the rebels for what he described as the deponents "not being in the best of health" after questioning.[39] In the cases where torture appears obvious, I have not employed the testimony for my analysis, or I have used the information with extreme caution.

Authorities also had incentives to restrict their coercive techniques. A dead deponent could not provide any information. Moreover, Rendón insisted that one of the leaders scheduled for execution should be given "nutritious food, spirits, and a comfortable bed" to aid his convalescence prior to hanging.[40] A weak, frail, humble rebel at a public execution could send the message that powerless and feeble insurgents had almost overthrown the government, revealing colonial officials' tenuous rule over the island. Further, the execution of a visibly injured revolutionary could perhaps generate sympathies among spectators that might rapidly convert the insurgent into a martyr.

Slaves and free people of color interrogated for their suspected involvement in the Aponte Rebellion realized that not only their answers but, just as importantly, the statements by others against them would determine their guilt or innocence. Free black Francisco Javier Pacheco creatively attempted to discover from his prison cell what his fellow rebels said about his role in the insurrection. While held in prison, his brother Manuel regularly visited him and brought him additional food and news of the investigation. Authorities later discovered that when Manuel delivered food to his brother he sent him "notes sewn into the corner of a tablecloth," to inform him about the people who provided testimony against him.[41] Francisco Javier relayed information from his prison cell back to his brother Manuel about the investigation via folded notes hidden in "cloth napkins and inside loafs of [unfinished] bread" that he returned to his brother after their brief visits.[42] In the note intercepted by prison guards, Francisco Javier advised Manuel to discover information about "my case with the notary Don Juan de Dios Corona," the legal official in charge of transcribing the court testimony.[43] Francisco Javier instructed his brother to obtain a copy of the court testimony in order to help him prepare for his interrogation by learning of prior testimony against him. Once authorities learned of the information that passed between the two brothers, they concluded it indicated Francisco Javier's guilt and promptly sentenced him for execution.

Slaves and free people of color realized that they played an active role in creating the trial record and, by extension, the historical documents I have employed to write the history of the Aponte Rebellion. In this sense, they not only attempted to write their own history through the bold action of insur-rection but also influenced how that history would and could be told by later historians.

THE APONTE REBELLION of 1812 represents a crucial episode in early nineteenth-century Cuban history, when the initial development of the sugar-plantation economy transformed the island from its long established role as a port of call for ships trading in the Atlantic, to the most prized colony in the rapidly disintegrating Spanish empire. In 1789, the Spanish Crown declared free trade in slaves throughout the empire.[44] No colony in Spanish America capitalized on the decree more than Cuba. While a scholarly consensus has yet to emerge over exact figures, historians appear to agree that from 1790 to 1820 at least 300,000 slaves entered Cuba, if not more. The massive importa-tion of slaves and the radical transformations in Cuban society are all the more apparent given that in the previous 280 years only 100,000 slaves had been imported into the island. In the span of thirty years, the overall volume of the entire history of the Atlantic slave trade to Cuba had increased three-fold.[45] The figure of 300,000 slaves in thirty years is even more staggering when compared to the United States, which imported roughly 400,000 slaves during its entire history. The expansion of slavery during the last decade of the eighteenth century and the first decades of the nineteenth century caused radical social, political, economic, and cultural transformations of Cuban society; these changes, in turn, gave birth to the 1812 Aponte Rebellion.

Ever since the leaders' executions in 1812, the Aponte Rebellion has been regarded as an important event in Cuban history. Stories about the insurrec-tion circulated immediately following the movement's suppression, making it a common and well-known event in Cuban popular consciousness. One year later, Antonio Valdés included a discussion of the Aponte Rebellion in his book *Historia de la isla de Cuba*.[46] Cuba's foremost novelist of the nineteenth century, Cirilo Villaverde—the son of a doctor who lived on a Cuban sugar plantation born in the same year as the Aponte Rebellion—included a discus-sion of the movement in his novel *Cecilia Valdés* (1839). Regarded by many literary scholars as the most important Cuban work of fiction from the nineteenth century, the novel powerfully addresses slavery and Spanish colo-nialism. The author recognized how the memory of the Aponte Rebellion served to limit the aspirations of white Cuban creoles to fight for indepen-dence. According to Villaverde, "There still remained, the vague if not sad recollections of past conspiracies. All that survived of the revolt of 1812 was the name of the rebel leader, Aponte, for whenever they wished to describe some wicked or abominable person, the old women would exclaim: 'Worse than Aponte!' "[47] Later in the novel, Villaverde has one of the characters repeat the common phrase again as an insult: " 'You're worse than Aponte,' as my grandmother used to say."[48]

Historians began to study the Aponte Rebellion during the last decades of the nineteenth century, motivated by the need to find historical roots for the Cuban wars of independence. When the first sustained war against Spanish colonialism, known as the Ten Years War, began in 1868, Spaniard Justo Zaragoza wrote a two-volume history of insurrections in Cuba to flesh out the origins of the anticolonial movement. Zaragoza noted that the legacy of the Aponte Rebellion remained fresh in Cuban minds through the "adage 'worse than Aponte' that is still used to indicate wicked people."[49] In 1894, José de Jesús Márquez, a well-known writer with a reputation for defending the interests of Cuba's working class, published a brief article based on published primary documents, which he partially reprinted at the end of his article. Márquez focused on Aponte and "the revolutionary junta of Havana that communicated by emissaries with subaltern juntas, and these then transmitted the plans to centers established in all points of the island." Márquez's description of the "revolutionary juntas" more accurately described the formation of the Cuban Revolutionary Party in 1892 to coordinate the independence movement than it did the Aponte Rebellion of 1812. As did so many historians who would follow him, Márquez simply stated these networks extended throughout the island but did not demonstrate how they operated.[50]

After Cuban independence had been achieved, Aponte and his rebellion captured the attention of novelist and intellectual Francisco Calcagno. One of the most influential scholars of the late nineteenth century, Calcagno studied Cuba's past to construct a unified national identity through writing novels and memoirs and compiling Cuba's first biographical dictionary in 1878.[51] Calcagno exemplified the conservative abolitionism of many white Cuban intellectuals who favored neither immediate emancipation nor strengthening human bondage.[52] For Calcagno, Aponte represented the nightmare of black rule that terrified intellectuals of the infant Cuban republic as they constructed the nation's identity in their preferred image. According to Calcagno, "Aponte endeavored to found a black empire on the ruins of a white colony, proclaiming himself Emperor in the manner of Dessalines or Christophe . . . and this would be obtained by assassinating all the white males and leaving the white females for domestic service and other uses."[53] After reading Calcagno's harsh portrayal of Aponte explicitly designed as a historical novel to strike more fear in the reader of the real possibility of a "black empire," few readers would have been able to repeat the popular phrase "worse than Aponte." After Calcagno had finished with Aponte, nobody could have been described as "worse than Aponte."[54]

Few topics related to the study of Afro-Cuban history and culture escaped the interests of Fernando Ortiz, Cuba's foremost anthropologist and perhaps the most influential Cuban social scientist of the twentieth century. Aponte was no exception. Ortiz's scholarship served to legitimate Afro-Cuban studies through his concept of "transculturation" that stressed that both the Spaniard and the African formed the Cuban national character, although he clearly preferred the former and pejoratively described the latter.[55] Ortiz did not analyze Aponte's movement with the purpose of explaining the origin of the phrase "worse than Aponte," which had preoccupied other scholars. Rather, he regarded the insurrection and other revolts as a strong commitment on the part of slaves to gain their freedom.[56] Ortiz's scholarship and his prominence as an author and intellectual validated the importance of the Aponte Rebellion for Cuba's past, providing an opportunity for other scholars to take the study in different directions.

The triumph of the Cuban Revolution in 1959 furnished a powerful purpose for studying history. After the revolution turned Marxist, an examination of the Cuban past required finding the origins and precursors to explain Fidel Castro's victory. "Indeed," as historian Louis Pérez Jr. has written, "the national past served as a major source of moral subsidy, conferring on the process of revolution a sense of continuity out of which was derived the claim to legitimacy."[57] Moreover, Antoni Kapcia has emphasized that the 1960s' historiographical emphasis on Cuba's revolutionary past "now gave the Revolution much of its historical legitimacy, direction and purpose."[58] Several black scholars and intellectuals seized upon the image of Aponte and his movement to assert the important role of Afro-Cubans in their country's past. Study groups formed in Havana where Afro-Cubans met to discuss and debate the contemporary problems of racism and their historical roots.[59] Out of these reunions, a group headed by Juan René Betancourt published a workbook that devoted an entire chapter to "José Antonio Aponte a martyr and hero denied and forgotten" by history. He argued that Aponte's abilities as a "conspirator and organizer" offered them the lessons of unity necessary for a "revolutionary cause" by his ability to bring together "not only the rural and urban slaves, and not only the different antagonistic African tribes, but also the mestizos and the free people of color."[60]

The black intellectual Walterio Carbonell also seized upon Aponte to make a radical argument about the origins of Cuban national identity. According to Carbonell, Cuban identity and culture (encapsulated in the term *cubanidad*) did not originate with the founding fathers José Antonio Saco, Domingo del Monte, Felix Varela, and Francisco Arango y Parreño who had long been placed in the nation's pantheon by hagiographers. Carbonell argued from a class perspective that Cuban culture originated with the masses and that, in the early nineteenth century, slaves and free people of color represented the revolutionary masses. Aponte acted as the political leader of the African masses who converted their "religious organizations" into a "true political" force.[61] Despite the radical transformations and the rhetoric of the 1959 Cuban Revolution, replacing the fathers of the nation with the black revolutionary Aponte asked for too much. The works of Carbonell, Betancourt, and others quickly disappeared from circulation.[62] Still, the Revolution did embrace the Aponte Rebellion as a historical link with the political struggle of 1959. The weekly revolutionary publication *Bohemia* celebrated the 150th anniversary of Aponte's movement in 1962 by portraying him as a precursor to the 1959 revolution.[63]

The Aponte Rebellion finally received its first and only book-length historical treatment with the publication in 1963 of the fifty-six-page *La conspiración de Aponte* by mulatto José Luciano Franco.[64] A prolific writer and historian, Franco nearly lived to be a centenarian (1891–1989). According to an autobiographical letter from his personal papers, Franco stated: "I owe my ability to read and write to my mother . . . [as] there were no schools for the children of workers during the Spanish colonial period."[65] By the age of fifteen, Franco worked in the tobacco industry and became involved in the labor movement. During the 1920s he went into exile in the United States for his political opposition to the Machado dictatorship that likely influenced his concern with American racial problems and their similarities and differences with Cuban ones.[66] In the 1930s, he began his career as a historian by working for Emilio Roig de Luechsenring, the "Historian of the City of Havana." Franco participated in scholarly discussions about Cuban history with Juan Gualberto Gómez, Fernando Ortiz, and Joaquín Llaverías at the Hotel Ambos Mundos, which Ernest Hemingway made internationally famous with his inspired writing and drinking there around the same time period. During the late 1930s, Franco began working at the Cuban National Archive and played a leading role in the direction of such scholarly organizations as Sociedad de Estudios Afrocubanos and Sociedad Cubana de Estudios Históricos e Internacionales.[67]

The common thread that runs through many of Franco's numerous publications is an interest in slavery, race relations, and what he specifically mentioned as the "rebelliousness of Afro-Cubans."[68] Franco led a new generation of Cuban historians into the archives where he spent long hours working almost exclusively with manuscript sources. Franco also used what he referred to as the "popular tradition maintained in the [Havana] neighborhood of Pueblo Nuevo" for his study of the Aponte Rebellion.[69] Consulting many, but not all, of the judicial records housed at the Cuban National Archive, Franco placed Aponte as the forefront leader of the movement that had the political goals of ending slavery and destroying Spanish colonialism. Franco took certain liberties in constructing the narrative and focused too narrowly on Aponte as the leader, which I will address in subsequent chapters. Overall, though, Franco correctly identified the basic events, plans, and goals of the movement. Cuban revolutionary intellectuals such as Roberto Fernández Retamar praised the book for being "written with the seriousness and passion that your admirers have come to know from many years of scholarship."[70] Franco's narrative of the Aponte Rebellion became incorporated into primary and secondary school texts as a political movement with an "advanced and revolutionary character" that understood "to accomplish abolition it was necessary to struggle for independence."[71] In 1977, the publishing house of the Cuban Revolution, the Editorial de Ciencias Sociales, issued a twenty-four-page abbreviated version of Franco's 1963 study along with 180 pages of documents in a small pocket-size paperback edition intended for massive distribution.[72] Franco's work had firmly placed Aponte in the antechamber to the 1959 revolutionary pantheon.

Ever since Franco's initial study appeared in 1963, no other scholar has focused exclusively on the Aponte Rebellion and worked through the documents in Cuban archives. Studies that feature the Aponte Rebellion in histories of Cuba largely follow Franco's pioneering study to serve two broad purposes. The Aponte Rebellion is often cited as an example of slave and free people of color insurrection.[73] Or, the Aponte Rebellion is used to show that the fear of slave revolution checked the desires for independence among white creoles while the rest of Spanish America struggled for liberation.[74] Historians Gloria García, Philip Howard, and Alain Yacou have conducted archival research in Cuba and featured the Aponte Rebellion in their studies, but they have not diverted or departed from Franco's analysis.[75] Literary scholar Sibylle Fischer analyzed Aponte's explanation of his book of drawings to provide keen insights into how he appropriated the ideas of the Haitian Revolution and placed them in a Cuba setting.[76] Stephan Palmié's detailed examination of Aponte's book of drawings relies exclusively on Franco's printed testimony and raises new and important questions, but he consciously avoids making any conclusion and even states that "such an answer to the question, What in the world is Palmié trying to argue? is not just unproductive, but ultimately arrogant." Consequently, Palmié purposely offers a series of deductive speculations that focus on Aponte the artist, and not the rebellion that bears his name.[77] My study of the Aponte Rebellion builds upon the pioneering work of Franco, yet explores the actions and motivations of not just Aponte but those of his followers as well.

I have situated my study of the Aponte Rebellion within the literature that examines the motivating forces behind slave and free people of color rebellion during the Age of Revolution. While masters, slaves, and free people of color in Cuba recognized the powerful symbol of the Haitian Revolution in igniting insurrection, scholars have yet to reach a consensus on this subject. Historians tend to share David Brion Davis's conviction that the "Haitian Revolution was indeed a turning point in history."[78] However, scholars disagree over for what and for whom it was a turning point. Eugene Genovese has shaped the scholarly debate by arguing that the Haitian Revolution brought about a decisive change in the history of slave revolts from maroon runaways who rebelled against enslavement to revolutionary movements aimed at societal reorganization through the destruction of slavery as a system.[79] Michael Craton and Michael Mullin recognize the qualitative differences in the overall character of slave resistance during the Age of Revolution from runaways to revolution but argue the change is a result of the dual process of closing the frontier and the demographic shift in the slave population from African to creole.[80] Whereas some scholars argue ideology is the driving force behind slave and free people of color revolution based upon natural rights, others have argued creolization explains the increase in rebellion.

The scholarly debate has been extremely productive in prompting historians to examine revolts and conspiracies throughout the Caribbean and Atlantic world during the Age of Revolution. Few scholars have published as widely on the topic as historian David Geggus. He concludes that abolitionism, not the ideology of the French and Haitian Revolutions, most frequently stimulated rebellion. Moreover, Geggus argues that the most receptive audience to the ideology of natural rights was not slaves but free people of color.[81] Julius Scott has examined slave revolts in the 1790s to conclude that the Haitian Revolution represented "A Common Wind" that connected rebels across national, linguistic, ethnic, and geographic boundaries in their resistance to slavery.[82] Robert Paquette has strongly asserted that the divisions between African and Creole forms of resistance argued by Craton and Mullin or the distinctions drawn between abolitionist and French Revolutionary ideology by Geggus "simply will not do." Paquette insists, "African-born slaves and American-born slaves, privileged slaves and field hands, blacks and mulattoes, slaves and free people of color, slave men and slave women could at a specific historical moment under a common experience of oppression come together to attack a common target."[83] The Aponte Rebellion offers a critical case to analyze what role the ideas from the Age of Revolution, and the Haitian Revolution in particular, played in catalyzing slave and free people of color revolts in the Americas.

Scholarly work linking cultural, ethnic, and ideological changes in slave regimes to causative arguments about the forms and functions of slave resistance has greatly broadened our overall understanding of the dynamic nature of slavery and provided a useful narrative framework to connect studies spread across geographic and chronological boundaries. These works, however, have also shown certain limitations. By focusing on African versus Creole or rebellion versus revolution, scholars have largely emphasized the structural and ideological aspects of slave societies. These approaches tend to discount the activities of the slaves and free people of color themselves precisely at the moment when they most powerfully demonstrated action by their own accord. Anthropologist Sidney Mintz has called for studies of slave resistance that move away from broad structural and ideological explanations toward a more detailed understanding of the historical specificity and context of a revolt as a way of comprehending the immediate concerns, aspirations, and agency of the rebels.[84] My analysis attempts to answer the "challenge" that historian Laurent Dubois identifies facing scholarly analysis of slave rebellion: "The challenge is to write an account that places the Caribbean people of African descent, both free and enslaved, at the heart—rather than on the margins—of the political and intellectual transformations of the age."[85]

EACH CHAPTER OF THIS STUDY explores a different dimension of the Aponte Rebellion and the revolutionaries involved to situate the revolt and its larger significance within multiple contexts. The introductions to all the chapters of this book begin with the execution of someone involved in the movement. This is done to structure the analysis and narrative of the rebellion and to emphasize the extreme odds and dangers the revolutionaries knew they faced. I have also begun with executions to address the concerns of several historians who have identified a recent trend in slave studies that ignores or minimizes the "brutalization of slaves." According to African American historian Robert Harris, one of the consequences "in large measure, [of] our zeal in examining the agency of the oppressed has deflected attention from the actions of the oppressors."[86] Scholars of slavery such as Herbert Aptheker, Alice Bauer, and Raymond Bauer pioneered the history-from-below approach in the 1940s that focused on the quotidian agency of slaves through what they described as "Individual Acts of Resistance" and "Day to Day Resistance to Slavery."[87] Recently, this approach has gained a wide audience without recognizing its historiographical origins. Scholars influenced by the work of James Scott and what he labels "weapons of the weak" have deftly argued that social relations are constantly reworked, making it important to recognize small acts such as foot dragging, dissimulation, false compliance, pilfering, feigned ignorance, slander, arson, poisoning, and sabotage as effective forms of resistance. As a result of such an approach, scholars now know more about the "everyday forms of resistance" by peasants, slaves, and the working class that paved the way for larger events such as rebellion. However, recent scholarship has not sufficiently emphasized the unequal power relations common to all slave societies.[88]

By structuring each chapter to begin with an execution, the purpose is not to emphasize the defeat of the Aponte Rebellion. The important story of all revolts and conspiracies involving slaves and free people of color in the diaspora is not why they failed or why they did not rebel more often, as some scholars ignorant of the power relations that operated on plantations once asked.[89] Oppression in and of itself does not produce what E. P. Thompson mockingly labeled "spasmodic" impulses to rebel, in reference to scholars who explained English riots by hunger pangs.[90] The major focus of my analysis of the Aponte Rebellion is to explain the operation of social, cultural, and political processes whereby free people of color and slaves, the rural and urban populations, Africans of diverse ethnicities such as Kongos, Minas, and Mandingas, and men and women made the decision to put their risky plans of liberation into action. My study analyzes the event known as the 1812 Aponte Rebellion to engage in what cultural historian Robert Darnton has methodologically labeled "incident analysis." My work shares a common historiographical approach with a growing body of literature that "focuses on an incident, relates it as story, and then follows its repercussions through the social order" to delve into the lives, motivations, and actions of the people involved in the event.[91] In reconstructing the event, my goal is to contribute a cultural history from below to rectify that "the study of mentalities" is "without a doubt, the field least developed within Cuban social historiography," according to Cuban historian Oscar Zanetti.[92]

The first chapter charts the Atlantic worlds of the Caribbean, Europe, Africa, and the Americas to examine the contradictory forces landing in Cuba from the Age of Revolution that heralded individual liberty at the exact moment when racial slavery expanded and intensified across the island. Cuban slavery and sugar cane cultivation expanded at a precarious moment in the world history of slavery. The Age of Revolution that inspired radical political changes in Europe and wars for independence in the Americas ushered in the beginning of the end for Atlantic slavery. Cuban masters recognized the global trends in slavery and attempted to insulate the island from the radical ideas crisscrossing the Atlantic as a strategy of self-preservation. Slaves and free people of color also knew about the larger transformations operating outside of Cuba and the possibility for radical changes. The contradictions generated by the dramatic increases in sugar production and slave labor precisely when the institution of slavery came under question provided the political opening for the 1812 Aponte Rebellion.

In order to understand the background of slaves and free people of color

Introduction

involved in the rebellion, and more broadly the social and cultural worlds they lived in, chapter 2 focuses on the transformations in Cuban society caused by the massive importation of slaves. Although slavery in Cuba dates to the early 1500s, by 1800 the institution had been completely transformed, drawing new and increasingly rigid lines of hierarchy and social division. The dramatic increase in slave imports and the expansion of plantation agriculture transformed Cuba into a racialized plantation society. Racial identity ever more rigidly defined the barriers of inclusion for the white population of European ancestry and exclusion for the black population of African ancestry. The new plantation society, however, did not immediately eclipse the previous forms of social relations that historically shaped interactions between masters, slaves, and free people of color. Ironically, the expansion of plantation agriculture worked by slave labor provided economic opportunities for manumission. By working on weekends, marketing goods, participating in contraband trade, and performing services that whites (either by their absence or choice) would not do, slaves earned money to buy their freedom. Yet, the same economic transformations that presented opportunities for freedom also set strict limitations on the meaning of liberty for free people of color. The rise of a racialized plantation society in the 1790s corroded the special niche and limited privileges that free men and women of African ancestry previously enjoyed in Cuba's hierarchical society. The expansion of slavery made the distinction between the free population of white European ancestry and the enslaved population of black African ancestry all the more clear, and the contradictory position of free people of color such as Aponte ever more apparent.

The next chapter investigates the rebels' worlds by focusing on organizations that proved instrumental in planning the rebellion: the militia and mutual aid societies. Spain fielded the free men of color militia to compensate for the lack of able-bodied white soldiers to protect the island from European rivals and pirate attacks. The militia could trace its origins to the sixteenth century and had long served as a distinct corporate body that provided social mobility for free men of color. The dramatic increase in slave labor and the expansion of plantation agriculture in the 1790s served to dilute the distinctions and privileges of militia service. In a hierarchical society of stratified orders, the black and mulatto militia provided essential assistance against foreign invasions and maintained domestic stability. In the racialized plantation society of the late eighteenth and early nineteenth centuries, however, the militia came under attack by colonial officials as a possible ally for slaves. Aponte and others decided to turn their military training in the service of Spanish colonialism into a weapon to destroy it. The militia provided crucial access to arms and weapons necessary for the rebellion to be a success.

The camaraderie of soldiers and their elevated social and economic position within their own community presented them as leaders to unite the free and enslaved populations of African ancestry.

The issue of racial and ethnic identity is examined through the African based fraternal societies known as *cabildos de nación*. These organizations united both free people of color and slaves who shared a common linguistic, cultural, and geographic heritage rooted in Africa. *Cabildos de nación* provided services, such as education, artisanal training, housing, loans, burials, festival celebrations, and even purchased freedom for enslaved members. People of African ancestry in Cuba chose to join these associations to define themselves in cooperation with others who shared a similar ethnicity. In this sense, these organizations show the importance of understanding that Africans in the Americas did not immediately or exclusively adopt a racialized identity of blackness. Although notions of blackness and whiteness undoubtedly represent the most important legacy of slavery in the New World, they cannot be considered the single defining characteristic from the very beginning or even as late as the nineteenth century. *Cabildos* offered a limited sense of autonomy from master control and independence from the supervision of colonial authorities that free people of color and slaves utilized to organize their insurrection. Several of the leaders of the Aponte Rebellion participated in *cabildo* functions and employed the societies to plan the revolts.

Chapter 4 turns to narrative history by providing a detailed account of the revolts that spread across the island from the east-central city of Puerto Príncipe to the eastern towns of Bayamo and Holguín to the capital of Havana in the west. The battlefields of the Aponte Rebellion spread over 500 miles, qualifying it as one of the most extensively planned revolts in the Americas. In particular, the chapter assesses whether the revolts and denounced conspiracies truly represented one coordinated movement or several separate rebellions.

Chapter 5 explores the ideological influences on the rebellion through an analysis of how emancipation rumors and the Haitian Revolution served as a radicalizing and unifying force for the rebels. Free people of color and slaves involved in the Aponte Rebellion called upon images of the Black Republic to give meaning and guidance to their own forms of resistance. The voluminous testimony from the Aponte Rebellion provides an unusual glimpse into the multiple meanings of the Haitian Revolution for slaves and free people of color. The Haitian Revolution became interwoven into a rumored monarchical decree of abolition on the eve of the Aponte Rebellion. The liberating monarch, however, confounded authorities tracking down the rumors as he took the form of the kings of Spain, Britain, Haiti, and the Kongo. The conclusion places the Aponte Rebellion within a hemispheric context of slave revolts and uses the insights from the movement to analyze the anomaly of Cuban loyalty to Spain while the Latin American colonies struggled for their independence from 1808 to 1830.

We now turn to an examination of the multiple contexts of the rebels' lives by analyzing the Atlantic World they inhabited during the era of the Aponte Rebellion.

# 1

## The Present Time Period Is Very Delicate

Cuban Slavery and the
Changing Atlantic World,
1750–1850

On the morning of 9 April 1812, a crowd of spectators gathered next to the military fort of La Punta, which to this day guards the western entrance to the Bay of Havana. Men, women, and children waited for the public execution of the conspirators who had attempted to overthrow Spanish colonialism and destroy Cuban slavery. According to the island's captain general, the crowd responded to the execution of the leaders "with applause from the public who desired the quick satisfaction of repressing the [movement], and [it] provided an example to others of the horror of their excess."[1] Among those on the execution scaffold with José Antonio Aponte, the leader of the rebellion, stood a free black named Juan Barbier. After inflicting a painful death by hanging, the executioner severed Barbier's head from his body. Colonial authorities then placed Barbier's head in a steel cage, secured it to the top of a pole, and placed it at the entrance to the Peñas-Altas plantation outside of Havana where the revolt had erupted on 16 March 1812.[2]

While judicial figures quickly, confidently, and authoritatively executed Barbier, privately they revealed their anxiety in attempting to identify Barbier and his specific role in the rebellion. Like the millions who shared the same tragic distinction of being part of the largest forced migration in human history, Juan Barbier crossed the Atlantic Ocean as a slave, undoubtedly with a different name. After his arrival in the Americas, unlike the vast majority who would die laboring on plantations, he managed to gain his freedom. Judicial officials could not determine how and when Barbier earned his freedom. They did suggest, however, that he had lived in Charleston, South Carolina, and concluded that he had spent considerable time in the former French colony of Saint Domingue where he learned how to read, write, and speak French before settling in Cuba.[3] His identification with the former

French colony only recently transformed into the independent republic of Haiti by slave revolution terrified authorities and caused them to investigate further.

Several slaves and free people of color questioned for their involvement in the rebellion had singled out Barbier as one of the leaders. Clemente Chacón, a free black from Havana, identified Barbier as "an admiral who has served in Haiti and demonstrated papers written in French."[4] Tiburcio Peñalver, a slave from a plantation outside of Havana, reported a similar story that Barbier "said he was a general and read some papers declaring [that] by order of his King, he had come to give the blacks their freedom."[5] Another slave from the same plantation told judicial authorities that, during a meeting where they discussed the rebellion, "Barbier took out some French papers and read them in his language saying he would explain them later."[6] José Joaquín Machado, a slave of Maca ethnicity from the Lower Guinea region, encountered Barbier on the road leading from Havana to the plantations outside the city. Barbier told José to prepare for the rebellion because "two generals from Haiti had come to Cuba to aid the rebellion."[7] Several of the arrested recalled seeing Barbier dressed in a "blue military jacket," mounted on a horse, and greeting slaves with "camarada, como va? [comrade, how is it going?]."[8] Barbier's image of a military figure speaking and reading in French resonated with slaves and free people of color in Cuba as a crucial event in the preparation for the rebellion. As authorities continued their investigation they discovered that many slaves identified Juan Barbier and several others of the arrested rebels as "French," such as the free black Juan Tamayo from Bayamo, known as "el Francés."[9]

Juan Barbier symbolized the radical changes circulating in the Atlantic world during the first decades of the nineteenth century. The attention Juan Barbier attracted from slaves and free people of color, as well as the officials who suppressed the movement, illustrates how Haiti provided contrasting images of fascination and fear for different sectors of Cuban society.[10] Slaves and free people of color connected to maritime commerce had routinely traveled throughout the Caribbean and crisscrossed the Atlantic since the sixteenth century.[11] By the late 1700s and early 1800s, however, the same currents that had carried ships for centuries now transported a revolutionary cargo of ideas, literature, and people that Cuban officials feared would infect a society based on slave labor.[12] The American, French, and Spanish American Revolutions directly and indirectly confronted the legitimacy of slavery by questioning the rights of monarchical authority and colonialism. No single political event in modern history, however, revealed so dramatically the contradiction between slavery and the political right of individual liberty as the Haitian Revolution. This chapter analyzes what ideas and influences emanating from the Age of Revolution had on the Aponte Rebellion of 1812.[13] The contradictions generated by the dramatic increase in Cuban slave labor at the exact time period the institution of slavery came under question as an organizing principle for New World colonies fueled the aspirations for liberation by free people of color and slaves.

## CUBAN SLAVERY DURING THE ATLANTIC AGE OF REVOLUTION

From roughly 1750 to 1850, the continents bordering the Atlantic Ocean witnessed a series of civil wars, bloody revolutions, independence struggles, and battles for political dominance that forced cartographers to work at a feverish pace for decades. Just as modern nation-states signed constitutions that chipped away at monarchical authority and colonial rule in favor of expanding individual autonomy and sovereignty, the people living in the increasingly interconnected Atlantic world found themselves more vulnerable to dramatic changes in their daily lives caused by events thousands of miles away. For some, these changes marked the birth of a new era; for others, they signaled the passing of an old one. Benigno López, a Spanish colonial official who advised the crown on foreign affairs, feared the changes circulating in the Atlantic world would disrupt three centuries of Spanish supremacy in the Americas. In 1796, he argued for the need to fortify the Spanish islands of the Caribbean against the contagion of slave insurrections from Hispaniola and Coro, Venezuela, as well as from an uprising of Native Americans on the Darien peninsula of Panama. López blamed the rebellions on the political ferment created by the English and the "new republic of the United States" with their "dominant and conquistador spirit" found in the "hearts of Englishmen and Anglo-Americans as they are the children of the same mother."[14] While Spanish officials feared these political changes, slaves and free people of color in Cuba embraced the time period as a revolutionary era.

The French, British, American, and Spanish political and economic elites of the era recognized the radical changing times. Bryan Edwards, an astute English planter from Jamaica, in a speech to the British Parliament in 1798, warned that "a spirit of subversion has gone forth that set at naught the wisdom of our ancestors and the lessons of experience."[15] The American revolutionary John Adams revealed more than he could have imagined with his response mocking his wife Abigail's plea to "remember the ladies" when drafting the Declaration of Independence: "As to your extraordinary code of laws, I cannot but laugh. We have been told that our struggle has loosened the bonds of government everywhere; that children and apprentices were disobedient; that schools and colleges were grown turbulent; that Indians slighted their guardians, and negroes grew insolent to their masters."[16] As independence struggles called into question the relationship between crown and colony, individuals also began to rethink their relations with their superiors and the hierarchical divisions that ordered societies. The Age of Revolution that swept the Atlantic world would involve, to different degrees, numerous nations, various social classes, and diverse races and ethnicities in the fight to end colonization, servile labor, and monarchical authority in order to expand political rights, citizenship, and individual liberty.

The Seven Years' War (1756–1763), the first global war that marked the rise of Britain as the undisputed leader in overseas colonization, accelerated interactions among different people in the Atlantic world. The battlefields of the Seven Years' War blanketed Europe and extended around the globe to the Caribbean, North America, South America, the Philippines, and the Indian Subcontinent. After Spain and France signed the third Bourbon Family Compact on 15 August 1761, the British navy targeted Havana, the largest port city of the Spanish Caribbean and the gateway to the Spanish mainland.[17] During the summer of 1762, an invasion force of over 12,000 soldiers supported by 200 warships commanded by the Earl of Albermarle, laid siege to Havana and after two months of bombardment, conquered the city.[18] The British only occupied Cuba for a year until the Treaty of Paris ended the Seven Years' War in 1763, returning the island to Spain in exchange for Florida.

Although brief, the British occupation initiated a series of changes that would fundamentally alter Cuban society. The British maritime supremacy that helped ensure victory in the Seven Years' War also strengthened the British as the leading force in the Atlantic slave trade. Although British control of Cuba lasted less than a year, perhaps as many as 4,000 African slaves arrived on the island in that period, comprising an amazing 8 to 10 percent of all slaves imported over the previous 250 years.[19] The British occupation further expanded Cuba's plantation system and strengthened the chains of human bondage and racial slavery. At the same time, the political rivalries of the Seven Years' War also provided the opportunity for some slaves to obtain their freedom. English officials reported that during their attack on Havana "five mulattoes, eighty-four negroes, and one Indian" sided with the invaders in exchange for their freedom.[20] Slaves could navigate the political openings caused by international warfare to inject their own strategies for liberation into the battles.

Once Spain regained control of the island in 1763, colonial official Julian de Arriaga realized the danger "of the increasing number of slaves that could become partisans of enemies if they are offered freedom." In order to diminish the anticipation of such a future "promise," the Spanish Crown decided to grant freedom to slaves who could demonstrate they had participated in the

The Present Time Period

defense of Havana.[21] During the siege, the British had encountered a committed defense at Morro Castle by the Cuban standing army and the numerous volunteers who took up arms. The captain general of Cuba, the Conde de Ricla, granted twelve slaves their *cartas de libertad* (letters of liberty) upon issue of the decree in 1763. Over the next year, fourteen additional slaves successfully documented their participation in the defense of Havana and earned their freedom. The slave José Aponte (perhaps a relative of José Antonio Aponte, the leader of the 1812 Aponte Rebellion) participated in the defense of Havana. During the battle, José Aponte "captured seven prisoners and killed two white English soldiers."[22] Despite four witnesses testifying to José Aponte's participation in the defense of Havana, the judge ruled that because "he had waited fifteen years to apply for his freedom, his request could not be granted," and he remain enslaved.[23]

While it is unclear if José Aponte of the Seven Years' War and José Antonio Aponte of the slave rebellion of 1812 shared a common ancestry, the latter included several sketches of family members who participated in the defense of Havana in his book of drawings. Judicial official Juan Ignacio Rendón grilled Aponte on the meaning of the book for three days, attempting to understand the images of blacks soldiers defeating whites. Aponte explained that one of the drawings portrayed his grandfather, "Captain Joaquín Aponte[,] in battle" against "six hundred men and an English Battalion that landed" in Havana.[24] José Antonio Aponte also elaborated on a drawing of the free black militia led by his father, "Nicolás Aponte, . . . demonstrating the carrying away of white male prisoners that were the English who entered the city at six in the morning."[25] In another drawing, Aponte depicted his grandfather wearing the medal "of the royal effigy of Carlos III," king of Spain (1759–88), for his service in battle.[26] While the English occupation of Havana represented a decisive blow to the Spanish imperial system in the Americas, the images of black soldiers heroically defending the city and the capture of white prisoners represented a source of pride for Aponte and probably numerous other free blacks and slaves.

Military records from Spanish archives confirm some aspects of Aponte's drawings of his grandfather Joaquín and father Nicolás. Joaquín Aponte served in the free black militia for most of his life. In 1775, at the age of sixty-one, he had served for nearly forty-three years. While employed as a mason, he worked his way up the military hierarchy climbing the ranks of soldier, sublieutenant, second lieutenant, lieutenant, artillery captain, and finally captain of the grenadiers. Joaquín Aponte's service record applauded his "defense of this Plaza [Havana] during the time it was occupied by the British nation, in which he had two encounters with the enemy, one in the bay and the other on the large bridges." Joaquín Aponte earned recognition from his superiors and, according to his military file, "for such merit obtaining the medal of royal effigy."[27] Unlike his grandfather, Aponte's father Nicolás does not appear to have distinguished himself with the same valor. Spain only compiled individual service records for high-ranking military officers of the free black militia, and Aponte never referred to his father holding a military title. Although no extant service records have been found for Aponte's father, in April 1790 the sublieutenant of the free black militia, Isidro Moreno, reported the arrest of "Nicolás Aponte, voluntary of the battalion, for being a debtor in the quantity of 50 pesos that he had borrowed" from the regiment on 20 September 1787.[28] Joaquín Aponte's service record and the reference to Nicolás Aponte's continued service in the free black militia indicate that José Antonio Aponte's drawings glorifying his grandfather's and father's service during the English occupation represented a heroic moment in the Aponte family album.

Following the Seven Years' War, the European colonial powers began to centralize their power by tightening the relations between the metropolis and colonies. Spain was no exception. Charles III enacted a series of commercial, economic, military, fiscal, and social policies known as the Bourbon Reforms. Historian Allan Kuethe argues that at the "root of the colonial reorganization lay the risky decision to arm and train Americans through the disciplined militia system."[29] Consequently, these reforms entailed a fundamental shift of military power into Cuban hands, particularly the white Creole elites who came to command the newly organized and expanded regiments and battalions. Further, the cooperation shown by Cuban Creole planters with the British invaders resulted in Spain increasing slave imports in order to guarantee Cuban loyalty. After traveling across the island to assess changes required after the British occupation, Spanish field marshal Alejandro O'Reilly concluded that the "happiness of this island, for the most part, depends on the importation of slaves . . . and when the vassal is wealthy what more could the Sovereign need?"[30] O'Reilly's conclusion on the reinforcing links between the Atlantic slave trade and the legitimacy of Spanish colonialism in Cuba would be echoed for over a hundred years. As late as the 1860s, African slaves arrived at Cuban ports long after all other nations of the Americas abolished the Atlantic slave trade, and the first sustained war for Cuban independence would not erupt until 1868, nearly fifty years after most of Spanish America began its struggle for liberation.[31]

The Bourbon Reforms of the second half of the eighteenth century accomplished much more in Cuba than an increase in militia regiments and cautious expansion of the Atlantic slave trade. Whereas in other parts of the Spanish Empire new and onerous taxes along with the persistent circumvention of local customs engendered opposition to the crown, Cuba emerged

The Present Time Period

ever more firmly linked to Madrid.[32] The reception and implementation of the Bourbon Reforms in Cuba appears quite distinct when compared to mainland Spanish America. Various scholars have observed that the Creole patriciate of Cuba "enjoyed a level of intimacy with the royal administration that escaped American elites located in the distant inland centers of colonial life," and that Cubans had largely succeeded in "nationalizing decision making" within the existing imperial structure.[33]

While the Bourbon Reforms did not create the same antagonisms between white Creoles (American-born) and Penisulares (Spanish-born) that would later fuel calls for independence throughout Latin America, the general dissolution of the corporate society of orders, known as the *sociedad de castas*, also occurred in Cuba. Scholars continue to debate the rigidity and flexibility of the *sociedad de castas* in ascribing corporate identities, limiting political and legal rights, restricting opportunities for economic advancement, and establishing and enforcing socioracial hierarchies.[34] After the 1790s, the expansion of Cuban plantation agriculture divided the population ever more clearly by race between the white population of European ancestry and the black population of African descent. While scholars of Cuba correctly emphasize an intimacy between white Cuban Creoles and Spanish officials as a result of the Bourbon Reforms, free people of color, slaves, mulattos, and blacks found themselves subject to an ever more rigid set of rules and regulations, as well as intensified racial discrimination.

Cuba once again became involved in an international conflict when the Spanish army battled the British in the American Revolution. After several years of fighting between the Americans and the British, Charles IV signed a formal declaration of war on 21 June 1779. Spain sought to push the British out of the Gulf of Mexico, to secure the Mississippi River, and to regain control of Florida.[35] Soldiers from the mulatto and black militia of Havana participated in the Caribbean theater of the American Revolution. In addition to the heroic scenes José Antonio Aponte had sketched of his father and grandfather in the Seven Years' War, he also included autobiographical drawings of his own participation in the American Revolution. Aponte explained to judicial official Juan Ignacio Rendón that he and other soldiers of the "black regiments" had served in the Caribbean theater and took part "in the year 1782 . . . in the invasion of Providence island . . . at eight in the morning."[36] Aponte participated in the 1782 assault on Providence Island, which included 202 militiamen of color.[37]

Aponte and other free colored soldiers from Cuba joined a larger fighting force of African ancestry from different regions of the Caribbean that gained crucial combat experience in the American Revolution. The French colony of Saint Domingue sent several hundred free blacks and mulattoes to participate directly in the war for North American Independence. Later leaders of the Haitian Revolution, such as André Rigaud and Henri Christophe, acquired vital military training and expertise.[38] Many blacks and mulattos joined the American Revolution from the nearby French colony of Guadeloupe. Among them, Jacques Gruel later drew upon his fifteen years of militia service and experience in the American Revolution to demand the extension of the French *Declaration of the Rights of Man* to him and all free coloreds.[39] From the Caribbean coast of Central America, Manuel Huevo earned his freedom by battling the British at the fortress of Omoa.[40] The experiences of black soldiers fighting in the American Revolution with its stated goals of political independence and individual liberty resonated with their own subordination as residents of plantation colonies built on the twin pillars of racial slavery and racial inequality. When judicial authorities raided Aponte's house to collect evidence of his participation in the revolts, they discovered an "effigy of general Guasinton [Washington]" that Aponte explained he "collected like any other curious thing."[41] Aponte, unfortunately, did not provide any other information on the effigy of Washington. Nonetheless, we can conclude that it obviously held special importance and most likely resonated with Aponte's own political goals of personal freedom and political independence.[42]

The American Revolution never directly confronted the problem slavery posed to reconciling property rights and political rights. Knowing the divisions slavery could cause, in drafting the Constitution the Founding Fathers of the United States cowardly opted not to mention the word "slavery" at all. The American Revolution, nonetheless, had transformed American slavery into the "peculiar" institution of the South by drawing a geographic line that subsequently divided the country into slave and free.[43] Francisco Arango y Parreño, the individual most responsible for promoting Cuban agriculture and expanding slavery, realized the implications of the division of the United States into slave and free states. When comparing Cuban slavery with other countries and colonies throughout the Americas, only for the United States did Arango provide data for individual states grouped into the North and South.[44] The weakening of slavery in the North created a social class not directly tied to the institution that slowly chipped away at human bondage from without, while the day-to-day resistance of slaves corroded masters' rule from within.

As the American Revolution and the ideals of men such as George Washington presented a "curious" question to slavery in the New World, forces in England which had percolated for years now began to reject the institution outright. Based more on parliamentary consent than on the divine right of kings, the political authority of the Hanoverian regime of the eighteenth century cast relations between king and subject and master and servant in the new light of contractual relations. At the same time, market relations created a new class of masterless laborers—heralded in Adam Smith's *Wealth of Nations* (1776)—that demonstrated the feasibility, and in some cases, the superiority of wage labor. The Quakers proved more forceful and consistent in questioning slavery, drawing their strength from evangelical Christianity. In 1787, they established the Society for Effecting the Abolition of the Slave Trade. The Abolition Society attracted influential new recruits: Thomas Clarkson and William Wilberforce, who used their political muscle in Parliament; and two former slaves, Olaudah Equiano (Gustavus Vassa) and Ottobah Cugoano, who spread word of their cause by relating slavery's horrors with authority and experience. After the slave revolution erupted in French Saint Domingue, colonial officials began to voice a heightened sense of danger and the need for Parliament to act quickly. Stephen Fuller requested that Parliament "devise some method of taking the sense of Parliament upon the abolition of the African Trade, as early as possible, in order that this horrid scene may be speedily and effectually closed; and that our colonies in general as well as Jamaica, may be relieved from a state of suspense so inviting to the Negroes and so dangerous to the White Inhabitants."[45] Given the previous three centuries of the Atlantic slave trade to the Americas and the lucrative profits it generated for British businessmen, especially during the eighteenth century, the abolition of the British trade in 1807 represented a remarkable achievement. The United States followed quickly behind, banning the Atlantic slave trade within its borders in 1808.[46]

Cuban slaveowners anxiously followed the antislavery debates and acts in America and Britain because the two countries had provided a constant source for imported slaves to work the rapidly expanding plantations of the island.[47] Francisco Arango lobbied the Spanish Crown to become more involved in the slave trade to protect its colonies from foreign dependence and vulnerability to what he described as the "very distinct English language" of commerce that can easily "confuse an honorable man of wealth and means for a wicked liar."[48] Cuban planters depended almost entirely on foreign slave traders; only two Spanish ships could be counted among the 343 that arrived at Cuban ports between 1804 and 1808.[49] In 1809, Arango remarked that "in these last years there has been a total transformation in the commercial system" of the slave trade. Disappointed, Arango concluded that with the English and the United States "eternally abolishing" the slave trade, it "leaves no other capable foreign flags that can be employed in such traffic other than the Portuguese and Sweden." Actions taken by the British Parliament and the American Congress threatened the institution of slavery and isolated Cubans slaveowners, causing them to decide that "all of our hopes are to consist of our own and of all our attention must be directed" to remedying this "unfortunate age."[50] The search and seizure of cargo from Sierra Leone by the British navy illustrated one of the consequences of this new age for Spanish slave traders.[51] Cuban elites responded to the changes in the slave trade by taking issues into their own hands. They petitioned the Spanish Crown to form their own slave-trading company to carry out slaving "expeditions with greater ease, especially today when we can not be assured of England or the United States of America."[52] Despite the abolition of the transoceanic slave trade elsewhere in the Atlantic world during the first decades of the nineteenth century, it continued to thrive in Cuba until 1867. Of the estimated one million slaves imported to Cuba, 85 percent arrived in the nineteenth century.[53]

In addition to Britain and the United States, other countries grappled with the question of slavery at the turn of the nineteenth century. Radicals of the French Revolution associated with the abolition society *Amis des Noirs* confronted the contradiction slavery posed to human liberty, proposing its destruction at the meeting of the Estates General in 1789. French abolitionist Hodey de Saultchevreuil advocated the immediate abolition of slavery and the slave trade, stating that "the annihilation of property, bankruptcies, disorder and insurrections, are perhaps the least evils we shall have to fear."[54] Despite Antoine Barnave's insistence that "the commotions propagated from the Metropolis to the Colonies, bear the same impression, and have preserved the same character," it would take five years for French Revolutionary radicals to declare abolition and extend the political rights of "citizens" to the slaves.[55] The emancipatory legislation from the National Assembly in 1794 simply recognized the freedoms already seized by slaves across the Atlantic on French Caribbean islands. Spaniard Isidro Antillon, who cautiously advocated the gradual abolition of slavery in Cuba, recognized how the insurrection in Saint Domingue accelerated the emancipation of slaves: "France, after being converted to a Republic . . . [and] some decrees obtained by the influence of the colonists, declared publicly to Europe that the blacks are free."[56] The "colonists" Antillon referred to represented the slaves, because the overwhelming majority of white French colonists and wealthy free people of color accorded citizenship rights opposed the abolition of slavery. Antillon feared that political turmoil in the metropolis would result in empowering slaves to decide the course of emancipation in Cuba.

Unlike Antillon, Cuban slaveholders took comfort from explaining slave insurrections in the Caribbean as the result of radical politics in the faraway cities of Europe. Cuban officials found reassurance in pointing out that some of the causes of the Haitian insurgency stemmed from the turbulent uprising in France. The Havana *consulado*, an economic and judicial institution that represented slaveholder interests in commerce, concluded that "whoever knows the origin of the republican revolution in France, knows that

The Present Time Period

the discord born in the metropolis over political opinions resulted in a war between the rich and the poor, and this same principle is what stripped the slaveowners of Guarico [Haiti] of their dominion over slaves by a declaration of liberty for four hundred thousand slaves."[57] Arango argued that French "masters had taught their servants" about the French Revolution, "and by their own hands they had built their own ruin. Authors of anarchy should not complain."[58] By blaming the slave insurrection on the politics of the French Revolution, Cuban slaveowners avoided the consideration that the slaves' own desire for freedom accounted for the Haitian Revolution. Since the slave revolt merely reflected revolutionary politics and "anarchy" in far away Europe, Cuban planters denied that their slaves held similar aspirations for liberation and would risk rebellion to attain it. José Antonio Aponte apparently did not share the simplistic reasoning of Cuban elites who traced the influence of the French Revolution strictly along imperial lines from the mother country of France to her colonies in the Caribbean. Aponte's book of drawings included a depiction of various "snakes [climbing over] a staff and a broken crown" of a king. Aponte told authorities he "had drawn [the sketch] during the time of the French Revolution."[59] As with so many other drawings, his interrogators asked no other questions, and he provided no additional details. At the very least, and all that we can know for certain, Aponte had some knowledge of the French Revolution.

The mainland colonies of Spanish America soon followed the example of Haiti with their own battles for independence, although the commitment to slave emancipation would not be nearly as swift or as clear. From 1808 to 1830, Spanish America witnessed a series of military and political battles that ended with most of the continent breaking the colonial chains that tied them to the Crown. The "liberator" of South America, Simón Bolívar, received military aid and refuge from the Republic of Haiti under the leadership of Alexandre Pétion. In exchange, Bolívar agreed to free the slaves who served in the rebel army to "forge the instruments of their captivity into weapons of freedom."[60] The expediency of war and the recruitment of slaves into the military ranks of the rebel armies delivered a devastating blow to slavery throughout Spanish America. Although slavery survived the wars of independence to accompany the birth of nations from Mexico in the North to Argentina in the South, the long and gradual process of slave emancipation had begun from which the institution would never recover.[61]

Colonial officials and slaveowners in Cuba protested the imprisonment in Havana of revolutionaries from the wars of independence in Spanish America. As early as 1802, insurgents from Venezuela began to fill the dungeons of Morro Castle that guarded the Bay of Havana.[62] The town council of Puerto Príncipe feared that the "promoters of such bold antipolitical and anticolonial acts," causing the "scandalous excesses of Caracas" and the "ignorance of Buenos Aires," would "open the eyes of the gullible."[63] The town council of Havana shared the same opinion that "not one favorable circumstance could be derived" from imprisoning rebels from New Spain and the "revolutionary interior."[64] Andrés Jáuregui, the Cuban representative to the Spanish parliament at Cádiz, Spain, realized the "present time period is very delicate" and pledged to limit the shipment of revolutionary prisoners to Havana.[65] Despite the concerns of elites about the revolutionary contagion carried by rebels from Spanish America, Cuba survived the wars of independence with the title the "ever faithful island." Contemporaries, historians, and even Fidel Castro have emphasized that the fear of slave insurrection and Cuba turning into another Haiti delayed independence until 1898.[66]

The impact of military and political battles that shaped the Atlantic world for Cuba—from the Seven Years' War to the American, French, Haitian, and Spanish American Revolutions—must also take into account events in Africa and their relation to the Aponte Rebellion. From 1600 to 1800, the military and political leaders of West-Central Africa attempted to consolidate large areas into centralized states through the forceful incorporation of small polities. By 1800, although these consolidations drastically reduced the number of "stateless societies" all along the Atlantic basin, no large single empire emerged to exert political influence over the region as a whole. The dominance of the Kingdom of Kongo declined throughout the seventeenth century as a result of civil wars, leaving in its wake smaller political entities and the rise of local warlords. The simultaneous process of political inclusion of small states and political fragmentation of larger ones in Africa, combined with the rapid expansion of sugar plantations in Brazil, Jamaica, Saint Domingue, Barbados, Antigua, Martinique, Guadeloupe, St. Kitts, and Cuba, constituted a deadly confluence in which the Atlantic slave trade flourished. Unsurprisingly, the Atlantic slave trade reached its peak in the eighteenth century with the transportation of more than six million Africans across the ocean.[67]

The link between political and military conflict in Africa and the demand for slave labor in the Americas often created clearly defined migration patterns. This relationship brought thousands of slaves from the Yoruba region of West Africa to Cuba. During the eighteenth century, Oyo rapidly built a political empire by extending its influence through military conquests that funneled slaves into the Atlantic slave trade, many of whom arrived in Cuba as war captives. By the 1790s, the Oyo Empire began to decline, but the process of exporting war captives from Yorubaland only accelerated with the incessant fighting there lasting until 1836.[68] Samuel Ajayi Crowther, seized during one of the many battles that ravaged the Yoruba country, recalled "in

The Present Time Period

many cases a family was violently divided between three or four enemies, who each led his [captives] away, to see one another no more. Your humble servant was thus caught—with his mother, two sisters, and a cousin—while endeavoring to escape."[69] Historians John Thornton and Paul Lovejoy have argued that the military and cultural background of African slaves shipped to the Americas represented a central, if not decisive, feature of the 1739 Stono Revolt in South Carolina, the Haitian Revolution, and the 1835 Malê revolt in Brazil.[70] Given the high influx of Africans into Cuba as a result of the collapse of the Oyo Empire, and the ability of Yoruba culture to have "an impact out of all proportion to its relative demographic weight," according to historian David Eltis, the military background of slaves may have likely contributed to a proclivity for rebellion.[71] The marked increase in revolts during the decades of 1790 and 1800 testifies to a heightened commitment to resistance by Africans in Cuba. Political events in the Atlantic world, from revolution in Europe to independence in the Americas to civil wars in Africa, all exerted an influence in Cuba that polarized society by strengthening a commitment to racial slavery for masters, while cracking the foundations upon which Spanish rule rested.

## STRENGTHENING CUBAN SLAVERY BY REFORM
## DURING THE AGE OF REVOLUTION

Cuban slaveowners recognized that the tumultuous political changes in the Atlantic world that they described as the "enlightenment of the time in which we live" challenged slavery. While they admired Europe for trying "to resolve the question of slavery with the simple principle of *natural justice*," masters suspected the actions of abolitionists "were animated by the interests of power and ambition in the race of nations to possess power and wealth." Cuban elites preferred not to question slavery because "it is a very complicated question of people's rights, of civil, public and private law, of politics, of economics, and morals as well."[72] Like their counterparts in Brazil and the U.S. South, Cuban slaveholders stood firmly against the tide of history that ushered in the gradual abolition of slavery, and instead looked to the past to legitimate the present.

During the years when Britain, France, and the United States began to question, and eventually abolish, the Atlantic slave trade, and the slaves of Saint Domingue took matters into their own hands through violent revolution, masters in Cuba frequently defended slavery by emphasizing the institution as a ubiquitous feature in human history. A Catholic official came to the defense of the master class by reassuring them "that the condition of bondage has been recognized and practiced since the beginning of the world."[73] Just as

The Present Time Period

the intellectual construction of European political legitimacy in the New World found historical justification in the Roman Empire, Cuban slaveholders frequently emphasized that their institution of human bondage could trace its lineage to the classical civilizations.[74] Cuban slaveowner Francisco Zavedra, for example, took comfort in noting that the ancient Greeks long ago reconciled political rights with slavery: "The harmony between the right of humanity and slavery has been observed since the most remote of times by the philosophy and legislation of the Greek republics whose insights have survived more than twenty centuries."[75] In particular, Zavedra singled out the "Athenians among the ancients who treated their slaves the best" by "providing indulgences" that later served "as a model for the Romans."[76] As the heirs of Greek and Roman laws, Zavedra reasoned that slaves in the Spanish dominions received the "most gentle treatment without comparison."[77] The need for Cuban slaveholders to seek out legitimacy in the ancient past (despite three centuries of human bondage on the island in the recent past) revealed their anxieties over how slavery was changing at the turn of the nineteenth century. Contemporary events provided few examples, however, to confirm Zavedra's Greek harmony between humanity and slavery. Rather, they indicated the real possibility of a Greek fire.

With a rigid hierarchical vision of the past, masters in Cuba could think of no other way to organize their plantation society than African slave labor. In 1792, Juan Baptista Valiente wrote to Spanish colonial authorities on the urgent need to develop agriculture. "Without a single doubt," he wrote, "these lands need numerous laborers, and these will be provided by slaves" as they are the only "utensils" that will suffice.[78] Several years later a colonial official from Bayamo echoed these sentiments when he wrote that "the only hope" to end the poverty of the island and to expand sugar plantations required the expansion of slave labor.[79] As loyal subjects of the Spanish Crown, most Cubans made their request for the expansion of slavery to benefit the king and his dominions. José Coppingeros wrote the Cuban captain general to complain of the "decadence of agriculture" near the eastern town of Bayamo that deprived "our Sovereign" of wealth. His solution for enriching the coffers of Madrid, and undoubtedly his own, required the establishment of a slave market in the central plaza of Bayamo, as well as in other cities across the island.[80] When Juan Baptista Valiente petitioned the Council of the Indies to expand the slave trade, he succinctly explained the dynamics of plantation slavery: "Money is the blood of countries."[81] The blood of African slaves would be sacrificed in the name of Cuban wealth.

The numerous requests by slaveholders in the 1790s and 1800s to urgently increase the slave trade indicate how changes in the Atlantic world provided an opportunity to expand plantation agriculture. Only three months after the slave revolt began on the northern plain of Saint Domingue in 1791, Francisco Arango urged Cubans to take advantage of the insurrection to expand sugar production. "It is necessary to look [at Saint Domingue]" wrote Arango, "not only with compassion, but with political eyes . . . to give our agriculture . . . advantage and preponderance over the French." Arango recognized the dominance of the French colony on the international sugar market and stated that "only in this case can we be within their reach. An atom at the side of a colossus is what we represent in respect to our neighbor."[82] Not only had the Haitian Revolution eliminated the dominant world producer of sugar, the decline in production resulted in a dramatic rise in prices and the "most happy situation" for Cuban plantation owners, as Arango wrote one year later.[83] Cuban medical doctor and scientist Tomás Romay remembered that "when the opulent colony of Guarico [Saint Domingue] was converted to ruins," the inhabitants of the island of Cuba gained "the prosperity that disappeared from the neighbors."[84]

While planters, merchants, and colonial officials welcomed the chance to catapult Cuba to the top of the sugar market, they also voiced trepidation over explaining why they suddenly had the opportunity to do so. The bishop of Cuba questioned what the future held if the "island of Cuba reached with the increase in laborers the same wealth of the French part of Saint Domingue?" The bishop warned that Cubans could share the same fate as French masters: "The end of the same neighboring colony has provided us with the most decisive answer."[85] Cuban slaveholders realized the dangerous position of expanding slavery across the island at the exact same time when slaves had decisively overturned it in Haiti, and others began to question the institution politically and philosophically.

In an effort to insure that slavery would continue to exist for years to come, slaveholders proposed several defensive reforms to prolong human bondage. In many respects, their actions resembled Southern slaveholders in the United States who attempted to reform and regulate slavery as it came under attack in the nineteenth century.[86] The initiative for reform came on the part of the Spanish Crown in 1789 just as the demand for slaves began to rise in Cuba. As a result "of the considerable increase in slaves," the king issued a *Real Cédula* (Royal Decree) known as the *Código Negro Español* (slave code) that specified food and clothing provisions, limited work hours, required religious instruction, protected marriages, and limited punishments for slaves.[87] Several historians have persuasively demonstrated that the rosy picture of slave rights provided by legislation rarely conformed to reality.[88] Consequently, the examination of Spanish slave laws by scholars has largely focused on showing the discrepancy between legislation formulated in the metropolis and the slave experience in the colonies, which often rendered the laws irrelevant. Masters, however, perceived the legislation as a threat to their authority and protested the law designed to curb their power over human chattel.[89]

Shortly after the *Código Negro* crossed the Atlantic and reached the colonies, prominent slaveholders in Cuba and other locations in the Spanish Empire held meetings to discuss the implications of the new law. Diego Miguel de Moya drafted a letter responding to the *Código Negro* signed by "almost all of the masters of sugar plantations in this jurisdiction." Cuban slaveowners did not protest all the articles of the *Código Negro*, "only proposing to point out the extremely grave inconveniences" that would result from putting into effect some of the new regulations.[90] Another slaveowner responded that the new slave code "is not anything else other than an amplified repetition of our ancient laws," but nonetheless felt threatened enough to reject its amplification.[91] Cuban masters did not reject the provisions that called for better material conditions, guaranteed the sanctity of marriage, or protected the slaves' right to manumission, but rather the "useless attempts always made by human prudence to fix limits between human bondage and domination."[92] Slaveowners regarded the legislation as the Crown's intrusion into their personal lives to dictate relations between master and slave.

Cuban slaveowners regarded the clearest indication of domination over another human being as the ability to threaten or inflict physical punishment. The *Código Negro* specified that whippings "could not exceed twenty-five" and would be carried out "with a gentle instrument that would not cause serious bruises or bleeding."[93] In contrast, the general desire by slaveholders to increase plantation output did not call for a relaxation in terror as a force to compel labor; as the bishop of Cuba claimed: "They [slaves] will only work with the threat of the whip always raised above their backs, and if this disappears for one moment, work will be interrupted."[94] Masters feared that any limits placed upon their ability to inflict physical punishment would be perceived by slaves as a sign of weakness, resulting in resistance: "Of this law the firm concept that will be left with slaves is that we cannot impose severe punishment, and having lost absolute fear, they will take no part in subordinating themselves to their masters and overseers . . . abandoning the plantations."[95] The response of Cuban slaveholders stressed that their authority rested upon the coercive power to command labor by both the threat of violence and brutal physical punishment. Masters' unease over slaves taking courage from such benevolent legislation revealed how political actions in Spain could reformulate the master-slave relationship for the colonies.[96]

In addition to the rejection of limits placed on whippings and punishments, Cuban slaveowners protested other aspects of the *Código Negro* that they perceived as a check on their power. In reference to work hours, the new

The Present Time Period

legislation required that slaves "should begin and end their work from sunrise to sunset."[97] Plantation owners responded to the restricted hours with detailed explanations of the cutting and processing of cane that required twenty-hour workdays during the long harvest season. Diego Miguel de Moya wrote the king and simply stated that if slaves only worked from sunup until sundown, sugar plantations "would be abandoned forever."[98] Zavedra's response to the *Código Negro* bordered on insulting the king and his ministers for their ignorance of sugar-cane cultivation. He insisted that "in this part it is clear that the decree will have to be modified according to circumstance, because [its] literal execution would destroy a large part of the settlements in the Indies."[99] Spanish colonial officials from the beginning of the conquest drafted tome after tome of legislation that rarely specified or provided any means for enforcement. Despite a long history of sterile legislation, Cuban slaveowners felt compelled to respond immediately to the *Código Negro* as an oblique attack on the institution of slavery.

Masters regarded the new code of laws as unnecessary because they argued Cuban slaves received the most benevolent treatment of all the slaves in the Americas. Spokesman for the planter class Francisco Arango y Parreño compared Cuban slave treatment with the "French who regarded slaves as beasts, while the Spanish see them as men." According to Arango y Parreño, Cubans' slaves were "the happiest in the world" as a result of "civil laws perfectly balancing the two extremes of the abuse of owners and the subordination of slaves."[100] The *consulado* of Havana echoed Arango's praiseworthy remarks: "We are fortunate to have a slave code, written with more humanity than those of foreigners, providing slaves with the aid of religion, and opening the doors to manumission."[101] Such laudatory remarks notwithstanding, slaveowners protested the *Código Negro* and especially the articles limiting work hours that would paralyze sugar production during the harvest season.[102]

While slaveholders did not agree with all the provisions of the *Código Negro*, they recognized that forces in the Atlantic world threatened the institution of slavery and required reforms to ensure its continued existence. After the British and American Atlantic slave trade ended in 1807 and 1808, a series of calls in the name of "humanity" to reform, but not abolish, the slave trade came from the island. Cuban slaveowners increasingly voiced concerns about the high mortality rate of the middle passage. According to Ignacio María de Alva, public attention in Havana focused on the ships docked in the bay and especially the poor health of slaves and the numerous deaths from transoceanic voyages. He wrote to the *consulado* of Havana to investigate the issue "in favor of humanity" and "the true interest of commerce."[103] Tomás Romay conducted an investigation of the survival rate of slaves on the middle passage in the name of "humanity, religion, and a sensible heart." Romay discovered that one-fourth to one-third of the human cargo died during the Atlantic crossing. He advocated the writing of a slave code for the slave trade because "what are the advantages gained by these unhappy [slaves] with slavery, if as soon as they are taken from their homes, they are buried in the abyss of the sea?"[104] With fewer nations participating in the trans-Atlantic slave trade, the economic costs of such a high mortality rate would have to be remedied.

British abolitionists who had labored since 1787 to end the Atlantic slave trade introduced several bills into Parliament that later caught the attention of Cuban slaveholders.[105] Tomás Romay forwarded a British law from 1793 to the Havana *consulado* on shipping slaves from Africa to the Americas to "avoid such abuses [deaths] with a rule that prescribes the number of slaves that can be transported in proportion to the tonnage of each ship."[106] In order to increase the survival rate on the middle passage and to encourage better care of the human cargo, the *consulado* offered rewards to ship captains for a mortality rate below 10 percent.[107] Francisco Arango recommended increasing the female slave population to minimize Cuba's dependence on the Atlantic slave trade. In recognized imitation of the British, Arango advocated a six peso tax on imports of male slaves while exempting females as a strategy to foster the growth of an enslaved Creole population.[108] In September 1809, the town council of Havana advocated advertising in the newspaper for slave traders to "bring one-half female" slaves from Africa.[109] In addition, to increase the survival rate of slaves once they arrived in Cuba, a Havana newspaper published instructions for overseers and a contest awarded a 2,000-peso prize for the best-run plantation on the island.[110] Faced with the rising tide of abolition cresting from the Age of Revolution, Cuban slaveholders devised a defensive strategy to prolong human bondage across the island to prevent the liberating waves of emancipation from crashing on Cuban shores.[111]

## ISOLATING CUBAN SLAVERY FROM THE CHANGING ATLANTIC WORLD

Attempting to reform slavery to prolong the institution required isolating Cuba from the transformative currents circulating in the Atlantic world. When insurrectionary movements began to spread across the Caribbean in the 1790s, the captain general of Cuba issued a decree prohibiting "any person from carrying on correspondence with foreigners, especially relating to the present disturbances."[112] Attempts by colonial authorities to suppress any information on insurrection and rebels revealed how loosely they regarded their grasp of power over society. Rumors, stories, and hearsay of revolution could now serve as catalysts for rebellion. Attempts to suppress information only caused stories of invasion by external forces to reach paranoid levels. In

The Present Time Period

1808, the town council of the landlocked city of Puerto Príncipe called for a "state of defense" in preparation of a suspected invasion force of "20,000 men from England."[113]

The slave insurrection that engulfed the French Caribbean offered a far more terrifying specter to Cuban elites than an English invasion. The most obvious defense against slaves emulating the example of the Haitian Revolution involved preventing the transmission of any news about the successful revolt. Slaveholders throughout the Americas had "nothing left but to *guard against the mischief which threatens us,*" according to a British colonial official after the revolt erupted in Saint Domingue.[114] On 15 January 1796, Captain General Luis de Las Casas reiterated a decree applicable to all Spanish colonies in the Americas that "prohibited the entrance of slaves to ports of the island that were not *bozales* [slaves born in Africa] brought from the coast of Africa." In addition, Las Casas insisted that any "slaves from the French colonies imported after the month of August of 1790" had to be "withdrawn from the island in the span of three months."[115] After slave revolts erupted in the British Caribbean, Spain extended the expulsion to human cargo imported from the English islands after 1794.[116] German naturalist and traveler Alexander von Humboldt, who spent time in Cuba intermittently from 1800 to 1804, remembered how "the upheavals in Santo Domingo in 1790 and Jamaica in 1794 caused such alarm among the slaveowners" that they eagerly discussed "what measures could be adopted to conserve tranquility."[117] The Cuban captain general reported in 1800 that extra vigilance against the clandestine introduction of French slaves by smugglers had already resulted in the "apprehension of several individuals and jail sentences."[118] Despite the increased security measures to isolate the island, many slave traders ignored the restrictions and opted to pay fines and penalties. The clandestine introduction of slaves from nearby Caribbean islands without authorization became so widespread that Cuban officials established a fixed set of increasing fines for repeated violations.[119] Captain General Someruelos optimistically suggested that "by these measures," they would hopefully evade "the contagion" of insurrection that spread throughout the Caribbean in the 1790s.[120]

Slaves, however, were not the only people who brought information on the Haitian Revolution to Cuba. The slave insurrection scattered refugees to various ports of the Caribbean and the Atlantic seaboard where they told and retold stories of the Haitian Revolution.[121] In the 1790s and 1800s, thousands of French émigrés fleeing the slave insurrection arrived in Cuba, settling mainly in Oriente.[122] To Cuba's white population, the arrival in the 1790s and 1800s of thousands of French émigrés offered an ominous reminder of the potential dangers of relying on slave labor.[123] Cuban slaveholders and colonial authorities expressed their "compassion" for the émigrés, promising to "cry perpetually" about the revolution on the nearby island.[124] The empathy of Cuban elites allowed French colonialists to bring their slaves to Cuba and purchase land to transplant their sugar plantations across the island.[125] When the French finally admitted defeated in 1804, and Haitians declared their independence, stories about the plight of white refugees spread throughout the Caribbean. Jamaican resident Maria Nugent recorded in her journal that she heard from people who had been in Cuba of the "dreadful account of the suffering of the poor people in St. Domingo."[126] By 1804, Captain General Someruelos reported that over 18,000 French émigrés resided in Cuba, concentrated in the eastern city of Santiago, with many others spread throughout the island.[127]

The French refugees quickly adapted to their new Cuban environment and showed little eagerness to return when British officials attempted to recruit soldiers to reconquer the island in 1795.[128] Cuba continued to accept many of the exiles from the Haitian Revolution until 1808, when Napoleon invaded Spain. Shortly thereafter, anti-French sentiment spread throughout the island, resulting in the expulsion of thousands of French men, women, and children and their resettlement in places such as Jamaica, Charleston, New York, and Philadelphia. The largest exodus of French émigrés from Cuba arrived in New Orleans, which received over 9,000 migrants, amazingly doubling the entire population of the city with their arrival in 1808–9.[129] Although brief, the French émigré presence in Cuba served to circulate and transmit through word of mouth news and stories of the Haitian Revolution that slaves and free people of color could appropriate and refashion to speak to their own interests.

If the daily presence of French refugees and their slaves provoked uneasy feelings among Cuban planters, requests by military leaders of the Haitian Revolution for arms and ammunition caused grave concern. French military officials battling the slave insurrection in Saint Domingue often sought refuge and supplies in Cuba's nearby harbors.[130] More alarming to Cuban authorities, however, was a letter by Miguel de Arambarri, a subaltern to Toussaint Louverture, to Captain General Someruelos requesting "twenty thousand rifles . . . in order to arm volunteers" to battle the British. In exchange, Louverture offered to help Spain reconquer Jamaica. The "special agent" wrote that "General Toussaint and I have at our command troops accustomed to defeating all of the obstacles . . . of war." Arambarri urged Someruelos to act immediately, insisting that "it is not necessary to wait for orders from the King of Spain when there was such a beautiful occasion to hit the enemy of humankind."[131] As a loyal servant of the Spanish Crown, Someruelos responded that he could "not and will not authorize any expedition without the blessing of the King."[132] Haitian leaders also sought aid from

Cuba to pursue the internal wars of the revolution that pitted André Rigaud against Louverture. Rigaud requested arms and money from Someruelos to fight his archrival.[133] Military requests by Louverture and Rigaud starkly illustrated how radically the Caribbean and Atlantic worlds had changed during the era of the Haitian Revolution. A former slave coachman and a mulatto goldsmith now functioned as major political power brokers among the European powers operating in the Caribbean.[134]

Attempts by Cuban slaveholders to avoid the contagion of revolt by isolating the island from news, ideas, and rebels from the Age of Revolution stood in contrast to more than three centuries of Caribbean history. In fact, the colonial powers of the New World had a long history of selling rebellious slaves to the Caribbean, as occurred after the 1741 conspiracy in New York and the 1822 Denmark Vesey conspiracy in Charleston.[135] While mercantilist economic philosophy sought to strengthen ties between colony and crown, the Caribbean region proved resilient to such a policy with the Spanish, British, French, and Dutch all occupying islands within close proximity. The slave trade, in fact, represented the great unifying force of the Caribbean and the early precursor to the modern transnational corporation. Rarely did a slave ship dock only at one port or trade exclusively with one nation. For example, when the British occupied Havana and investigated Spanish fiscal policy they discovered that the contraband trade in slaves involving various European nations and colonies had not only been tacitly recognized but organized with a tax equal to the one placed on legally imported slaves without penalty.[136]

Cuban slaveholders never directly confronted the contradiction of attempting to isolate an island organized for producing plantation agriculture for export, worked by imported African labor, and tied to Atlantic commerce. Cuban Francisco Arango shared the French physiocrat conviction that "the experience of three centuries . . . has established that the returns" of agricultural products and "not precious metals from American colonies" are what enrich the metropolis.[137] Cuban agriculture connected the island to, rather than isolating it from, a larger Atlantic world through the importation of slave labor and the exportation of plantation crops.

The clearest indication of the interdependence among the major European powers operating in the Caribbean surfaced during the outbreak of rebellions on nearby islands. Often the colonial forces of one nation did not have sufficient arms, personnel, and resources to suppress an uprising.[138] The Haitian Revolution, again, provides the most dramatic example. In a failed effort to stop the rebellion before it engulfed the entire region, the British, French, and Spanish armies all battled against the slaves, turning Hispaniola into an Atlantic graveyard. Captain General Someruelos provided refuge to the French General Ferrand after he requested aid in the name of the Catholic majesty and their common struggle to "suppress slave revolts."[139] Francisco Arango offered French General Rochambeau assistance in his plan to reestablish slavery in Saint Domingue.[140] The British and the Spanish regularly shared information on the alarming increase in the size of the Haitian navy, which they perceived as part of a plan for invading neighboring islands and disrupting commerce.[141] Despite never-ending political differences, European powers in the Caribbean remained united in aiding each other in suppressing slave rebellions as an effective strategy of self-preservation.

As cooperation, commerce, and sympathy united European powers in the suppression of slave insurrections, Cuba developed its own specialty that quickly earned itself fame in the plantation regions of America. Alexander von Humboldt remarked that "this hunting of men, has given an unfortunate fame in Haiti and Jamaica to the dogs of the island of Cuba."[142] For reasons of effectiveness and reputation, slave catchers throughout the Caribbean regularly made trips to Cuba to purchase dogs for chasing runaways and ending insurrections. Cuban dogs gained notoriety for the ferocious aid they provided the British in suppressing the Second Jamaican Maroon War of 1795.[143] British officials in Jamaica praised Captain General Luis de Las Casas of Cuba for acting "with the most Civility and Cordiality" by providing 100 dogs, resulting in "negroes all over the island [being] struck with horror at hearing of this measure." The dogs proved so effective in suppressing the Maroon War that the Earl of Balcarres suggested turning them on the "Brigands of St. Domingo to do the same there."[144] The French employed Cuban dogs during the Haitian Revolution and, according to some accounts, set up a miniature Roman coliseum where soldiers made sport of the starved animals that devoured black flesh.[145] More than fifty years later during the U.S. Civil War, Cuban dogs aided the Confederacy in its attempt at secession by pursuing runway slaves as battlefields reached the plantations zones of the South.[146]

Atlantic powers eagerly aided neighboring colonies when an insurrection broke out as an opportunity for financial gain and as a security measure to prevent a rebellion from engulfing the entire Caribbean. The ability to lend arms, resources, and personnel to repress an uprising, however, depended on domestic stability. For example, the Maroon War of 1795 indirectly aided the Haitian Revolution by requiring British troops destined for Santo Domingo to remain in Jamaica. The Jamaican Assembly acknowledged the extended assistance offered by the British troops "for having detained a considerable part of the forces destined for the service of Santo Domingo on occasion of the Insurrection of the Maroons." Their expression of gratitude represented a sigh of relief that they did not share the same fate as their fellow French planters. Cuban slaveholders eased their anxiety and preoccupation about the contagion of revolution that spread through the Caribbean by claiming they

The Present Time Period

had isolated the island from surrounding rebellions. Their own experience, however, had taught them a truth that they could not likely face alone. Should a rebellion break out, Cuban planters might need assistance in suppressing the insurrection.[147]

The new policy of isolation also required reversing a long tradition of freeing slaves who reached Cuba to profess the Catholic faith. Runaway slaves from Protestant to Catholic countries became the beneficiaries of one of the unforeseen consequences of the European Reformation. Dating back to the seventeenth century, and especially after the British had firmly established colonies in the New World, the Spanish king decreed "to place in liberty all black slaves that flee the English and Dutch colonies to my dominions with the pretext to embrace our Holy Catholic Faith."[148] Where slave populations of Protestants and Catholics existed within close proximity, the possibility of flight and the expectation of freedom presented major problems, even contributing to revolts. Part of the motivation for the 1739 Stono Revolt in South Carolina stemmed from the Catholic background of the Angolan slaves in the rebellion who most likely planned to seek refuge in Spanish Florida.[149] When Britain returned Florida to Spanish control after the American Revolution, and the slave population increased in Georgia, runaways repeatedly crossed the border causing the Council of Indies to consider reversing the policy.[150] Just as political differences among European powers could provide opportunities for freedom through militarily aiding one side or the other during wartime, so could religious differences between Catholics and Protestants.

While slaves undoubtedly had an easier time crossing by land from Protestant to Catholic territory, a steady stream made the passage by boat from Jamaica to Cuba. In 1750, three slaves from Jamaica arrived in Santiago, whereupon the governor immediately granted them their freedom.[151] During the 1780s, the number of slaves seeking refuge in Cuba increased markedly. The Jamaican Assembly sent troops to Cuba in an attempt to reclaim "the parties of negroes who had deserted in a similar way from the north side of the island." Jamaican masters hoped to put an end to what they described as such a "distinct and public an avowal of encouragement to the slaves of this island to desert the services of their master, [causing] the ruin of many industrious individuals."[152] Slaves in Jamaica probably learned of the policy from individuals connected to maritime commerce who regularly traveled throughout the Caribbean. For example, in 1789, six slaves left Jamaica for Cuba in a canoe. Juan Baptista Hipolito testified that he convinced the others to go with him to Cuba after he learned of Spanish policy while living as a free man in the colony of Saint Domingue. During a trip to the Dutch colony of Curaçao, an English slave trader seized Juan Baptista and then sold him to Jamaica. Likely drawing upon his knowledge of the trading and shipping routes of the

Caribbean, combined with his ability to speak French, English, and Spanish, Juan Baptista and five other slaves successfully fled Jamaica for Cuba.[153]

In 1789, Alfred Clarke attempted to persuade the Cuban captain general, José de Espeleta, that the policy "may eventually be productive of danger to the properties of the inhabitants of both islands, if the slaves of the other are harboured and detained on the other."[154] Despite Clarke's pleas, Espeleta responded that the slaves "eloped from Jamaica" could not be returned as they had been granted "absolute freedom" to "instruct themselves in the Catholic religion, which was their object in coming here."[155] For Spanish colonial officials a trickle of runaways from Jamaica to Cuba did not present a significant threat to the security of the island and even provided a sense of Catholic pride from slaves' determination to leave their Protestant masters behind. Further, the additional presence of what Cubans described as "black Englishmen" only complemented the eastern portion of the island heavily tied to the British Caribbean.[156] Several plantations had large populations of Jamaican slaves that required English-speaking overseers to direct the laborers who understood little Spanish.[157] Hidden behind the rather harmless migratory patterns, an elaborate network of travel and communication routes indicated the degree to which the Caribbean had developed into an integrated region and, just as importantly, how knowledge of changes in one region shaped the experiences of slaves in another.[158]

After slave revolts erupted in the Caribbean in the 1790s and new restrictions were placed upon the importation of slaves, Spanish officials suddenly cooperated with the British in returning runaways to Jamaica. In 1795, Cuban authorities in the eastern city of Bayamo arrested a "suspicious negro from Jamaica" and quickly deported him.[159] Cubans no longer praised slaves from Jamaica for embracing the Catholic faith. Rather, they now described them as "legitimately owned . . . by the Island of Jamaica" and immediately returned them to the British colony.[160] The request by British vice admiral Mosley to return slaves that "have either deserted to the island of Cuba, or been inveigled away by illicit traders," suddenly received a response of eager cooperation.[161] Spanish officials promptly returned three runaways named Bavo, Sipion, and Santiago to Jamaica and began to patrol Cuban waters for slaves traveling from island to island.[162] The change in policy may have also reflected metropolitan politics. Spain had fought with Britain from 1796 to 1802 and 1804 to 1808 in the First and Second British Wars. Once Spain and Britain allied against Napoleon, the two countries appeared more inclined to cooperate in the international pursuit of runaways.[163]

The Aponte Rebellion of 1812 sent a shocking answer to elites who hid from their fears of a radical change by clinging to the belief that they could isolate Cuba from the revolutionary contagion circulating in the Atlantic world. Just as the arrest, interrogation, and execution of free black Juan Barbier that began this chapter indicates how the Haitian Revolution shaped the movement, the presence of numerous "English slaves" in the Aponte Rebellion reveals that events in the British Caribbean likely informed the rebels' actions. In the days before the outbreak of the rebellion in Bayamo, many of the arrested later reported to have had meetings where they spoke English.[164] Simply, knowledge of the English language provided enough proof for judicial officials to place free black Antonio Tamayo and Kongo slave Juan Farriol in jail.[165] Felix Corral informed Captain General Someruelos that "in virtue of having discovered the cause of the insurrection of slaves, many of them were from the English nation and others proficient in the [English] language."[166] The influence of events in the French and English Caribbean on the Aponte Rebellion of 1812 revealed the intimate knowledge slaves and free people of color had of liberation struggles in other parts of the Atlantic world. In planning their rebellion in Cuba, the leaders took courage and inspiration from the Age of Revolution by linking their actions with movements elsewhere.

CUBAN SLAVERY EXPANDED at a precarious moment in the world history of slavery.[167] The Age of Revolution that inspired radical political changes in Europe and wars for independence in the Americas ushered in the beginning of the end for Atlantic slavery in the New World. Cuban masters were not impervious to the global trends in slavery and attempted to insulate the island from the radical ideas crisscrossing the Atlantic as a strategy of self-preservation. Slaves and free people of color, as well, did not remain ignorant of the larger transformations operating outside of Cuba and the possibility for radical changes. The Aponte Rebellion of 1812 would confirm masters' fears of these external influences and their failed attempt at isolation, illustrating the need, according to the town council of Puerto Principe in 1811, to "guard against domestic enemies."[168] The next chapter turns its attention from the wider political changes in the Atlantic world to focus upon the transformation of Cuban society as slavery expanded.

# 2

## Nothing Worse in the World than to Be a Slave

Slaves and Free People
of Color in Early
Nineteenth-Century Cuba

The slave Tiburcio Peñalver suffered the same fate as José Antonio Aponte and Juan Barbier when the Havana military escorted him to the execution scaffold for his participation in the revolt. Unlike numerous male slaves who labored in the countryside, Tiburcio's master, Don Nicolás Peñalver, exempted him from the arduous task of cutting cane on his plantation named Trinidad, located outside of Havana. Tiburcio and a few other slaves held the privileged position of wagon drivers who delivered processed sugar cane to Havana merchants. Each time Tiburcio traveled to Havana, however, he delivered more than sugar cane. Tiburcio carried news from the countryside to friends and associates in Havana and relayed information back to the plantation from the city. While in Havana, he regularly stayed over night in the Guadalupe neighborhood where José Antonio Aponte and Juan Barbier lived. Authorities learned that during Tiburcio's trips to Havana he informed the urban leaders of the rebellion's preparation in the countryside. Tiburcio later confessed that he told the Havana leaders of the revolt that it "was agreed upon by his companions . . . to burn all the sugar plantations." On the night of 13 March 1812, Barbier and Tiburcio left Havana together at 10:00 P.M. for the countryside to make the final preparations for the planned insurrection.[1]

The next day Tiburcio arrived at the Trinidad plantation as normal, but not by himself. According to slave Tomás Peñalver, Tiburcio and Barbier recruited slaves from the plantation Trinidad to participate in the revolt, before heading to the Peñas-Altas sugar estate to ignite the insurrection. According to Tomás, Barbier commanded Tiburcio "to set fire to the slave quarters." During the uprising, Tiburcio and three other slaves broke down the door of the overseer's house and "delivered several blows with a machete" to him and his wife. Tiburcio managed to elude capture when authorities crushed the rebellion and arrested hundreds during the night and following day. When overseer Alejandro Pérez counted slaves at the Trinidad plantation on 15 March, Tiburcio was noticeably absent.[2]

Unlike the Frenchman Juan Barbier, who Cuban authorities quickly caught and then speedily executed on 9 April 1812, Tiburcio proved elusive. His knowledge of the surrounding terrain, plantations, villages, roads, and hide-outs he acquired while making deliveries to Havana most likely assisted his evasion of the patrols, just as the same skills acquired as a coachman served Toussaint Louverture as he traversed the countryside building alliances during the Haitian Revolution.[3] As remarked in the nineteenth-century novel *Sab* by Gertrudis Gómez de Avellaneda, slaves and free people of color who worked as carriage drivers and muleteers "know these roads" and "every inch of this country . . . to find shelter."[4] For several weeks military officials reported with frustration that they could not find Tiburcio. Martín Aróstegui wrote to Captain General Someruelos from a plantation that, despite "more than ten men . . . searching without stop to capture Tiburcio," he remained at large.[5] Nearly two weeks later, judicial authorities continued to report that Tiburcio eluded capture.[6] Aware of the nearly two-month-old manhunt that pursued him and his likely execution as soon as he would be captured, Tiburcio decided on 10 May to "voluntarily turn himself in at the plantation Trinidad," as authorities closed in on his hiding places. Shortly thereafter, Cuban officials shipped him under tight guard for interrogation at La Cabaña military fortress in Havana.[7]

The long search and the incriminating testimony by numerous slaves and free people of color caused judicial officials to demand Tiburcio's execution. Juan Ignacio Rendón recommended to Captain General Apodaca that Tiburcio be "condemned to capital punishment because not only did he take part in the conspiracy, but he was also one of the principal leaders who burnt the plantation and committed the murders at Peñas-Altas."[8] Apodaca agreed, labeling Tiburcio one of the "principal agitators" who deserved the death penalty "with the promptness that humanity recommends."[9] Judicial officials postponed Tiburcio's punishment until they had caught and questioned other slaves and free people of color in order to stage a collective execution. Five months later on 23 October 1812, at six thirty in the morning, a militia regiment and several Catholic priests escorted Tiburcio through the streets of Havana to the scaffold at La Punta military fortress. After announcing their crimes and informing the crowd of their punishment, the hangman executed Tiburcio and others for their leadership of the rebellion.[10]

Tiburcio Peñalver's personal involvement in the Aponte Rebellion illuminates several changes in Cuban society that will be examined in this chapter to establish the social and cultural background of the slaves and free people of color who joined the movement. At the time of the Aponte Rebellion, Cuba stood between two histories: the imperial service colony of the past and the plantation society of the nineteenth century divided ever more rigidly by race and legal status. Tiburcio's delivery of sugar to Havana for sale on the international market provides a glimpse into the expansion of plantation agriculture and the noticeable increase in slave labor as a result of the Atlantic slave trade. The sugar boom created clear distinctions between rural and urban society, but deliveries from the countryside to the city demonstrate the two areas remained linked together by the flow of commerce. The massive importation of slaves transformed Cuban society by emphasizing racial divisions that increasingly and with more clarity attempted to separate the black and white populations. The formation of rigid racial divisions fostered a collective identity by uniting, albeit tenuously, the historically disparate rural and urban and free and slave populations of African ancestry.

## THE SLAVE TRADE AND THE DEMOGRAPHIC TRANSFORMATION OF CUBAN SOCIETY

Slave labor represented the single most important factor for slaveholders in transforming their colony into a plantation society. Spanish economic policy from the sixteenth century generally demanded that colonists could purchase goods only from the mother country. The slave trade to Spanish America, however, had long escaped such restrictive regulations. Recognizing its inability to provide its American colonies with slave labor from the very beginning of the conquest in the sixteenth century, the Spanish Crown contracted out the slave trade to individual foreign companies through the system known as the *asiento*. The Portuguese dominated the *asiento* through the seventeenth century before Dutch, French, and then English traders took control of the trade for most of the eighteenth century. The Spanish Crown began to recognize the limitations of monopolistic slave-trading contracts to provide its colonies with slave labor as both the Seven Years' War and the America Revolution interrupted the *asiento*.[11]

During the second half of the eighteenth century, Spain reorganized its colonial administration through the Bourbon Reforms. Among other innovations, the Bourbon Reforms eased restrictive commercial regulations within the empire and attempted to increase administrative efficiency. Cuba provided the testing ground for the intendancy system in the 1760s that reinforced the captain general as the political head of the island and created the position of intendant who oversaw royal revenues, fortifications, and trade with the aim of rooting out corruption and centralizing royal control. The economic policy of the Bourbon Reforms no longer restricted Cuban trade to the ports of Cádiz and Seville, but allowed free trade within the Spanish American empire. The change in commercial regulations inspired Cuban slaveholders to push for opening the slave trade to all nations and end the *asiento* system.[12]

On 28 February 1789, the Spanish Crown acknowledged the great importance of the slave trade to commercial expansion, and the development of the Spanish Caribbean colonies in particular, by declaring free trade in slavery.[13] Spanish subjects could go to any foreign country to buy slaves that could then be brought to designated ports free of duty. More importantly, foreigners could now import slaves free of duty as Cuban slaveholders did not possess the expertise, ships, capital, or infrastructure to participate in a significant manner in the Atlantic slave trade, despite initial attempts.[14] Unlike the former *asiento* system that had set the price for imports, now buyer and seller would negotiate slave prices on an individual basis. When the two-year trial period of free trade in slaves ended in 1791, Francisco Arango y Parreño lobbied to have the policy extended, stating "with all frankness . . . the free introduction [of slaves] has allowed the island to prosper."[15] In the span of fifteen years, from 1789 to 1804, the crown issued eleven decrees aimed at expanding the slave trade.[16] Although the Cuban slave trade dates from the first decades of the sixteenth century and stands out as the longest in the history of New World slavery, only during the period from 1789 until its final abolition in 1867 did it fundamentally alter the social, racial, and ethnic composition of the island.

Cuban efforts to increase the imports of human cargo from 1790 to 1820 displayed a general trend of almost constant growth, with fluctuations that resulted from the Napoleonic wars (see table 2.1). While no consensus has emerged over exact figures, scholars agree that from 1790 to 1820 at least 300,000 slaves entered Cuba, and possibly more. The massive importation of slaves and the radical transformations of Cuban society are all the more apparent given that in the previous 280 years only 100,000 slaves had been imported. In the span of only thirty years the volume of the trans-Atlantic slave trade to Cuba increased threefold.[17]

Merely noting the correlation among changes in Spanish commercial policy, plantation agriculture, and the importation of hundreds of thousands of Africans to supply expanding sugar and coffee plantations cannot adequately capture the individual experience of enslavement. The narrative of William Thomas provides one of the few firsthand accounts of the Cuban trans-Atlantic slave trade to grasp the traumatic experience from capture, shipment to the African coast, crossing the Atlantic, being sold in Cuba, and then working as an unpaid laborer. Born near the West African coast in Cameroon

TABLE 2.1. Estimates of Cuban Slave Imports, 1790–1820

| Year | Humboldt | Saco | García | Pérez | Eltis |
|---|---|---|---|---|---|
| 1790–94 | 27,501 | 27,501 | 32,713 | 40,000 | 36,700 |
| 1795–99 | 22,915 | 23,045 | 24,238 | 52,000 | 30,800 |
| 1800–1804 | 38,230 | 38,230 | 40,650 | 59,800 | 50,900 |
| 1805–9 | 14,728 | 14,728 | 16,519 | 24,000 | 19,600 |
| 1810–14 | 28,193 | 28,193 | 31,308 | 46,500 | 37,700 |
| 1815–20 | 93,907 | 104,928 | 137,980 | 147,000 | 139,800 |
| Total | 225,474 | 236,625 | 283,408 | 369,300 | 315,500 |

Sources: Alexander von Humboldt, *Ensayo político sobre la isla de Cuba* (1826; reprint, with an introduction by Fernando Ortiz, Havana: Fundación Fernando Ortiz, 1998), 102; José Antonio Saco, *Colección de papeles científicos, históricos, políticos, y de otros ramos sobre la isla de Cuba ya publicados, ya inéditos* (Paris: D'Aubusson y Kugelman, 1858), 2:70; Gloria García, "Importación de esclavos de ambos sexos por varios puertos de Cuba, 1763–1820," in *Historia de Cuba: La colonia, evolución socioeconómica y formación nacional de los origines hasta 1867*, ed. María del Carmen Barcia, Gloria García, and Eduardo Torres-Cuevas (Havana: Editorial Política, 1994), 471–73, table 11; Juan Pérez de la Riva, *El Monto de la inmigración forzada en el siglo xix* (Havana: Editorial de Ciencias Sociales, 1979), table 3; David Eltis, *Economic Growth and the Ending of the Transatlantic Slave Trade* (Oxford: Oxford University Press, 1987), 245.

at the Bight of Benin around 1800, Thomas recalled that one day when his older brother left him unattended, "I was seized by a man, who sent word to my brother to come and redeem me for 100 goats." After waiting "two moons," Thomas's captors sold him for "gun, powder, and cloth" to the coast because his "brother had not so many goats."[18] Thomas then made the forced trek to the West African coast for sale to Atlantic slave traders. He recalled that after the merchant "sold me to the Spaniards," he was loaded "with a great many others until the vessel was quite full." Shortly after leaving the African coast, however, an "English man of war" intercepted the ship near Sierra Leone. Thomas remembered that after the British captain, Hagan, boarded the ship, he "took the slaves out of irons, when all [became] very glad and danced too much." Several years later the Atlantic slave trade ensnared Thomas again. While delivering goods by river transport in what he described as "a large canoe, carrying iron bars, muskets, tobacco, beads, powder &c., to exchange for gold, rice, cattle &c," he was seized again. Similar to his first enslavement, Thomas's captors sold him to a Spanish slave trader bound for Havana, Cuba.[19]

Once the ship left the African coast, "all cried very much at going away from their home and friends, some of them saying they would kill them-

Nothing Worse in the World

selves." After three weeks at sea, several of the Africans began plotting to "rise and kill the captain, and take the ship back to Africa." Thomas, with a less courageous spirit and perhaps a more sensible head, told them "that they did not understand 'sailor palaver,' and if they took the vessel, 'big wind would come, and she would capsize, and then all of us would die.'" One month after leaving Africa, the ship arrived in Havana where they "were placed in a baracoon [barracks], and sold, as purchasers offered us." Thomas spent the next twenty years of his life in Cuba owned by several masters and working in a wide variety of jobs ranging from general laborer on a sugar plantation to hat maker to domestic servant. After several years of scheming to escape Cuba and return to Africa, Thomas gained passage to London with the help of the British consul in 1842. In February 1843, after visiting with British abolitionists and providing his narrative for publication in the *Anti-Slavery Reporter*, Thomas prepared to make his return trip to Sierra Leone.[20]

The story of William Thomas is just one of millions of Africans who crossed the Atlantic. The documentary record has left more evidence for historians about the demographic and economic aspects of the slave trade. The absence of material on the individual experience of slaves such as William Thomas tragically indicates how people of European ancestry most commonly valued Africans as commodities that could be quantified, rather than as distinct individuals valued for their human qualities.[21] While we will never understand the scope and magnitude of the largest forced migration in human history without a quantitative assessment (just as we cannot comprehend the Jewish Holocaust or atomic warfare without body counts), it is important to approach the study of slavery and the slave trade with qualitative sources because these few sources tell us something numbers cannot.

Slaveholders readily purchased slaves as soon as they could, but Spanish policy called for a distinction between the importation of *bozal* slaves directly from Africa and the importation of *bozal* slaves from other ports and colonies of the Americas. The 1789 free trade in slaves allowed slave traders throughout the Atlantic world to supply Cuba with slaves. As described in the last chapter, after insurrections erupted in the French and British Caribbean colonial officials began to distinguish between *bozal* slaves who came directly from Africa and *bozal* slaves who had spent time in the Americas. Spanish colonial officials prevented the importation of slaves from French and British colonies because they feared slaves would spread the contagion of rebellion. The long history of legal and illegal interactions among the colonial powers of the Caribbean resulted in regulations for bozal imports from American ports being circumvented on a regular basis.[22] Less than one year after the Spanish Crown prevented the importation of human cargo from Saint Domingue, the captain general of Cuba allowed a French trader to sell 197 slaves in

Havana. Slaves from the French and British colonies continued to routinely arrive at Cuban ports during the 1790s and 1800s despite prohibitive decrees.[23]

When slave-trading ships arrived from Africa or other ports of the Americas, several procedures and inspections occurred before examination by prospective masters. In Havana, slave ships normally docked outside the harbor until they received official clearance to deliver their cargo.[24] As part of the new series of laws that regulated the slave trade and slavery in the Americas, the Spanish Crown issued a royal decree in 1784 abolishing the previous practice of branding slaves on the "face or back" to distinguish them from "fraudulently imported slaves" before placing them on display to buyers.[25] In Havana, soldiers from the white and free men of color militias, as well as the regular infantry army, escorted slaves from the ships to prevent uprisings and violent confrontations.[26]

Soldiers also carried away slaves who died during the middle passage. The burial of Africans presented grave sanitary and health problems for Cuban residents. Unscrupulous slave traders often dumped dead slaves overboard to avoid burial costs of thirty-two *reales* per body. The captain general issued a new law in 1809 to enforce burials on land and prevent entombment at sea. He insisted that the Africans be buried "in solid ground . . . and the body be covered with earth so that animals cannot discover the body." The captain general did not appear alarmed that slave traders routinely threw dead African slaves overboard, bodies regularly washed ashore from sea, or scavenging animals often unearthed Africans from hastily dug shallow graves. He complained that the difference between those buried on land and "those dispatched to the sea is that [slave traders] do not have to pay" for the burial.[27] Even after death, slaves represented a revenue-generating commodity for the Spanish state.

The Cuban militia vigilantly escorted the slaves from the docks to the large military-like barracks called *barracones*.[28] In Havana, the neighborhood of San Lázaro beyond the city walls housed the recently arrived Africans.[29] Lorenzo Clarke from Lagos later reported that when he arrived in Cuba sometime during the 1830s "slaves were taken to the government baracoons [sic] on the Alameda, [across from] the Morro."[30] Miguel Marino, who arrived in Havana during the same time period, was taken "to the baracoons at the Havana, called Castilo [sic] Príncipe."[31] The confined spaces of the barracones and the numerous Africans who temporarily passed through the buildings before a master purchased them represented a continuity with their experience in the middle passage. Just as slave traders routed Africans through slave forts in West Africa, sold them to Atlantic merchants, and then housed them in the crowded hull of ships for the trans-Atlantic voyage, upon arrival in Havana, slaves disembarked to cramped barracones run by Cuban slave mer-

Nothing Worse in the World

chants before being sold to Cuban masters. As historian Paul Lovejoy has emphasized, the middle passage did not just represent the Atlantic crossing, but the "middle" period of the entire enslavement process form capture in West Africa to trans-Atlantic crossing to sale and labor in the Americas.[32]

As a response to the high mortality rate after arrival in Cuba and the dwindling number of nations participating in the Atlantic slave trade, medical doctors began to voice concerns about the slaves' health. Physician Tomás Romay voiced medical concerns about the death rate on the middle passage and convinced Spanish officials to vaccinate slaves as soon as they arrived.[33] In 1808, the captain general established a vaccinating committee that campaigned for the "most zealous propagation of the vaccine" by requiring the inoculation of all African slaves prior to sale in Cuba.[34] The town council of Havana decided to establish infirmaries in all the slave barracones of the city to vaccinate slaves and examine their health upon arrival from Africa.[35]

The required medical treatment for *bozales* just to keep them alive and their vulnerability to diseases because of their weakened physical strength indicates the devastating toll the middle passage had on their health. In the 1810s medical doctor J. L. F. de Madrid investigated the health of slaves by visiting several Havana barracones. The doctor drew a sharp contrast between "the growing wealth and prosperity of this country as a result of agriculture and free trade" with what he observed when he "entered one of the barracones located outside the city walls that presented a very different spectacle." Madrid remarked at the horror that struck him to see "a number of dying blacks naked and spread out on wooden planks, many of them reduced to skin and bones, and inhaling an intolerable stench." Dysentery represented the major cause of death in the barracones, causing the "muscles and the skeleton to weaken, perfectly distinguishing the configuration of bones." The placid numbness of the Africans shocked the doctor who noticed that "some only complained a little or not at all and appear in a stage of tranquility" even while they "urinated and defecated in bed, sometimes just pure blood, often becoming cold as marble, and then dying." The doctor identified unsanitary living quarters, diseases, and an inadequate and unhealthy diet as the causes for dysentery. He concluded his report, however, by observing that it was the institution of slavery as a whole and not strictly medical, sanitary, or dietary reasons that caused dysentery. "There is nothing worse in the world than to be a slave: violence, punishing work, meager and terrible alimentation, terror, and demolition of the spirit, these are the causes that predispose Africans to dysentery."[36] His stark observations, unfortunately, did not find sympathetic ears.

J. L. F. de Madrid was not alone in recognizing that Cuban economic prosperity based upon African slavery had two perspectives. The structure of

Cuban slave society delineated along class and racial lines for the purposes of production whereby one segment of the population received the benefits from another's unpaid labor produced conflicting benefits of economic growth. For white Cuban Creoles and Spaniards, the increase in the slave trade and plantation production brought new wealth and prosperity. Rebel leader José Antonio Aponte, however, had a different perspective. In his book of drawings, he included images of various trading ships in Havana, customs houses near the harbor, and, in particular, a boat from Spain carrying news of the ending of taxes and new regulations for commerce. On the docks where goods were loaded and unloaded, Aponte cryptically described his drawing as depicting "a sloop . . . attacking the greed of the dock with death." Cuban judicial officials demanded Aponte elaborate on his puzzling description of Havana commerce. José María Nerey asked Aponte, "How can you content yourself with what you have explained about the development of commerce with what is indicated by the drawing . . . when on the dock you see death . . . which indicates destruction of this, not advancement." Aponte explained that "death only destroyed greed," not commerce.[37] Nerey asked no other questions about the drawing so it remains uncertain what specifically Aponte intended by drawing an image that depicted the increase of commerce in Havana's harbor juxtaposed with death. At the very least (and perhaps all we can know with certainty), the economic growth of Cuba as a product of expanding plantation agriculture and the importations of slaves were not universally embraced but depended on who received the benefits.

The impact of the slave trade on Cuban population growth did not just affect the people of African ancestry. Census data for the period shows a marked increase in the population across the island. In the twenty-five years between 1792 and 1817, the population on the island doubled (see table 2.2). The overall trend shows the population of slaves and free people of color growing faster than the white population.[38] The 1792 census marked the first time in Cuban history that the combined slave and free people of color population outnumbered the white.[39] It was clear to an observer in 1799 that the "progressive increase in the [slave] population by reason of natural increase and the introduction of blacks" explained the dynamic demographic growth of the island.[40] The free population of color also showed remarkable growth and doubled in the same time period. Of the overall increase in the population from 1792 to 1817, the combined slave and free population of African ancestry comprised 62 percent of the growth while the white population represented 38 percent.[41] Francisco Barrera y Domingo exaggerated the role of Africans in Cuba's population growth when he repeated in 1798 the popular phrase that "of the four parts of the Cuban people, three and a half can be attributed to them [Africans]."[42] His point recognized how the

Nothing Worse in the World

TABLE 2.2. Cuban Population Figures, 1755–1817

| Year | White (%) | Free People of Color (%) | Slave (%) | Total |
|---|---|---|---|---|
| 1755 | no data | no data | 28,760 (17) | 170,000 |
| 1774 | 96,440 (56) | 30,847 (18) | 44,333 (26) | 171,620 |
| 1792 | 133,559 (49) | 54,152 (20) | 84,590 (31) | 272,301 |
| 1804 | 234,000 (46) | 90,000 (18) | 180,000 (36) | [504,000] |
| 1810 | 274,000 (46) | 108,600 (18) | 217,400 (36) | 600,000 |
| 1817[a] | 239,830 (43) | 114,058 (21) | 199,145 (36) | 553,033 |
| 1817[b] | 259,260 (41) | 154,057 (24) | 225,131 (35) | 638,448 |

*Sources*: 1755, 1817: B. Huber, *Aperçu statistique de l'ille de Cuba, précède de quelques lettres sur la Havane, et suivi de synoptiques* (Paris: Chez P. Dufart Libraire, 1826), 228–33; 1774, 1792, 1817: Ramón de la Sagra, *Historia económico, político y estadística de la isla de Cuba* (Havana: Imprenta de las Viudas de Azora y Soler, 1831), 3–10; 1804, 1810: Alexander von Humboldt, *Ensayo sobre la isla de Cuba* (Paris: Joules Renourard, 1827), 108–13. Humboldt claimed the total population in 1804 numbered 432,080. This does not correspond to his figures on the racial breakdown of the population. The number in brackets indicates the corrected total.
[a]These 1817 figures are from de la Sagra.
[b]These 1817 figures are from Huber.

importation of slaves fundamentally changed the racial characteristics of the Cuban population.

The rapid demographic transformation of Cuba produced an uneasy tension among elites that society was growing beyond their control. During the 1790s and 1800s, local officials throughout the island regularly gathered census data to track the population. Unfortunately, they did not collect the data in a systematic or consistent manner to allow for a detailed analysis of the demographic structure of Cuba.[43] Nonetheless, the numerous censuses themselves indicate a conscious effort to track the population and a noted obsession with demographic figures because of a fear over the rising slave population. The functionary in charge of synthesizing and presenting the information to the captain general in 1799 recognized the inaccuracies of the data: "the current censuses should always be regarded with suspicion."[44] Alexander von Humboldt reached similar conclusions about Cuban statistical data from the 1774, 1792, and 1817 censuses that he described as "very inaccurate."[45] The recognized flaws of Cuban statistical data do not invalidate it as a historical source. All censuses whether from nineteenth-century Cuba or twenty-first-century United States have mistakes from undercounting, overcounting, or mathematical errors. The important point is that contemporaries anguished over census errors. They believed they could only control the rapidly growing population through accurate quantification.[46]

The disappearance in the 1800s of census categories that did not describe European or African phenotypes pointedly indicates how the Cuban population became categorized ever more clearly along racial lines. Warfare and contagious diseases annihilated the vast majority of indigenous population during the sixteenth century. As late as the eighteenth century, however, scattered Native American groups continued to exist in Cuba, mainly in the eastern portion of the island. The 1775 census for the eastern city of Holguín and its surrounding territory, for example, counted an almost equal number of Indians, free people of color, and slaves, in addition to the overwhelming majority of Spanish and white Creoles. Nearly thirty years later and after the establishment of some small plantations and the growth of Holguín, the category of "Indian" disappeared from the census all together. Censuses now divided the population into whites, blacks, and free people of color.[47] Neither the political correspondence from the time period nor local, national, or imperial archives provide any explanation for the "disappearance" of the indigenous population by warfare or contagious diseases. Rather, as Cuba's population became increasingly divided along racial lines as a result of the slave trade, the "Indian" population became collapsed into the category of white or mulatto. For example, in order to enlist additional soldiers at the end of the eighteenth century, the subinspector general declared the Indians of Bayamo "white" for purposes of military service despite colonial law that viewed them as perpetual minors.[48] The disappearance of the category demonstrates how identity in Cuba became increasingly divided between free and slave by race at the end of the eighteenth century.

SLAVES, SLAVERY, AND THE RACIAL TRANSFORMATION
OF CUBAN SOCIETY

The terms that contemporaries used to describe the Cuban populations of European and African ancestry did not correspond only to census categories. According to the female slave María Belen, questioned for her involvement in the revolts in Puerto Príncipe, Africans came up with their own designations to refer to white people. María told judicial officials that when slaves talked among themselves they would use the term *el mundo* (the world) to designate white people.[49] From their testimony in court, slaves and free people of color also indicated how they referred to each other beyond racial categories. The Kongo slave Benito, owned by Tomás Valdés, reported to authorities that he had dinner and drank wine with his *compañero* (close companion), the black slave Pablo.[50] Likewise, the African-born slave Francisco González, also from the Kongo region, greeted a stranger of African ancestry on the plantation

Nothing Worse in the World

with *camarada* (comrade).[51] Through categories that designated whites and blacks, slaves in Cuba created their own terms for the populations of European and African ancestry that showed a degree of commonalty with each other and their distance from the white population that represented another *mundo*.

The Spanish and white Cuban population limited their descriptions and categories for the slave and free people of color population as they related to work. According to the bishop of Cuba, "only blacks can resist all day the strength of the sun while working." The bishop elaborated that while Africans lived a "healthy and robust" life on the plantation, when the "Spaniard, Canary Islander, or American" carried out the same work, "diseases appear that lead them to the grave."[52] Luis de Las Casas, the captain general of Cuba from 1790 to 1796, knew only slightly better. He encouraged the migration of Canary Islanders to offset the dependence on slave labor in the countryside because, he reasoned, their familiarity with the tropical climate made them suitable to the Cuban environment. According to Las Casas, "previously almost all of the migrants from the Canary Islands worked the land." "Now," the captain general complained, "they have taken the pleasure of occupations less tiresome" even though they "were permitted to migrate to America with the expressed condition to work in the countryside."[53] The rapid increase in the slave population and the beginnings of the sugar boom resulted in racializing labor. Previously, Canary Islanders worked on plantations. By the 1790s, however, almost all of the tasks carried out in agricultural production and the most labor-intensive work had been relegated to African slaves. The comment made by the mulatto slave Sab in the 1840 antislavery novel that "this virgin soil did not need to be watered with the sweat of slaves to be productive" would have fallen on deaf white ears.[54] Indeed, the governor of Bayamo referred to Africans working on plantations as "their natural state."[55] By the beginning of the nineteenth century, plantation labor in Cuba became synonymous with African slavery.

The instruments of authority and domination encoded by slavery with racial connotations changed the meanings of physical punishment in Cuba during the 1790s and 1800s. Certain actions emblematic of the violent treatment of slaves became regarded as inappropriate for the white population. Perhaps no single action more powerfully represented the authority slavery provided whites over blacks as the ability to inflict physical punishment with the lash. In 1809, military officials arrested Juan de la Cruz and placed him in jail for a fight with his wife, not because of the physical harm he inflicted on her, but because he beat her like a slave "with a leather whip."[56] The whipping of humans did not represent a crime, and even received the blessing of the Spanish Crown, as long as the lash landed on African backs. As slavery began to define ever more clearly the paradigm of Cuba's hierarchy, the use and threat of force in the form of punishments for slaves and whites had to be separated.

The restrictions placed upon some abusive husbands also extended to teachers who whipped unruly children in public schools. Teachers had the authority to physically reprimanded white school children, but no longer with a whip.[57] British traveler James Alexander remarked capital punishments also took on racial connotations that made them inappropriate for the white population: "The Spaniards have a great objection to see a white person executed at Havanah [sic], because it degrades their orders in the eyes of the coloured inhabitants."[58] Slavery clearly represented the lowest position in colonial Cuban society. Consequently, to treat any white like a slave represented the greatest insult. As slavery came to be associated exclusively with blackness, punishments took on racially specific connotations that made them applicable only to Africans and inappropriate for Europeans.

Cuban officials also worried that just as slavery could unleash the tyranny of masters on family members, it would also project the island to the world as an "uncivilized" country. Beginning in the nineteenth century, the Cuban government sponsored programs that expanded public education throughout the island. The leaders of the education program made explicit appeals to promote Cuban education to foster an image of a "civilized" country. The necessity to define Cuba as a civilized and educated country revealed a tension among the elite of the island that slavery and the large African population represented a backward institution.[59] Although the policy largely focused on cities, educators established several schools in rural areas. Francisco Arango y Parreño and Nicolás Calvo funded a school near the plantation district of Güines outside of Havana "to improve the education and soften the rough customs of the whites in the countryside."[60] As Cuba's population changed demographically and racial divisions became more apparent, education and physical punishment increasingly took on racial connotations.

Unsurprisingly the complaints of whippings by teachers or the arrest of abusive husbands rarely carried over for masters who beat slaves, despite the legal limitations imposed by the *Código Negro*. Travelers' accounts, archival sources, slave testimonies, novels, and secondary sources leave little indication about the brutality of Cuban masters, their overall regard for slaves as property, and their complete authority to inflict physical punishments.[61] When Francisco Barrera investigated the health conditions of slaves on plantations he sarcastically noted that "their breakfast is a lash of leather."[62] Masters in Cuba recognized that the Spanish Crown expressed concerns over their brutal treatment of slaves. Slaveholders attempted to persuade the Crown that their financial interests dictated kind treatment of their human property. A group of Cuban slaveowners simply stated, "It is profitable for masters to

Nothing Worse in the World

treat slaves well because it is slave labor that provides the wealth and development of our haciendas."[63] According to masters, since slaves represented capital and instruments of production, it did not make rational sense to destroy and damage their property. Human calculation, to the liberal economists' dismay, however, is rarely so rational.[64] Punishments of slaves provided a disciplinary tool that not only shaped and formed the behavior of an insubordinate slave but also served as a threat for the entire slave community. When Abiel Abbot visited plantations near Matanzas in the late 1820s, he noticed that the overseer assembled all the slaves in front of the master's house "to see correction by the mayoral. I heard the snap of the lash, but no other noise; and the negroes retired from the parade in Indian file."[65] Likewise, when French traveler Julian Mellet visited plantations on the eastern end of the island, he also commented on how masters forged punishments and the threat of punishment into a disciplinary tool to control slave behavior: "All of the whites . . . are required to reach the harshest extremes to inspire terror and respect and not become themselves victims of the slaves' rage."[66] Slavery above all rested on either actual or threatened force. In order for punishments to have power in shaping master-slave relations, whippings were routinely applied to show such threats would and could be enforced.

Masters in Cuba walked a fine line between enforcing punishments to demonstrate their ultimate authority and showing restraint for fear that such cruelty not only damaged their personal property but even more dangerously engendered rebellion. Following the Haitian Revolution, the colonial state appeared especially worried about this dilemma because it would ultimately fall upon the government to put down an insurrection. Occasionally, the state investigated the abuse of masters who overstepped the written and unwritten norms that characterized slave punishment. In 1811, Luisa Montaño from Santiago requested sale to another master because of the constant whippings she received from her owner. Luisa's master, Luis Gerbet, defended himself, remarking she was "a thief, runaway, drunk, and begged money from my friends." The lawyer concluded that Luisa's alleged vices did not "justify the excessive punishment," because she only escaped "to see her husband," but nonetheless denied her request for a new master.[67]

In some cases, judicial officials did strip slaveowners of their human property. In 1812 the captain general of Cuba ruled that Juan Gómez and his wife could no longer be "served by slaves . . . for the punishment [they had] given to a black female."[68] Even though the state occasionally interceded on slaves' behalf and contested the authority of slaveowners, it should not be regarded as an example of early antislavery thought and action. Rather, just as the colonial government attempted to isolate Cuba from the contagion of revolt circulating in the Atlantic as a strategy of self-preservation, the efforts to standardize and restrict masters' punishments displayed a reformist position to guarantee the stability and future of slavery.

For every action brought against masters for excessive and cruel punishment, hundreds if not thousands went unreported. Cuban officials threatened to investigate masters' abuses more frequently than they actually investigated such crimes. In 1809, Captain General Someruelos wrote to the Havana town council requesting that they investigate why, despite the prohibition, masters continued to employ "the punishment of an iron collar around the neck with three iron neck ties." He reminded the council members of the "considerable time that has passed" since the implementation of the 1789 *Código Negro*. Someruelos emphasized that, if the practice did not stop, judges would investigate "any slave's complaint of poor treatment by their owner."[69] Several months later the captain general once again requested action by the town council on "the cruel punishments that some masters have given to their slaves against the prohibitions" of the *Código Negro*.[70] The Havana town council showed no inclination to investigate such abuses and would only remind masters that slaves had the right to ask the government to investigate cases of excessive punishment.[71]

With the duty placed upon the slaves to report excessive punishment by masters, it is surprising any found lawyers to investigate such accusations. Undoubtedly, masters attempted to prevent slaves from filing complaints. This makes the petition of people such as Luisa Montaño against her master all the more forceful and desperate. Cuban officials often learned of cruel punishments through the discovery of mutilated dead bodies, rather than from slaves reporting crimes to a lawyer or judge. José Mederos informed the local military official at Jesús Monte, a small city outside of Havana, that a terrible odor emanated from the neighboring yard of Esteban González. According to the surgeon's death certificate, a dismembered body "was found in four sacks."[72] Rural patrols often found bodies of dead people of African ancestry, some of them likely the result of abusive slaveowners.[73] The common reports of self-mutilation and suicide by slaves provide further indication of the abuse by masters and the horrific mental trauma caused by slavery.[74] Cuban anthropologist Fernando Ortiz remarked that the "Mandingas were known for their tendency toward group suicide: in this way they freed themselves from their labors and had the last laugh on the master with a strike for which there was no settlement, and their successful escape to the other world."[75] The last laugh may have settled old scores and prompted investigations to prevent the loss of property, but the tragedy of suicide pointedly revealed how slavery produced incredible and often desperate desires to escape the earthly world.[76]

Not only did the trans-Atlantic slave trade and the abuse of masters con-

Nothing Worse in the World

tribute to a high mortality rate, slaveowners literally and consciously worked their slaves to death. German traveler Alexander von Humboldt shockingly reported that Cuban slaveowners "discussed with the utmost calm" whether it was not more economical to overwork slaves and derive "from them all of the possible profits in a few years."[77] The *consulado* of Havana bluntly remarked that the twenty-hour workdays of the harvest season resulted in the high mortality of slaves.[78] William Thomas recalled from his own enslavement that the normal workday for slaves in Cuba spanned from "four in the morning till seven in the evening."[79] Margarita Cabrera reported that slaves at the sugar plantation where she labored for fifteen years worked "from three in the morning till noon" stopping for lunch, and then "they returned to their work, and went on till sunset, and often later."[80] Agustín Acosta reported that, during the harvest, workdays began at "about four in the morning, to midnight, one hour being allowed in the middle of the day for meals."[81] Cuban officials estimated that the long work hours resulted in most slaves not living beyond ten years on sugar plantations.[82] Indeed, anthropologist Sidney Mintz accurately described Caribbean plantations as "agroindustrial graveyards" with their regimented work schedule and high mortality rate.[83]

Fueled by the slave trade, Cuban society underwent radical social, demographic, and economic changes beginning in the 1790s. In the relatively short span of thirty years, Cuba imported more than 300,000 slaves, amazingly tripling the entire volume of the trans-Atlantic slave trade for the previous three centuries. The massive importation of slaves and the expansion of plantation agriculture began a transformation of Cuba into a plantation society worked by slave labor that would continue throughout the nineteenth century. A new slavery emerged in Cuba after 1790. Racial identity became the primary category that defined the barriers of inclusion for the white population of European ancestry and exclusion for the black population of African ancestry. The racial plantation society, however, did not immediately eclipse the past cultural and political structures that provided special rights and privileges for free people of color and slaves. The two societies existed side by side and contradicted each other. Despite the atomizing work regimes of the "agroindustrial graveyards" some slaves became free people of color by creatively and resiliently drawing upon the contradictions produced by a society in transition to improve, however small, their subordinate position.

"KNOCKING OF THEIR CHAINS LINK BY LINK":
FREE PEOPLE OF COLOR

Free person of color Juan Bautista Lisundia added another conspirator to the executioner's list along with rebel leader José Antonio Aponte, Frenchman

Juan Barbier, and the slave Tiburcio Peñalver. Aponte informed authorities that Lisundia frequently visited his house and that they had lunched together in the past.[84] Judicial officials learned that Lisundia attended meetings with Aponte when the rebels planned the revolt.[85] Lisundia had been spotted with the Frenchman Juan Barbier in Havana and on plantations outside the city during the insurrections.[86] According to slave Antonio Cao, Barbier and Lisundia directed the insurrection by brandishing "machetes in the air and ordering the plantation to be burnt."[87] Lisundia had also met with slave Tiburcio Peñalver in Havana and in the plantation districts for the purpose of planning the rebellion. When the revolt erupted, Tiburcio followed Lisundia's orders and set the Peñas-Altas plantation on fire.[88] Juan Bautista Lisundia's involvement in the insurrection and his association with Aponte, Barbier, and Tiburcio resulted in colonial officials sentencing him to death by hanging on the morning of 9 April 1812.

Just as the slave Tiburcio connected the rural and urban worlds of the Aponte Rebellion by delivering sugar cane to Havana for sale on the international market, free person of color Juan Bautista Lisundia served as an important link between the slave and free groups involved in the insurrection. Lisundia may have traced his family ancestry to Central Africa because he often associated with Kongo slaves.[89] Sometime during his life in Cuba he gained his freedom and took up a residence in Havana with his father Clemente Chacón.[90] Although Lisundia lived in Havana as a freedman, he regularly made trips to the plantations where he often worked as a contract laborer alongside slaves.[91] He traveled frequently between rural and urban areas with a license that authorized him to leave Havana to work on plantations. Lisundia extended his mastery of literacy to the illiterate by providing licenses for slaves and free people of color to travel between Havana and the countryside.[92] Lisundia appears to have carried on a close friendship with several plantation slaves, frequently fraternizing and drinking cane alcohol with them, according to several sources.[93] Lisundia's camaraderie and friendship with people of color held in bondage may have stemmed from his own previous position as an enslaved laborer.

Judicial officials never bothered to ask Lisundia how he obtained his freedom or why he associated with slaves when they interrogated him. They also did not question how other freedmen and freedwomen in the rebellion had achieved their liberty. Authorities did not bother to ask because manumission commonly occurred throughout Cuban history, even if it remained difficult for the slave to achieve. By the time of the Aponte Rebellion in 1812, the free people of color population represented nearly 20 percent of the entire Cuban population. The expansion of plantation agriculture worked by slave labor ironically provided economic opportunities for self-purchase. By working on

Nothing Worse in the World

weekends, marketing goods, participating in contraband trade, and performing services that whites either by their absence or choice would not do, slaves earned money to buy their freedom. The same economic transformations that presented opportunities for freedom also set strict limitations on the political and material meanings of liberty. The rise of a racialized plantation economy in the 1790s forced masters and colonial officials to reconsider the economic and social roles performed by free men and women of African ancestry in nineteenth-century Cuba. The expansion of slavery made the distinction between the free population of white European ancestry and the enslaved population of black African ancestry all the more clear, and the position of free people of color ever more tenuous.

The ability of rebel leader Lisundia to earn his freedom and of other slaves to become free people of color does not indicate masters' benevolent treatment or the roles of the church and state in protecting the humanity of slaves, as scholars once claimed. Earlier historians correctly emphasized the varied experiences of slaves and the possibility for liberation, but they erred in suggesting, without investigation, that the institutions of the state and the church alone explained why. Subsequent historians have shown the failure of laws and Catholicism to curb master domination, but in refuting such ideas they shared the approach of focusing on the church and the state by describing them as weak institutions, rather than examining the actions of slaves.[94] German traveler Alexander von Humboldt observed a crucial aspect of Cuban slavery that subsequent historians have often overlooked, even though many have consulted his work. Humboldt concluded that "in no part of the world, where slavery exists, is manumission so frequent as in the island of Cuba; for Spanish legislation, directly the reverse of French and English, favors to an extraordinary degree the attainment of freedom, placing no obstacle in its way, nor making it in any manner onerous." Yet, at the same time, Humboldt recognized that the relatively high incidence of manumission did not indicate benevolent slave treatment, or that all slaves had equal access to manumission.[95]

Cuban slavery in the early nineteenth century was the product of a long colonial tradition born out of Spanish medieval society that came into conflict with a plantation mode of production.[96] Cuban slavery in the nineteenth century traced its origins to a corporatist tradition that guaranteed certain segments of the population rights through political, legal, and judicial channels. The plantation regime of the nineteenth century, however, created a new hierarchy that made gaining access to these rights ever more difficult. The two slave societies that existed in Cuba were the product of a constant and ongoing battle. Masters attempted to impose a nineteenth-century racialized system of bondage. Slaves, in contrast, defended themselves against plantation exploitation by employing past cultural practices and legal rights that challenged the rigid societal divisions between the free and enslaved.

Hardly unique to Cuban history, the right for slaves to purchase their own freedom represented a common feature in all the Iberian colonies of the Americas. The legal provisions for slaves to accumulate capital and property to buy their own freedom had its origins in Roman law. The practice later became codified in Spain through an extensive legal code called the *Siete Partidas* in the mid-thirteenth century.[97] As early as 1526, the Spanish Crown attempted to set a scale for the price of freedom based upon age and physical condition to regulate the already common practice in the Americas.[98] Throughout Spanish and Portuguese America, wherever slavery existed, local notaries recorded "letters of liberty" (*cartas de libertad, cartas da liberdade*), marking the transition from a slave to a free person of color. Slaveowners employed self-purchase as an incentive for slaves to conform to their will. Over time, however, slaves transformed the master-bestowed reward into a right.

From the early colonial era slaves had the right to initiate the purchase of their own freedom by making a down payment on their market value. In Cuba (as in other parts of Spanish America), the legal procedure of self-purchase initiated by the slaves became known as *coartación*, literally, the process of cutting ties.[99] British traveler Robert Jameson attributed Cuba's large free population of African descent to the practice of *coartación*: "There are many coloured people whose freedom is the purchase of the extra earnings allowed them by law." During his time in Havana, he observed that "every slave, under Spanish colonial law, who tenders his master the sum he was bought at, is entitled to enfranchisement, nor can his master refuse it. It is equally permitted him to purchase a portion of his freedom, by installments, as his ability allows, being then said to be *coartado* or cut." The slave thus bought his freedom "by knocking of his chain link by link," according to Jameson.[100]

Contemporaries as well as historians have tended to concur that manumission by self-purchase largely represented an urban phenomenon and rarely extended to the plantations. For example, in 1800 Havana slave Antonio José paid 200 pesos for his freedom, money he earned in his "free" time apart from working at the military fort, Casa Blanca.[101] Urban slaves had easier access to courts and notaries to initiate self-purchase, could market goods to earn money to buy their freedom, and could draw upon free people of color to assist in the process.[102] Although there are few quantitative studies of manumission for Cuba and none which makes a systematic comparison between rural and urban areas, it appears that self-purchase in one payment or through a series of installments by a *coartación* agreement had become widespread by

Nothing Worse in the World

the nineteenth century. Historians Laird Bergad, Fe Iglesias, and María del Carmen Barcia have demonstrated that for every four slaves sold in the markets at Havana, Santiago, and Cienfuegos from 1790 to 1880, one slave gained freedom.[103]

Self-purchase by slaves represented such a common form of manumission that over time *coartado* became a special juridical status.[104] *Coartados'* legal rights fluctuated somewhere between a slave and a free person of color. Before a slave became a *coartado*, a local government official known as the *síndico procurador* decided the slave's value. For example, when judicial officials questioned María Antonia Antola for involvement in the 1812 Puerto Príncipe rebellion, they listed her legal status as "coartado" and not as a slave, even though Don Pedro Antola had been recognized as her master.[105] Once the slave made the first payment and began to chip away at their bondage, each installment reduced the price of the *coartado*.[106] The master retained the right to sell the *coartado*, but the price could not exceed the assessed value minus whatever payments had been made towards freedom.[107] The new master had to honor the existing *coartado* agreement and accept any future payments for liberation. Thus, what began as a self-purchase agreement between a single master and a slave, became transferable to any master.

As *coartado* represented a distinct, albeit ambiguous legal category between slavery and freedom, it remained unclear whether a child born to a *coartado* mother inherited a slave, *coartado*, or free legal status. The disagreement focused on whether the child received the mother's status of *coartado*, and how to assess the value of the newborn. According to Spanish legal officials, the majority of lawyers in Cuba had "judged that the legitimate value of the child should be reduced equal to the quantity paid by the mother for her freedom, leaving the difference the just price of the child." Apparently through custom and tradition, the amount *coartado* mothers had paid toward their freedom had also been applied to children at birth in assessing the slave's value. In 1789 the Spanish Crown decided to reverse the previous customary practice and issued a royal decree to instruct lawyers that *"coartación* by mothers is only for them. . . . It cannot be transferred to children in order that they can obtain the same benefit."[108] In 1795 the point had to be reemphasized in Cuba when María Antonio attempted to have a notary in Bayamo sanction her freedom and that of her two children born during her status as a *coartado*.[109] The 1789 royal decree also emphasized the increasing importance of slave labor to the Cuban economy. According to the edict, transferring *coartado* status from mother to child "would reduce the laborers so necessary in these precious lands."[110] The change in the previous practice of lawyers deciding *coartado* status for mother and child on a case-by-case basis without any ruling from Spain reveals the somewhat flexible nature of slavery prior to the sugar boom. In 1789, however, the same year in which the Spanish Crown declared the slave trade open to all nations, legal officials decided to settle any ambiguity over *coartación* by declaring it a noninheritable status.

For slaves the possibility for freedom by self-purchase depended above all on access to money. The sugar boom worked by slave labor would make Cuba the world's principal producer by 1840 and home to the first railroad in Latin America, amazingly more than a decade before the "mother" country of Spain.[111] Slaves and free people of color operated most of the urban market stalls and domestic servants normally made the purchases for their masters' households. As slaves and free people of color often represented both the buyer and seller, this placed considerable marketing and purchasing power in their hands.[112] Indeed, markets throughout the island may have more accurately reflected African trading customs rather than Spanish or Cuban ones. When the Kongo-born slave María Antonia went to purchase food for her master's dinner at the Plaza Mayor in Puerto Príncipe, she conversed with fellow Kongo slave José in what authorities described as "their language."[113]

Cuban officials were not impervious to the dangers of placing considerable marketing and purchasing power in the hands of people of African ancestry. As elsewhere in the Americas, urban residents expressed alarm over the large number of urban slaves and suggested sending them to the disciplined labor regimes of the plantations and mines.[114] When Pascual Ferrer visited Cuba in 1798, he remarked that the people "normally found walking on the streets were only blacks and mulattos."[115] Juan Domingo Caballero brought attention to the Puerto Príncipe town council of "the large number of Blacks working for wages and engaged in illicit commerce." According to Caballero, masters recklessly "cast their slaves to the streets" without attempting to "cure or restrain their bad habits." Caballero asked the Puerto Príncipe town council to transfer urban male slaves to "the haciendas and countryside and for the females to be returned to the houses for useful and honest occupation."[116] Likewise, the Havana town council regularly checked markets for illicit goods and received complaints about the numerous black female fruit vendors "uniting with others of their class" and "the trouble created by their clamor and obscenities."[117] As complaints mounted, the captain general requested that Leonardo Del Monte investigate the practice and offer solutions for what could be changed. Despite the problems created by what Del Monte referred to as the "corrupting liberty" of independence from master control, and the even more threatening problem of "shelter offered to fugitives," he did not recommend any laws to prohibit slaves from working on their own. Del Monte simply stated that, whatever problems created by the urban slave labor system, "there are many honorable women and men who survive on the labor of one, two, or more of the slaves." To take

Nothing Worse in the World

away their slaves' ability to work for wages would deprive the owner of a crucial source of revenue, and thus "submerge them in the most deplorable misery . . . forcing them to robbery and other vices."[118] Slaves working on their own and contracting out their labor generated substantial revenues for their masters that offered them the security of not having to engage in manual labor.

While masters and Cuban authorities could recognize the necessity of allowing slaves to work for wages and hire out their own labor, they had more difficulty determining what to do with slaves who lived on their own. Slaves who promptly and routinely paid their slaveowners wages escaped close scrutiny and monitoring in exchange for putting cash in their owners' hands. In 1810 Juan de Dios Molina arrested a slave found "sleeping with a woman who was not his wife," during his night patrol of the Guadalupe neighborhood in Havana. Despite producing a note written by his master that authorized him to work on his own, the official arrested the slave as a suspected runaway because the note was three months old.[119] When the slave's owner, Luis Roca, heard of the arrest, he quickly wrote a letter protesting the imprisonment because "there was no other reason other than that the license was old." Roca took it as a personal offense that Juan de Dios Molina arrested his slaves as it reflected on his character as a master. Roca emphasized that he had five other slaves who all lived on their own and exemplified "loyal conduct." Cuban officials promptly released the slave after the captain general personally intervened in the case. He stressed that to avoid such problems in the future, slaves should always carry current licenses.[120] Whether earning their own wages through selling goods or living on their own outside of the immediate supervision of their masters, slaves could participate in the market economy to acquire money for their freedom.[121]

Although Cuban authorities and slaveowners recognized that slaves could and often did possess a significant amount of money, they always appeared perplexed about how they had acquired it. In 1812 a slave named Trinidad recorded with a local notary that a loan originally given to free black Ignacio Montero for 100 pesos be transferred to Montero's "legitimate wife" for repayment.[122] In Puerto Príncipe, authorities investigated a rash of pig thefts on plantations that eventually arrived clandestinely at city markets. As they probed the causes of the disappearing pigs, they discovered that working class whites had recruited several slaves to steal the animals.[123] In Santiago, authorities arrested slave Luisa Montavlo for stealing a bag of wheat from her master that she then sold to a store for three pesos.[124] The slave José owned by Domingo Reyes stole chickens from nearby plantations with his master's knowledge to buy his freedom.[125] The clandestine and unregulated nature of the informal economy provided a degree of shelter for slaves to engage in contraband trade as a strategy to increase their revenues and buy their freedom.

The rise of the plantation economy undoubtedly placed new constraints on slaves for obtaining their freedom. The rapid expansion of sugar plantations created an insatiable demand on slaves as bound laborers that made manumission all the more costly for masters. Slaves, however, utilized the laws and institutions that had long provided avenues for freedom such as *coartación*, working and living on their own, and engaging in contraband trade to knock of their chains. Numerous slaves became free, and by their existence, offered hope and a real example that freedom could be obtained. While liberty brought a new legal status and freedom from master control, free people of color were not isolated from the transformation of Cuban society by the expansion of slavery.

## FREE PEOPLE OF COLOR AND THE LIMITATIONS OF LIBERTY

Cuban masters pointed to the free population of color as a stabilizing force for a rapidly expanding slave society. The presence and active role in Cuban society of free people of color made the division between an enslaved African population and a free European population function not as one of polarized extremes but as a spectrum marked by varying degrees of freedom and material conditions. The ambiguity of the free population of color as "neither slave nor free," or a group representing "slaves without masters," as historians have labeled them elsewhere in the Americas, served as an example to the enslaved of the real possibility for emancipation, regardless of how difficult it was to achieve.[126] Masters idealized the loyalty of free people of color to offer themselves a reassuring image of their benevolent treatment and the legal divisions among the population of African ancestry. In Cuba, as in most slave societies with the notable exception of the United States, free people of color militated against a clear polarization along racial lines as slavery was not a status shared by the entire population of African descent. In order to avoid confronting the possibility of solidarity between the free and slave populations, government officials often assumed their divergent legal statuses automatically created divisions. For example, the involvement by the free black Joaquín in the Aponte Rebellion shocked judicial officials because they believed "his free condition" fostered "his adherence to whites."[127]

Their surprise at the alliance among free people of color and slaves in the Aponte Rebellion was not without justification. Numerous free people of color joined the master class through slave ownership.[128] The mulatta slave María Ramona Cabrera provided no distinction between the cruelty of white

Nothing Worse in the World

and black masters. She appeared before judicial officials "completely bathed in blood as a consequence of the injury inflicted" by her black master José María Moreno with a butcher's knife.[129] No matter how eager their ambition or how strong their loyalty to white slaveholders, however, free people of color continued to be defined primarily by their racial status even though they were no longer human chattel. They were defined as "free people of color", not as "free people." The category "free white," in fact, sounds ridiculously redundant. We should not assume so, however, without first recognizing how race and freedom had become intricately linked by 1800 throughout the Atlantic world, as Haitian scholar Michel-Rolph Trouillot has emphasized.[130] The category "free white" never appeared in Cuban censuses or legal documents for the late eighteenth and nineteenth centuries because there was no need for it. All white people were automatically understood to be free. As the development of plantation agriculture and the massive importation of slaves transformed Cuban society, colonial officials defined people of African ancestry first by their racial identity, and second by their legal status.

Just as Spanish officials made a concerted effort to track the ever-increasing slave population, they also closely monitored the rapidly growing free population of color. The advent of the sugar economy altered the demographic makeup of Cuba, causing a decline in the percentage of the white population while the percentage of slaves and free people of color increased throughout the country. The free population of color had long been established in Cuban history and grew from a substantial 18 percent of the population in 1774 to 24 percent of the population by 1817 (see table 2.2). Census data from 1791 to 1810 for several cities of the island display the same general trend. In Havana, for example, free people of color increased from 22 percent of the population in 1791 to 27 percent in 1810, whereas the white population decreased from 54 to 43 percent in the same time period.[131] The free black population thrived in urban areas, as possibilities for manumission were greater. In addition, the relative freedom of cities and towns represented a clear contrast with plantation society and its highly regimented slave-labor work regimes.[132] As Francisco Arango y Parreño remarked in 1811, "the hatred free people of color have for agriculture," and its association with slavery, partly explained their migration to the city.[133]

Contemporary Cuban demographers showed mixed emotions of security and apprehension over the growth of the free population of color. Not only did slaveholders point to the free population as an indication of the benevolent nature of Cuban slavery, but they also made comparisons with other slave societies to argue that the island would not erupt in violent rebellion. Cuba's first demographer, Antonio del Valle Hernández, compared the ratio of free people of color to slaves for the British and French Caribbean from available statistical data in 1813. Valle argued that unlike the French Caribbean, which had a ratio of free people of color to slaves of 1:33, or the British Caribbean of 1:65, Cuba's ratio of 1:1.86 would prevent a broad based racial movement.[134] Valle's demographic logic assumed that the divergent legal statuses of the slave and free populations automatically separated them into opposing groups that would not unite through insurrection. While free people of color most certainly guarded their freedom and defined themselves in contrast to slaves, the legal differences between the two groups did not necessarily divide them.[135]

Demographic arguments for the racial and legal division of Cuban society depended on identifying and separating slaves and free people of color. Racial and legal identity in everyday life, however, did not correspond as neatly and as uniformly to census categories. Cuban official Francisco Jurco assumed the slave Tomás González was free when he arrested him in 1805. According to Jurco, Tomás acted as a free man by not showing humility and creating a "big scandal" by shouting "various dishonorable insults." Jurco reported that in the Havana neighborhood Jesús Monte there lived "various free blacks of considerable pride," but he suspected they might be slaves.[136] Jurco then compiled a list of all the free people of color and their professions to easily identify them and separate them from the enslaved population.[137] In order to more closely monitor the interactions between the free and enslaved, the Cuban colonial government created committees known as "neighborhood watchmen" to perform policing functions.[138]

That white Spaniards and Cubans could not always determine the difference between a free and an enslaved person but had little trouble in categorizing them by their African ancestry reveals the degree to which racial identity influenced social interaction. Slaves such as Tomás González could assume an impostor role as a freedman, but free people of color, with the rare exception of some mulattos and *chinos* (the Cuban term for the offspring of a mulatto and a black), could not assume the role of whites. Most free people of color did everything they could to separate themselves from slavery and give concrete meanings to their own freedom, but colonial officials often identified and treated them as slaves.

Similar to slaves who labored and lived on their own, free people of color were required to carry licenses.[139] Pedro López imprisoned free black Luis de Zayas for failure to produce a license, assuming he was a runaway slave.[140] The colonial state often extended periodic labor levies, through which masters provided slaves for the construction of roads and bridges, to the free population of color.[141] Like slaves, free people of color could not own guns. Even the possession of such necessary work tools as machetes among two or more free people could provide grounds for arrest.[142] Slaveholders indicated

Nothing Worse in the World

much more than they realized when they claimed slaves were treated "equal" to free black laborers.[143] As racial slavery ever more clearly defined the dominant social relations of production, society often assumed free people of color were to be treated as slaves.

Regardless of attempts to circumscribe their mobility, free people of color gave substantial meaning to their freedom by their own labor. Free people of color did not have to turn their wages over to a master. As a product of the expanding economy and the scarcity of skilled white laborers, free people of color dominated the artisan and skilled trades. Men worked as blacksmiths, silversmiths, shoemakers, carpenters, sculptors, tailors, musicians, painters, bakers, hatmakers, masons, and in other skilled trades. Women most commonly found employment as domestic servants, water carriers, nurses, seamstresses, laundresses, midwives, wet nurses, and market vendors. Several free people of color attained master rank in their respective trades and directed artisan shops that employed several apprentices.[144] Artisan training often represented a family business. For example, after the Barbucea brothers had gained their freedom by working as carpenters, they opened their own shop in the Guadalupe neighborhood of Havana to specialize in building horse-drawn carriages.[145] Artisan trades and other professions provided avenues for advancement that people of African ancestry eagerly filled to improve their own social position.

The success of free people of color in the skilled and artisan trades resulted in a certain degree of bargaining power with the state because of their relative prosperity and wealth. In 1800 the master blacksmith José Dolores, a free black, landed in jail for what authorities described as illegal gambling. José protested his arrest by claiming he did not participate in any gambling activity but had only "been near the shell game run by others of his class." Past arrests for the same vice resulted in the judge giving little credence to José's plea of innocence. Unlike the others slaves and free people of color arrested and then sentenced to the city's public prison, José served out his sentence at the city arsenal because of his blacksmith skills. The arresting officer sent José to the arsenal "because of an absence of those of his profession." José, in fact, had first suggested the idea and requested to be "transferred to the arsenal." He almost certainly had a contact at the arsenal and had perhaps been imprisoned there during a past arrest. José realized that a prisoner who provided a valued and relatively scarce service would likely receive better treatment.[146] Trapped between a world of slaves and masters, free people of color such as José Dolores could use their economic power to bargain, albeit unequally, for an improved situation even while in prison.

The new policy of the state actively preventing interracial marriage clearly revealed the limitations placed upon free people of color and the growing racial divisions in nineteenth-century Cuba. Scholar Verena Stolcke has pointed out that, with the rise of the plantation economy in the nineteenth century, the Cuban elite placed a new emphasis on preventing miscegenation and protecting whiteness as an indicator of social status. On 15 October 1805 the Council of Indies promulgated a decree requiring that people of known nobility who desired to marry with members of the castes, blacks, or Indians seek permission from the viceroys and audiencias throughout the Spanish Empire. Shortly afterwards, the audiencia of Puerto Príncipe in Cuba reiterated the Council of Indies' decree and extended the meaning of "known nobility" to mean all persons of "pure blood." This significantly widened the definition, making it applicable to a much larger audience. Of further importance, the 1805 decree required persons of known nobility or pure blood to seek permission from civil authorities and not the church. Cuban elites welcomed the policy because they opposed the church's practice of sanctifying interracial marriages and even encouraging marriages among whites and the population of African ancestry who lived conjugally. Previously, intermarriage among whites and people of color, while undoubtedly a social taboo, had not demanded a petition to colonial authorities. Following the transformation of Cuban society by slavery, however, the Cuban elite regarded interracial marriages as capable of stigmatizing the status and distinction of whiteness.[147]

Despite the legal obstacles and social barriers to interracial marriages, numerous couples attempted to legalize their nuptials through civil proceedings and church ceremonies. In 1811 retired military soldier Vicente Pérez attempted to legalize his marriage with Guadalupe Carrión, a free black. Captain General Someruelos denied the petition on the simple grounds that interracial marriages "did not have a place" in Cuban society.[148] When a man and woman of different races attempted to marry, a family member of European ancestry often protested the marriage. In 1810 María Gertrudis Rivafecha asked the captain general to prevent the marriage of her son Santiago, a soldier in the white militia, with María Eusebia, a free black. Captain General Someruelos advised that María and Santiago should "not be given a license" because of "the very such inequality to be seen" by their different racial identities.[149] The Cuban colonial state did not deny marriage for this reason alone, but it appears to have been the main reason. Santiago and María, however, did not give up, or decide to live conjugally, as other interracial couples did. Two years later they tried once again to marry legally by soliciting the new captain general, Apodaca. Their new petition for marriage did contain one important change to encourage approval. Santiago and María both stated they were mulattos. Apparently, the previous petition had been lost in the bureaucracy of the colonial government as it went unmentioned in

Nothing Worse in the World

the new case. Captain General Apodaca approved the marriage petition, stating "as a result of the two being mulattos, their marriage should not be prevented."[150]

The long walk to the marriage altar by Santiago and María through two separate petitions reveals both the flexibility and rigidity of race relations in the early nineteenth century. Captain General Someruelos denied their first petition because the elite of Cuban society had little tolerance for interracial marriages. Despite the desire for colonial officials to ascribe rigid racial categories to the Cuban population, the ability for Santiago and María to "become mulattos" in their second marriage petition starkly reveals how race represented a fictive identity based on social circumstances. A marriage request by two mulattos (just like a marriage request by two whites or two blacks) did not automatically require an investigation or the consultation of family members to determine if anybody opposed the union. The different phenotypes that marked Cuba's cultural landscape continually presented scenarios that often made racial ancestry suspect. The anxiety among colonial officials and masters over the ethnic and cultural diversity of Cuba prompted them to simplify racial categories in an effort to create a clearly divided society. The limits of a socially constructed identity based upon visual representations of different degrees of whiteness and blackness created flexibility within categories but also constructed boundaries that could not be crossed. María and Santiago resubmitted their marriage petition as mulattos, not as whites or blacks. María apparently could not pass as white and Santiago could not pass as black. The degree to which people could manipulate racial categories given their own extremely restricted circumstances (just as *coartados* could fashion their legal status somewhere ambiguously between slavery and freedom) reflected keen cultural and legal maneuverings by slaves and free people of color to not let others determine their identity.

A volunteer in the white militia of Santiago who attempted to have his son removed from the mulatto regiment provides another example of how the changing social conditions in Cuba influenced racial identity. Manuel José Velásquez served as a soldier in the 3rd Company of the white militia of Santiago. His three sons upheld the family military tradition and also served as volunteers. Only two of Manuel's three sons, however, served in the white militia. Manuel's son José Antonio had been placed with the mulatto militia because of his physical appearance even though his "other brothers [served] in the white battalion."[151] Manuel wrote to the governor of Santiago emphasizing that "by Divine Providence I enjoy the quality of being white, and for which I am notoriously known and considered in this community."[152] Manuel provided notarized copies of records from the "Baptismal Book of White People" and the "Marriage Book of White People" to substantiate his status as a white person.[153] In addition, Manuel Velásquez submitted a copy of José Antonio's baptismal record, also registered in the "Baptismal Book of White People."[154] The confusion over José's racial identity as a mulatto stemmed from his mother who had been classified as an "Indian" when baptized. In addition, she had two brothers who served in the mulatto militia.[155] Authorities investigating the case recognized that the situation "was something very distinct" but nonetheless decided that José would remain enlisted in the mulatto militia.[156]

The judge explained his ruling on the basis of the mother's unclear status as an "Indian" and her brothers identification as mulattos. According to Antonio Vaillant, "we have, in the end, brothers who were and are mulattos, so the sister would be one as well, and not an Indian." The judge had no proof of their mulatto identity such as baptismal or marriage records but based his ruling on the "fact" that their physical appearance did not resemble the indigenous population of Cuba. Judge Vaillant argued that "in [Santiago de] Cuba there still lives an Indian named Francisco Xavier, and if you call him you will see the face of an Indian." The judge decided "by the same means you will realize the truth by seeing that José Antonio Velásquez" has the face of a mulatto, and not an "Indian."[157] Social identity in Cuba became defined by European or African racial features regardless of documentation that could demonstrate otherwise. José Antonio remained enlisted in the mulatto militia, and based on the extant documents his two brothers continued to serve in the white battalion. All three brothers were apparently the offspring of the same mother and father; the court never challenged their family lineage during the proceedings. Authorities did not identify José, his brothers, or his mother as "Indian" because in a society divided between Europeans and Africans, everyday social interactions did not provide space for identities that would complicate the racial hierarchy constructed around degrees of whiteness and blackness.

The necessity for colonial officials to order Cuban society into rigid hierarchical categories of subordination also affected some segments of the white population. Colonial officials throughout the island began to pay increased attention to poor whites and their possible interactions with slaves and free people of color.[158] Cuban authorities focused their attention on rooting out and ending gambling activities because they attracted a diverse audience of slaves, free people of color, and poor whites. Both religious and government officials routinely conducted investigations into gambling activities that they vaguely described as "banned games."[159] In Havana, the local military official in charge of the neighborhood of Jesús María had heard of a house with a "hidden door" where "an uncertain number of blacks" carried on gambling activities. When he arrived at the house he surprised the players who were

Nothing Worse in the World

"circled around a table . . . with four decks of cards." The seven gamblers reportedly scattered before they could be arrested, but conveniently left behind their money.[160] When it came to arresting wealthy Cubans for involvement in similar illicit activities, Cuban officials appeared willing to look the other way. Authorities did not arrest Don Ramón Rodríguez who ran illegal waging activities inside his house despite complaints by the local priest of the "infinite harm to this neighborhood" by the "scandalous behavior" of those who assembled at the house.[161] Cuban authorities opted to not enforce gambling prohibitions when they involved the "señoras in white robes, and Dons in striped gingham coats," according to James Alexander, who attended several gambling houses in the early 1830s.[162] When gamblers represented the "poorly educated," however, such as those who gathered at a local bar or a general store, neighborhood police officers did not offer friendly warnings before making arrests.[163]

Part of the increased attention to monitoring the activities of the lower classes reflected the state's apprehension that poor whites, slaves, and free people of color would become partners in crime. Military and police officials attempted to crackdown on the theft of animals, such as horses, donkeys, chickens, and pigs, agricultural products, and material goods that arrived clandestinely at markets. When authorities did arrest thieves they discovered that whites and people of color sometimes collaborated in the crimes. For example, in 1811 Captain General Someruelos reported the arrest of José María Bravo, Manuel Fablada, and the slave Tomás Portuondo for various thefts.[164] Perhaps the most alarming example of collaboration among whites and slaves in committing robberies occurred in the west central province of Puerto Príncipe. Vicente Cañizares had recruited slaves from Miguel de Cespedes's and Carlos de Quesada's plantations to steal foodstuffs, livestock, and material goods. Most terrifying to the judge investigating the case, Cañizares encouraged slaves to foment rebellion to make theft easier if necessary. According to the slaves Juan Francisco and Pedro, Cañizares had promised to buy their freedom once they delivered the stolen goods. It remains unclear from the investigation to what degree Cañizares coerced the slaves into acting as contract bandits, or if they voluntarily took advantage of the opportunity. They certainly did everything they could to convince the judge that they were the victims of an unscrupulous ringleader who took advantage of innocent slaves. In the end, the judge sentenced Cañizares to one year in jail, while the slaves returned to their masters unpunished, but under orders to be closely watched.[165]

Colonial officials showed a particular interest in preventing alliances and associations between the rural and urban and slave and free populations of African ancestry. In 1809 the town council of Puerto Príncipe "cautioned masters of plantations to prohibit the unrestricted communications of slaves with others who did not serve on their haciendas."[166] Masters in Cuba recognized rural plantations did not operate as isolated fiefdoms. The expansion of plantation agriculture that began in the 1790s extended a chain of production that strongly linked together laborers, goods, and information in rural zones with cities. The specialization of labor, the seasonal nature of cultivation, and the technology required for refining and processing sugar cane resulted in skilled free people of color routinely traveling to the countryside to work on a contract basis.[167] In addition to labor and commerce, family relations often bridged the different rural and urban worlds for slaves and free people of color. For example, free black María de la Luz Sánchez lived in Havana but earned her living by selling bread in the countryside so she could visit her husband who toiled as a slave on a plantation.[168] As a colony of Spain, Cuba had always been connected to a larger world beyond its immediate environs. The increased anxiety in the 1790s and 1800s over the links between the rural and urban and free and slave populations indicated the threat of revolt loomed large in the minds of elites and colonial officials.

For nearly three centuries Cuba had been characterized by rural and urban populations of slaves and free people of color without a noticeable concern by whites for possible alliances among the disparate groups. The sudden attention to such possibilities reflected fear over racial conflict, but also a well-founded suspicion given the changing circumstances for rebellion exemplified most dramatically by Haiti. Daily social interaction provided conflicting examples of the possibility for racial solidarity among people of African ancestry. Slaveholders could allay their apprehensions over racial conflict by taking comfort from people of African ancestry who decided to become masters once freed. Further, the numerous arrests by local military officials in Havana for fights between the free and enslaved, blacks and mulattos, and Africans and Creoles provide little indication of an overarching racial solidarity.[169] At the same time, Cuban officials noticed examples that could counter these reassuring beliefs of division. In 1804 the governor of Holguín had discovered a meeting of free blacks in an urban house that assisted runaway slaves.[170] In Santiago, military officials began to question the allegiance of free blacks they employed as "runaway spies" to hunt down maroon communities. The spies often failed to find the camps, and when they did, the hideouts had already been abandoned.[171] Authorities later concluded after reflecting on the Aponte Rebellion of 1812 that "the regular division between the free and slave" was breaking down in dividing the population of African ancestry in Cuba.[172] Colonial officials and slaveholders increasingly talked openly about the real dangers of the growing slave and free people of color populations that could lead to race rebellion in Cuba. The alliance between individuals such as the

Nothing Worse in the World

slave Tiburcio Peñalver and the free black Juan Bautista Lisundia when they acted in concert by burning the Peñas-Altas plantation showed that, however divergent their legal positions, they could unite in insurrection.

Whether real, a product of imagined potential, or most likely a combination of both, fear of slave rebellion resulted in everyday acts of insubordination attracting the attention of the Cuban government. Military officials guarding the entrance to the city of Havana arrested slave José Gordillo in 1811 for "resistance" and "lack of respect" when ordered to stop before leaving Havana.[173] Similarly, José María Ruan in Puerto Príncipe requested an investigation into the activities of free mulattos who addressed him without the deference he demanded.[174] Spanish officials also expressed concern over the frequency with which slaves and free people of color wielded knives and machetes in individual fights with their masters and employers.[175] Acts of resistance by slaves and free people of color to their subordinate position in Cuban society undoubtedly occurred before the expansion of slavery. Indeed, such acts of disrespect, resisting arrest, or individual fights certainly did not begin or end in nineteenth-century Cuba. The significance of such acts in the context of the changing demographic structure whereby the population of African ancestry both free and enslaved came to outnumber the white population for the first time in the 1790s, however, caused such actions to take on a heightened sense of danger.

MANY AFRICANS and their descendants in the Americas did not accept enslavement regardless of how many times masters justified human bondage as part of the natural order of things. Slaves, with incredible ingenuity, hard work, and years of savings—testifying to their skills as "Napoleons of finance," to quote Caribbean historian C. L. R. James—purchased their own freedom through the practice of *coartación*.[176] Freedom from a master, however, did not provide equality in Cuban society. Free people of color continued to be defined by their African heritage and associated with slavery. Racial identity increasingly became the primary but not the only factor in defining the hierarchy of Cuban society. But just as slaves did not accept their subordinate position born out of the middle passage, free people of color gave concrete meaning to their liberty through work, social relations, and above all independence from master control. Slaves and free people of color would make a common alliance in the Aponte Rebellion stemming from their common experience with racial subordination. The next chapter examines two of the most important institutions in colonial Cuban society that the rebels refashioned into organizational centers for the insurrection: the militia and the *cabildos de nación*.

# 3

## Organizing
## the Rebellion

The Overlapping Worlds of the
Militia and the *Cabildos de Nación*

The executions for involvement in the revolts did not end with the leader, José Antonio Aponte, the Frenchman Juan Barbier, the slave Tiburcio Peñalver, or the freedman, Juan Bautista Lisundia. Judicial officials added the name of the free black militia soldier Clemente Chacón to the hangman's fatal list. When the rebels gathered early on the morning of 9 April 1812, it was not their first meeting, but it would be their last. The slave Tiburcio Peñalver testified that he stayed at Chacón's boarding house and tavern in the neighborhood of Guadalupe when delivering sugar cane to Havana.[1] Free mulatto José Manuel Santa Ana lived next to Chacón and informed judicial officials that "Juan Barbier lived in the same house and would leave in the company of Chacón or his son Juan Lisundia."[2] José Antonio Aponte admitted accepting invitations to "eat at the house" of Clemente Chacón.[3] Several other slaves and free people of color reported various meetings at Chacón's and Aponte's houses attended by as many as fifteen people.[4] Judicial officials focused on the gatherings at Aponte's and Chacón's houses that brought together Juan Barbier, Tiburcio Peñalver, Juan Bautista Lisundia, and others as the key meetings in planning the rebellion.

The meetings at Chacón's house prior to the rebellion attracted little attention from authorities. Local police officials did not regard the gatherings as irregular, as Chacón's house also served as a tavern, a grocery, and a boarding house. Chacón lived with his freed son, Juan Bautista Lisundia, and his enslaved wife, María de la Trinidad. When authorities asked María if "she was the wife of Chacón," she responded that "although she lives with him and has an indecent friendship, they have not made their relationship legitimate."[5] Chacón, however, listed his marital status as widowed (most likely to hide María's knowledge of the meetings and possible involvement in the rebellion).[6] Police reports for the neighborhood provide no indication of any altercations at Chacón's establishment before the rebellion. His criminal arrests prior to 1812 resulted not from any wrongdoings at his tavern but instead from the attempted theft of a horse in 1808 and an unspecified offense in 1790 related to his participation in the militia.[7] When the lawyers investigating the rebellion learned of the meetings at his tavern, they focused their questions on the individuals that patronized the establishment.

The planning of the rebellion at Chacón's tavern involved male members of the population of color whom colonial officials regarded as among the most loyal to the Spanish Crown: the black militia. At the time of the Aponte Rebellion, Clemente Chacón had more than twenty years of service in the black militia and had achieved the rank of captain.[8] Local police officials likely did not view the gatherings with any suspicion precisely because his tavern served as a meeting place for soldiers. Chacón's wife, María, reported that "on several occasions she heard conversations about the captains, sergeants, and others of the battalion without understanding anything in particular."[9] Black militiaman José Sendiga later confessed that he assisted the "leader Aponte and his companion Chacón . . . with the collection of ammunition" for the rebellion while serving in the artillery division.[10] In particular, judicial officials found it most troubling that, not only did black militiamen assist in the preparation for the uprising by gathering arms, ammunition, and recruits, but despite their knowledge of the rebellion, they did not inform their superior officers.[11] Authorities learned from interrogated rebels that Chacón planned to direct the attack on the Havana military fort, Castillo de Atares, to prevent Spanish troops from leaving the city to suppress the plantation uprisings.[12]

The alliance between black militiamen and slaves in the Aponte Rebellion sent a horrifying shock to colonial authorities of the dangers of arming the population of African ancestry. The free men of color militia had long occupied a corporate position in Cuba's colonial hierarchy since its formal organization in the sixteenth century. The militia protected the island from rival European powers and pirate attacks, and it suppressed internal uprisings. The changes in Cuban society as a result of the massive importation of slaves and the growth of plantation agriculture caused slaveholders and government officials to voice concerns about the military training and arms provided to men of color. The transformation of Cuba into a plantation society worked by slave labor resulted in casting the function and purpose of the militia in a dangerous new light. The specific role and privileges of militiamen that historically served to separate them from other free people of color and the enslaved population began to dissolve as race became the primary marker of social status with the expansion of slavery. The alliance between the black militia and slaves in the Aponte Rebellion confirmed slaveholders' worst anxieties about arming and training free men of color and destroyed any belief that the free and enslaved would not unite in a common cause.

## THE PRIDE AND PRIVILEGE OF MILITIA SERVICE

Judicial official José María Nerey focused on Clemente Chacón's role in the rebellion because soldiers met at his house and he had detailed knowledge of Aponte's book of drawings. Chacón testified that Aponte had shown him his book and described it as "large without being able to give its specific measurements, with an unfixed cover, and that he could recognize it if the book was presented to him."[13] Nerey then placed Aponte's book before Chacón and asked him to explain the drawing that "depicted two armies in battle." The image displayed "white and black soldiers, with one of the blacks on a horse with the head of one of the [whites] . . . and another black that also had a bleeding severed head."[14] Chacón indicated that Aponte "had shown [him] the book before, but he [Aponte] did not explain the significance of the drawings," or why "armed black soldiers" were shown "escorting tied" white soldiers.[15] To various questions about the meanings of the drawings Chacón responded he "could not give any information on its significance"; he did "not understand anything in those drawings"; and he "ignored their allusion."[16] Chacón denied any specific knowledge of the meanings of the drawings. Any detailed information Chacón provided to explain the purpose of a book depicting black soldiers defeating and butchering whites would most certainly have been regarded by judicial officials as evidence of his involvement in the rebellion.

Chacón did elaborate on one drawing portraying an image of two black soldiers appearing before a king. Nerey asked for him to elaborate on the meaning of a "page that depicts a king placing his right arm on the head of two black soldiers." Chacón explained that, "according to Aponte, it represents the King of Spain when [the crown] established the black battalion."[17] Blacks soldiers had participated in the militia since the sixteenth century, but only after the English attack on Havana and the Bourbon military reforms of the 1760s did an all black battalion of 800 soldiers form.[18] According to Chacón's description of the drawing, Aponte informed him that the "two captains from the indicated [black battalion] unit" had been sent to Spain for an audience with the king. In Aponte's drawing, Chacón explained, the king honored the service of the black battalion "by placing his royal hand" on their heads, "indicating that they did not have to remove their hats for his majesty."[19] The respect accorded the militia by the king of Spain in Aponte's drawing had special symbolic meanings related to military rules that required black soldiers to show deference to whites. According to the regulations that governed the militia, black soldiers had to stand with heads bowed and with hats in hand in the presence of white soldiers, as a reminder of their subordinate position in colonial society.[20]

Not limited to Cuba, the resentment free soldiers of color expressed over the symbolic act of deference to whites also surfaced in Panama during the 1770s. Mulatto soldiers complained that white officers sought them out merely to demand removal of their hats as an act of social submission. The white militia commander, Félix Martínez Malo, insisted on hat removal with bowed heads in deference to whites because not doing so would "foment the unjust pretensions of those mulattos who aspire to leave the condition of their birth to which they should be subject." Martínez further elaborated that "subordination, courtesy, and respect are the fundamental bases on which the good order of this militia must be preserved." The insistence on demonstrating deference by removing hats makes Aponte's selection of the king of Spain all the more important. All soldiers, regardless of rank or race, would have had to stand with their hats in hand and heads bowed in front of the monarch.[21] Aponte's drawing showed no deference to the king. Rather, the king displayed respect and admiration for the black militiamen.

When judicial officials interrogated Aponte on the meaning of his book of drawings, he too showed little eagerness to explain the images of blacks battling whites. Aponte did elaborate with considerable detail and pride on the black militia, and in particular, the image of black soldiers before the Spanish king. According to Aponte, the drawing represented "our king Don Carlos III (who is with God) placing his hand on the head of one of the black soldiers belonging to the lieutenant Antonio de Soledad and second lieutenant Ignacio Alvarado."[22] As with the drawings of Aponte's father and grandfather discussed in chapter 1, service records from Spanish archives confirm Antonio Soledad's service as a soldier in the black militia. By 1791, at the age of seventy-six, Soledad had served more than fifty-four years in the militia. He steadily climbed the military ranks from volunteer soldier to sergeant to lieutenant to captain to the highest position of commander. His service record also confirmed his audience with the king, as depicted in Aponte's drawing. Like other soldiers, Soledad's received recognition for his bravery in "the defense of this city [Havana] when it was occupied by the British Nation." For his leadership in battle, he had traveled to Spain and "had the high honor of kissing the royal hand of his majesty and receiving a medal."[23] Antonio Soledad became so well-known for his military exploits that the government-issued official guide to the city, *Guía de forasteros*, listed him as the commander of the free black militia in 1795.[24] Unsurprisingly, the service record does not mention the point, emphasized by both Chacón and Aponte in the drawing, that "his majesty did not permit [Soledad] to remove his hat."[25] The brief descriptions of the drawing from court testimony and Antonio Soledad's service record reveal the sense of distinction that military service provided. Soledad's trip to Spain and an audience with the king fostered racial pride for soldiers such as Aponte, Chacón, and others serving in the militia.[26]

Colonial officials regarded some of the drawings in Aponte's book as subversive even though their depiction of loyalty to the Spanish Crown confirmed the exact reason for the formation of the militia regiments. Beginning in the sixteenth century, Spain established militia companies throughout the Americas that enlisted black and mulatto volunteers to compensate for the absence of able-bodied white soldiers. By the eighteenth century, armed militia soldiers of African ancestry could be found in Cuba, Puerto Rico, Santo Domingo, Margarita, Venezuela, Colombia, Peru, Central America, Mexico, Uruguay, Argentina, Louisiana, and Florida. Wherever free people of color existed, a militia unit could be found. Men of color, as well as Native Americans who served the Spanish Crown, made sure they received certain privileges and benefits in return for their loyalty.[27]

The first organization of regimented militia companies of African ancestry in Havana occurred as a result of an attack in 1586 by English corsairs under the direction of Francis Drake. In 1600, the governor of Havana established a 100 soldier militia company of free mulattos. Throughout the seventeenth century, volunteer militia regiments formed across the island separated into black, mulatto, and white companies to reinforce the racial caste structure of colonial society. Following the English seizure of Havana in 1762, Spain ambitiously expanded the militia to include three battalions of 2,400 soldiers and sixteen separate companies with roughly 100 soldiers in each. Historian Herbert Klein has estimated that by 1770 one out of every five adult males among the free population of color served in the militia.[28] Free people of color often took the initiative in petitioning for the formation of companies. During the American Revolution, the free black Manuel Blanco raised a 100 man artillery company, and had the privilege to name his own subordinate officers, hold the rank of captain, and receive a salary of thirty-four pesos per month.[29] Likewise, during Bernardo de Gálvez's expeditions against the British at Pensacola and Mobile, José Uribe and Pedro José de Oporto of the Cuban battalion proposed raising a black and mulatto company of 100 soldiers each.[30] The restructuring of the Cuban military as part of the Bourbon Reforms and, in particular, the notable expansion in black and mulatto militiamen served as a model for other regions of the Spanish Empire in the New World.[31]

At the end of the eighteenth century and during the first decades of the nineteenth century, the militia continued to expand as the Cuban population increased and foreign and civil wars in the Atlantic world became more numerous. Colonial officials made specific plans to increase the militia companies in the eastern portion of the island. In 1809 Manuel Atraso, the commanding military officer attached to the black and mulatto battalion of Santiago, wrote to Captain General Someruelos expressing "the considerable need for the formation" of additional companies.[32] In 1810, military officials drafted proposals to increase the number of soldiers serving in the militia in the jurisdiction of Havana and Santiago. One year later, army officers drafted a plan to defend the eastern portion of the island against an attack that they suspected might come from the independent republic of Haiti.[33] The governor of Santiago requested information on the training and battle readiness of the militia in his jurisdiction to prepare for any attack or internal uprising.[34] The new emphasis on Santiago and the vulnerability of the eastern portion of the island revealed an uneasy realization for military strategists that only the narrow Windward Passage separated the largely unguarded Cuban coast from the nearby island of Haiti.

Free men of color eagerly joined the militia because membership provided special privileges and distinction within Cuban society. Militia privileges, known as *fuero* rights, included access to military courts, exemptions from certain taxes, tribute payments, and labor levies, and the right to bear arms, something long denied to the population of African ancestry.[35] Originally, only white militia units enjoyed *fuero* rights. The military reforms after the Seven Years' War and the necessity to expand militia regiments resulted in extending the right to all soldiers as a recruitment strategy.[36] Militiamen who had faithfully served for more than twenty years could request retirement and continue to receive *fuero* rights and a small pension.[37] Only high-ranking officers received a salary for their service, but soldiers who fought in combat received a monthly stipend that reflected the hierarchy of color. Mulatto captains earned forty pesos while black captains received thirty-eight.[38] Militia duty also provided the opportunity for volunteer soldiers to apply for loans based on their service records.[39] In addition, the networks of friendship and trust among commanding officers gave rise to the practice of making informal loans to fellow soldiers.[40] Special privileges and tax exemptions for militiamen often extended to family members.[41] Captain General Someruelos honored Lucas Zorrila's request to have his criminal case turned over to military authorities after he emphasized his father's service as a captain of the mulatto battalion.[42] By serving the Spanish Crown and taking advantage of opportunities for military service, free men of color used their special juridical status to secure basic limited rights for themselves and their family members.

For soldiers such as José Antonio Aponte, militia rights and benefits were never far from their minds. Authorities found handwritten copies of royal decrees spelling out *fuero* rights when they raided his house after the rebellion. In particular, the documents related to the pensions for retired militia officers. In two of the documents, a passage stated that "all of the sergeants, subalterns, and captains that serve in my army will retire with a pension."[43] Spanish military regulations specified that militiamen who served for more than twenty years would receive a monthly pension and enjoy the privileges and benefits of the *fuero* for life.[44] For José Antonio Aponte this militia right may have had particular importance because in 1800 he had been forced to retire from his position as captain in the 2nd Company of the Havana black battalion after twenty-three years of service. The retirement list vaguely described Aponte's "reason for exclusion" as "lacking strength," likely indicating poor physical health.[45] Aponte most certainly guarded the copies of the royal decrees to assert with legal authority his rights as a retired military officer and pensioned veteran.

Judicial officials suspected that the handwritten copies detailing militia rights served an additional purpose. They demanded that Aponte explain how he obtained the decrees and if others had knowledge of them. Clemente Chacón testified that he "had not seen or had knowledge about . . . a Royal Decree in three copies or drafts . . . authorizing various things relating to the officers of the mulatto and black battalion."[46] Aponte stated that he had obtained copies of the documents from "José Domingo Escobar, a retired sergeant of the black battalion." According to Aponte, Escobar received the copies from black militia captain Cristóbal de Zayas who had fifteen decrees from a "dispute about the formation of the regiment."[47] Aponte had been a longtime associate of Escobar and learned his carpentry trade while studying as an apprentice under him when they both served in the militia. Escobar denied providing Aponte with copies of the decrees but did recall in 1812 having heard "eighteen or twenty years ago, Cristóbal de Zayas read . . . a copy of a royal decree with the same meaning."[48] Soldiers in the militia such as Aponte and Cristóbal de Zayas apparently collected, copied, circulated, and guarded decrees that specified their special rights as militia soldiers.

Aponte may have played an important role in copying and circulating the decrees among soldiers in Havana. According to his testimony, he had ordered his decrees "transcribed by his own apprentice named Agustín Santa Cruz."[49] When authorities questioned Agustín, he testified that at age eleven or twelve his godmother, Carmela Santa Cruz, arranged for him to study for "four years as an apprentice with Aponte." Before beginning his training in carpentry, Agustín recalled that his godmother had him "perfect his ability to read and write for two or three months with the same master [Aponte], after which he dedicated his time only to learning his trade." Part of Agustín's training in learning how to read and write involved studying and copying the royal decrees on the militia. Agustín identified the royal decrees seized by

Organizing the Rebellion

authorities as drafted in his own handwriting. When authorities asked why the decrees had been employed as a teaching tool, Agustín responded that Aponte did not explain the purpose for making the copies other than to instruct him how to read and write. Judicial officials suspected that Aponte circulated the copied decrees to other soldiers in Havana, but could not figure out why or for what specific purpose.[50]

As with Aponte's drawings of the militia defending Havana against the English in 1762 or Antonio Soledad's audience with Carlos III, the decrees on militia rights by themselves did not contain any subversive meanings. If anything, the decrees and the drawings emphasized loyalty to the Spanish Crown and appreciation for rewards and privileges accorded to the militia. The context of discovering the causes for the rebellion clearly made the images of black soldiers defeating whites and the implicit assertive demands for militia rights threatening. More broadly, it also revealed larger changes in Cuban society at the turn of the nineteenth century. The need for Aponte to craft a history of the militia's important role in Cuba's history and the accompanying rights and rewards for loyal service indicated how the status of free people of color had declined with the expansion of plantation slavery. The reaction by judicial officials to the images and decrees as subversive also revealed how their perceptions of the militia had changed. By the 1790s, an alliance between the slave and free population of African ancestry appeared more dangerous than ever. In addition, the grave concern authorities had with the images derived from their uneasy recognition that as the population increased and foreign wars multiplied during the Age of Revolution, colonial society had become, to a certain degree, dependent on militiamen of color for defense. This problem resulted in the difficult decision to expand the militia despite the dangers of arming and training more men of color. The militia had its origins in an earlier colonial era that increasingly appeared at odds with the expansion of a racialized plantation society in the nineteenth century.

Judicial officials focused on Aponte's three copies of militia rights because free men of color when arrested often displayed assertive confidence in demanding special treatment. For colonial officials, militiamen seemed determined to flaunt their immunity and show contempt for civilian authorities. When police officers attempted to arrest Agustín Martínez for a stabbing, he would not let them enter his home on grounds that he was a soldier. Juan de Dios Hernández reported that Agustín felt so confident in his rights as a militia member that he would "not converse with proper words, but reserved insults for them" as they dragged him away.[51] On a different occasion, another soldier in the militia created a "scandalous scene" when a police officer attempted to arrest him for carrying a sword without a sheath.[52] Several soldiers simply refused to cooperate with criminal investigations handled by civil authorities or requested, and often received, special consideration because of their militia status.[53] The captain general honored the requests by suspected Aponte rebels Francisco Andrade and Hiliario Santa Cruz for transfer from Havana's public prison to military quarters because the *fuero* guaranteed their right to be jailed only in a military guardhouse, barracks, fortress or defensive tower.[54] The special treatment accorded militia soldiers for minor offenses such as theft and fighting became widely known and led others to claim the privilege. Occasionally, black criminals falsely claimed membership in the militia with the hope of escaping arrest and fines.[55] Militia service (or even the claim to militia service) instilled confidence in free people of color in their daily interactions with colonial officials that the government regarded as arrogant and even threatening.

Military exercises and drills provided the opportunity for soldiers to display publicly their status as militiamen that entitled them to distinction and preferential treatment. Failure by volunteers to attend weekly militia drills could result in small fines, and repeated absences could even end in imprisonment.[56] When the militia performed their weekly exercises, usually on Sundays, they could attract a large audience of interested observers.[57] Juan Francisco Manzano recalled in his autobiography that, as a young slave living in Havana in the early 1800s, he attended "military drills with my godfather, Javier Calvo, a first sergeant in his battalion."[58] The mulatto militia of Havana repeatedly requested that colonial officials repair the street in front of their barracks. They wanted to perform their military drills outside of their quarters in the street to allow the general population to observe them.[59] Militia members received a special uniform that they kept at home and wore for military exercises when they performed and paraded with weapons.[60] Black militias throughout the island carried a banner that read "Conquer or Death," and the mulatto militia flag displayed the declaration "Always Forward in Glory."[61] The legal rights and degree of social distinction accorded to militiamen provided an institutional framework for creating a cadre of leaders.

The service records for commanding officers in Cuba indicate that military officials recruited leaders from the most talented and economically independent segments of the free people of color community. The captains, sergeants, lieutenants, and commanders most commonly earned their living as masons, blacksmiths, shoemakers, carpenters, tailors, artists, and musicians, among other skilled trades.[62] In particular, carpenters of African descent appear to have established a strong link with the militia. After a riot erupted in Havana and destroyed several blocks in March 1809, the black militia received orders to rebuild the houses.[63] José Antonio Aponte represented just one of many officers who owned and operated his own carpentry shop.[64] Artisan training as an apprentice resulted not only in learning a trade,

Organizing the Rebellion

but often led to enlistment in the militia. Javier Pacheco and José Sendinga, for example, joined the militia after studying carpentry with black military officer Daniel Ribero.[65] As observed elsewhere in Spanish America, almost all officers in the free people of color militia had learned a skilled trade and most artisans could be counted on the regiments' enlistment roster.[66]

## THE AMBIGUITY OF MILITIA RACIAL IDENTITY

The special status accorded to militiamen could serve both to foster a sense of racial pride and at the same time create a noticeable degree of separation from the larger population of African ancestry. Racial identity in the militia reinforced Cuba's corporate hierarchy of orders. The special privileges granted to soldiers, however, conflicted with the primacy placed upon the subordination of all people of African ancestry with the expansion of slavery and plantation agriculture in the nineteenth century. The very existence of the militia tended to militate against the racial subordination a slave society demanded. The presence of men of color in the militia, even though subordinate to whites, stood in contrast to the regulations that prevented Africans and their descendants from bearing arms. Just as free people of color demonstrated that slavery was not the only position for blacks and mulattos in Cuban society, the militia could project a sense of parity with whites through their common military service. In brief, by belonging to the militia, free men of color had the potential to transcend some of the racial and class-based barriers that increasingly defined Cuban society with the expansion of slavery.

The clearest method for black militia soldiers to separate themselves from the enslaved population involved enforcing slavery as a social system. Privileges bestowed by colonial officials to militiamen rewarded loyalty to the Crown and the economic priorities of Spain's New World empire. The militia enforcement of slavery began as soon as Africans arrived on Cuban soil. In addition to white militia units, the mulatto and black battalions guarded the slave ships docked in Havana's harbor that arrived from other ports of the Americas and Africa. The militia companies escorted the human cargo from the ships, standing guard while prospective buyers inspected slaves at the *barracones*.[67] The image of black soldiers guarding slaves served to reinforce colonial authorities' belief in the loyalty of militia troops to the Spanish Crown regardless of race.

As in other parts of Spanish America, militiamen of African ancestry played a vital role in the defense of slavery by hunting down runaways, conquering maroon communities called *palenques*, and denouncing rebellions.[68] In the 1790s, colonial officials raised a new concern regarding the capture of runaways and the destruction of *palenques* as a result of the dramatic increase in the slave population and the insurrection in Haiti.[69] On the eastern portion of the island, runaway slave communities flourished, raiding plantations and intercepting deliveries on roads.[70] In 1809, Cuban captain general Someruelos authorized eight companies of the mulatto battalion to hunt down and destroy *palenques* near the eastern city of Santiago.[71] During the 1790s, military officials in Santiago reluctantly enlisted mulatto militiamen because of the "many free people and slaves who had come from Santo Domingo with knowledge and experience of events on the island."[72] The priority placed on capturing runaways and the need to protect the island from a possible foreign attack necessitated the recruitment of additional militiamen of color, despite reservations.[73] The militia also aided in the suppression of insurrections and the capture of criminals.[74] The role of black and mulatto militiamen in capturing runaway slaves, rebels, and criminals vividly reveals the restricted, contradictory, and complex nature of freedom and rights for the population of African ancestry in Cuba. In order to receive the special rights and privileges denied to the black population as a whole, militiamen of color suppressed the actions and desires for freedom of other people of African ancestry.[75]

Perhaps nothing more forcefully allayed reservations about a possible alliance between slaves and militiamen than black and mulatto soldiers who eagerly joined the ranks of slaveholders.[76] Militia soldiers represented the upper echelon of free people of color in Cuba, causing some historians to describe them as a "petty bourgeoisie of color."[77] Given their financial resources and economically independent status, in addition to the common practice of human bondage in West and Central Africa (albeit distinct from New World racial slavery) from where many of these soldiers could trace their family ancestry, we should not find slave ownership surprising, regardless of how startling it may appear to the modern observer. Agustín Martínez, for example, a militia soldier in the black battalion of Havana, caught the attention of authorities because of his abusive practices as a slaveowner, not because of slave ownership per se. Authorities arrested him for the "not so light injury he inflicted upon the leg of his Ganga slave Francisco" with a knife.[78] In Bayamo, the sergeant of the mulatto militia, Juan de la Luz Márquez, sold his Creole slave Juan del Rosario (who had the "special flaw of a runaway") to Blas Rodríguez.[79] Several soldiers owned numerous slaves whom they employed in their houses and plantations. At the time of his death in 1827, black militia captain Atanasio Oquendo owned twenty-three slaves who worked on his coffee plantation outside of Havana.[80] As Cuban society became ever more rigidly divided between freedom and slavery at the turn of the nineteenth century, the clearest indication of free status paradoxically represented the ownership of another human being.

Emphasizing militia soldiers' slave ownership illustrates the complexity of race relations in Cuba. The appearance of slave ownership among people of African descent raises the important question of why other wealthy and prosperous free people of color chose not to join the ranks of masters when they had the material resources to do so. Rebel leaders Clemente Chacón and José Antonio Aponte both employed several laborers to work under their direction and owned property that likely indicated sufficient financial resources to purchase slaves. Yet, they did not own slaves. Even though free people of color undoubtedly guarded their freedom and sought to define themselves in contrast to slaves, some shared common experiences with those in chains that helped to foster a collective identity and antislavery ideas and actions.

Family relations could intimately bridge the divide separating free and slave status. Some Cuban militia soldiers married enslaved women and came to personally know the extreme limitations slavery placed on the establishment of stable families.[81] José Andrili emphasized his loyal service in the black militia of Havana when he wrote to the captain general for assistance in freeing his enslaved wife, María Gertrudis Palomino. Andrili had worked out an arrangement with his wife's master, Francisco Cabrera, to purchase her freedom by paying thirteen pesos every month for two years. Cabrera later decided to sell María to a priest, who prevented Andrili from seeing his wife and would not accept any money for her freedom.[82] Clemente Chacón did not marry María de la Trinidad, but they lived together as husband and wife despite her enslaved condition.[83] Extended and consensual family relations fostered a common identity between enslaved and free people of color. In 1812, Felipe Vásquez, the second captain of a mulatto battalion in Bayamo, paid 100 pesos to free his goddaughter Isabel.[84] Free militiamen of color shared a tenuous bond with slavery. Many had family relations or associations with the enslaved, and thus, intimately understood how slavery adversely affected the life not only of slaves, but also of the free.

## DECLINING MILITIA PRESTIGE WITH THE
## RISE OF PLANTATION SOCIETY

The associations and common experiences between slaves, free people of color, and black and mulatto militiamen increased at the end of the eighteenth century because of a decline in prestige and benefits associated with military service. The Haitian Revolution and the expansion of slavery caused colonial officials and slaveholders to express openly their reservations about arming free people of color. Francisco Arango y Parreño, the individual most responsible for expanding the slave regime in Cuba and gaining concessions for slaveowners, petitioned the Crown to disband the militia in the 1790s. In his influential treatise on Cuban agriculture in 1792, Arango prefaced his discussion of the militia by urging "from this moment" to "begin taking precautions" to prevent an uprising similar to the "insurrection of slaves in Guarico [Haiti]."[85] Arango praised the black and mulatto battalions for their service, describing them as "without dispute among the best soldiers in the world." He acknowledged that in the past these soldiers served an essential function for external defense against pirates and rival nations, but we "should not risk their use for internal defense" as the number of slaves in the countryside increased. For Arango it "was not the armed battalions that most frightened" him, but militia veterans no longer attached to a specific unit or company that "retired in the countryside."[86] The changing demographics in the countryside that favored the population of African descent caused Arango to fear militia soldiers might not carry out the suppression of a slave insurrection, and might even start such an uprising.

Numerous slaveowners and military officials did not believe an alliance between the free people of color and slaves would materialize. Arango recognized their doubts, noting that "some have said the difference between the free and the slaves separates their interests and will provide a formidable barrier" for solidarity. He regarded such ideas as naive and dangerous for they failed to understand the common grievances born from racial oppression. According to Arango, whether slave or free, "all of them are blacks." He further elaborated that despite their different legal status, slave and free "have more or less the same complaints and the same motivation for living disgusted with us." While Arango undoubtedly simplified the differences between slaves and free people of color, he correctly identified that their subordinate position in society could "dispose them to destroy the object they attribute to their degradation," namely the white population. Unsurprisingly, Arango did not propose any reforms that might have alleviated black disgust for whites because it would cut into his profits and prestige as an elite. Rather, Arango's solution simply called for making it more difficult for people of African ancestry to oppose racial oppression by disbanding the black and mulatto battalions.[87]

The captain general and colonial officials did not grant Arango's petition or the requests by others to disband the militia. Captain General Luis de las Casas argued that the interests of free blacks and mulattos were not the same as those of slaves. He provided the example of militia members who owned slaves to emphasize that soldiers often viewed those in bondage with contempt.[88] Despite the government's refusal to disband the militia, other requests soon followed. In 1799, the Havana *consulado* requested that the Spanish Crown "diminish or extinguish the militia of color, or at least the black"

Organizing the Rebellion

regiments. They echoed Arango's plea "never to have them in the countryside and always with the precaution of not providing them weapons."[89] Armed free blacks and mulattos provided contrasting images of stability and destruction in the eyes of different sectors of Cuban society. Government officials pointed to the three centuries of loyal service that defined the militia as a distinct social class with special privileges. Slaveowners, however, realized how the rise of the plantation economy eroded the special status of the militia in the Spanish colonial order and could engender racial solidarity. The Cuban government may have refused requests to disband the militia, but they also voiced their own uneasiness with training free blacks in armed combat. In 1808 Captain General Someruelos advised recruiting free men of color for the Trinidad militia but cautioned against "instructing them, when possible, in the use of weapons."[90]

Although the efforts to disband the militia failed, they undoubtedly contributed to a decline in prestige and appreciation for black and mulatto soldiers. In Mexico, Viceroy Revillagigedo disbanded most volunteer militias in the 1790s. He only retained militia regiments operating in areas of the highest strategic value and need.[91] As Havana served as a port of call for ships transporting goods, news, and people to Mexico, military deserters often hid in Havana's free people of color neighborhoods. Aponte and other militia soldiers likely knew of the debates over the future of the militia and would have followed them closely.[92] Disbanding the militia would have meant an end to the special legal status and pensions for free soldiers of color. Aponte included in his book of drawings a map of all the major military forts of Havana, streets, cathedrals, and the house of "Señor Don Franc[isc]o de Arango." Aponte explained that he "had made the drawing without any other purpose than to entertain himself."[93] As with so many other drawings, judicial investigators asked no other questions about the specifics of the drawing. Aponte may have drawn the map to identify targets to attack for the rebellion. All of the fortresses represented strategic military locations that would have to be taken for the revolt to be a success. Francisco Arango's house likely had been singled out and included in his map because he was among the most influential political figures in Cuba at the time. His house would have been commonly known and served as a popular reference point in navigating the city and providing directions. If the map had been drawn to plan the rebellion, Arango's house may have been a target for attack because of his labors to expand slavery and his opposition to the militia.

While calls to abolish the militia went unanswered at the turn of the nineteenth century, the rise of slavery caused a decline in esteem for black and mulatto soldiers in Cuban society. The *fuero* specified that soldiers arrested for crimes would serve out their punishments in military prisons. In 1807, however, mulatto and black soldiers convicted of minor offenses had been ordered to work on public roads, often side by side with slaves.[94] Captain General Someruelos did not grant Felipe Aristiga, a black soldier in the Havana battalion, any special consideration when he sentenced him to four months of public service for an unspecified crime.[95] Colonial officials often assumed black and mulatto soldiers were slaves until they could prove otherwise. Pedro López and Benito Conderos arrested black and mulatto soldiers because they did not have a license verifying their free status and militia service.[96] In Puerto Príncipe, the question over whether militia soldiers should be addressed with the honorific title of "Don" created such a debate that it became discussed in sermons.[97] As the prestige and benefits associated with militia service declined, the burdens of military drills and absence from home undoubtedly became an additional weight to shoulder. Militia privileges such as pensions and exemptions from taxes helped foster a cohesive group identity, but the limitations of these benefits revealed the social barriers that segmented colonial society by race.[98]

Perhaps the greatest insult to black and mulatto soldiers involved sharing their military barracks with slaves. The rapid increase of imported Africans resulted in the black and mulatto barracks doubling as *barracones* for slaves after their arrival in Cuba. In Santiago, government officials converted the military barracks of the militiamen of color into slave housing-pens. Soldiers in the militia immediately complained because their barracks provided a residence for officers during military exercises, temporary housing for soldiers who traveled from the countryside, and a location for meeting and socializing.[99] Cuban officials explained that the deteriorated state of the barracks and their construction primarily of hay made the quarters more suitable for slaves.[100] The decision to provide the same quality of housing for slaves and free soldiers further indicates the declining prestige of the militia and how the government often regarded and treated all people of African descent equally, regardless of their distinct legal status. Despite the captain general's strong encouragement to build new barracks for the free people of color battalion because "some of the militia are armed and the actual circumstances make it indispensable to prevent any event" from transpiring, neither the colonial government or city officials in Santiago would pay for the construction of new quarters.[101] Despite the loyal service of soldiers and their long history of protecting the island from foreign invaders and maintaining internal peace, the rise of plantation agriculture worked by African slave labor chipped away at their corporate privileges. The colonial state saw no reason to provide different living quarters for people of African ancestry in Cuba regardless of whether they had recently been imported as slaves or had long served in the militia.

Organizing the Rebellion

In addition to the decline in militia prestige from demographic and economic changes with the expansion of plantation slavery, the Haitian Revolution provided a dangerous reminder about the military potential of arming African descendants in Cuba. During the early years of the Haitian Revolution, Spain allied itself and provided arms to slaves who battled the French under the command of black leader Jean François. The inability of Jean François to develop a strategy of slave emancipation or identify with the French National Convention's declaration of abolition, as had Toussaint, resulted in his declining influence. In July 1795, Spain and the Directory of the French Republic signed a peace treaty ceding western Hispaniola to France, leaving Jean François and his troops without a country. In 1796, Jean François and his forces had been forced into exile and attempted to settle in Cuba. Havana's town council barred him from living in Cuba because "several blacks had prepared functions to celebrate the arrival of Juan Francisco [Jean François] to show their affection toward him and his officials without ever meeting them."[102] The exiled troops from Saint Domingue stayed only a brief time at the port of Havana, prohibited by officials from disembarking and docked on the other side of the harbor to minimize their interaction with the local free people of color and slaves. After a short stay in Havana, Jean François left for Cádiz, Spain; Georges Biassou, for Saint Augustine, Florida; Gil Narciso, for Guatemala; and other troops scattered throughout the Spanish Caribbean.[103]

Authorities suspected that some of Jean François' troops had managed to settle permanently in Cuba. Four years after their banishment in 1796, Someruelos believed that "some of the division of the caudillo Juan Francisco from Santo Domingo still lived" on the island. Any of Jean François' troops remaining in Cuba would be "expelled from the island" for the "ease with which they could cause distrust, hide themselves, and much more in this country."[104] Ten years later, Someruelos again rejected the request of Jean François' troops to settle in Cuba with their families after living in Cádiz, Spain, because "they should not be trusted because of the notions they bring from their country of origin."[105] Although prevented from settling permanently in Cuba, Jean François and his troops left a long-lasting impression on the slaves and free people of color, because of their military achievements. For government officials, the troops also served as an ominous portent about the dangers of arming and training people of African ancestry in societies dependent on slavery.

Colonial authorities such as Captain General Someruelos recognized that they placed themselves in possible danger by training, fielding, and arming free men of color. The success of the Haitian Revolution provided new respect and fear for the military capability of black soldiers that demanded greater monitoring of their activities. Military regulations generally required rifles and guns be locked away and guarded at the barracks, but many soldiers often took their weapons home with them for personal use. When the captain of the mulatto militia, Santiago Caravallo, died in 1804, several of the missing guns from the Bayamo company turned up in his will.[106]

Authorities often suspected and sometimes arrested soldiers for stealing weapons and ammunition. In 1800, Carlos de Ayala "placed José Aponte in the public jail for stealing" from the arsenal.[107] The arrests perhaps indicates that Aponte had been planning his insurrection and gathering weapons as early as 1800. Aponte was not alone among soldiers who had militia ties and participated in the revolts. As authorities investigated the Aponte Rebellion of 1812, they learned that numerous soldiers had planned to use their militia connections to gather arms and ammunition from their barracks.[108] Cuban officials and economic elites remained divided about the future of the militia because it represented both the loyalty of the free men of color to the Spanish Crown and an institution that could lead an armed insurrection by people of African ancestry.

The changing reactions to the militia at the end of the eighteenth century and the beginning of the nineteenth century reflected the larger transformation of Cuban society brought on by the expansion of racial slavery. The militia could trace its origins to the sixteenth century. The dramatic increase in slave labor, however, served to dilute the distinctions and privileges of militia service. Regardless of militia soldiers' attempts to distinguish themselves from the enslaved population by guarding slaves ships, hunting down runaways, or becoming masters, many colonial officials regarded them above all as blacks. Increasingly, colonial authorities began to emphasize less the differences between free militiamen and slaves, and more their similarities. Undoubtedly, soldiers chafed under the increased racial hostilities and their declining social prestige, revealed most dramatically by their military quarters being converted into slave *barracones*. In the racialized plantation society of the late eighteenth and nineteenth century, however, the militia came under attack as a possible ally for slaves.

Soldiers such as José Antonio Aponte and Clemente Chacón came to understand the declining prestige of the militia in the 1790s and 1800s. They served the Spanish Crown and took pride in the service of black soldiers as revealed by their explanations of the militia depicted in Aponte's book of drawings. By the nineteenth century, however, militiamen of color represented a contradiction for Cuba's slave society. The special legal and social status accorded to black and mulatto militiamen no longer seemed so secure. Aponte and others decided to turn their military training in the service of Spanish colonialism into a weapon to destroy it. The militia provided crucial access to arms and weapons necessary for the rebellion to be a success.

Organizing the Rebellion

The camaraderie of soldiers and their elevated social and economic position within their own community presented them as leaders to unite the free and enslaved populations.

## CABILDOS DE NACIÓN: AFRICAN ETHNIC ASSOCIATIONS AND IDENTITY IN CUBA

Among the rebels crowded on the execution scaffold with José Antonio Aponte on the morning of 9 April 1812 stood the free black militiaman and director of the Mina Guagni fraternal society, Salvador Ternero. Judicial authorities learned that Ternero and his fellow rebels shared more than just the same punishment for insurrection. Reportedly, Aponte frequently came to Ternero's house as they resided in the same Havana neighborhood.[109] Like Aponte, Chacón, and others involved in the rebellion, Ternero served in the black militia and earned his living as an artisan. Authorities believed Ternero drew upon his militia connections to store ammunition in his house. Javier Pacheco reported that "Ternero was to have 300 to 400 armed men" at his command for the rebellion.[110] The crucial evidence of Ternero's involvement in the Aponte rebellion came from reports of secret meetings that took place on the roof of his home and his own admission of conversations about whether "there would or would not be a revolution."[111] Captain General Someruelos likely agreed with free black Melchor Chirinos's belief that Ternero represented "a demon with butchering thoughts," when he sentenced him to death by hanging.[112]

The Aponte Rebellion of 1812 was not the first time Spanish officials had come across the name Salvador Ternero. Four years earlier José Augustín Jurco, arrested Ternero for a fight with a black Ganga slave named José Antonio. Ternero emphasized his militia service and *fuero* rights, resulting in his release due to his service as a soldier in the second company of the battalion.[113] One year later, authorities arrested Ternero again for involvement in a Havana riot targeting the French residents of the city. Ternero recalled "being imprisoned" for what he described as the "revolution of the blacks when they attacked and robbed the French." For his role in the urban revolt, Ternero served one month of hard labor at La Cabaña military fortress. In the same year, authorities once again detained Ternero for a fight with a tailor, immediately releasing him for unspecified reasons.[114] Ternero's record of individual fights and participation in an urban riot undoubtedly contributed to his guilt in the mind of colonial officials investigating the Aponte Rebellion.

In addition to criminal procedures, Ternero also attracted the attention of authorities from civil investigations. Salvador Ternero served as the leader of the Mina Guagni fraternal society that based its membership on a shared cultural and geographic heritage rooted in the Gold Coast of West Africa.[115] Prevalent in colonial society, these collective organizations became known as *cabildos de nación*, reflecting the voluntary grouping by common ethnic identity of the numerous African "nations" forcibly imported to Cuba. Cuban contemporaries as well as others from the plantation zones and port cities of the Atlantic world used the term "nation" for Kongos, Lucumies, Minas, and others to indicate African ethnic identity. To clarify, "nation" is here used to connote a group of individuals bound by a common language, culture, history, and geographic origin. In this context, "nation" is used as it was historically in the Afro-Atlantic world of the fifteenth to mid-nineteenth centuries to refer to African ethnicity, and not to project anachronistically backward the modern definition of "nation," linked primarily to the formation of political states.[116] Historian David Bell in discussing "nation" and "nationhood" for the early modern era offers the following operational definition that can be applied to Cuba: "As far as definitions go, I cannot do much more here than state that eighteenth-century authors most often used the 'nation' to mean a community that satisfied two loose conditions. First, it grouped together people who had enough in common—whether language, customs, beliefs, traditions, or some combination of these—to allow them to be considered a homogenous collective. Second, it had some sort of recognized political existence."[117] While discussions of African ethnicity and "nations" may conjure up ideas of "tribes" and "tribalism," Joseph Miller has emphasized that all too often scholars unsuspectedly (and sometimes intentionally) use the term "tribe" uncritically for African ethnicity and nationhood that echoes a pro-colonialist ideology.[118] It is not by coincidence these African associations became known as *cabildos de nación* in Cuba. The Spanish term *"cabildo"* represents the English language equivalent of a town council or a town government. Consequently, the labeling of these societies as *cabildos de nación* provides some indication of how they functioned as representative bodies for African "nations" by providing political and administrative services.[119]

On three separate occasions in the 1790s, several members of the *cabildo* Mina Guagni challenged Salvador Ternero's authority as *capataz* (a term meaning steward or leader but also used for an overseer or foreman) to direct the financial affairs of the society. Unnamed members wrote to the captain general in 1794 complaining that *"capataz* Salvador Ternero . . . had sold the *cabildo"* house where the society regularly held reunions and bought a new house without consulting the members.[120] Three years later members of the Mina Guagni nation discovered that Ternero had purchased their new house in what amounted to a silent partnership with a free mulatta, Juana de Mesa, who demanded payment for revenues the *cabildo* generated by renting out

Organizing the Rebellion

rooms. The judge investigating the case ruled that Salvador Ternero as *capataz* of the Mina Guagni nation would have to pay 700 pesos to Juana de Mesa.[121] After selling the old *cabildo* house, purchasing a new one, and then being forced to pay 700 pesos, several members of the Mina Guagni nation petitioned to have Salvador Ternero removed as *capataz*.[122]

For some members, Ternero's actions recklessly jeopardized the existence of the *cabildo* Mina Guagni. The ownership of a house uniting slaves and free people of color by common ethnicity provided a sacred space for solidarity in a society increasingly divided along racial lines between slavery and freedom. Almost all the activities of the Mina Guagni nation revolved around the cabildo house that served numerous functions vital to the society: a home which rented rooms; a conference center for holding meetings and reunions; a school for education and training in the artisan trades; a bank through collection of membership dues, offering loans, and purchasing the freedom for slaves; a restaurant through food services such as the "plate of the day"; a theater for dances; and even a funeral parlor. As a consequence of the investigation into the divisions of the Mina Guagni nation, authorities prevented the *cabildo* house from carrying out its regular functions. Catarina Barrera and eight other members of the society pleaded with the captain general of Cuba to reopen the *cabildo* house "because it has been more than a year and a half since there has been amusement on the festival days."[123]

Ternero's abuse of authority and violation of the members' trust represents a story of graft and corruption common to many organizations, *cabildos* or otherwise. Ternero, in fact, never specifically denied the accusations nor felt compelled to elaborate on his purchases. Upon learning of the charges brought against him by fellow *cabildo* members, he requested the investigation be taken over by a military court, where he hoped to find a more sympathetic jury as a militia member.[124] Ternero turned to the highest-ranking militia officer, Antonio Seidel, who oversaw and supervised the operation of the black militia in Havana, to intervene on his behalf and have the case moved to a military court.[125] Seidel confirmed "Salvador Ternero as a soldier of the 5th company," which entitled him to the military jurisdiction of the *fuero* court. Ternero provided a copy of the letter authorizing him as the elected *capataz* to administer the financial, legal, and material affairs of the *cabildo*, to demonstrate he had not exceeded his authority.[126] He then proceeded to direct the investigation away from his purchases by focusing on the issue of identity and membership rights as criteria for challenging his leadership.

Ternero defended his position as *capataz* of the *cabildo* on the basis of his birth in Africa. According to Ternero, it was "the intention of some black Creoles that endeavor to destroy" the *cabildo* that created the division.[127] He dismissed the complaints as irrelevant because they were made by "Creoles who are not members of the national body [*no son miembros del cuerpo nacional*]." Ternero further argued that "the Creoles and slaves do not have a voice or a vote in *cabildo*" functions.[128] Ternero explained that slaves of Mina Guagni ethnicity could be members and take part in the functions of the society. However, the rules and regulations of the Mina Guagni society did not grant them the right to vote, because the "touch of slavery" prevented them from always "attending *cabildo*" functions, according to Ternero. Only upon becoming free did they enjoy full membership rights.

As for the free Creoles who challenged Ternero, he argued that "according to the constitution of the *cabildo*, and according to general custom they are prohibited representation . . . even if they are the children of black members of the nation." Creole Manuel Vásquez raised the loudest voice calling for Ternero's removal as *capataz*. "Ultimately," Ternero reasoned, "the defects (speaking with reservation) of being a black Creole" rendered Manuel Vásquez's complaints illegitimate because he was not born in Africa of the Mina Guagni nation.[129] Ternero reversed the standard explanation of colonial society that structured hierarchical privileges by place of birth from the white Spaniard at top of the hierarchy followed by the white Cuban, mulatto Cuban, black Cuban, and then the "pure-blooded" African on the bottom. Puzzled as to how to respond to Ternero's argument of legitimate African identity based on place of birth and full membership in the Mina Guagni nation, Captain General Luis de las Casas ordered officials to investigate other *cabildos* to determine if Creoles also participated and received voting rights.[130]

After receiving the order, Francisco Faveda and notary José Díaz Velásquez visited several *cabildo* houses and knocked on their doors to inquire if they had Creole members. According to Juan de la Torre and José de Jesús, the *capataces* of the Kongo Masinga nation, Creoles "were not represented in the *cabildo*." Upon inquiring at the *cabildos* Kongo and Karabali Osso, Faveda and Velásquez learned that Creoles were members but "did not have votes" for deciding the societies' functions.[131] Believing that the organizations drew their membership only from the African-born sectors of Cuba's population, the presence of Creoles in *cabildos* perplexed authorities and revealed how little they knew about the societies. Behind closed doors, *cabildos* provided relative autonomy and distance from master and government supervision that could shelter the planning of the rebellion.

Ternero keenly observed that Cuban officials disapproved of Creole participation in *cabildos* and expressed shock upon learning that they joined African societies. Masters and colonial officials believed the African and Creole populations did not socialize and would not make common cause in rebellion. Consequently, Ternero deftly emphasized Creole participation in

Organizing the Rebellion

the Mina Guagni nation to discredit their challenge to his leadership. Ternero acknowledged that "it is true [Creoles] dance and amuse themselves in the *cabildos*, but it is not by a right that they have, but by permission."[132] For Cuban authorities, *cabildo* dances represented the clearest indication of the cultural differences between Africans and Europeans. Black Creoles who voluntarily participated in the ethnic-based *cabildos* contradicted the ideological justification for slavery that supposedly saved Africans from "heathenism" and "backwardness" with the benefits of Western culture. It further called into question the comforting belief of slaveowners that the African-born and Cuban-born populations remained culturally distinct and would not make common cause. Despite the evidence of financial mismanagement, the captain general dismissed the charges against Ternero and allowed him to retain the title of *capataz*. He ruled that "black Creoles should not vote," according to "the custom of such communities," and therefore had no grounds for a complaint.[133]

Outraged over the ruling, Manuel Vásquez protested that Ternero had denied Creoles and slaves their "rights to vote" within the *cabildo* for his own benefit. Realizing Cuban authorities discouraged fraternization between *bozales* and Creoles, Vásquez dropped the complaint on behalf of Cuban-born blacks, but continued to protest Ternero's leadership for denying slaves the right to vote. Vásquez emphasized that "Augustín Morales, being legitimate of the nation" should not be "excluded for his servile condition."[134] Further, since slaves contributed financially to the *cabildo* without enjoying voting rights, Vásquez compared their treatment by Ternero with that of the "extensive violence" committed by their masters who also did not recognize their rights.[135] Despite prohibiting slaves from voting, fifteen members supported Ternero by pointing out that "Augustín Morales who is of the nation . . . is the only slave who follows the band of Vásquez."[136] Overall, the investigation into the financial affairs of the Mina Guagni nation revealed that the vast majority of both free and enslaved members continued to regard Ternero as the rightful leader of the *cabildo*.

The dispute among members of the Mina Guagni nation provides crucial insights into both the process of identifying others and self-identification in early nineteenth-century Cuba. Spanish authorities sought to separate the African and Cuban-born populations and, therefore, discouraged Creole participation in *cabildos*. In the same vein of preventing a broad racial identity, government officials encouraged the formation of *cabildos* because they emphasized distinct African ethnicities. Despite official discouragement and even limited political rights, some Creoles joined *cabildos* and continued to identify with the nation of their parents and ancestors. Although Cuban society at large tended to privilege Cuban-born blacks over Africans, within *cabildos*, *bozales* exerted more authority by claiming "legitimate" ethnicity as members of the nation. Social identity for Africans in Cuba showed a great degree of variation in the processes by which certain groups became identified legally and culturally by others and in the way people self-identified individually and collectively; *cabildos* provided opportunities to build solidarity that transcended the boundaries of birth, ethnicity, gender, and legal status.

## "KINGS AND QUEENS TO WATCH OVER THEIR INTERESTS"

The formation of ethnic groups based upon African nations represented a common feature of slave societies in the Americas. Masters throughout the New World recognized that Africans did not represent an undifferentiated mass of laborers but brought with them forms of social organization and cultural differences that they perpetuated and refashioned in the Americas as survival strategies. Robert Jameson, a British observer in Cuba, recognized how both master and slaves identified Africans by nations in the early nineteenth century: "The different nations to which the negroes belonged in Africa are marked out in the colonies both by the master and the slaves; the former considering them variously characterized in the desired qualities, and the latter joining together with a true national spirit in such union as their lords allow."[137] Masters often stereotyped certain nations for possessing distinguishing characteristics that some historians regard as offering a few "glimmers of truth" about African cultural traits.[138] Regardless of what masters' stereotypes can tell us specifically about African identity in the New World, it is clear that profits depended on an awareness of cultural differences. Historian David Eltis has soundly observed that "[w]hile the planters' basic requirement was slave labor from anywhere in Africa, no one can read the transatlantic correspondence of the early modern slave systems without recognizing the importance of African nationhood in the shaping of the plantation regimes."[139] African ethnic categories that came to be known as "nations" in the diaspora provide an analytic lens to examine how slaves and free people of color defined themselves and were defined by Europeans.

Depending on the nature of the documentation and the quality of reporting, the existence of societies based upon African nationhood can be found throughout the Americas for the whole period of slavery. Scholars have begun to revise the emphasis placed on the heterogeneity of the slave population that was once described as a "crowd" of diverse African ethnicities and have pointed toward specific cultural groups that can be tracked in the diaspora.[140] For the slave societies of Anglo-America, the action of Africans grouping

Organizing the Rebellion

themselves by nations normally became known in the context of a rebellion, often among Gold Coast slaves known as Coromantees.[141] The Iberian slave societies have left a particularly rich documentation related to African ethnicity, compared to the Anglo colonies in the New World. The Portuguese colonies in Brazil and Africa often recognized African nations through religious ceremonies.[142] The common appearance of Angolan and Kongolese ethnicity among African and Afro-Brazilian Catholic brotherhoods likely indicates religious traditions slaves took with them and transformed when they crossed the Atlantic.[143] For example, "Angolan Kings and Queens" received payments for directing the brotherhood of Our Lady of the Rosary in Recife.[144] According to Tomás Treolar, who worked at a Brazilian gold mine, Africans chose "kings and queens to watch over the interests and welfare of their respective nations."[145] Throughout the Americas, Africans created associations, relationships, and networks by looking back across the Atlantic to their cultures of origin to create survival strategies in the New World.

Spanish America appears to follow the same general pattern as Portugal of recognizing national differences among Africans through the church. At least a century before the conquest of the New World, municipal authorities in Seville appointed a steward to settle disputes between slaves and masters, and the African population formed religious brotherhoods that gathered on feast days to perform their own dances and songs.[146] These practices were then carried to the Americas and expanded when introduced to a larger African slave population. Sodalities in Lima, Peru, often reflected African ethnicity, such as the Dominican brotherhood for the "negros Congos," and the brotherhood of Nuestra Señora del Socorro for Angolans.[147] In addition, organizations formed along lines of African ethnicity expressed their desire to separate from church control. In Buenos Aires, for example, Africans in the nineteenth century regularly petitioned the police department for permission to form societies based upon their common national backgrounds to better serve their spiritual, cultural, and financial needs.[148] Whether through the church, informal organizations on plantations and mines, or state-sanctioned societies, Africans in Latin America grouped themselves along lines of African ethnicity and culture.

In Cuba, Catholic brotherhoods included Africans as early as the sixteenth century. In 1573, the town council of Havana reported that Africans took part in the procession of Corpus Christi, and wills indicate they regularly made donations to sodalities.[149] The Mandinga, Karabali, Lucumi, Arara, Ganga, and Congo nations proliferated in Havana and organized important brotherhoods. Most of the organizations selected a patron saint that they honored on his or her feast day with elaborate festivals and ceremonies.[150] In 1755, Bishop Morell de Santa Cruz wrote with shock at the lack of interest in Christianizing "these miserables [slaves and free people of color who] have been left totally abandoned as if they were not Christians and incapable of salvation."[151] In particular, the bishop's report emphasized the "scandalous and grave disorders" created by the "cabildos . . . when they congregate on festival days."[152] Apparently, during the span of the sixteenth and seventeenth centuries some cabildos had separated from the brotherhoods and taken on a social role independent of the church. The bishop planned to bring the "lost sheep of the flock to the Good Shepherd [by] . . . administering to the cabildos the sacrament of confirmation, reciting the Holy rosary," and appointing lay religious officials to instruct and supervise the societies.[153] Despite the bishop's protest, it does not appear the nations became "converted to temples of the living God," as he optimistically predicted.[154] For example, although the cabildo Karabali Induri affiliated itself with the Catholic Church Nuestra Señora del Buen Viaje, it does not appear as if any religious officials oversaw their activities or intervened to settle disputes among members in 1800.[155] By the mid-eighteenth century, if not earlier, cabildos likely outnumbered brotherhoods.[156]

Various scholars have traced the origins of the cabildos to religious holidays and Catholic brotherhoods of Spanish origin, but Philip Howard pointed out that analogous societies were common to West and Central Africa.[157] At the port of Old Calabar and surrounding regions in the Bight of Biafra, an all-male secret society known as Ekpe formed as early as the second half of the seventeenth century. Identified with the leopard, Ekpe members paid dues assessed by their rank in the organization. According to historians Paul Lovejoy and David Richardson, Ekpe society created an "interlocking grid of secret associations [that] served to regulate the behavior of members."[158] The secret organization crossed the Atlantic and resurfaced in nineteenth-century Cuba through an altered form with a different purpose as the Abakuá society.[159] In the Yoruba kingdom of Oyo there existed a semisecret organization known as the Ogboni society that advised the king on religious and political matters. Scholars disagree about the founding date of the Ogboni society and the extent of its influence. However, it is almost certain that because the war-torn region of Yorubaland funneled thousands of Africans to Cuba in the nineteenth century, some knowledge of the organization likely crossed the Atlantic and influenced the Yoruba-based cabildos.[160] Associations, organizations, and secret societies in West and Central Africa provided an institutional framework that enslaved and free Africans could mold to their New World surroundings in Cuba.

Various other societies could be found in West and Central Africa that performed charitable, recreational, political, and economic functions for members who often shared the same language, ethnicity, and nationality. The collective and communal organizing principles of these organizations often

Organizing the Rebellion

translated into mutual aid societies in the Americas. The African-born and American-born populations of African descent displayed a strong tendency to socialize and meet with those who shared a similar ethnicity, and to form some sort of organization, formally or informally, to keep in touch with and look out for each other. In Cuba and elsewhere in the Americas, the association of Africans who shared a common language, culture, history, and identity often functioned as a mutual aid society that linked the more fortunate and well-placed members with their poorer and severely exploited members through patron-client networks.[161] The Yoruba in West Africa, for example, operated mutual aid societies as early as the eighteenth century through the Ajo and Esusu saving institutions. Each member paid dues into a collective fund that would then be made available for individual loans. When Yoruba slaves began to be exported across the Atlantic, the Esusu savings association emerged in the Caribbean.[162] Spanish colonial administrators and Catholic priests regarded African *cabildos* in Cuba as a natural and safe extension of their own religious sodalities. The organizations for Africans, however, surely did not represent something entirely of Spanish or Cuban origin, but an Old World institution modified in a New World setting.

## "THOSE FROM ETHIOPIA WHO WANT TO JOIN TODAY": THE GROWTH OF *CABILDOS*

Over the last forty years a great expansion has occurred in the knowledge of the forced migratory process linking the Americas and Africa. As a result of collaborative efforts, computer assistance, and the construction of data sets, it has become easier for scholars to eschew the generic nondescriptive terms "Africa" and "African" and identify more precisely the origins of slaves and their New World destinations. David Eltis, David Richardson, Stephen D. Behrendt, and Herbert S. Klein have compiled an easily accessible database of more than 27,000 slaving voyages that now makes it possible to trace the Old World origins and American destination of Africans with greater precision than ever before.[163] For example, two out of every three slaves imported into the British Caribbean from roughly 1650 to 1710 left from a 200-mile stretch of territory on the Gold / Slave Coast of Africa.[164] Despite the greater precision in specifying African origins and New World destinations, at least two salient problems face the scholar studying African ethnicity and the Atlantic slave trade. First, most records reveal only the ports where ships left from, not the origin of slaves brought to the African coast. And second, Europeans who authored the documents, while cognizant of ethnic differences, often confused one group with another.[165]

Unlike other slave-importing regions of the Americas, tracing a particular dominant African culture in Cuba through census data from the Atlantic slave trade remains difficult because no single exporting region provided more than 31 percent of the migrants. The most recent scholarship has shown that "[o]f all the receiving areas in the Americas, Cuba received the greatest mix of African peoples."[166] For reasons that remain unclear, slave purchasers in Spanish America showed less concern for regional preferences than their counterparts elsewhere in the Americas.[167] Examining *cabildos* in the era of the Atlantic slave trade provides an opportunity to study how African ethnicity in Cuba was a product of the middle passage, but from an angle other than migration records. As Africans formed *cabildos* and defined their own ethnicity, these sources provide a rare view into how they identified themselves. Salvador Ternero, for example, did not need to know the percentage of Mina Guagni slaves imported to Cuba to understand how the slave trade shaped ethnic identities in his *cabildo*. He simply recognized that "when they founded the *cabildo* in 1731 there had not come those from Ethiopia who want to join today."[168] The increase in the slave trade and the spread of sugar plantations across Cuba strengthened the importance of Mina Guagni ethnicity within the *cabildo* and made African fraternal associations all the more important in daily interactions.

The same process occurred in the *cabildo* of Lucumies, as the population of Yoruba ancestry was known in Cuba. As the war-torn region of Yorubaland began to funnel slaves to Cuba at the end of the eighteenth century, a "confederation of Black Creoles" formed within the *cabildo*, representing the sons and daughters of the original founding members. Creole Manuel Blanco attempted to prevent the sale of the *cabildo* house that his parents had helped purchase. The marked increase of *bozal* Lucumi members, however, resulted in the Africans winning the case by their numerical superiority.[169] Cuba (along with Brazil) represents something of an anomaly for African identity transformation in the Americas during the late eighteenth and nineteenth centuries. In other parts of the New World, a broad-based racial identity began to eclipse African ethnicities with the ending of the slave trade, the growth of a Creole slave population, and the gradual abolition of slavery. In Cuba, however, African ethnic identity remained strong due to the dramatic increase in slave imports.

Charting the overall growth of the number of *cabildos* and the membership in each society proves difficult because no single governmental institution supervised the associations for the early nineteenth century, further revealing the relative autonomy these societies enjoyed. As a result, historians have yet to find a concentrated corpus of records on the societies. While quantifying the growth of *cabildos* remains difficult, qualitative sources indicate a noticeable increase in these societies from 1750 to 1820. In 1753, the Cuban bishop complained of the "noisy shouting of males mixed with females amusing themselves in extremely clumsy and provocative dances . . . that sanctify the festivals in this city." The bishop counted twenty-one *cabildo* houses that he emphasized "served the devil": the Karabalies owned five; the Minas, three; the Lucumies, two; the Araras, two; the Kongos, two; the Mondongos, two; the Gangas, two; the Mandingas, one; the Luangos, one; and the Suangos, one.[170] Scattered references to more than thirty *cabildos* found in civil disputes for the years spanning 1790 to 1820, along with frequent mentions of associations in official correspondence and criminal proceedings, suggest the number of Havana societies increased to at least fifty by 1812.[171]

The division of several *cabildos* provides a qualitative indication of the growth of the societies as a result of what Ternero described in the 1790s as the "arrival of those from Ethiopia who want to join today." In the 1780s, a dispute surfaced within the Lucumi *cabildo* between the diverse ethnicities that claimed membership. One member recalled that "the *cabildo* was erected by the Lucumi nations, specifically the Nangas and the Barbaes," but also included members from the Chabas and Bambaras.[172] By the seventeenth century Yoruban culture and language had become a lingua franca along the Western African coast, promoting what John Thornton has described as "cultural intercommunication."[173] In Cuba, this process apparently expanded the cultural boundaries of inclusion that facilitated the collaboration of several nations under a broad Lucumi identity. Near the end of the eighteenth century, however, with the increase of slaves from the Yoruba region, the society divided into separate *cabildos* represented by the Nangas and Barbaes in one house and the Chabas and Bambaras in another. A similar division emerged in the *cabildo* Kongo Musolongo in 1806 as indicated by their request to Cuban authorities to separate into two different societies.[174] Likewise, as a result of a contested election, Juan Gavilan and a group identifying themselves as the Karabali Osso desired to separate from the Karabali Umugini *cabildo* despite "fourteen years more or less of unity."[175] The ability to incorporate members from different nations at one moment and then at another draw lines of exclusion corresponding to fluctuations in populations among West Africans in Havana demonstrates the flexibility of African ethnicity and culture in the New World and the ever-changing ways Africans viewed each other.

Cuban slaveowners clearly understood the important functions of *cabildos* in a slave society dependent on the Atlantic slave trade. The existence of societies sharing a common language and culture served to mitigate slightly the horrific experience of the middle passage through collective solidarity even as they also prepared slaves for their new lives as unpaid laborers. As discussed in chapter 1, in 1789 the king of Spain issued a slave code that sought to protect slave marriage, limit work hours, specify food and clothing rations, and prohibit excessive punishment. In addition, the code held implications for the activities of the *cabildos* by emphasizing the need for slaves "on holidays to . . . be instructed in the Christian doctrine" and prevent the "uniting with others . . . in simple and natural diversions [and] to avoid excessive drinking."[176] Cuban slaveowners immediately protested all the provisions that curtailed their authority as masters, yet these same slaveowners surprisingly defended the rights of slaves and free people of color to form *cabildos* and perform their dances. Diego Miguel de Moya authored a petition signed by "all of the masters of sugar plantations in this jurisdiction" that argued by "taking away now the slaves' right to holidays that they count on to leave their enslavement (*salir de su esclavitud*), would for certain be an infallible principle of their resentment."[177] Cuban slaveowners, obviously, did not mean that all the slaves who participated in *cabildos* became free. Rather, they recognized that some slaves survived the brutal daily life of slavery with the hope that participation in a *cabildo* could lead to liberation.

Masters also revealed more than they realized. Participation in *cabildo* functions allowed slaves, however briefly, to "leave slavery" and the confines of master dominion. Further, when masters emphasized that the "inclined diversion of the Blacks is to dance in the barbarous style of their countries," they recognized "that if this [right] is denied them, it will cause an irresistible pain and produce bad consequences."[178] Cuban masters convinced themselves that by providing slaves and free people of color with a limited sense of autonomy, they would not rise in rebellion. Indeed, the town council of Havana reasoned that French slaveowners destroyed by the Haitian Revolution had only encouraged insurrection by "making slaves work on holidays."[179] In a society fueled by the forceful importation of thousands of Africans every year, slaveowners quickly realized the benefits of allowing organizations that fostered African ethnic solidarity to round off the sharp edges of the master-slave relationship.

## "CHILDREN OF THE SAME NATION": THE DIVERSITY OF *CABILDO* MEMBERSHIP

*Cabildo* membership served to strengthen networks and resources weakened by living in a slave society that showed little hesitation in destroying kin relations. The common practice of referring to fellow *cabildo* members by words with familial connotations reveals how the organizations served as a surrogate for an incomplete family structure.[180] Francisco Alas, the "emperor" of a Mina and Mandinga *cabildo* in Bayamo, described a meeting attended by his "*parientes* (relatives), free Blas Tamayo, slave Mateo and his

Organizing the Rebellion

wife, and the slave Candelaria Dolores."[181] One member of a *cabildo* reported that while he "was sick, all of his relatives had come to visit him."[182] José Caridad Perrera, a free black of Karabali ethnicity, ate dinner during festival days in "the house of Antonio José Barraga the Captain General" of the *cabildo* together with "various other relatives."[183] Other *cabildos* simply referred to members as part of one family. Cristóbal Govín, the second captain of the *cabildo* Karabali Oquella, complained of the new discord caused by an election "between a family that has always carried on with the utmost peace and harmony."[184] Still others described their fellow *cabildo* members with the more general *"compañero"* (companion) that conveyed a sense of the shared camaraderie that developed from being part of a community.[185] Whether described as "family" members, "relatives," or "companions," *cabildos* provided a widened network of associations that fostered collective solidarity.

Rebel leader Salvador Ternero's dispute with the Cuban-born Creoles in the Mina Guagni *cabildo* indicates that within a nation, the rights and benefits accorded to "family" members, "relatives," or "companions" could vary widely. While African ethnic identification tended to define who could be counted on *cabildo* membership lists, evidence from various societies suggests that the treatment of mulattos, Cuban-born Creoles, and slaves depended on the regulations and customs of each society. Contemporary documents leave little indication that mulattos participated in *cabildos*. Given that nations in Cuba based their membership on a shared African ethnicity, *cabildos* may have excluded mulattos. Cuban officials may have also prohibited them from joining *cabildos*, as they sought to prevent blacks and mulattos from making common cause. Despite the tendencies that worked to exclude mulattos, some may have participated in the *cabildos* or visited houses during festival days. On 25 February 1811, authorities arrested José Montero, Felipe Santiago, and Rafael Rodríguez, all soldiers in the free mulatto militia, for attending a meeting at a *"cabildo* of Blacks."[186] Other than this brief reference, there is not enough evidence to conclude that mulattos regularly participated in *cabildo* functions, just as there is no evidence to argue that the nations specified their exclusion.

Ample evidence suggests that Cuban-born blacks regularly participated in the nations. For example, the free Creole Juan Bautista Valiente, appropriately known as "el Cubano" to reflect his place of birth among Africans members of the society, participated in the Mina *cabildo*.[187] The *cabildo* Musolongo allowed Creole participation and recognized Juan Ruíz as a member, "even though he is a Creole, son of a father and a mother of the nation, and married to a free black of the nation."[188] Regardless of Salvador Ternero's bitter dispute with Manuel Vásquez over Creole voting rights, he recognized Creoles as members and described them as "children of the same" nation, and never proposed their expulsion.[189] While the differences between African-born and Cuban-born members could lead to rivalries within organizations, colonial officials appeared more alarmed than the *cabildos* that the two groups fraternized. Judicial authorities chastised rebel leader and free black Clemente Chacón for allowing his son Juan Bautista, "a free black Creole, to play the drums with the Kongo nation" during what they suspected were meetings to coordinate the uprising.[190]

While some Creoles actively participated in ethnic associations, others began to separate themselves from the African-born population. Leaders of the Lucumi *cabildo* complained of the formation of a Creole group that opposed the interest of the *bozales*. As Cuban authorities settled disputes within *cabildos* and became cognizant of Creole participation in the associations, they came to suspect that "there had formed a *cabildo* of black Creoles." The free black José Herrera denied any association with the society and insisted that he had no knowledge that his "sister-in-law Manuela González had been elected Queen of the Creole *cabildo*." Further, Herrera elaborated that "should one [*cabildo*] form, he would not join, because he was not a man of *cabildos* . . . and could not make the movements of the *bozales*." Rather, Herrera emphasized, he was somebody who "danced the minuet, as is the custom of Creoles."[191] Herrera's contrast between the minuet and *cabildo* performances drew a clear distinction between African and Creole dances. He also revealed, perhaps simplistically, the degree to which some Creoles defined themselves in contrast to *bozales*, and the complexity of racial and ethnic identity in Cuba.

Slaves and Creoles alike, in contrast to *bozales*, had limited rights and privileges in *cabildos*. The *cabildo* Karabali prevented slaves from voting for leaders; the organization's electoral roster listed only free members.[192] Likewise, other societies prevented slaves from participating in elections and deciding the financial expenditures of the nations.[193] Given that the distinction between free and slave represented the primary division of Cuban society, and given the prevalence of slavery in Africa, it should not be surprising that *cabildos* defined membership rights based upon legal status.

A few *cabildo* members even owned slaves. In 1807, Antonio Ribero, a member of the Lucumi Llane nation, purchased a slave for 500 pesos. The transaction caught the attention of the *cabildo* not because they opposed the purchase on moral grounds but because they suspected Ribero had bought the slave with money stolen from the society.[194] In 1804 Cristobal Govin, *capataz* of the Karabali Oquella nation, opposed remodeling several dilapidated rooms of the *cabildo* house, because he "would have to transfer my habitation during the construction" to the one of "Rafaela, slave of Teresa Barreto who lives in another room of the same house."[195] When Salvador

Organizing the Rebellion

Ternero assumed the title of *capataz* of the Mina Guagni *cabildo*, the nation authorized him to administer "whatever quantities of maravedíes, gold pesos, silver pesos, jewelry, slaves, merchandise, agricultural products, and other goods."[196] Although nations fostered ethnic identification and a community beyond the immediate supervision of white masters, the ownership of slaves by some *cabildo* members and the limited voting rights extended to human chattel illustrated how slavery pervaded every aspect of Cuban society.

Whereas some nations limited the participation of slaves in *cabildo* functions because of their enslaved condition, others attempted to overcome the barriers that blocked active participation. Festival days represented crucial events that allowed for a collective solidarity to be expressed through ceremony and dance. While masters might grant their slaves permission to participate in a *cabildo* as a reward, they also benefited from such participation. The nation Karabali Osso recognized the important participation of slaves in *cabildo* functions. In 1803 their account book recorded this entry: "payment for slaves' daily wages of our nation" to masters in order to secure their participation at *cabildo* events.[197] The Karabali Osso nation, in effect, hired the attendance of its enslaved members by paying wages to their masters. As slavery represented obstacles to full participation, generated additional expenses through payment of wages to masters, and undermined collective strength, *cabildos* often provided loans to emancipate members.[198] The *cabildo* Kongo, for example, reported that Cayetano García owed "80 pesos of the 200 that he was given for his freedom."[199] Free members could not only participate more actively in *cabildos* than slaves, but as the rightful owners of their own labor, they could contribute more generously to the nation's financial resources.

Some societies accepted members from other nations. Authorities assumed the free black Antonio from Bayamo was Karabali because he participated in the nation's festival days and "lived among them," but he described his ethnicity as Kongo.[200] Although the Mina and Mandinga could trace their nations to the distinct geographic areas of the Gold Coast and the upper Niger Valley respectively, they formed a joint *cabildo* that extended membership to both groups.[201] Members of different nations could even gain considerable authority within a *cabildo* with which they did not share a common ethnicity. In 1803 the *cabildo* Karabali Induri elected Juan Echevarría to the position of second *capataz* by an overwhelming majority. Jesús Sollazo, the leader of the *cabildo*, immediately declared Echevarría's election "null . . . because he is not of the nation Induri." The captain general sided with Echevarría because he had won the election outright and because of "the fact that he had been admitted to the *cabildo*" long before the election took place.[202] Although not an African-born member of the Karabali Induri nation, he apparently had enough supporters within the *cabildo* who did not define leadership qualities exclusively by ethnicity. For the leader of the nation, however, it was precisely his lack of ethnicity that made him unsuitable to serve as an elected officer. Echevarría's election pointedly reveals both the contested nature and flexibility of identity defined by African ethnicity in Cuba.

*Cabildos* routinely extended membership to people of diverse ethnicities, but as with Creoles and slaves, tended to restrict their voting rights. Salvador Ternero had dismissed Manuel Vásquez's complaint as "not having legitimate representation of the nation" because he was a Creole and had the support of only one slave. In addition, Ternero emphasized that among Vásquez's supporters was "María de la Luz Romero who is of a different nation."[203] The Karabali Apapa, like other nations, did not limit membership to only one ethnic group. When a dispute divided the *cabildo* over buying a new house, however, only those members of Karabali Apapa ethnicity and those who had been extended voting rights could debate the purchase. The leaders of the *cabildo* explained that members of other ethnicities "do not have representation in the *cabildo* according to the resolutions of this government, *without obtaining the right and permission from us*, and the others who make up the nation."[204] Voting rights in *cabildos* appear to have been universally granted to free African-born members who represented the ethnicity of the *cabildo*. For Creoles, slaves, and *cabildo* members of other ethnicities from the dominant group, generalizations prove elusive because the practices and customs of each society tended to differ, illustrating the diverse experiences of people of African ancestry in Cuba.

Although *cabildos* often restricted participation in their associations along ethnic lines, they also recognized commonalties with larger cultural groups common to areas of the slave trade. Manuel Blanco explained to authorities that the division of the Lucumies into separate nations reflected the different homelands of the members while recognizing their common Yoruban culture. According to Blanco, "the truth is that among the blacks who call themselves Lucumies, some are Chabes, others Barbaes, Bambaras and Nangas . . . all of them take the name Lucumi, but some are from one homeland and the others from another." The same recognition of a larger shared culture can be observed among the different groups of Kongolese in Cuba. Blanco observed that "there are many Blacks who call themselves members of the Kongo nation, but as they are from diverse homelands they have in this city diverse *cabildos*."[205] The Karabali also identified themselves as part of a larger cultural group, but divided their *cabildos* to reflect a specific homeland of the members. In addition to choosing leaders for each Karabali *cabildo*, they also elected "José Aróstegui as the *capataz* of the five Karabali nations" to coordinate activities among the organizations.[206] The Lucumies,

Organizing the Rebellion

Kongoleses, and Karabalies formed associations based on a broadly shared cultural identity rooted in Africa. They then limited *cabildo* membership to build close solidarity among those of their same nation and homeland, whom they affectionately described as their "paisanos" (countrymen).[207]

"WHO MOVES ALL OF THESE MACHINATIONS?":
THE LEADERSHIP OF *CABILDOS*

Within each *cabildo*, several members held administrative positions that strengthened the *capataz*'s leadership. The *cabildo* Karabali, located in the city of Matanzas, elected Rafael as their new leader in 1814. They then decided upon a general staff that resembled a king's court. They agreed that Rafael's wife would serve as queen mother; María Rosario Domínguez as princess; Diego as first minister, Nicario as second minister; Bernardo as first captain; Miguel de la Cruz as second lieutenant; Manuel del Portillo and Felipe as musicians; and Francisco as treasurer.[208] In addition to these titles, other *cabildos* created positions such as governor, emperor, sergeant-at-arms, queen of war, and captain of war.[209] Although denied voting rights within *cabildos*, slaves often attained leadership roles. The slave Patricio served as "captain of the Karabali slaves" and Alonzo Santa Cruz held the position of "King of the Kongo slaves."[210] The captain general of Cuba attempted to prevent the establishment of an elaborate leadership structure and recommended that "there should not be positions other than first, second, and third *capataz*."[211] The captain general attempted to restrict the *cabildos'* ability to provide members with titles because of the dangers of allowing slaves and free people of color to create their own hierarchical structures.

Cuban authorities remained torn over how to deal with the leadership organization created by *cabildos*. They recognized the important role of *cabildos* for a rapidly expanding slave society, as they provided crucial cultural adjustment for slaves recently imported from Africa. Further, a single leader provided the important function of serving as an intermediary between colonial officials and African laborers. Nonetheless, the Cuban government continually voiced concerns over the power that came with being a *capataz* of a *cabildo*. In 1759, the captain general of Cuba informed Spanish officials that, "as a precaution for certain disorders, it has been established by this government to name for each [*cabildo*] a Captain to watch and supervise their functions and meetings, who is of the same nation, and of old and mature age."[212] By the late eighteenth and early nineteenth centuries, the previous policy of the colonial government appointing leaders had been replaced by the *cabildos* electing their own leaders. *Cabildo* elections ultimately required approval by the colonial government which, in turn, shaped who would and would not be an acceptable candidate. However, there are not any known extant examples of authorities overturning an election. The change in policy from government-appointed to *cabildo*-elected leaders reflected the ability of nations to create a leadership structure acceptable to colonial officials. *Cabildos* expanded their restricted autonomy to determine the internal affairs of their societies by selecting leaders who did not attract the government's close scrutiny.

While government officials referred to *cabildo* leaders as *capataz* or captain, some nations came up with their own titles. The free black José Caridad Herrera described Antonio José Barraga, the leader of the Karabali *cabildo*, as "Captain General."[213] Authorities learned that "inside the house" of the Kongo nation, members called the *capataz* Joaquín "the Kongo King."[214] The difference between the government-given title of *capataz* and the chosen title, by some *cabildo* leaders, of captain general or king probably did not represent any vast difference in the function of nations. Nonetheless, the distinction does reveal the tension that informed the process of identification and self-identification. The decision by the Kongolese to give their leader the title of king might be considered as something more than a generic reference to monarchical authority. Throughout the eighteenth century one of the central claims to legitimate rule in the Kongo region was made by asserting "I am the King of the Kongos."[215] Civil wars split the Kingdom of Kongo into various camps that claimed adherence to a military king or a blacksmith king, which may have informed who became selected as a leader of a *cabildo* in Cuba. Some *cabildos* eschewed the leadership titles of *capataz* and captain provided by the colonial government. Perhaps they did so in reaction to how colonial society disproportionately shaped the discourse of identity, from stripping Africans of their birth names to deciding what titles could be given to *cabildo* leaders.

Many of the leaders of the *cabildos* earned their elected position by distinguishing themselves as militia soldiers. Manuel Blanco rose to a leadership role within the black militia by commanding a 100 man company that fought in the American Revolution. He also served as a leading force in directing the financial affairs of the *cabildo* Lucumi.[216] Retired militia soldiers of the black battalion of Havana, Tomás Poveda and Clemente Andrade, served as the elected leaders of the *cabildo* Karabali.[217] Juan Gavilan, also a retired soldier, emphasized his military service when he wrote to the captain general to resolve a dispute within the *cabildo* Karabali Umugini.[218] Military distinction and service helped to single out these soldiers as leaders among people of color and within their own communities.[219] For many soldiers, the militia represented an opportunity for social advancement and a steppingstone toward achieving what some scholars have regarded as "social whiteness" through the acquisition of legal rights denied to blacks and mulattos.[220] The acquisition of rights and special privileges accorded to soldiers, however, did not necessarily preclude identification with slaves and free people of color. The common appearance of militiamen as elected *cabildo* leaders likely indicates their military status did not automatically separate them from slaves and free people of color, but rather could elevate them to leadership roles.

*Cabildo* leaders tied to the militia would often have their *fuero* rights extended to the associations. Domingo Acosta, the *capataz* of the Karabali Apapa nation, drew upon his connections as a retired militia soldier to request that a military court settle a dispute within the *cabildo*.[221] Captain General Someruelos recommended that a "military tribunal" investigate the financial affairs of the Mina Guagni nation after Esteban Torres and Salvador Ternero emphasized their militia service.[222] When Manuel Blanco became involved in a property dispute with the *cabildo* Lucumi over selling the nation's house, he hoped to win the case by mentioning his volunteer militia service and stressing that he did it "without receiving a salary or any gratification."[223] The selection of *cabildo* leaders from the ranks of the colored militia served to present colonial authorities with individuals they regarded as loyal subjects of the Spanish Crown. By electing leaders acceptable to government officials, the *cabildos* would suffer less scrutiny and supervision.[224]

An examination of the electoral process indicates that female members often guided the affairs of the nation, not the elected *capataz* as Cuban officials believed. Because of their numerical superiority among the *cabildo's* voting members, women often decided the selection of new leaders. For example, of the forty-two eligible voters who participated in the *cabildo* Karabali Oquella elections of 1804, thirty-one were women.[225] Although the majority of males cast their votes for Cayetano García as the new *capataz* for the *cabildo* Kongo Macamba in 1807, Antonio Diepa won the election because of six females votes.[226] Of the forty-seven votes cast in favor of Juan Echevarría for the position of second *capataz* of the *cabildo* Karabali Induri, thirty-two came from women, guaranteeing his margin of victory by a ratio of two to one. The *capataz* of the *cabildo* Jesús Sollazo attempted to overturn Echevarría's election on the basis that he was not of Karabali Induri ethnicity, "but also because the general customs observed in the *cabildos* of this city for the elections of *capataz* do not admit the votes of women."[227] The captain general ruled against Sollazo's motion to not accept the women's votes for *capataz* because it was "contrary to what is daily observed."[228] The *capataz* of the Karabali Oquella, Cristobal Govin, shared Jesús Sollazo's opinion that female participation in *cabildos* should be limited because Lázaro Rodríguez won the election with "only the assistance of Teresa Barreto's supporters."[229] As women actively participated in the urban economy and made up a noticeable percentage of the urban free population of color, they played a decisive role in determining who led the *cabildos*.

While some *cabildo* leaders felt threatened by the authority women could exert in shaping the leadership of African societies, others recognized their important role in maintaining the unity of nations. In 1805 José Arostegui of the *cabildo* Karabali Osso informed the captain general of the death of Rita Castellanos who held the leadership position among the female members of the nation. Shortly thereafter, Barbara de Mesa "occupied her place with all the support of the nation for her recommendable" characteristics. Arostegui requested that the captain general "give his recognition to Barbara de Mesa as *capataza*" so that she could "govern the women of said *cabildo* with authority" to insure "perfect peace and harmony."[230] Other *cabildos* not only recognized the important role of women in governing female members but acknowledged their crucial role in promoting a unified organization. When the queen of the Kongo Macamaba nation, Rafaela Armentaras, died, the *cabildo* recognized that without her leadership "the disorder has increased," and they could no longer resolve disputes by themselves but required government intervention.[231]

Not only did females in *cabildos* exhibit considerable authority in determining leaders, they also influenced financial expenditures. Through membership dues, renting rooms, collecting alms, and hosting festivals, *cabildos* normally held savings in cash that varied from 300 to 1,000 pesos. These savings represented a significant amount given that the prices for slaves in Havana newspapers usually ranged from 300 to 500 pesos.[232] The important duty of guarding the safe that contained the *cabildo*'s money usually fell upon the queen. When the *cabildo* Karabali Osso became involved in a dispute that required paying a legal fine, Barbara de Mesa would not turn over the safe to the neighborhood commissioner José Castillo "until she had been threatened with prison."[233] When members of the *cabildo* Karabali Oquella challenged the financial expenses of the *capataz*, the whole nation went "to the house of Teresa Barreto, queen of said *cabildo*," to count the money in the safe. The *cabildo* leaders pulled from the safe "a bag full of money and in the presence of the nation . . . counted 946 pesos."[234] Most *cabildos* entrusted the queen of the nation with guarding their money, but they took precautions to insure that it would take more than one person to open the safe.

*Cabildos* used a safe modeled on the Spanish coffer that required three different keys to prevent one person from making a withdrawal.[235] The *cabildo* Karabali Induri distributed its "three different keys" to the "First *Capataz*," the "Second *Capataz*" and "an elected person in consultation with all the nation." The three key holders could only open the safe in the presence of "twenty people, men or women, of the nation" to explain the purpose of

Organizing the Rebellion

withdrawals.[236] Likewise, the *cabildo* Kongo Macamba also required its safe to be opened in the presence of its members to "avoid future disputes, objections, and suspicions of the *capataz*."[237] Female leaders of *cabildos* guarded the safe, but they did not hold the keys to open it. The Kongo Macamba nation stated very clearly that whoever "takes on the task of treasury" would have to be a "black male."[238] The leader of the *cabildo* Karabalí Oquella, Cristóbal Govín, feared that "the funds of the *cabildo* held by Teresa Barreto, a rebellious women with bad ideas," would jeopardize the stability of the nation.[239] Govín feared she could get a hold of "the common money of the nation," which would empower her to "move all of these machinations."[240] Whether through deciding elections or guarding the safe, females decisively shaped *cabildo* functions.[241]

## "ENTERTAINMENT, FOOD, AND DRINK":
## UNITY THROUGH COLLECTIVE IDENTITY

The *cabildos* showed remarkable flexibility in maintaining an overall sense of unity despite their divisions. While it is important to emphasize distinctions of ethnicity, place of birth, legal status, and gender, given that the members of the nations themselves made these distinctions, it is just as important to recognize that *cabildos* continued to support the collective efforts of the nation as a whole. Moreover, the documentary record is biased to show divisions because the archival sources were created when the colonial state intervened to settle disputes. As with many organizations representing lower-class interests in a society controlled by a powerful elite, the tension between the specific needs of individual members and the unity of the *cabildos* created friction within the associations. *Cabildos* could recognize and address dissent within their own ranks without causing the complete dissolution of their societies, indicating that collective needs often superseded individual interests. The organizations represented the only institutions that permitted voluntary grouping along ethnic lines by Africans and Creoles, men and women, and slaves and freedpersons in Cuba. For a colony rigidly divided between white European masters and black African slaves, *cabildos* stood in contrast to the racial slave-free paradigm that defined the circles of inclusion and exclusion for most of Cuban society.

*Cabildos* also broke down the division between rural and urban society. Although the urban *cabildo* house provided the center for the nations' activities, members represented both the city and countryside. When the *cabildo* Kongo Musolongo elected Augustín Pedroso to the position of *capataz* in 1806, the rural members of the nation could not travel to Havana to participate in the election. Before Pedroso could assume leadership of the *cabildo*, however, the nation recognized—in something akin to an absentee ballot—that the members "absent in the countryside agreed with the election of Pedroso."[242] Not only could *cabildos* break down rural and urban division by both groups participating in elections, but housing could also link the two distinct geographic areas. The free black María Francisca Duarte lived in the *cabildo* house of the Karabali Apapa located outside the city walls of Havana. She shared the room on weekends with her husband who worked in the countryside. "On the first day of the month," according to María Francisca, she paid five pesos in rent to the *capataz* of the *cabildo* when, "as customary, [her] husband came from the countryside."[243] Temporary housing on weekends served to unite rural and urban members of the nation and likely facilitated their attendance at *cabildo* functions in the city. In addition, and perhaps more importantly for María Francisca and her husband, the *cabildo* house offered temporary marital unity. The geographically gendered division of labor often separated spouses. Females most commonly found employment as market vendors and domestic servants in urban areas, whereas male laborers tended to dominate rural plantations.

The *cabildos'* cooperative methods of raising revenues and deciding expenditures revealed an emphasis on collective rather than individual goals. During three months in 1801, the *cabildo* Karabali Osso raised 576 pesos from membership donations. Apparently, the *cabildo* did not require a specific amount for all members to pay. Domingo Alcántra made the largest donation of 72 pesos, while Trinidad de Medina contributed the smallest amount of 29 pesos. Given that only fourteen members (six women and eight men) made donations to the *cabildo's* safe, it is likely that participation in a nation did not require paying dues. According to Manuel de Jesús, who participated in an unnamed *cabildo* in Puerto Príncipe, slaves "were poor blacks who could contribute [only] one coin for the festivities."[244] The *cabildos* Karabali Induri and Karabali Oquella realized some members could not contribute from their own pockets but could provide money to the nation by begging for alms.[245] *Cabildos* represented diverse economic backgrounds such as free landowners, artisans, market vendors, and unpaid slave laborers. Consequently, a universal membership fee of any substantial amount for joining a nation would have been difficult to collect.

*Cabildos* often redistributed their money back to members. The society would hold a special meeting, and the members who had voting rights would then decide the financial affairs of the *cabildo*. Nations commonly provided loans to members and even purchased freedom for slaves who participated in the *cabildo*.[246] The account books of the *cabildo* Karabali Umugini recorded loans to José María Rebollo, María Dolores Méndez, and Josefa for unspecified reasons in December 1801.[247] In addition, *cabildos* offered medical and

Organizing the Rebellion

financial assistance to sick members. The Karabali Osso paid ten pesos to rent a "carriage to take a sick [member] of the nation to the village of Guanabacoa" located on the eastern side of Havana harbor.[248] Tomás, the king of Karabali Induri nation, recorded that the *cabildo* gave four pesos to "Matías Billalta who was sick."[249] The *cabildos* also paid for burial services that normally fell upon the lay brotherhoods of the Catholic Church.[250] Loans, medical assistance during periods of illness, or a solemn burial, brought the nation together by pooling their limited financial resources.

Festivals, more than any other activity, served to unite the nation. Almost all *cabildos* held elaborate celebrations on 6 January, the Day of the Kings. In addition, on other religious holidays, Sundays, and to transfer power to a newly elected leader or commemorate the death of a past one, *cabildos* hosted reunions at which they performed music and danced. During the festival days of San Blas in Bayamo in early February, all the *cabildos* of the city held gatherings and parades.[251] According to British traveler Robert Jameson, *cabildo* performances on Sunday could be observed throughout the city of Havana. "At these courtly festivals (usually held every Sunday and feast day) numbers of free and enslaved negroes assemble to do homage with a sort of grave merriment that one would doubt whether it was done in ridicule or memory of their former condition. The gong-gong—(christianized by the name of diablito), cows-horns, and every kind of inharmonious instrument, are flourished on by a gasping band assisted by clapping of hands, howling and the striking of every sounding material within reach, while the whole assemblage dance with maniac eagerness till their strength fails."[252] Jameson's musical preferences led him to describe the performances as played on nothing more than crudely fashioned instruments that revealed neither musical talent or purpose. It is likely that colonial authorities held the same opinion, and therefore, saw nothing threatening in the collective gatherings.

The view of *cabildos* as Africans engaged in simplistic savage dances depended, of course, on who witnessed them. When asked why a *cabildo* member from Bayamo participated in the festivals held by his nation, he told authorities that he had "entered for entertainment, food, and drink."[253] Juan José Moroto of the Lucumi nation, who grew up in Philadelphia, explained his participation in *cabildos* as an opportunity to express a collective ethnic solidarity not permitted in North America. Moroto told colonial officials that he "had been raised in North America where the blacks do not dance in *cabildos* and are not permitted to have dances, on the days of work they are working and on Sundays they are in the church praying."[254] In order to hold a dance, the *capataz* of the *cabildo* had to notify the neighborhood military officer and purchase a license; otherwise, they could be fined. For example, in 1796 military commissioner Juan García fined the Karabali Apapa nation eight pesos for "dancing in the *cabildo*" without a license.[255] Although *cabildo* festivals ultimately required approval from colonial authorities, they allowed Africans to identify themselves as members of ethnic-based organizations by performing rituals and customs they had brought across the Atlantic and transformed in Cuba.

*Cabildo* dances served to bring the members of the nation together to express a collective identity and solidarity and, at the same time, raise money for the nation. During festival days *cabildos* often opened their doors to nonmembers. For a small entrance fee, nonmembers of the *cabildos* could become spectators to the dances and ceremonies and purchase food and drink. *Cabildos* attracted a wide audience that included not only members of their own ethnic groups, but other Africans, people of African ancestry born in Cuba, and even curious white observers, according to European travelers.[256] Depending on the size of the festival, the *cabildos* could raise a substantial sum. In 1808 the *cabildo* Lucumi Llane collected fifty-seven pesos from entrance fees for a fiesta held in March.[257] The *cabildo* Karabali Osso raised 240 pesos over several religious holidays celebrated during Christmas in 1805.[258] The revenues, derived from selling tickets for *cabildo* performances, provided financial resources to fund the nation's other activities. Further, the attendance by members of different nations at *cabildo* houses during festival days provided the opportunity for the diverse African populations in Cuba to share the cultures they held in common. At the same time, the festivals also demonstrated what made the nations different from one another based on their place of origin. As the next chapter will analyze, *cabildo* members involved in the Aponte Rebellion would employ the shelter of festival days around Christmas in 1811 to collectively meet, plan, and organize the rebellion.

MEMBERS OF *cabildos* chose to join associations to define themselves in cooperation with others who shared a similar ethnicity. In this sense, they show the importance of understanding that Africans in the Americas did not immediately or exclusively adopt a racialized identity of blackness. While *cabildos* above all emphasized ethnic identity, they did not ignore that whites were not slaves and that the ruling class of Cuba was not African. At meetings inside *cabildo* houses when nations discussed the needs of their members, they surely addressed the problems their organization faced of existing in a society based upon a racial hierarchy that privileged the European over the African. As a result, African ethnic identity was not necessarily in conflict with a New World racial identity of blackness. By providing a network of alliances and an institutional structure that offered a limited sense of familiarity for Africans in Cuba, *cabildos* helped their members to survive in a society based upon racial oppression.[259]

The process by which *cabildos* and the free people of color militia could address the specific needs of their own nations and fellow soldiers, and also serve the common interests of all people of African ancestry, became apparent in the Aponte Rebellion of 1812. Militia member and *cabildo* leader Salvador Ternero drew on his experiences as a soldier to gather arms, and he discussed and organized the rebellion in the security of Mina Guagni *cabildo* house.[260] Cuban authorities encouraged free people of color to participate in the militia and provide armed assistance for the colonial state, as this tied individuals to the Spanish Crown. Likewise, Cuban officials allowed the formation of *cabildos* because they believed African ethnic identification would prevent the formation of a broad-based racial movement. The Aponte Rebellion, however, revealed the flexibility and innovative nature of African identity in Cuba. Africans in Cuba could define themselves by simultaneously emphasizing both their Old World ethnicity and their New World racial identity, revealing the strength—not the weaknesses colonial officials assumed and some present-day observers fear—of cultural diversity.

# 4

## Burn the Plantations

The Cuban Aponte
Rebellion(s) of 1812

The hangman's noose tightened once again during the early morning of 9 April 1812. The executioner added another name to the fatal list that included the leader of the rebellion, José Antonio Aponte, the Frenchman Juan Barbier, who had been to Saint Domingue, the slave Tiburcio Peñalver, who routinely traveled from the countryside to the city, the freedman Juan Bautista Lisundia, the militia soldier Clemente Chacón, and the *cabildo* leader Salvador Ternero. Estanislao Aguilar, a free mulatto from Havana, also suffered execution by hanging for his involvement in the rebellion.[1] Aguilar shared much more with his fellow rebels than having his life end by public execution. He lived in the same Havana neighborhood of Guadalupe outside the city walls where Aponte, Chacón, Lisundia, and Ternero all had their homes.[2] The proximity of the rebels' houses made it easy for judicial officials to search them for clues and evidence indicating their participation in the revolts.[3]

The free mulatto Estanislao Aguilar served as a crucial link between the urban leaders of the revolt and the slaves and free people of color who toiled on plantations outside of Havana. As a literate artisan of an unstated profession, Estanislao Aguilar regularly forged passes for himself and others to facilitate travel between Havana and the countryside.[4] Apparently, Aguilar's routine trips from the capital to the plantations hid his secretive activities in planning the insurrection. He often escorted urban slaves and free people of color, such as fellow conspirators Juan Bautista Lisundia and Juan Barbier, to the plantations.[5] Aguilar had developed close associations with several slaves and free people of color who worked on plantations and routinely traveled to the city where they often stayed overnight in the Guadalupe neighborhood of the leaders.[6] Aguilar made his last trip from Havana to the plantations with Barbier, Lisundia, and the slave Tiburcio Peñalver on the night of 14 March 1812.[7]

Barbier and Aguilar returned to the plantations armed with knives, which judicial officials suspected they purchased from retired carpenter Tomás Gómez, who often sold meat and poultry on plantations.[8] Once Aguilar, Barbier, and Lisundia arrived, they "gathered all the slaves together" and informed them of their plans for rebellion.[9] Aguilar later recalled that when they explained the insurrection would provide "freedom" for the slaves and "burn the plantations, they became very happy and joyful."[10] According to slave Tadeo Peñalver, after they announced the start of the uprising, the rebels engaged in a ceremony where "Lisundia, Barbier, and the mulatto Estanislao Aguilar . . . played [music] and danced."[11] Aguilar later confessed that the slaves "played small drums . . . [Barbier] danced . . . and Lisundia beat a drum."[12] According to the lawyers Francisco María Agüero and José María Ortega, the rebels then committed themselves to insurrection by offering a toast of *aguardiente* [sugar cane alcohol], and making a pact *"to fight for liberty, to kill anybody who attempts to stop their hopes, . . . offering to end slavery, and make them [slaves] happy."*[13]

Estanislao Aguilar and the other leaders from Havana played a leading role in directing the insurrection when the revolts erupted on the night of 15 March 1812. Free black Francisco Javier Pacheco stated that after Aguilar, Barbier, and Lisundia arrived at the Peñas-Altas sugar plantation, they immediately set fire to the living quarters of the master and his staff, the boiling houses for processing sugarcane, the stacked and cut sugarcane ready to be milled, and the slave quarters.[14] The plantation quickly burnt to the ground. Aguilar, Barbier, and Lisundia gave no quarter in dealing with the white inhabitants of the plantation who did not escape. With machetes and knives, the leaders killed five whites and injured two others in front of the slaves.[15] According to Lisundia, Barbier then announced to the slaves that they "would cut off the heads of anyone who did not join them" as they organized to spread the rebellion to other plantations.[16] Barbier and Aguilar commanded the rebels to carry the insurrection to the neighboring plantations of Santa Ana and Trinidad.[17]

Before the rebels reached their destinations, the government had called out the militia and armed the local citizens. By the early morning hours of 16 March 1812, the rebellion had been suppressed. Military authorities quickly arrested hundreds of slaves and free people of color, while numerous others scattered throughout the countryside. Over the next several months most of the rebels would be hunted down, tried, punished, and many executed. Among those quickly caught and speedily executed was Estanislao Aguilar.

The rebellion that broke out at the Peñas-Altas sugar plantation led by

Aguilar, Lisundia, and Barbier figures as one of the many revolts and aborted insurrections throughout the island collectively known as the Aponte Rebellion. The insurrections by slaves and free people of color began in the east-central region of Puerto Príncipe during January 1812. The rebels then escaped to the east and attempted to extend their movement to Bayamo in February. But before the revolt erupted in Bayamo, a slave had denounced the rebellion. By early March, Holguín and other destinations had been rocked by reports of insurrection. Then, in the middle of March, the insurgents rose in rebellion on several plantations outside of Havana. This chapter provides a detailed narrative analysis of the various movements that occurred throughout the island from January to March 1812. It concludes with an analysis to assess if indeed the revolts and denounced conspiracies formed part of one coordinated movement, as historians have long concluded, or several separate rebellions.

THE REBELLION IN PUERTO PRÍNCIPE

The opening battle of the Aponte Rebellion of 1812 occurred in an area with a heightened sense of alarm to black resistance. As a result of the Haitian Revolution and the conquest of the Spanish portion of Hispaniola, the audiencia of Santo Domingo transferred to the Cuban city of Puerto Príncipe in the 1790s, known today as Camagüey. The hundreds of Spanish bureaucrats, officials, and émigrés who settled in Puerto Príncipe and oversaw colonial policy for the Caribbean brought to Cuba their fears and terrors of slave revolution. The expansion of plantation agriculture and slave labor in the region only served to magnify these concerns. Census data for the plantation areas of Puerto Príncipe is not available, but the urban slave population had grown by 61 percent from 1791 to 1810 from 8,226 to 13,265.[18] The increase of slave labor on plantations undoubtedly grew by an even larger percentage. Rebellions and alleged conspiracies in the region that broke out in 1795, 1796, 1797, 1798, 1799, 1805, and 1809 further exacerbated their concerns.[19] The frequency of such planned rebellions most certainly made the émigrés feel that they had not escaped the possibility of destruction by insurrection.

The heightened paranoia of Puerto Príncipe's white residents made it difficult to determine when plans for the rebellion began. Masters and colonial officials constantly intimated that slaves and free people of color intended to rise in revolt. Francisco Sedano, the governor of Puerto Príncipe, later recalled that he had heard "rumors during the month of September 1811 that the slaves of the region planned to gain their liberty by taking the province."[20] In October, another rumor circulated that British abolitionists would aid the slaves in rebellion. Captain General Someruelos claimed that the reports of abolitionist assistance "caused more harm than if Napoleon had sent his emissaries."[21] The repeated rumors of revolt, somewhat paradoxically, created an uneasy relaxation. The constant discussion about the possibility of insurrection resulted in catching authorities off guard when the rebellion began.

Over the course of two days, beginning on 15 January 1812, slaves and free people of color rose in rebellion on five plantations, all located within three miles of Puerto Príncipe. The first insurrection began at the Najasa plantation and immediately involved all the slaves. The rebels burnt the master's house, killed three whites, and then spread the movement to the neighboring plantations.[22] Within a matter of hours, slaves had revolted at the Daganal plantation, where they killed the white overseer, Pedro Cabrajal. The insurgents then moved to the sugar estate San José and killed two whites, followed by another uprising at the Santa Marta plantation where they killed another white and seriously injured two others. The uprising ended at the Montalban plantation where the rebels killed one white and injured another before the local militia, standing army, and armed citizenry finally suppressed the insurrection.[23] By the time the rebellions ended, slaves and free people of color had killed eight whites, injured numerous others, and burnt or partially destroyed several plantations.

The rebellion had been planned and organized during weekends and the holidays from Christmas until the Day of the Kings on 6 January. Kongo slave Máximo utilized a two-week pass from his master to leave the plantation on Christmas to organize the insurrection with other slaves and free people of color in Puerto Príncipe.[24] Karabali slave Simón received a travel pass at Christmas that he used to leave the plantation and stay with his enslaved wife, Susana, in Puerto Príncipe until the Day of the Kings.[25] Authorities later learned that at taverns, festival celebrations, and small gatherings on weekends and holidays, slaves and free people of color took advantage of their limited opportunities to travel and collectively meet to plan their rebellion.[26] At one meeting after the rebels drank several bottles of *aguardiente*, slave José Miguel reported that Máximo proclaimed "if they were to be captured, it would not be alive, but dead."[27] During the meetings between 25 December and 6 January the rebels had agreed that the Karabali slave Fermín, owned by Isabel Rabelo, would serve as the "motor of the conspiracy for the meetings he had organized and [he] named himself captain of the movement."[28] Slave José Miguel informed authorities that the participants in the insurrection had decided that after the plantation uprisings had liberated the slaves, they would form "four separate columns to attack the town."[29]

The *cabildos de nación* played a crucial role in organizing the insurrection in Puerto Príncipe. The holiday season provided additional opportunities for *cabildos* to have meetings that normally would have raised suspicions among colonial officials and masters. The slave Luis reported that he had been told that the captain of the Karabali *cabildo* had recruited "blacks to fight against the rich whites."[30] Free black Joaquín Belaguer, who served as the "King of the Kongos" in Puerto Príncipe, admitted to talking about the rebellion in his *cabildo* house and even toasting the triumph of the Haitian Revolution and the coronation of Henri Christophe as emperor of Haiti.[31] Manuel de Jesús left his master's plantation at Christmas to stay at the *cabildo* house where his fellow members—whom he described as his "muchachos"—elected him captain of the organization during their discussions about the rebellion.[32] *Cabildos* offered a limited sense of autonomy from master control and independence from the supervision of colonial authorities that free people of color and slaves utilized to organize their insurrection.

Judicial officials in Puerto Príncipe expressed a keen interest in a specific meeting among slaves on a coffee plantation when they talked about the rebellion. Authorities learned from several of those arrested that while the slave Pedro Francisco had "sharpened his machete, he grabbed a plantain, stabbed it," and then announced to others, "This is how I will run my machete through the whites."[33] Judicial officials interrogated five slaves about Pedro Francisco's bold action and declaration. The Mandinga slave Vicente told authorities that he had heard that after Pedro Francisco cut up the plantain with his machete, he announced, "And this is how I will run it through the stomachs of the whites."[34] Francisco Guerra reported that he had seen Pedro Francisco cut up the plantain with his machete, "but could not hear if he said 'this is how I would stab the whites,' as he was a far distance away."[35] The slave Nicolás told authorities that Pedro Francisco "expressed that just as I have finished sharpening my machete and cut up this plantain, the same will happen to the stomach of the whites."[36] When judicial officials questioned Pedro Francisco, he unsurprisingly claimed the stories "were absolutely false."[37] The amount of time, effort, and money judicial officials dedicated to discovering if Pedro Francisco had indeed sliced a plantain in illustration of what he would do to whites pointedly indicated how terrified masters and the colonial government had become of slave revolution. Although Pedro Francisco did not participate in the rebellions when they erupted, authorities nonetheless sentenced him to fifty lashes for his reported "scandalous expressions" during the everyday act of sharpening his machete and preparing food.[38] The reactions of masters and colonial officials to what could be regarded as a harmless conversation reveal how tenuously they regarded their control over Cuban slave society. In the early nineteenth century, the slicing of a plantain served as a small but metaphorical act in the destruction of slavery and Spanish colonialism.

Burn the Plantations

The terrified panic expressed by Puerto Príncipe's white inhabitants over the insurrection demanded that the colonial government act quickly and authoritatively. The town council held emergency meetings to authorize an increase of 200 militia soldiers for patrolling the countryside to extinguish the "inflamed desires of the blacks to achieve their freedom."[39] They also purchased extra military supplies in the belief that the slaves and free people of color planned to revolt again.[40] The zealous persecution of the revolted slaves resulted in Puerto Príncipe prisons rapidly becoming overcrowded. Local military officials stated that they could not "completely control the copious number of blacks" crammed into the town prison. They warned that the overcrowded prisons could possibly "cause another and more serious rebellion."[41]

The show of force by the local military served not only to suppress the insurrection and deter future plans of rebellion but also to restore public confidence in the authority of the colonial government. The Cuban captain general wrote to the Council of the Indies justifying the excessive costs created by fielding the extra militia as necessary to "calm the fears of residents."[42] Colonial officials voiced concerns over allowing the mulatto and black militia to participate in the suppression of the rebellion. They hoped, however, that soldiers of African ancestry squashing the desires for freedom of people with whom they shared a common heritage would militate against racial solidarity.[43] The colonial government took the opportunity of the insurrection to demonstrate that masters and citizens were dependent on the state for protection against their "domestic enemies."[44] The town council of Puerto Príncipe received donations and rewards from local residents for suppressing the insurrection and disciplining slaves and free people of color because the "owners of ranches, haciendas, and sugar plantations" had failed to instruct "their slaves in the conservation of domestic discipline."[45] Just one month after the uprising began, Captain General Someruelos wrote to his superiors in Spain informing them that they could "safely consider the event extinguished."[46] Francisco Sedano, the governor of Puerto Príncipe, did not share Someruelos's optimism. He concluded that although the movement could be "called extinguished . . . public tranquility had not returned to its previous state." To extinguish the fires of insurrection that razed several plantations, more action was required.

One of the clearest methods for symbolically ending a movement that attempts to overthrow the existing order is to stage a public execution of the leaders. On 29 January 1812, a large group of citizens gathered in the central plaza to observe the public execution of the rebels. The governor of Puerto Príncipe oversaw the execution by hanging of eight rebels during a ceremony that lasted over two hours. According to the governor, the executions were

Plaza in Puerto Príncipe (present-day Camgüey) where fourteen leaders of the 1812 rebellion were executed. Photograph by Matt D. Childs.

greeted by an "enthusiasm almost impossible to forget," which certainly left a long-lasting impression on all those present.[47] Two days later on 31 January, the governor sentenced two more slaves to death. Instead of hanging, Governor Sedano decided to test a new machine for administering the death penalty called a garrote. Execution by garrote occurred by slowly tightening an iron or leather collar around the neck until the victim either died of suffocation or a broken neck. The governor reported that either as a result "of a defect of the instrument or the inability of the minister of execution," the rebels "were left more choked than dead." In order to complete the execution after several failed attempts by garrote, the army shot the insurgents.[48] More than a month later, rural patrols captured several escaped slaves and free people of color. Governor Sedano sentenced four of them to their deaths by hanging for their involvement in the insurrections. The governor hoped the last executions would satisfy "the suspicions of the local inhabitants" who did not think the "barbarous project had been extinguished."[49] Suppressing an insurrection and executing the leaders may stop a rebellion, but these do not address why leaders rose in revolt in the first place.

In addition to the fourteen executions, authorities arrested more than 170 slaves and free people of color, then whipped, imprisoned, and banished many of them from the island. Colonial officials transported over 100 free people of

Burn the Plantations

color and slaves to Saint Augustine, Florida, to serve prison terms that varied from one to ten years.[50] Free black Joaquín Belaguer unsuccessfully appealed his four-year prison term in Florida for a reason that would have surprised the retired and elderly in the twentieth century. According to Joaquín, Florida was "a cold country that would cause an old black man to become sick."[51] Public executions and punishments provided the opportunity for the colonial government to powerfully reassert its authority. The town council of Puerto Príncipe, in a closed meeting, however, candidly remarked that executions alone would not end rebellion: "Who is capable of believing that after the contamination" of the slaves with rebellion that "they will return to their duties because we have killed ten or twelve of the principal leaders?" Council members recognized that the "contamination" from the uprising could last a long time, recalling that "more than five years" of insurrection "passed in the other colony [Saint Domingue] until it finally ended in catastrophe."[52] Repressing an uprising did not exterminate the idea of insurrection.

### THE CONSPIRACY IN BAYAMO

The prediction of continued rebellions by the town council of Puerto Príncipe quickly came to fruition in the eastern town of Bayamo. Like Puerto Príncipe, Bayamo had experienced dynamic population and economic growth during the last decade of the eighteenth century and the first decades of the nineteenth century due to the expansion of slavery. From 1791 to 1810, the population had more than doubled, from 23,003 to 52,084. By 1810, slaves made up 32 percent of the town's inhabitants; free people of color, 40 percent; and the white population accounted for 28 percent.[53] As in Puerto Príncipe, insurrections by free people of color and slaves had also erupted in the region. In 1795, mulatto militia officer Nicolás Morales planned a rebellion, protesting that a royal decree granting mulattos and quadroons equality with whites in holding public and ecclesiastic offices throughout the Spanish Empire had not been implemented in Cuba. The local government responded to the calls for mulatto "liberty" with "extra vigilance" to prevent "claims of equality from the many ignorant plebes."[54] Ten years later in 1805, a reported slave conspiracy, organized on plantations with the intention of attacking the city, terrified local officials. After a long investigation and the questioning of numerous slaves and free people of color, judicial authorities could only prove that the intended rebellion had involved a small maroon community talking about the Haitian Revolution and insurrection.[55] Masters and colonial officials in Bayamo displayed the contradictory actions of expanding slave labor to increase their wealth while simultaneously decrying the dangers of the growing population of African ancestry.

The governor of Puerto Príncipe publicly assured the local inhabitants that the execution of the leaders had ended the rebellion. Privately, however, he sent a very different message to Lieutenant Governor Corral of Bayamo, urging him to patrol the countryside for rebels that had eluded capture. In February, rumors, stories, and reports circulated, including that as many as "180 of the revolted blacks from the Najasa" plantation in Puerto Príncipe were heading toward Bayamo, according to one terrified resident.[56] Panicked white residents were not the only people to express an interest in rebels heading toward their town. Free black Juana Villegas told judicial officials that she had heard conversations about the arrival of "many blacks from [Puerto] Príncipe."[57] Freedwoman Gertrudis reported that "the blacks from the city of Puerto Príncipe" were headed toward Bayamo to spread the rebellion.[58] The arrest of several slaves and free people of color, previously unknown in Bayamo and without travel licenses, at the end of January and the beginning of February fanned the suspicions of a rebel invasion.[59]

The planned rebellion in Bayamo came to an end on the night of 7 February 1812, when the slave Antonio José informed his master, Lorenzo Vásquez Tamayo, of the uprising.[60] According to Antonio José, "Many blacks from the town and others that came from elsewhere were going to unite . . . burn various houses . . . block the entrances [to the city] . . . and attack the military headquarters to seize gunpowder, bullets, and rifles."[61] Colonial officials in Bayamo quickly made several arrests and searched houses and slaves' quarters on plantations. One of the leaders of the rebellion, a free black, José María Tamayo of Karabali ethnicity, had purchased six pounds of gunpowder in preparation for the insurrection. In addition, authorities discovered several of the rebels had stockpiled arms and ammunition.[62] The Mina slave María Francisca, owned by Miguel Barriaga, heard that the leader was "José María Tamayo, known as 'Matamuchos'" (literally, "kills a lot"), who "persuaded many to kill the whites."[63] Bayamo's lieutenant governor Corral concluded from the interrogations that "the blacks from the Hacienda Najasa in the jurisdiction of Puerto Príncipe had proceeded in agreement with those of this city" when they began the uprising.[64] The discovery in José María Tamayo's house of two rebels who had escaped capture for their role in the insurrection in Puerto Príncipe provided the crucial evidence linking the two rebellions.[65]

The insurgents planned the Bayamo conspiracy during holidays and festival days, similar to the Puerto Príncipe rebellion. During the first week of February, the local inhabitants of Bayamo, both slave and free, celebrated the festival of La Candelaria on the second, San Blas on the third, and San Blas Chiquito on the fourth. Just as the holidays from Christmas until the Day of the Kings offered travel opportunities and relaxed supervision in Puerto Príncipe, the festivals of La Candelaria, San Blas, and San Blas Chiquito enabled

Burn the Plantations

slaves and free people to visit friends and relatives. The Kongo slave Antonio, who had been raised in Jamaica before being sold to Cuba, told authorities that he traveled to Bayamo on San Blas to "spend time with a black Englishman named Pedro owned by Don Juan Antonio Trelles."[66] The slave Candelaria, owned by María Teresa Barreto, took a special interest in the festival days, as she shared the name with the Catholic feast day of La Candelaria (Candlemas in English), commemorating the purification of the Virgin Mary and the presentation of the infant Jesus in the temple. Candelaria attended several festivities that included "numerous Minas and Mandingas," where they "talked about the blacks who had revolted in Puerto Príncipe."[67] Judicial officials later learned that numerous slaves and free people of color held meetings to plan and discuss the rebellion during the festival days.[68]

Between 2 and 4 February, slaves and free people of color sang several songs as part of the festival. Only after authorities discovered the conspiracy did judicial officials regard the songs as having revolutionary connotations. The festival of La Candelaria involved a procession throughout the city, the blessing and burning of candles, and a large bonfire.[69] Slaves and free people of color had repeatedly chanted during the procession: "dale fuego al Bayamo," which would translate directly as "burn Bayamo."[70] An unidentifiable suspected rebel told judicial officials that they repeated "dale fuego al Bayamo as a result of joy and happiness."[71] Whatever the specific meaning of the chant "burn Bayamo," authorities regarded it as an incendiary slogan to spark the rebellion. Slaves and free people of color had also been heard singing:

| | |
|---|---|
| Francisco Mandinga, se murió | Francisco Mandinga died; |
| donde come mi amo, | Where my master eats, |
| como yo; | I eat; |
| donde duerme mi amo, | Where my master sleeps, |
| duermo yo; | I sleep; |
| donde jode mi amo, | Where my master fucks, |
| jodo yo.[72] | I fuck. |

Judicial authorities investigating the rebellion concluded the songs represented fiery verses to ignite the insurrection. In addition, they believed the songs revealed the intentions of slaves and free people of color to become the rulers of Cuban society. While the evidence is scant and lacks detail, it appears that songs and chants played an important role in organizing the rebellion that went unnoticed until the slave Antonio José denounced the movement. Similarly, slaves working in the boiler house of a sugar plantation on the British Caribbean island of Tobago in the 1770s signaled the beginning of their rebellion through song and verse.[73] Historian Robert Darnton's observation on the importance of songs for pre-Revolutionary Paris would apply equally to the conspiracy in Bayamo. According to Darnton, "Parisians commonly composed verse about current events and set it to popular tunes. . . . In a society that remained largely illiterate, they provided a powerful means of transmitting messages."[74] Songs and verses within the context of the Bayamo festivals could spread information on the revolt and mask revolutionary intentions.

The African *cabildos* of Bayamo also played a central role in organizing and planning the rebellion during the festival days of early February. For several days, slaves and free people of color from Bayamo held meetings in their *cabildo* houses and discussed the rebellion. The free black, Blas Tamayo, reported that "all of the slaves and free people of color who are Mandinga and Mina in this city [Bayamo] met together." They celebrated the holiday with a large feast, including "the killing of a cow."[75] A member of the Karabali *cabildo* informed authorities that his society had several meetings "night and day in which they had conversations in their Karabali language."[76] Patricio served as the "Captain of the Karabali slaves" for his *cabildo*. He traveled from his master's plantation to Bayamo in order to "play the drums and sing."[77] Likewise, the Kongo slave Rafael Infante, owned by Juan Tamayo, reported that he "sang and danced" with fellow *cabildo* members.[78] Several *cabildos* chose new leaders with special titles for the rebellion. The Kongo *cabildo* held a meeting to decide who would be the "Captain of War." The Minas and Mandingas chose members for the positions of "Captain," "Queen Mother," "Sergeant," and "Queen of War."[79] The *cabildos* of Bayamo utilized the three-day holiday of La Candelaria, San Blas, and San Blas Chiquito to meet collectively and make the final preparations for the rebellion.

On the night of 3 February, authorities raided the Karabali house in search of runaway slaves from Puerto Príncipe who may have attempted to spread the rebellion to Bayamo. Karabali *cabildo* member José María Tamayo provided shelter for two individuals whom he described as "two free blacks from Puerto Príncipe." Tamayo explained that the "only reason he was moved to offer them housing was because of the language [Karabali] that they spoke, indicating they were his relatives."[80] When authorities discovered the runaways in the house, they whipped all those present and arrested the leaders of the *cabildo*.[81] The public whipping of all the *cabildo* members, both slave and free, and especially the leaders, created a sensation among the other African fraternal organizations of the city. *Cabildos* created their own system of hierarchy by electing leaders as kings and queens. The public whipping of all members, regardless of position or title, demonstrated that authorities did not recognize or respect the *cabildos'* membership structure. The next day, leaders of the Karabali, Kongo, and Mina and Mandinga *cabildos* held a meeting to protest the treatment. According to Caridad Echevarría, a free black

Burn the Plantations

who attended the meeting, the *cabildo* leaders announced they "were going to send the whites to hell" by "burning the town . . . and the same would happen as in the island of Santo Domingo."[82] According to a member of the Karabali *cabildo*, the leaders of the rebellion had been chosen because of their service as the directors of *cabildos*.[83] A Karabali arrested for knowledge of the rebellion attempted to shift the guilt of his involvement to the *cabildo* leaders because, he explained, they "had given the order, and the other Karabalies do what they command."[84] The Minas, Mandingas, Karabalies, and Kongos all held meetings, in the security of their *cabildos*, to discuss the rebellion among those that shared a similar ethnic heritage. The leaders of the *cabildos* then coordinated the activities of their members with the other ethnic associations to organize a rebellion that united the diverse African population in Bayamo.

In addition to the diverse African ethnicities involved in the Bayamo conspiracy, slaves and free people of color who had previously spent time on various islands of the Caribbean also participated in the movement. The eastern region of Cuba had always been closely tied to the islands of Jamaica and Hispaniola through commerce. Illegal trade from Jamaica and Saint Domingue flourished during the 1790s and brought hundreds (and likely thousands) of slaves to Cuba. In 1805, Bayamo judicial officials investigated a conspiracy involving numerous English-speaking slaves. In order to question the English-speaking rebels, the judge reluctantly swore in a slave named Joaquín to "fill the position of court interpreter" and translate from English to Spanish for the accused rebels. The judge investigating the case admitted that "the urgent necessity" of the situation did not permit waiting "for a person of better rank and hierarchy" to be sent from Havana or Santiago.[85] Because many slaves and free people of color had been born in Africa, crossed the Atlantic, sold to various colonies in the Caribbean ruled by the British, French, Dutch, and Spanish, they often represented a far more cosmopolitan and multilingual population than their masters.[86]

Several people involved in the Bayamo rebellion of 1812 spoke multiple languages. For example, the slave Patricio spoke Karabali, English, and Spanish.[87] Judicial officials asked the slave Felipe, of Kongo ethnicity, why "despite being a creole," he spoke what they identified as "Jamaican, Kongo, and Spanish?"[88] Masters and authorities automatically assumed—and too many historians studying slavery in the Americas have uncritically followed their assumptions—that creolization resulted in the loss of African languages. Lucumi José María Aguilera told lawyers investigating the case that in addition "to the language that they speak in his land [Yoruba], and in addition to what he learned here [Spanish]," he also "spoke English that he mastered when he was on the island of Jamaica."[89] Slave Juan Tamayo had been born in Saint Domingue and then sold to Bayamo, where he continued to speak fluent

French and Spanish.[90] Numerous others involved in the rebellion spoke multiple languages that judicial officials identified as Guinea, Kongo, Karabali, Lucumi, Mina, English, Jamaican (English Creole), Spanish, and French.[91] After learning about the multilingualism of the rebellion, Bayamo's lieutenant governor wrote to Captain General Someruelos and informed him that the conspiracy was as much a foreign invasion as a local insurrection because of the "many blacks from the English nation" and elsewhere who joined the rebellion.[92] Despite the diversity of languages and backgrounds that presented formidable barriers to unity, slaves and free people of color involved in the Bayamo rebellion drew strength from their disparate experiences.

The suppression of the Bayamo conspiracy and the subsequent punishments of slaves and free people of color were not nearly as severe or as extensive as in Puerto Príncipe. The lieutenant governor of Bayamo's initial ruling on punishments, however, called for executions administered with the same vengeance. He recommended that "José María Tamayo, alias Matamuchos, Antonio José Barriaga, Blas and Juan Tamayo, and the advisor, well-educated, and tempting Caridad Echevarría" suffer death by "hanging in the Royal Plaza." Afterwards, "their dismembered body parts would be placed at the entrances and the most public places of the city so that their presence will inspire terror in those of their class and extinguish their tumultuous thoughts." The governor then recommended that all those involved who were not the leaders receive fifty lashes and six-year prison terms in Florida.[93] Masters and judicial officials successfully petitioned Lieutenant Governor Corral to ameliorate the severity of the punishments because they owned many of the slaves charged with the crime of insurrection. Corral could justify changing his recommended punishments because the government quashed the Bayamo conspiracy before it began. He decided that only the leaders would serve prison terms in Florida, free people of color would work for two years on roads and public projects, and masters could reclaim their slaves with the condition that they remained chained at all times.[94]

Captain General Someruelos and other colonial officials across Cuba placed the military on alert after the eruption of the plantation revolts in Puerto Príncipe and the discovery of the Bayamo conspiracy. The standing army in Bayamo and the local militia made numerous urgent requests for arms and ammunition to establish patrols in the countryside and prepare for any future uprisings.[95] When news of the rebellion reached the city of Santa Clara in the center of the island, the town council formed "four patrols to keep watch and stand guard during all hours, night and day" to prevent "the contagion from spreading here."[96] Political leaders at the port of Manzanillo located on the southeastern end of the island also feared insurrection would spread to their city. Judicial officials arrested a runaway slave named José

Ramón Borrego from Puerto Príncipe, believing he had participated in the plantation revolts.[97] The town council of the small eastern city of Jiguaní, located thirty miles from Bayamo, requested arms for the local inhabitants to "calm them and maintain a prudent show of caution and vigilance."[98] Political authorities in Santiago assumed that the Bayamo conspiracy had connections with their town because the leader, José María Tamayo, had made two trips to the city where he purchased rifles for the rebellion.[99]

The fear of insurrection resulted in news of the rebellions spreading rapidly throughout Cuba, to other Caribbean islands, and to the capitals of Atlantic world empires. By 7 February 1812, news of the Cuban rebellions had reached Jamaica through the Spanish merchant Francisco Curado, who happened to be in Puerto Príncipe at the time of the insurrection. Curado informed English colonial officers at Montego Bay that "a few of the white inhabitants to the number of eight or ten were killed in the commencement, but that the inhabitants had been enabled to get possession of forty or fifty of the revoltens, twelve of whom were hanged at Port au Principe [Puerto Príncipe]." He further elaborated "[t]hat martial law was declared and [it was] ordered that all negroes found without a paper from their owners were to be taken up: if any resistance made, to be killed."[100] Jamaican governor Edward Morrison wrote to London informing the Colonial Office of the rebellion in Cuba. Morrison then followed the familiar policy of isolating the island from the contagion of insurrection by "adopt[ing] the necessary measures to prevent the introduction into this island of any persons of colour or negroes from the Coast of Cuba."[101] Captain General Someruelos sent news of the "evil intentions" of the uprisings across the Atlantic to his superiors in Spain.[102] American commercial agent in Havana Vincent Gray sent a warning of "the insurrection of the Negroes in every quarter of the island" to Secretary of State James Monroe, who had his own personal expertise with suppressing slave rebellions, having served as governor of Virginia during Gabriel's Conspiracy of 1800.[103] In the aftermath of the Haitian Revolution, few events created more of a sensation or spread more rapidly in the Caribbean and the Atlantic world than information about slave rebellion.[104]

THE EXAMPLE AT HOLGUÍN

The possibility of rebellion struck terror in most white minds throughout Cuba, but few showed as much apprehension about the insurrection as the inhabitants of Holguín. After the first execution of the eight leaders of the Puerto Príncipe rebellion, Governor Sedano wrote to Holguín lieutenant governor Armiñan advising him "to take the most active measures not only for the capture and extermination [of the rebels] in case they pass through your territory, but also to prevent at all costs any uniting" with other slaves and free people of color.[105] After witnessing the execution of the leaders in Puerto Príncipe and moving on to Jamaica, Francisco Curado became convinced that "the negroes in the environs of that town . . . and Olgene [sic; Holguín] were in insurrection."[106] Bayamo authorities extended their search for runaway slaves suspected of participating in the conspiracy to Holguín.[107] Colonial officials in Holguín decided to "exhaust all preventive measures" by "bringing the women from the countryside to the city until the movement has been pacified."[108] The town council of Holguín adopted measures to suppress any possible rebellion and calm the panic of white residents, acknowledging that "nowhere is an uprising of blacks more feared than in this city."[109] The threat of slave and free people of color insurrection terrified Holguín's white inhabitants, causing them to become extra vigilant in preparation for a possible revolt.

In contrast to the white population, the Holguín lieutenant governor initially seemed unalarmed. After being informed of the insurrection in Puerto Príncipe and the possible spread of the movement to his territory, he decided to "place fifteen men in arms" to patrol the countryside and protect the city.[110] Upon learning of these small measures, Armiñan's superior in Santiago demanded that he take the threat of rebellion seriously. Governor Urbina told Armiñan that he would have to enlist more soldiers, because "there is little that twelve armed men could do; you will say good-bye to this town with a pathetic demonstration of force that the blacks will not fear."[111] Governor Urbina sent 800 cartridges of ammunition and 100 pounds of gunpowder to Holguín to make his point about the necessity to arm extra troops.[112] In response, Armiñan gathered all the residents of Holguín to the central plaza to address them about the "scandalous uprising" that resulted from the "introduction of black bandits into our jurisdiction." He called upon "all the men who live within the city of whatever rank, class, or status, with the arms they have in good condition," to form militia regiments to patrol the city and rural areas.[113] With the local residents mobilized, judicial and political authorities in Holguín began to investigate the possibilities of rebellion.

Rumors of slave revolts and alleged conspiracies had circulated before in the region. In 1808, the town council of Holguín authorized the formation of extra volunteer militia units for the supervision of the slave population.[114] In 1809, the lieutenant governor ordered the formation of patrols to monitor the population and guard against any insurgent movements.[115] When the wars of independence began in continental Spanish America, Holguín residents feared the contagion of insurrection would spread to their region.[116] The Holguín town council later reported that since September 1811 "rumors ran through this jurisdiction of a black uprising."[117] By mid-February 1812, the

Burn the Plantations

lieutenant governor reported news had spread throughout the region of a planned uprising "by the shouts of a crazy [priest] during a sermon on the first Sunday that had greatly disturbed the courage of these inhabitants."[118] In order to prepare for a possible invasion of slaves and free people of color from the plantations, the town council decided "to position two cannons" at the entrance to the city.[119] In addition, the town council held extra meetings with the local residents, and more volunteers took up arms to patrol the urban and rural areas.[120] With the imminent threat of rebellion terrifying the white population, judicial officials began to question vigorously suspected rebels to get to the bottom of the planned insurrection.

During the last two weeks of February and the first week of March 1812, colonial authorities in Holguín made no progress in discovering any details or plans about the much talked about rebellion. Armiñan wrote to Urbina that the hysteria "has made it impossible to provide you with a portrait of the actual state of the population as a result of the plotted uprising of the black slaves." The Holguín lieutenant governor "was left without a doubt that the planned rebellion was real, with a prefixed day to strike, even though they had been unable" to discover anything.[121] The suspicion of possible connections with revolts in other towns only increased when a rural patrol arrested three runaway slaves from Puerto Príncipe near Holguín at the end of February.[122] The questioning of numerous slaves and free people of color finally produced some information. On 11 March a female slave (who authorities did not identify by name or master) "denounced the uprising that had been planned to take place on the 14th at night, or on the 15th in case the tumultuaries could not unite." Within "three hours," the standing army and the militia filled the local prisons with "more than fifty of the accomplices . . . and the principal leader" of the uprising.[123] Shortly thereafter, colonial officials in Santiago and Holguín concluded that the rebellion had been planned to begin on the plantations; then the insurgents would attack the city.[124]

Analyzing the planning, organizing, and motivations of the slaves and free people of color involved in the denounced conspiracy in Holguín remains difficult. The answers to basic questions are still elusive: What were the connections with the other rebellions? What role did the *cabildos* play, if any, in the planning of the insurrection? How did the unity between free people of color and slaves form? These and numerous others remain unanswered because historians and archivists have yet to find the testimony and trial records from the Holguín rebellion.

On 25 March 1812, Santiago Márquez, the judge in charge of the trial, wrote to Lieutenant Governor Armiñan stating he had concluded his review of the investigation and enclosed the court records. Unfortunately, the testimony and trial records are not included with the letter located in the Museum of Holguín Province Archive.[125] Neither the court testimony and trial records, nor copies of the documents that local magistrates often sent to the captain general in Havana and colonial officers in Spain, nor even mention of these in correspondence, has been found in local, regional, specialized, national, or colonial archives. Armiñan stressed his own direct involvement in the arrest and questioning of more than fifty people to "determine the true accomplices."[126] Armiñan, however, surely exaggerated when he mentioned that only "three hours" after the rebellion had been denounced, he "put in practice the most active proceedings to effectively justify with certainty" the involvement of "more than fifty of the accomplices with evidence."[127] Only with a large team of lawyers and notaries could the lieutenant governor have questioned more than fifty people in the span of three hours. It needs to be stressed that Armiñan had to convince Santiago governor Urbina that he was taking all the necessary measures to investigate the rebellion but also that he would put an end to it as soon as possible. A long, drawn-out, time-consuming judicial investigation was not what Armiñan needed to win Urbina's approval. Moreover, in their panic, the local white inhabitants called for immediate suppression of the rebellion and speedy punishment. As a result, Armiñan may have decided to forgo the standard judicial investigation and proceed directly to punishment.

Lieutenant Governor Armiñan may have also limited his investigation because of orders he received not to attract any unnecessary attention to the planned rebellion. Urbina advised him to "always proceed with the utmost reservation to avoid whenever possible that they [the slaves] understand the object of your investigation."[128] After the plantations had been burnt and whites killed in Puerto Príncipe, and the conspiracy discovered in Bayamo, colonial authorities began to recognize the dangers of openly talking about rebellion. Upon learning of actions elsewhere and of the terror and fear expressed by the white population, slaves and free people of color could become emboldened to revolt. Indeed, many slaves and free people of color may have first learned of the revolts when authorities asked if they had any knowledge about them.[129] Furthermore, the panic and fear of the white population certainly suggested to rebels that the Spanish colonial state did not have everything in order, pointing to a moment of weakness to strike for their own liberation. The Holguín lieutenant governor faced the difficult task of quickly and discreetly investigating the rumors of rebellion and then ending the alleged movement through swift punishments.

Local residents called for immediate castigations once authorities discovered the plan for insurrection. Urbina wrote to Armiñan, congratulating him on foiling the conspiracy and advising him "to go straight to a hurried conclusion" with a "quick punishment to serve as an example to the rest," which perhaps indicates that a complete judicial inquiry was not under-taken.[130] On 3 April 1812, Armiñan called all of the town residents to the central plaza to witness the execution of the rebel leader and the whipping of slaves and free people of color who had joined the movement.[131] Without the testimony and trial record, very little can be gleaned from the extant sources about the punished. Authorities concluded that the slave Juan Nepomuceno, owned by Francisco de Zayas, was the "rebel leader of the conspiracy" and would pay "for his crime on the gallows."[132] The lieutenant governor never specified the particular actions which merited Juan Nepomuceno's execution.

The scant biographical information available about Nepomuceno derives from an 1807 notarial document and his burial record. In February 1807, Don Cristóbal Hidalgo sold Juan Nepomuceno to Francisco de Zayas for 400 pesos. Apparently, Nepomuceno had resisted his condition in the past, as the bill of sale described him as a "black *ladino* [usually someone born in Cuba who had mastered Spanish, but could also refer to an African who spoke Spanish] with various scars, vices, faults, and sicknesses."[133] In slave sale transactions and advertisements, "vices" and "faults" often indicated that slaves ran away or showed insubordination. His various scars likely indicate whippings, further suggesting past acts of resistance. Nepomuceno had prob-ably been born in Africa because his burial record described him as an "un-married man, casta Congo."[134] Other than these few details, little else can be gleaned from the records about the leader executed as the organizer of the rebellion in Holguín. The most detailed portrait comes from literature. Hol-guín novelist, Pedro Ortiz, in his 1990 historical-fiction essay titled "La hora tercia," informed by Franco's accounts and apparent consultation of archival sources from Holguín, portrayed Juan Nepomuceno as inspired by the Hait-ian Revolution.[135]

Unfortunately, we know even less about the other slaves and free people of color involved in the revolt. According to Armiñan, the "blacks Federico, Mateo, Antonio, Miguel, and Manuel" received public whippings in the cen-tral plaza of an unspecified number of lashes.[136] Authorities never stated if they were slaves or free men of color. All five may have been free, as docu-ments often identified slaves by the names of their masters. On the other hand, inclusion of the surnames of free people of color was standard in legal documents.[137] Lieutenant Governor Armiñan sentenced the five to serve their prison terms in Florida.[138] In addition, Armiñan sentenced the black José Mauricio to the military fort of San Juan de Uloa to serve a life sentence at hard labor.[139] As for the more than fifty accomplices whom Armiñan men-tioned on several occasions, the extant documents do not record their fates. Without the court testimony and trial record, which would provide impor-tant details, we only have a limited understanding of the planned conspiracy in Holguín and what the rebellion may have meant to slaves and free people of color. Without more conclusive documentation of the attempted insurrection at Holguín, we cannot dismiss the idea that the planned rebellion might actually have been a product of white fears. What does remain clear from the fragmentary record, however, is that masters and colonial authorities confronted what they generally believed was the real possibility of a formidable insurrection.

## THE INSURRECTION IN HAVANA

At the same moment the military disassembled the gallows in Holguín, colonial authorities constructed another nearly 400 miles away in Havana. News of insurrection circulated widely in the capital in early January after the rebellion in Puerto Príncipe, increased with the discovery of the conspiracy in Bayamo in February, and then reached a fevered pitch with the investigation of the planned insurrection in Holguín. The town council of Havana hurriedly enacted additional security measures to monitor the rural and urban areas for signs of rebellion.[140] María de la Luz Sánchez, a free black of Kongo ethnicity, reportedly told her former mistress in February that "within a short period of time this land will be governed by blacks."[141] On 9 March 1812, Captain General Someruelos began investigating reports of slaves who were "soliciting others with the intention of conspiring against public tranquility and the lives of citizens, especially the masters to obtain their liberty."[142] The slave Pablo, owned by Melchor Valdéz, told judicial authorities on 10 March that Havana slaves had discussions about freedom and rebellion.[143] Havana resident Pablo Félix Tinoco later told authorities that he had overheard his slave Antonio mention to another in mid-March that "the hour has arrived to remove all of the tyranny by freeing all of the blacks."[144] News, stories, and rumors of a planned uprising circulated widely in Havana during the first two weeks of March 1812.

Although unnoticed at the time, a significant clandestine migration of rebels left Havana for the plantations outside the capital to spread the rebellion. Commerce, family relations, holidays, ethnic solidarity, and labor connected the rural and urban areas of Havana province on a daily basis. German traveler Alexander von Humboldt and the slave Juan Francisco Manzano correctly emphasized the difference between rural and urban society for Cuban slaves. The divergent experiences of free people of color and slaves in urban and rural society, however, did not mean the two regions existed in isolation. Manzano had painfully learned firsthand of the torturous experiences of rural slaves when his mistress sent him to the plantation on several

Burn the Plantations

occasions as a form of punishment.[145] Numerous slaves and free people of color who lived in Havana regularly left the city to work in the countryside. For example, carpenters contracted their specialized labor to plantations, food vendors from Havana daily made the rounds to sugar and coffee estates to sell such items as bread and meat, and urban masters often rented their slaves out for temporary agricultural service during the harvest.[146] Reverse migration from rural to urban areas also occurred. Rural slaves routinely visited Havana as a result of plantation produce delivery to wharves and warehouses for shipment to international destinations, travel privileges that allowed them to fraternize with family and friends on weekends and holidays, and their own small contributions to the market economy as vendors of crafts and food.[147] The multiple economic, social, and familial links connecting the countryside and Havana provided a network that could unite the two areas in rebellion.

Similar to the revolt in Puerto Príncipe and the conspiracy in Bayamo, slaves and free people of color in Havana planned their insurrection during holidays. Kongo slave Francisco González reported a conversation on the "Day of the Kings" with a "black dressed in a military jacket mounted on a horse" proclaiming he "would give freedom to the slaves."[148] Between the Day of the Kings on 6 January and 15 March, several free people of color and slaves left Havana, including Juan Barbier, Estanislao Aguilar, Juan Bautista Lisundia, Francisco Javier Pacheco, and others, to spread the rebellion to the countryside.[149] Authorities later arrested slaves and free people of color on the plantations with forged passes that had facilitated their travel from Havana to the rural areas.[150] Numerous insurgents who lived on plantations attended organizational meetings in Havana when the leaders planned the rebellion. For example, slaves Tiburcio Peñalver and Antonio Cao, who labored on sugar estates, traveled to Havana several times before the insurrection. While in Havana, they stayed with José Antonio Aponte and Clemente Chacón.[151] At the same time, as news of the planned rebellion circulated between the countryside and the city, a runaway slave voluntarily returned to his master after a five-month absence. Several days later, the same slave participated in an insurrection on the plantation, suggesting he might have returned to settle an old score.[152]

The captain general's suspicion of an organized insurrection began to yield some concrete leads in early March. According to the slave Cristóbal, owned by Miguel Solas, "two or three months ago, while he was standing in the doorway of his master's house, three blacks asked him how many servants were in the house and their names."[153] Cristóbal informed authorities that the three men asked him if he wanted to have his name added "to a book" that listed the participants for the insurrection.[154] The three unidentified blacks explained to Cristóbal that they were forming "a junta of blacks to rise in rebellion because they could no longer continue as slaves."[155] Cristóbal's statement that he had "heard many slaves say that they are free" terrified judicial officials already alerted to a possible rebellion.[156] The key witness lending credibility to the rumored conspiracy was Captain General Someruelos's personal carriage driver. This free black of Mandinga ethnicity named Luis told Someruelos that a black Creole asked him "if he wanted to write his name on a list that included 200 names of various black slaves who intended to leave the dominion of their masters by ending their [masters'] lives with arms."[157] Luis could not explain why he did not immediately inform Someruelos of the conversation, which caused judicial officials to suspect he planned to participate in the uprising. With the knowledge that the rebellion involved such trusted servants as Someruelos's own carriage driver, judicial officials began an extensive investigation.

When word spread through Havana and the countryside that several slaves and free people of color had denounced the rebellion, it only accelerated the rebels' plans for insurrection. By 11 March, news circulated in Havana that the rebellion had been foiled. Over the next several days, various free people of color and slaves made their way with urgency to the countryside to launch the insurrection rather than call off the uprising.[158] Free black militia soldier Francisco Javier Pacheco later reported that "José Antonio Aponte requested" that he and others go to the plantations.[159] Juan Barbier, Clemente Chacón, and Juan Bautista Lisundia all stated that Aponte authored a letter describing the plan for the rebellion, commanding them to take it to the plantations and read it to the slaves.[160] While the urban leaders of the rebellion secretly left Havana, slaves on plantations held meetings to coordinate their activities.[161] Authorities later learned that the key meeting for organizing the revolt had occurred on the night of 15 March 1812 when slaves from several plantations gathered to discuss the rebellion.[162] A mulatto slave, Carlos Aguilar, left the Santa Ana plantation with Barbier and Lisundia to spread the insurrection to another location.[163] The leaders of the rebellion acted quickly in putting their plan into motion. They realized that since the movement had been denounced, authorities would quickly track them down.

The leaders may have selected the Peñas-Altas plantation to begin the rebellion because it provided special opportunities to enter the slave quarters undetected. Peñas-Altas bordered a common forest where local residents cut firewood and livestock grazed in the fields. Documents detailing property disputes reveal that in late November 1811 Juan de Santa Cruz, the owner of Peñas-Altas, had written to colonial officials complaining of the cutting of "all species of trees" by local residents, which he needed for firewood in refining

Burn the Plantations

Location of Peñas-Altas plantation outside of Havana where the rebellion erupted on the night of 15 March 1812. Photograph by Matt D. Childs.

his sugar cane. In particular, Santa Cruz complained of the "unbearable harm" caused by local residents who "cross the hacienda" and the "excitement they cause among the black slaves."[164] Santa Cruz took it upon himself to preserve the forest exclusively for his needs by attempting to prevent local residents from traversing his plantation. As a result of his actions, over thirty local residents of both European and African ancestry called upon Captain General Someruelos to resolve the dispute over who should have access to the forest and grazing fields.[165] Leaders of the rebellion may have chosen Peñas-Altas with the hope that the local residents would not report unknown individuals in the area, as this would only draw more attention to their own unauthorized use of the forest and grazing fields.[166]

On 14 March, Aguilar, Barbier, Lisundia, and Tiburcio Peñalver recruited slaves from Peñas-Altas to join the insurrection. Once the uprising began, they immediately set fire to the plantation. In a matter of hours, the rebels razed the entire estate.[167] According to the slave Baltasar Peñalver, Juan Barbier posted two slaves to guard the bell of the plantation to prevent the whites from sounding an alarm.[168] During the uprising, the insurgents killed the technician in charge of refining sugar, his two children, and two white overseers.[169] The slave Alonzo Santa Cruz, of Kongo ethnicity, later informed authorities that, once the rebellion began, "not a white person could be

Remnants of the smokestack from the boiling house of the Peñas-Altas plantation. Photograph by Matt D. Childs.

seen."[170] After the rebels killed the whites and burnt the plantation, Juan Bautista Lisundia, a free black from Havana, gathered the slaves to direct them to the neighboring plantations.

During the night and early morning hours of 15–16 March, slaves and free people of color attempted to repeat their success at Peñas-Altas at three other nearby plantations: Trinidad, Santa Ana, and Rosario. At the plantation Trinidad, the slave Amador lit the bagasse (residue of sugar cane after the extraction of juice) on fire once the group from Peñas-Altas arrived.[171] During the course of the uprising at Trinidad, the rebels killed five whites, including the overseer and his family.[172] Authorities later learned that slaves from the plantation Rosario had planned the insurrection to occur at the same time as the revolt at Peñas-Altas. As soon as the revolt erupted at Peñas-Altas, several slaves at Rosario were heard stating "we are going to do the same at this plantation as had been done at Peñas-Altas."[173] Doña María Lusado overheard one of her slaves talking about the insurrection, stating that the rebellion

Burn the Plantations

would "begin by killing the master, overseer, and others."[174] Before the revolt had reached Rosario, however, the military and armed citizenry firmly suppressed the insurrection at Santa Ana. On horseback and commanding the slave army, Barbier, Lisundia, and Aguilar directed the rebel slaves to the Santa Ana plantation. The local militia, standing army, and armed citizens successfully "repelled the first attack at Santa Ana," according to the Karabali slave Ziprián Santa Cruz.[175] Shortly thereafter, the rebels dispersed and took refuge in the countryside. Over the next several months, the Cuban army and militias hunted down most of the rebels, subjected them to trial and punishment, and then executed many of them.

A flurry of conspiratorial activity occurred in Havana when the revolts erupted in the countryside. After Barbier, Lisundia, Aguilar, and Tiburcio Peñalver left Havana, the urban leaders held several meetings to make the final preparations for the rebellion. The Karabali slave Juan de Dios Pacheco reported that Aponte, Chacón, and Ternero regularly held meetings at Aponte's house to plan the rebellion.[176] Several people later arrested for their involvement in the revolts testified that Aponte hosted reunions at his house between 15 and 17 March.[177] According to the free black Francisco Javier Pacheco, Aponte announced at a meeting "on Sunday 16 March at nine o'clock at night that for the planned rebellion . . . they would set fire to the neighborhoods outside the city walls and kill anybody who tried to contain it."[178] According to Clemente Chacón, the next day, 17 March, Aponte "was very happy" at a meeting at which he "assured all who attended that everything went well on the plantations and they have successfully met the challenges of the countryside."[179] Salvador Ternero informed judicial officials that "Aponte had informed him about the revolution he planned, advising him . . . [to come] to his house with all the people he could gather."[180] Aponte gained firsthand information about the insurrection in the countryside from the slave Antonio Cao, who participated in the Peñas-Altas uprising.[181] Antonio served as a crucial link between the countryside and the city, having stayed overnight at Aponte's and Chacón's houses in the past.[182] When lawyers asked Aponte about the meetings and whether they had discussed the rebellion and more specifically "the plan of operations," he replied "it is true that they [the meetings] occurred and dealt with what has been indicated."[183] Stephan Palmié's revisionist interpretation minimizes Aponte's role and incorrectly claims "all Aponte himself ever admitted was having had some knowledge of potentially seditious plans that some men with whom he was closely associated were hatching."[184] Aponte's house served as one of the key conspiratorial centers for planning and organizing the rebellion.

The home and tavern of free black militiaman Clemente Chacón also served as a nexus for organizing the rebellion. During the days immediately prior to the revolts in the countryside, slaves, free people of color, and militia soldiers held meetings to discuss their participation in the insurrection.[185] Chacón's enslaved wife María informed officials that slaves and free people of color regularly frequented the tavern for food, drink, and conversation.[186] When a lawyer investigating the rebellion asked Aponte "if he frequented the home or tavern of the aforementioned Chacón," he responded that "last week [9–16 March] Chacón had invited him to eat dinner."[187] It appears almost certain that Aponte went to the tavern to discuss the rebellion. Chacón's house and tavern, similar to Aponte's home, also served to link the urban leaders with rural slaves in coordinating the uprising. Plantation slaves Antonio Cao and Tiburcio Peñalver had visited Chacón's tavern and stayed overnight at his home during their trips to Havana.[188] Chacón's tavern and Aponte's house provided the necessary space and security beyond the scrutiny of masters and colonial officials to organize the insurrection.

Similar to the rebellion in Puerto Príncipe and the conspiracy in Bayamo, the African *cabildos de nación* played an important role in organizing the revolution in Havana. Salvador Ternero used the *cabildo* house of the Mina Guagni fraternal society, which he presided over as the highest elected official, to organize and plan the insurrection. According to the free mulatto Esteban Sánchez, at the time of the revolts on the plantations, Ternero had held a *cabildo* meeting at his house attended by "Clemente Chacón, José Antonio Aponte, a black captain whose name he does not know, the slave of Don Juan de Mesa, and ten or twelve more."[189] Aponte admitted that he had a close relationship with Ternero, having "known him for more than ten years," and confirmed that he went to his house to discuss the rebellion.[190] Ternero later confessed that at one *cabildo* meeting, the members of the Mina Guagni society had a conversation about "whether there would or would not be a revolution of the blacks."[191] Free black Melchor Chirinos informed judicial authorities that upstairs at Ternero's *cabildo* house they discussed the rebellion and "made a toast with *aguardiente*" to their success.[192] Juan Bautista Lisundia used his influence with the Kongo nation as a drummer to recruit members to join the rebellion.[193] When the rebellions erupted and authorities learned of the Havana connections to the plantations, the military raided several *cabildos* and questioned their members about involvement in the insurrection. As in Puerto Príncipe and Bayamo, members of *cabildos* used their limited autonomy to recruit, plan, and organize the rebellion.[194]

Based on the study of Cuban historian José Luciano Franco, various scholars have claimed José Antonio Aponte served as the head official of the Chango-Tedum *cabildo*.[195] Franco and most recently Philip Howard, in his study of the *cabildos*, have claimed Aponte was a member of the secret Ogboni society that originated in the Kingdom of Oyo in Yorubaland. No

Burn the Plantations

historian, however, has provided any Cuban primary sources to document this claim or evidence of Aponte's involvement in the Chango-Tedum *cabildo*. Scholars continue to debate the exact date of origin and extent of the influence of the Ogboni society in Yorubaland.[196] Clearly, we cannot assume Aponte's association with a society that has yet to be documented in Yorubaland prior to 1812 or, even more importantly, to have crossed the Atlantic and resurfaced in Cuba. If Aponte was a member of the *cabildo* Chango-Tedum or any other *cabildo* for that matter, it never entered the court record during his more than twenty hours of testimony. Moreover, authorities never asked him about his *cabildo* associations. This absence in the trial record is even more puzzling because the voluminous court testimony offers a wealth of detail on numerous *cabildo* members who had been interrogated about their involvement in the rebellion. Further, neither Aponte's name nor the *cabildo* Chango-Tedum could be found among the *cabildo* records detailing more than fifty societies that operated at the time of the rebellion. From the extant documents, it appears likely that Aponte never belonged to or served as a *cabildo* leader as other scholars have claimed. Nonetheless, this does not mean that Aponte had no knowledge of or associations with *cabildos*. On the contrary, he admitted going to Salvador Ternero's house and fraternizing with people who belonged to the African ethnic societies.[197]

During the process of questioning the hundreds of slaves and free people of color suspected of involvement in the rebellion, authorities slowly learned of the specific plans for the revolution in Havana. After the plantations had been burnt and the slaves liberated, Lisundia, Barbier, and Aguilar would lead an attack on the Havana military forts.[198] Havana had become the most fortified city in all of the Americas as a consequence of pirate attacks, the humiliating defeat by the English during the Seven Years' War, and the ambitious military plans of Carlos III (1759–88). In order to enter Havana from the plantations, the rebels would have had to take the military fortress of Atarés that guarded the southwest entrance to the city. When the leaders recruited slaves on plantations to participate in the rebellion, they carried with them a drawing of the Atarés fort to demonstrate visually the specific target to attack as they explained its location. Once they reached the outskirts of Havana, Clemente Chacón, a free black militiaman, would lead the revolutionaries' assault on Atarés.[199] Salvador Ternero would draw upon his expertise as a volunteer in the free black militia by directing the attack on the dragoon's quarters.[200] And free black militiamen Pilar Borrego and José Sendinga would lead the offensive on the artillery house. Afterward, they would redistribute the weapons to the slaves and free people of color.[201] The notable participation in the insurrection by the same men the colonial state had trained to defend the island against foreign attack and internal uprisings terrified judicial officials. Upon learning of the numerous black militiamen who joined the movement, the lawyer questioning Salvador Ternero candidly asked if they "had been ordered to join the movement [by their superiors] or participated voluntarily?" Ternero bluntly responded, "He who joined wanted to join."[202]

The goal of the Havana rebellion called for the destruction of slavery, just as had been reported in Puerto Príncipe and Bayamo. According to the free mulatto Aguilar, when Barbier arrived at Peñas-Altas he "informed the slaves that he had come to give them liberty."[203] Black slave shoemaker Cristóbal Solas had heard that the "blacks would rise in rebellion because they could not continue as slaves."[204] The lawyers representing slaves for masters who feared significant financial losses if the government "confiscated" their property for prison terms or "destroyed" their property by execution blamed the revolt on free people of color. Francisco María Agüero and José María Ortega argued that Barbier, Lisundia, and Aguilar had "seduced" the slaves into joining the rebellion by "proclaiming they had come to fight for liberty."[205] Masters and lawyers could only explain the slaves' motivation to join the rebellion as a result of the leaders' seductive promises of freedom. That hundreds eagerly joined the movement, however, clearly indicated they did not require much enticement.

Once the government quashed the rebellions, military authorities patrolled the countryside. Militiamen, the standing army, and armed citizens sent a steady stream of prisoners from the countryside to Havana for questioning. The interrogation of slaves and free people of color who participated in the rebellion led to the arrest of Aponte, Chacón, Ternero, and Juan de Dios Pacheco on 19 March, effectively ending the revolution. At first, Ternero would not provide a statement or answer lawyers' questions. He asserted that he "was a militiaman" and requested the *fuero* as he had done in the past when arrested on several occasions.[206] Regardless of his rights as a militiaman, the terror caused by slaves and free people of color precluded any special legal treatment. Aponte and Chacón knew better and did not even bother to request the *fuero*. Colonial officials arrested more than 200 slaves and free people of color over the next two months, rapidly filling the island's prisons.[207]

As in Puerto Príncipe, Bayamo, and Holguín, the government authorized the expansion of the local militia and the distribution of additional arms and ordered vigilant patrols to sweep the countryside and cities for possible rebels.[208] Captain General Someruelos requested a "supplement of 30,000 pesos" because of the "very urgent" and "highest necessity" to arm troops, man the military forts, and guard prisons as a consequence of the "events at Peñas-Altas by the blacks."[209] The town council agreed that "all of their power would be used against the rebels [because] the revolution had gained much

Burn the Plantations

ground with the events in Bayamo and Puerto Príncipe, . . . [offering] a favorable moment to destroy us."[210] The town council immediately authorized the investigation to move quickly. They recommended the rebels be "judged and punished instantly," setting aside the "sacred, respected rights that justice owes to humans."[211] Juan Ignacio Rendón, the main lawyer in charge of the investigation, later claimed that by the severity of the punishments, slaves and free people of color "relearned their fear and submission to whites."[212] The use of terror wielded by the state would restore order and demand submission from the population of African descent.

With executions already being demanded by the government and local inhabitants, it only remained for officials to identify rebels who merited the death penalty. The discovery of meetings at the homes of Aponte, Chacón, and Ternero, and the active recruitment of slaves to participate in the rebellion by Barbier, Lisundia, and Aguilar, provided more than enough evidence for judicial authorities to order the construction of an execution scaffold. Judicial authorities imprisoned more than 150 slaves and free people of color for suspected involvement in the Havana uprisings. Physical punishment varied from twenty-five lashes to as many as 200, the latter figure undoubtedly intended to cause death. Judicial officials sentenced rebels to prison terms, from one to ten years, in Cuba, with the others scattered to Spanish military forts throughout the greater Caribbean.[213] The Cuban representatives to the Spanish Parliament meeting in Cádiz agreed with the brutal punishments because the uprising was a "formidable insurrection" that could have involved "100,000 slaves in the countryside [near] the city." Moreover, according to the representatives, the "situation was even more serious." They argued the greatest "threat to the island of Cuba was the free people of color in the city; people with more ability than the slaves and a certain degree of intelligence that they used to promote the movement."[214] The first round of executions began on the morning of 9 April 1812, accompanied by a general report on the rebellion for distribution throughout the island. Captain General Someruelos firmly concluded that the plan for the rebellions across Cuba had been born in the "fatuous and heated brain of the black José Antonio Aponte." The captain general informed the residents of Cuba that since the leaders had been caught and executed, "everything now is perfectly tranquil."[215]

ONE UNIFIED REBELLION OR SEPARATE MOVEMENTS?

After providing an analysis of the various movements collectively known as the Aponte Rebellion of 1812, one crucial question to ask is whether it was one unified revolution or several separate uprisings and conspiracies. Colonial authorities and judicial officials simply concluded that Aponte and the others inspired and directed the rebellions from Havana without documenting or explaining in detail how they did so. Strong evidence indicates that the events in Bayamo and Puerto Príncipe were part of the same movement. Slaves and free people of color in the two regions had either contacted each other before January 1812 or decided to join forces once the rebellion began. The leader of the Karabali *cabildo* in Bayamo, José María Tamayo, explained that he provided shelter for two Karabali slaves who participated in the Puerto Príncipe uprising because they were his "relatives," referencing to their common African ethnicity.[216] The slave Gertrudis from Bayamo informed authorities that she had learned from several of her Karabali friends that they "collectively sang" about the rebellious blacks from Puerto Príncipe that had come to Bayamo.[217] Judicial authorities, colonial officials, and even foreign observers all concluded with sufficient evidence that the rebellion in Puerto Príncipe was linked to the denounced conspiracy in Bayamo.[218]

Establishing connections among events in Puerto Príncipe and Bayamo, the denounced conspiracy in Holguín, and the rebellion in Havana remains difficult, and ultimately only suggestive. All the political leaders of the eastern portion of the island believed the rebels from Puerto Príncipe would spread their movement to Holguín.[219] Bayamo resident José Antonio Alvarez had heard that as many as "180 blacks could arrive" in Bayamo or Holguín from Puerto Príncipe.[220] Military officials in Puerto Príncipe believed they confirmed the rumors of a rebel slave invasion in late February when they arrested three slaves who reportedly planned to spread the rebellion to Holguín.[221] Unfortunately, without the court testimony and trial record from the Holguín conspiracy, establishing connections between the movements with the extant records remains elusive.

When judicial officials investigated the rebellion in Havana, they surprisingly failed to ask about connections with other movements on the island. The interrogated conspirators certainly had every incentive not to mention any involvement with or knowledge of the other rebellions, as it would be regarded as a clear indication of guilt. Nonetheless, given the wide range of questions posed to the rebels, it is puzzling that little information about the revolts in Holguín, Bayamo, and Puerto Príncipe can be found in the Havana judicial proceedings. Suggestive evidence could indicate that the rebels coordinated the planned insurrection in Holguín and the plantation uprisings in Havana to start on the same day. Unknown to judicial officials in the two cities, who simultaneously conducted their own separate investigations, the denounced conspiracy in Holguín had been planned for the same day the rebellion erupted on the Peñas-Altas plantation in Havana.[222] Judicial officials either assumed that all the rebellions had been planned from the capital and felt no need to prove it, or possibly, but definitely less likely, the coordination from Havana was so well-known that it did not require an investigation and, thus, never entered the court records. Colonial officials and judicial investigators may have simply assigned the leadership to the Havana rebels to calm quickly the fears of white residents, terrified by a rebellion that had engulfed the entire island.

Perhaps even more surprisingly, colonial officials, judicial authorities, slaveowners, and others never questioned how the rebellions had been coordinated over a geographic area that spanned more than 500 miles from Havana in the west to Bayamo in the east. The lack of attention to this important detail pointedly reveals that although hundreds of miles separated the main cities of Cuba, the island functioned as an integrated political unit. Communication across the diverse regions certainly occurred. Frustrated efforts by colonial officials to prevent the flow of information and individuals from one region to another indicated the hidden communication networks of slaves and free people of color. In the aftermath of the rebellions and conspiracies, the governor of Santiago reprimanded Juan Falcón for his inability "to prevent communication among the blacks" in the jurisdictions of "Bayamo, Holguín, and this city [Santiago]."[223] Likewise, the town council of Puerto Príncipe called for the "utmost vigilance . . . [to] absolutely prohibit slaves from communicating with others."[224] Military officials and slave catchers often arrested runaway slaves and free people of color traveling without licenses far away from their homes. A slave patrol in Bayamo arrested the escaped slave Feliciano from Havana shortly after military officials discovered the planned conspiracy.[225] Many examples demonstrate that slaves clandestinely traveled throughout the island.[226] Free people of color also moved throughout the island with forged travel passes and could have spread the movement.[227] Logistically, planning and coordinating the rebellion throughout the island was clearly possible.

Orders sent out across the island for the arrest of Hilario Herrera, a resident of the village of Azúa on the Spanish border separating the island of Hispaniola, may provide key evidence of a single individual who linked the various rebellions. During the last days of February 1812, Governor Francisco Sedano of Puerto Príncipe concluded that "Hilario Herrera, alias, the Englishman," had been "the primary organizer of the bloody uprising" in the eastern part of the island.[228] Santiago Governor Urbina described him as "the author of the horrible catastrophe the island of Cuba would have suffered, from which, we have happily been saved."[229] Previously wanted for "stealing a cow," Herrera had escaped capture, spread the rebellion to the cities of Bayamo and Holguín, and was attempting to return to Santo Domingo to evade arrest, according to Sedano.[230] Colonial officials ordered a manhunt for Herrera in Santiago, Bayamo, Holguín, Puerto Príncipe, and even in Santo Domingo.[231]

Cuban political leaders sent physical descriptions of Herrera across the island so that he could be identified and arrested. Authorities described him as a "free black, Dominican, tall, robust, trimmed beard, somewhat gray-haired, more than fifty years old, always wears a bandanna on his head and jewels on his hands, he is called Hilario Herrera, alias, the Englishman."[232] The generic description of Herrera, which could have fit many people, combined with the panic created by the rebellions, resulted in several reported sightings of Herrera on different parts of the island. Bayamo resident and Santo Domingo émigré, Rosa de Matos informed Lieutenant Governor Corral that "Hilario Herrera passed through this town on his way to [Santiago de] Cuba during the past Christmas."[233] Judicial officials in Havana suspected Herrera may have been in the capital after Pablo Serra reported that his slave had talked with a "black who wore a bandanna on his head."[234] Cuban historian José Luciano Franco believed that Herrera "served as the agent of the conspiracy planned by Aponte in the eastern zone of the island," providing the link to the leadership in Havana. Herrera may even have attempted to coordinate "on the day of the rebellion the arrival in an undetermined place on the northern coast a boat from Haiti carrying three hundred rifles for the rebels."[235] The search for the elusive rebel in several cities only turned up the barren report that the "black Hilario Herrera boarded as a passenger on the Spanish sloop *Dos Amigos*," bound for Santo Domingo on "the first of February."[236] Herrera left behind a trail of unanswered questions for colonial officials and historians on his role in the Aponte Rebellion. He did not leave his revolutionary activities in Cuba; the same year Herrera escaped from Cuba, he participated in a slave revolt in Santo Domingo.[237]

THE APONTE REBELLION OR THE
REBELLIONS BLAMED ON APONTE?

Political movements always create leaders. It usually falls upon leaders to carry out the vital duties of coordinating plans, issuing orders, commanding followers, specifying goals, writing manifestos, inspiring obligations, and directing meetings. A cadre of leaders also provides an identifiable group for the existing order to focus on in suppressing the challenge to their authority. By concentrating blame for the movement on leaders, the ruling class denies that opposition might be widespread. Moreover, concentrating on leaders offers elites the comforting belief that had it not been for the influence of radical agitators, the masses would not have joined ranks. José Antonio Aponte's

Burn the Plantations

name became synonymous with the movement immediately after authorities suppressed the rebellions. Just one year later, Antonio J. Valdés's *Historia de la isla de Cuba* briefly mentioned the insurrections headed by the "Black Aponte and the other accomplices" that "disturbed the tranquility of the island's inhabitants."[238] "Aponte" the man entered history with the political movement known as the "Aponte Rebellion of 1812." What requires further examination is to determine if history has done justice to Aponte's role in the rebellion, or slighted the participation of others.

Regardless of evidence indicating meetings at Aponte's house attended by various slaves and free people of color involved in the rebellion, when authorities discovered the book of drawings that contained images of black soldiers defeating whites in battle, it was all the proof they needed to justify his execution. Even before they found the book, Juan Ignacio Rendón, the lawyer in charge of the investigation, had concluded from the interrogation of others that the book contained "references to the crime."[239] Aponte's own acknowledgement that the maps had been "copied with the exact attention to the entrances and exits of the military forts" of Havana, only confirmed Rendón's suspicion that the book served as a blueprint for locations to attack.[240] Before Rendón had concluded his investigation, he labeled Aponte and other free people of color as the leaders and charged them with seducing the slaves to revolt.[241] As slavery defined the patron-client networks and the asymmetrical reciprocity relations that governed Cuban society, "masterless" free people of color were especially vulnerable to the repressive authority of the colonial state.[242]

Colonial administrative changes in Cuba also favored quickly finding the leaders and ending the investigation. Someruelos ended his otherwise extremely successful twelve-year tenure as captain general with the difficult task of suppressing the rebellions. Undoubtedly, Someruelos did not want a long investigation that would delay the end of his rule and call into question his effectiveness as a colonial administrator. The execution of Aponte and others on 9 April 1812, represented Someruelos's last official act as captain general.[243] When he died over two years later, the printed eulogy praising his service in Cuba specifically singled out his "prompt and orderly" actions in suppressing the rebellion and executing the leaders.[244]

The transition of power meant that Juan Ignacio Rendón conducted the investigation with little supervision from either Someruelos or his successor, Apodaca. Rendón received his training as a lawyer in Spanish Hispaniola before emigrating to Cuba as a result of the Haitian Revolution. His personal experience with rebellion certainly provided a heightened sense of alarm to the images in Aponte's book. Rendón later stated that "within the span of four days," he had "discovered the conspiracy . . . led by the rebellious José

Antonio Aponte."[245] Rendón fell ill over the course of the investigation, which may explain why he asked very few questions about events in other parts of the island.[246] Less than one week after the plantation uprisings outside of Havana, Rendón declared José Antonio Aponte the leader of the islandwide movement.

The need to discover the leaders and administer swift punishments, and the exigencies created by the transition in colonial administrations, all made finding the authors of the movement an immediate necessity. Political expediency, however, does not mean Aponte had no role in the movement. Aponte hosted several crucial meetings at his house during the planning of the insurrection. The slave Antonio Cao from Peñas-Altas solidified the link between the plantation slaves and Aponte's home when he stayed there during his frequent visits to Havana.[247] Clemente Chacón reported that Aponte told him "he had more than *four hundred blacks* at his command" for the rebellion.[248] Several rebels testified that Aponte finalized the last details for the insurrection during meetings at his house between 15 and 17 March.[249] Given the life and death situation for the interrogated rebels, they most certainly did everything possible to direct guilt away from themselves. Blaming Aponte for their participation in the rebellion could save their lives. On the other hand, because any association with the leader would most definitely be interpreted as an admission of guilt, it is amazing how many admitted to talking about the rebellion with Aponte.

Court testimony—especially testimony of slaves and free people of color involved in conspiracies and rebellions, as American historian Winthrop Jordan has eloquently demonstrated—is inherently contradictory.[250] Slaves and free people of color questioned for their suspected involvement asserted their innocence by denying statements made against them and counteraccusing their accusers.[251] In the confusion of their own testimony they often contradicted their earlier statements. Aponte was no exception. At first, he denied any meetings at his house and his reported warning that "any man of color who did not join them would have his head cut off." Once Aponte realized he would be found guilty, he admitted that the conversations had taken place in his house. Aponte acknowledged "that it appeared just that all the people of color should unite, and they would only chop off the heads of those who resisted."[252] Aponte also admitted to participating in the rebellion when he answered "it is true" to statements identifying him as a leader. Aponte told judicial authorities that he "became involved in the project in concert with others, but always advised moderation." Aponte argued that he used his influence to place restraints on Ternero and Chacón, because he "could not commit atrocities with a heart of steel."[253] Later, Aponte also admitted to hosting meetings at his house at which the rebellion was planned and orga-

Burn the Plantations

nized.[254] After Aponte confessed his knowledge of the movement and participation in the project, Rendón and other lawyers only asked about the rebellion in Havana and not about the revolts and conspiracies in other parts of the island.

Aponte may have provided testimony on his association with insurrections across Cuba that have yet to be found by historians and archivists. After Aponte's execution, the investigation and questioning of suspected rebels continued for months. Judicial officials questioned free black Pilar Borrego with information from what they described as "the statements given by Aponte and Chacón the day before their execution, and with the knowledge they would die on the following day from their punishment."[255] When authorities interrogated free black Melchor Chirinos in May, they mentioned "Aponte's last confession" before his execution.[256] Military official Vicente de la Huerta later informed Captain General Apodaca in October that "in the afternoon on the day 8 April, at the time when José Antonio Aponte, Clemente Chacón, and the other prisoners were in the chapel" receiving their last rights, they "gave an interesting declaration." Huerta stated that he immediately called a "judge and a court clerk" to take their last testimony. Reportedly, the final confessions "lasted past eight at night." The next morning, on 9 April, the testimony was given to Someruelos.[257] The last confessions by Aponte, Chacón, and others are not included with the court testimony and trial record, which have been housed at the Cuban National Archive for more than a hundred years.

The crucial evidence for Aponte's role as the leader of the islandwide movement may be included in his last confession. The last statement given by Aponte the day before he died, perhaps with the incentive to clear his conscience, and even protect others by taking responsibility for the movement, remains absent from the extant documentation. Judicial officials might have misplaced the testimony when they requested the Aponte Rebellion court records from government archives during their investigations of other criminal activities. In 1839, Juan de Velasco requested the court records from the Aponte Rebellion to investigate the "clandestine meetings of blacks in this capital." Velasco suspected that Juan Ignacio Rendón had previously questioned some of the slaves and free people of color "for their involvement many years ago in the investigation of Aponte, Lisundia, and others for planning a conspiracy against the whites."[258] Several years later, when the extensive La Escalera conspiracy erupted in Matanzas and Havana during 1843–44, the military commission in charge of the investigation requested the Aponte Rebellion court records.[259] Reportedly, the military commission returned all the records to government archives, but they could have misplaced Aponte's testimony. Aponte's last confession was not included with the trial records for the later investigations. If Rendón and Someruelos agreed that Aponte had served as the leader of an islandwide rebellion based upon his last confession, the document could answer many crucial questions about the movement. Perhaps the most important question would be if indeed the revolts and conspiracies that rocked Cuba during January, February, and March deserve the title "the Aponte Rebellion of 1812."

CORRECTLY OR INCORRECTLY, the politics of blame turned to fame for José Antonio Aponte: history has known him ever since as the leader of the Aponte Rebellion of 1812. The rebellion began in Puerto Príncipe, with the insurrection of slaves on several plantations. The movement then spread to Bayamo, where the *cabildos* played an active role in organizing and planning the insurrection during festival days. Word of slave and free people of color rebellion terrified white residents throughout the island. In Holguín, this fear contributed to the questioning of slaves on several plantations and the movement's denunciation. Havana slaves and free people of color rose in revolt on 15 and 16 March through an elaborate plan that united the urban and rural populations. The available documentation ultimately does not provide enough evidence to argue that the rebellions represented one coordinated plan of revolution directed by Aponte and other leaders from Havana. However frustrating it may be for historians looking for conclusive evidence to get the facts straight, the primary concern of colonial officials was putting an end to the movement. Their goal was to suppress the rebellions, punish the leaders, and restore order. They focused on identifying specific individuals and the sequential chains of meetings that transformed conspiratorial plans to coordinated insurrections. Despite our need to look for proof that would pass as acceptable evidence in a modern courtroom, the records stubbornly resist such levels of verification; judges and lawyers simply did not apply these standards to their evidence. Connections and linkages, nevertheless, can be made among the various rebellions by examining the ideas and reasons that motivated the rebels to rise in revolt. The next chapter examines how the important ideological influences of the era represented by an emancipation rumor, stories of the Haitian Revolution, and more broadly changing notions of political liberty from the Age of Revolution served as a common unifying force among the rebels to bridge differences of geography, ethnicity, culture, and legal status, which single individuals alone could not cross.

# 5

## Vanquish the Arrogance of Our Enemies

Emancipation Rumors and Rebellious Royalism

And the executions continued for months. The hangman's list did not end with the leader José Antonio Aponte, the Frenchman Juan Barbier, the slave Tiburcio Peñalver, the free black Juan Bautista Lisundia, the black militiaman Clemente Chacón, the *cabildo* leader Salvador Ternero, and the mulatto Estanislao Aguilar. The executioner added free black Francisco Javier Pacheco's name to his deadly list. A Creole born in Havana who lived in the Salud neighborhood outside the city walls, Pacheco earned his living by working as a carpenter specializing in the repair of carriages. He also served as a volunteer militiaman in the black battalion of Havana.[1] Pacheco had been on the plantations at the time of the rebellions in March but eluded arrest until military authorities finally captured him on 7 May when he recklessly returned to Havana.[2]

After several days of questioning during May and June, Rendón sentenced Pacheco to death by hanging.[3] As with the slave Tiburcio Peñalver, mentioned in chapter 2, colonial officials postponed Pacheco's sentence until October to stage a collective execution of several conspirators. Early in the morning at 6:20 A.M. on 23 October 1812, an armed regiment of professional soldiers and volunteer militiamen escorted Pacheco and three others to La Punta military fort on the western side of Havana Bay. Captain General Apodaca reported that the crowd "applauded the gesticulations" of Pacheco and the other rebels during their last earthly moments as they dangled from the end of ropes.[4] The bodies were left hanging for nearly nine hours until at three in the afternoon, the Brotherhood of Charity removed them.[5] Afterward, the executioner severed Pacheco's head, affixed it to a pike, and placed it at the entrance to his neighborhood outside the city walls to serve as a grim warning for all to see.[6]

Pacheco had close associations with many of his fellow rebels. He informed authorities that he had "known Aponte ever since he was a small boy because he learned his [carpentry] trade with him as an apprentice."[7] Pacheco often visited Aponte's house and like many others had seen Aponte's book of drawings.[8] He also knew Clemente Chacón, testifying he visited "his house three times to eat lunch."[9] Authorities believed Pacheco and Juan Barbier organized the insurrection during several meetings at Chacón's tavern.[10] The slave Antonio Cao from Peñas-Altas informed officials that he met Pacheco at Aponte's house when they planned the rebellion.[11] Pacheco's connections with the important leaders of the Aponte Rebellion only further contributed to his guilt in the minds of colonial officials investigating the movement.

The crucial evidence for Pacheco's role as a leader of the movement related to a political manifesto tacked to the captain general's home on 15 March 1812, proclaiming independence, and attributed to his handwriting. Several people stated Pacheco had transcribed the proclamation from dictation by Aponte. The powerful message of the declaration stated in no uncertain terms that the revolution was on: "At the sound of a drum and a trumpet you will find us ready and fearless to end this empire of tyranny, and in this manner we will vanquish the arrogance of our enemies."[12] The bold action of nailing the manifesto to the captain general's house offered not merely an explicit warning to the colonial state of their intentions but a call to arms for their followers. Although not a formal political document composed by a congress or a junta, it should be regarded as a declaration for Cuban independence (if not Cuba's first). As explained in the previous chapter, slaves and free people of color denounced the movement in Havana on 10 March. Placing the declaration of independence on the residence of the highest-ranking Spanish official in Cuba sent a clear message to their partisans of a steadfast conviction to follow through with their plans for insurrection.

The Havana town council petitioned Someruelos to conduct an immediate investigation when they met two days later in the exact same building where the rebels had posted their insurrectionary declaration. The town council recognized that "the revolution," as they referred to the movement, was well planned, as seen "by what happened to the door of this house on the fifteenth." According to the Havana town council, the manifesto indicated an intent to repeat the same events as the "windward island," in reference to Haiti.[13] Aponte later confessed that he "dictated the manifesto to Pacheco, who transcribed it and assumed the responsibility for posting it."[14] Authorities found a draft of the proclamation at Clemente Chacón's house, which he reportedly planned to circulate prior to the rebellion.[15] The declaration posted on the captain general's residence, the draft found in Chacón's home, and knowledge of the document among rebels, caused authorities to believe the insurgents circulated the manifesto during the planning and organization of the rebellion. Despite Pacheco's claims of ignorance about the declaration, authorities concluded "Aponte dictated the seditious manifesto transcribed by Pacheco, who assumed the responsibility for placing it on the house of government."[16] For colonial officials investigating the rebellion, the political intentions behind the document that called slaves and free people of color to arms for what they regarded as a revolution required swift and severe punishments.

This chapter explores the rebels' motivations, hopes, aspirations, goals, and ideas that inspired the bold action of drafting a declaration of independence to announce courageously the beginning of their movement. Two political and ideological currents represented by royalism and racial revolution converged in the Aponte Rebellion. A series of rumors circulated throughout the island that a distant king had declared the slaves free, but their masters would not promulgate the decree. Emancipation rumors by royal decree became intertwined with stories and sightings of black military leaders from the Haitian Revolution. Reportedly, the Haitians came to Cuba to assist slaves and free people of color in their insurrection. Aponte and other leaders aligned their movement with these stories and rumors, circulated them, and refashioned them as a basis for legitimizing their cause and catalyzing the insurrection. In conjuring royalist approval for the insurrection and Haitian military and political power, they crafted a complex and seemingly contradictory political culture. Monarchical authority had the power to end slavery by decree, and the Haitian Revolution showed slaves how to claim their freedom with their own hands.

ROYALIST EMANCIPATION DECREES CRISSCROSSING
THE ATLANTIC WORLD

The reports of slaves being declared free circulated widely throughout the island at the end of 1811 and during the first months of 1812. As a result of the limited privileges slaves had to visit and socialize with friends beyond the confines of their own plantations, word began to spread rapidly among them about declarations of freedom during the Christmas holiday season. In the town of Puerto Príncipe, the slave Manuel de Jesús reported that during the Christmas "celebrations attended by the blacks" from various plantations, they talked of their freedom.[17] The twenty-five-year-old Mandinga slave named Francisco Xavier testified that during Christmas he and other slaves had "conversations about being given their freedom."[18] An unnamed slave reported that they had conversations discussing that "the King had given them their freedom but the Caballeros [in reference to the Cuban elite]" would not recognize the decree.[19] In the eastern town of Bayamo, slaves congregated on the festival days of La Candelaria, San Blas, and San Blas Chiquito, from 2 to 4 February, when they socialized and heard rumors of their possible freedom. According to a slave owned by Teresa Barreta, slaves and free people of color in Bayamo discussed that in Puerto Príncipe "the blacks had revolted" because "their freedom had been denied to them."[20] Through Christmas and other holidays that allowed slaves to temporarily step outside the bounds of master supervision, word of a reported decree of freedom began to spread rapidly across the island.

In Havana, authorities began to investigate the widespread talk about a slave emancipation decree before insurrections erupted on the plantations in mid-March. According to Pablo José, owned by Don Melchor Valdés, in February slaves began to discuss being declared free but denied the right by their masters.[21] The administrator of a coffee plantation outside of Havana reported to officials that an unknown black man spread news among slaves that a decree of freedom "had been hidden by the Governor and the [town] council and that he had come to call together all the people to go to Havana to obtain their liberty."[22] According to the slave driver on a coffee plantation owned by Santiago Malagamba, an unknown black man asked him to assemble the slaves so that "they could go to Havana to ask for their letters of freedom."[23] After insurrections erupted on several nearby plantations, authorities arrested Francisco Galano for inciting slaves to rise in revolt and march on Havana to claim their freedom.[24]

Emancipation rumors that circulated widely across the island traced some of their roots to the turbulent politics in Spain during the Napoleonic Wars. As a result of the French occupation of the Iberian Peninsula, the weakened regency had conceded parliamentary representation to the colonies. On 26 March 1811, a Mexican representative to the Cortes at Cádiz proposed that "slavery as a violation of natural law, already outlawed by the laws of civilized countries . . . should be abolished forever."[25] The shocking suggestion quickly crossed the Atlantic. Cuban captain general Someruelos wrote the Cortes urging them "to treat the issue with all the reserve, detailed attention, and thought that its grave nature requires in order to not lose this important island." News of the debate over slavery circulated in Havana and other cities through the *Diario de sesiones de Cortes*, causing "a significant sensation among the inhabitants of the capital, and a very sad series of grumblings . . . throughout the island," according to Someruelos.[26] The Cuban representative to the Cortes, Andrés de Jáuregui, wrote to the Havana town council informing them of the debate in Spain that "conjures up a storm so threatening to my country . . . it could degenerate into horrific conclusions."[27] Jáuregui recommended that if the Cortes had to debate the issue of slavery and the slave trade, it be done in "secret and with moderation . . . [to] not excite any

Vanquish the Arrogance

murmurings in our servants."[28] The Havana town council concluded that the discussions in the Cortes resulted in "exciting the slaves' aspirations to obtain their freedom with the confidence that it had already been given to them."[29] When word of the debate in the Cortes reached Puerto Príncipe in June, the council decided to increase the number and frequency of slave patrols in the countryside to guard against their "domestic enemies."[30]

Cuban slaveowners correctly concluded that any actions to end the slave trade and slavery threatened their economic prosperity and could result in financial ruin. The town council of Santiago emphatically protested that any discussion of abolition would result in slaves "emancipating themselves by their own hands and repeating in the island of Cuba the same catastrophe that covered in blood and ashes the largest and most opulent colony of the Antilles," an allusion to French Saint Domingue.[31] William Shaler, an American commercial agent in Havana, wrote to the United States government that the prospect of abolition moved Cuban planters to suggest to him that the "Island of Cuba ought to become part of the United States."[32] The question of the abolition of slavery attracted the attention of a wide and varied audience: masters concerned about their property; Spanish officials seeking to maintain the colonial status of Cuba; and pre-Monroe doctrine Americans eager to expand their power in the hemisphere. Perhaps nobody, however, showed as much interest as the slaves, who had the most to gain.

Cuban fears that the ongoing discussion of abolition in the Spanish Cortes could result in slaves making their own conclusions about the debate came to fruition during the first months of 1812. Captain General Someruelos claimed that the "contagion . . . of false and attractive news and promises that the Cortes had decreed the slaves free, and [that] the government of this island had concealed from them this extremely important point," resulted in "the slaves becoming involved in the criminal project."[33] Slaves such as María Candelaria explained their participation in the revolt "because in spite of having granted the slaves their freedom, it had been denied to them" by their masters.[34] Free black Juan Bautista Vaillant, who had been born in Jamaica and later moved to Cuba, reported that it was not the Cortes but the king who "decreed that all the blacks are free, but the whites . . . did not want to give them their freedom."[35] Slaves deftly crafted a response that stated their reasons for rising in rebellion centered on loyalty to misunderstood directives of the Spanish Cortes and king.

The repeated references to a declaration of freedom resulted in judicial officials recommending lighter punishments for slaves, since false rumors had motivated their actions. Lawyers Francisco María Agüero and José María Ortega reasoned that the slaves should not receive harsh punishments for believing their "owners had usurped the sovereign disposition of the Cortes," and that the Cortes "acted in their favor" with an emancipation decree.[36] Perhaps better than anybody, slaves understood the asymmetrical patron-client relations that defined Cuban political culture. By claiming royalist approval for rising in rebellion, slaves provided a recognized justification to explain their actions in a colony governed by a monarchical paradigm for political and social organization. Cuban officials increasingly narrowed their questions on why slaves rose in revolt to the Cortes decree because it explained the insurrection as simply a "misunderstanding" rather than a strike for freedom. Not all slaves, however, explained their participation as a result of a decree that originated in Spain.

Several slaves and free people of color arrested for their involvement in the rebellion explained that the king of England had declared them free. Free black Francisco Javier Pacheco, for example, reported that at the time of the rebellion a rumor spread throughout the plantation districts that the "King of England" had called for freeing all the slaves in Cuba. Pacheco elaborated that the "English had seized ships filled with slaves that came to Cuba because they did not want slavery . . . sending them [instead] to Santo Domingo [Haiti] because there they were ruled by a black King."[37] The African-born Kongo slave Francisco González repeated a similar story of England's role as an emancipating force on the island. During the planning of the insurrection, Francisco had been told "Havana was in rebellion because there had arrived an English General ordering the Captain General" of Cuba to provide "freedom for all the slaves." Similar to the story of the declaration of freedom by the Spanish Cortes, slaves emphasized that the "Captain General hid the decree." As a result, Francisco and other slaves planned "to join together and go to Havana to look for the letter."[38] Captain General Someruelos later suggested that the idea of England interceding on the slaves' behalf resulted from the widespread circulation of an article originally published in London in October 1811 critical of Cuban slavery that could be found in the "hands of everybody" on the island.[39]

Whether through overhearing masters talk about British abolitionist activities or through their own forms of information, slaves and free people of color came to learn of emancipation activities in other parts of the Atlantic world. As they planned their own rebellion, they connected their struggles for freedom to stories and rumors that an English king had declared them free. Slaves from the British Caribbean imported to Cuba through legal and contraband trade may have spread stories about an English king taking on a liberating role in the Aponte Rebellion. As plantation agriculture expanded across Cuba and the actions of the British Parliament led Jamaican masters to fear an immediate abolition by decree, an illicit slave trade from Jamaica to Cuba flourished. Colonial officials reported periodically on the illegal importation

Vanquish the Arrogance

of slaves from Jamaica and emphasized the need to take "all the proper precautions to not permit the landing of any slaves until they have been classified as pure *bozales*" direct from Africa.[40] Despite such precautions, transactions of individual slave sales reveal that Jamaica remained an important source for laborers in the eastern portion of the island throughout the first half of the nineteenth century.[41] Several plantations had large populations of Jamaican slaves that required English-speaking overseers to direct the laborers who understood little Spanish.[42] The large presence of Jamaican slaves was poignantly revealed in the 1805 Bayamo Conspiracy when an English-speaking slave took on the role of official court translator because no free person white or black could be found to perform the task.[43] In the 1840s, British abolitionists discovered that "so large is the number of British subjects held in slavery in one district in the island of Cuba that the English language is almost exclusively spoken among them."[44] As the slave population from the British Caribbean increased in Cuba, it appears that some slaves transformed the rumor from the Cortes declaring them free to one that reflected their own cultural background, represented by an English king.

The rumors and stories of emancipating monarchs aiding the Aponte Rebellion in the form of the kings of Spain and England also included the king of the Kongo. Among slaves of Kongo ethnicity in the town of Puerto Príncipe, word spread that the "King of the Kongo" had declared them free and was sending troops to aid the rebellion. According to the twelve-year-old female slave María Belen, slaves she identified as members of her same "nation" discussed the emancipation rumor during the Christmas holiday. María learned of the rumor from fellow Kongo slave José María while working in her master's kitchen. In a conversation that likely occurred in their native African language, María reported that José told the slaves that the "King of the Kongos had sent letters here to order freedom for the blacks." The blacks, however, remained enslaved because "*el mundo* [the world]," the term used by slaves to "designate white people," did not, according to María, want to grant them their freedom. As a result, the king of the Kongos "would send many Blacks to kill all the whites and give land to the slaves." María reported that she had heard similar stories from the slaves Francisco and Domingo, indicating that the rumor had apparently been discussed widely.[45]

Judicial officials then proceeded to question the slaves who had reportedly spread the rumor of Kongo assistance. José María did not deny that he told María Belen "while they were in the kitchen that the King had ordered the freedom of the blacks and that the whites here opposed" the decree.[46] María Belen even told her mistress, Ana Rita Coronado, about the decree for fear that she could get in trouble for having simply participated in the conversations. Upon learning of the discussion among the slaves about the king of the

Kongo, Coronado decided to disregard the rumor because she claimed "nobody believed it," as it came from the mouths that others regarded as "liars."[47] Slaves from the Kongo region decisively influenced Cuban society through their culture, social organizations, and political ideas that they brought with them that survived the horrific middle passage. Of the slaves and free people of color questioned for their involvement in the Aponte Rebellion who specified their African ethnicity in testimony, 40 percent, 56 out of 139, claimed a Kongo identity among various other West African groups such as Mandinga, Lucumi, Mina, Carabali, Ganga, Arara, and others.[48] This figure of 40 percent corresponds with the latest data that estimates west-central Africans represented 41 percent of the overall Cuban slave imports for the period 1806–20.[49] Only after the insurrections erupted on the plantations and Kongo slaves had been arrested for participating in the rebellion did authorities recognize that the stories they regarded as harmless conversations about the wishful assistance of the king of the Kongo could have influenced slaves to revolt.

The reference to the king of the Kongo and his role in aiding the Aponte Rebellion was not unique to Cuba. Historian John Thornton has argued that the civil wars in the eighteenth-century Kingdom of Kongo that funneled thousands of slaves across the Atlantic resulted in Africans bringing with them clearly defined notions of monarchical authority. Slaves' allegiance to the Kingdom of Kongo and explicit references to define themselves as subjects of the "King of Kongo," played an important role in the Haitian Revolution. Kongolese political ideology decisively shaped how some participants in the Haitian Revolution defined monarchial authority and served as a point of reference for slaves to legitimate their cause.[50] Similarly, on the nearby island of Martinique, rumors circulated in the 1760s and 1789 that the king of Angola would come with a powerful army to free the slaves and take them back to their country.[51] As many Cuban slaves had their primary political and cultural ideas formed by their experiences in Africa and not just the New World, we should not be surprised to find references to the "King of the Kongo" as a likely source for an emancipation decree and to the aid he would provide for the Aponte Rebellion.

"THE BLACK KING JOSÉ ANTONIO APONTE
HAD PAINTED"

A similar story of Cuban slaves being liberated by an order from a king with aid of military generals also found inspiration from the nearby island of Haiti. Several slaves reported that it was not the Spanish Cortes, the English king, or the ruler of Kongo that had declared them free, but the king of Haiti. At the time of the rebellion, some of the arrested were found in possession of proclamations from Saint Domingue that had reportedly been shown to others.[52] "Havana was very agitated," slave José Antonio had heard, "because some black generals from Haiti had come with an order from the black King to tell the governor of Havana to give the slaves freedom."[53] Another bondsman reported "one or two black captains from Haiti had ordered the Governor to free the slaves in the name of the King of Haiti."[54] Slave Joaquin Belaguer had reportedly "talked in his excessive inebriation" about the elaborate "coronation of [Henri] Christophe," only recently crowned emperor of Haiti in 1811, which resulted in slaves regarding him as the liberating king.[55] Cuban authorities who suppressed the insurrection remained convinced that Haitian agents planned to aid the rebellion. Captain General Someruelos told the successor to his office that "he believed without a doubt . . . there had been here several hardened black warriors that had served in Saint Domingue with military rank."[56] Planters reported to the town council of Havana that "external enemies" had been conducted to Cuba by an "emissary" from the "neighboring and close island of Santo Domingo [Hispaniola]."[57] Havana's representatives to the Spanish Cortes at Cádiz stated that "it was believed, and rumors circulated, that for the planned [revolt] the black Henri Christophe . . . would play a part with boats and arms."[58] In Puerto Rico, similar reports of Henri Christophe as a liberating monarch circulated throughout the island in 1812, which prompted Governor Meléndez to form slave patrols to monitor the plantations.[59] As the only nation to abolish slavery in the Americas, Haiti seemed, to many Cuban slaves, a logical point of origin for an emancipation decree.

Singled out among the presumed revolutionary generals from Haiti as one who would order the Cuban captain general to free the slaves was Jean François, known in Spanish-speaking Cuba as Juan Francisco. Several of the arrested rebels testified to seeing and talking with Juan Francisco at the time of the rebellion. Free mulatto Estanislao Aguilar told authorities that he had attended a "meeting in a tavern" near the "road that leads to the sugar plantations, accompanied by Juan Francisco, or Juan Fransura."[60] Juan Lisundia, a free black arrested for his involvement in a revolt on a sugar plantation outside Havana, had heard that "the black Juan Francisco . . . had arrived at the village of Guanabacoa."[61] Javier Pacheco reported that he "had dinner with other blacks and Juan Francisco, who brought two bottles of wine to toast their good success."[62] According to free black Clemente Chacón, José Antonio Aponte had told him that Juan Francisco "was an Admiral that served at the orders of the black king Christophe of Santo Domingo and came with his dispatches to seduce the free blacks and slaves of this island."[63] The "Admiral" was the title Jean François called himself while fighting with the Spanish against the French during the early years of the Haitian Revolution. Knowledge of his title may reveal the detailed information received by blacks in Cuba regarding events in Saint Domingue.[64]

Untangling the stories of who had seen, talked with, and talked about "Juan Francisco" and other revolutionaries from Haiti remains difficult. The life-or-death threat of imminent punishment greatly influenced how participants recounted the events of the past. Authorities later concluded from the testimony of other rebels, who knew him as "Juan Francisco," that Juan Barbier, a free black who had traveled to Charleston, South Carolina, and spent considerable time in Saint Domingue where he learned how to read, write, and speak French, assumed the identity of the famous agent to galvanize support for the insurrection.

Judicial officials at first assumed Juan Barbier was the Haitian agent "Juan Francisco" when they arrested him in March 1812. They quickly questioned him about his involvement in the rebellion and attempted to swear him into the criminal proceedings with the name "Juan Francicso." Juan Barbier stubbornly refused to answer any questions until he was sworn in as "Juan Barbier" and not "Juan Francisco." He emphatically asserted that his "true name is Juan Barbier" and "because he has his own true name he will not be called" Juan Francisco. Dumbfounded by Barbier's assertion and with no evidence but hearsay from other slaves and free people of color to prove otherwise, judicial officials followed Barbier's request and he was sworn in as "Juan Barbier," not "Juan Francisco."[65] What requires further exploration is placing within a Cuban context the numerous references by slaves and free people of color to an emancipation decree from Haiti and its association with Henri Christophe and Juan Francisco, to understand how it resonated with the rebels' own experience.[66]

"Juan Francisco" became intimately associated with the Aponte Rebellion for reasons stemming from his historical presence in Cuba. "Jean François" the historical figure had been an early leader of the Haitian Revolution who had allied with Spanish forces against the French. His inability to develop a strategy of slave emancipation or identify with the French National Convention's declaration of abolition, as had Toussaint Louverture, resulted in his declining influence. In July 1795, Spain and the Directory of the French Republic signed a peace treaty ceding western Hispaniola to France, leaving Jean François and his troops without a country. "In the year 1796," Captain General Someruelos later recalled, "Juan Francisco, *caudillo* of the blacks from Santo Domingo, with other military chiefs of his," namely Georges Biassou and Gil Narciso, attempted to settle in Cuba.[67] Havana's town council barred Jean François from living in Cuba because "several blacks had prepared functions to celebrate the arrival of Juan Francisco to show their affection toward him and his officials without ever meeting them."[68] Cuban governor Luis de

Vanquish the Arrogance

Las Casas wrote to Madrid in December 1795 protesting Jean François' plans to settle in Cuba because "his name rings in the ears of the mob as an invincible hero, redeemer of the slaves . . . and [one who] germinates the seeds of insurrection."[69] The exiled troops from Saint Domingue stayed only a brief time in Cuba, prohibited by officials from disembarking while docked for several weeks on the other side of the harbor to minimize their interaction with free people of color and slaves.[70] After a short stay in Havana, Jean François left for Cádiz, Spain; Georges Biassou, for Saint Augustine, Florida; Gil Narciso, for Guatemala; and other troops scattered throughout the Spanish Caribbean.[71]

Jean François' association with Cuba did not end with his brief Havana stay in 1796. Over the next fifteen years, there would be several reports of Jean François' soldiers visiting Havana or attempting to settle on the island.[72] In 1805, for example, authorities in Bayamo investigated a reported conspiracy among slaves who had talked about the Haitian Revolution. The slave Juan Bautista stated he would be "Captain" of the movement and "kill his master," just as "Juan Fransura" would have done.[73] Such stories may have served to transform Jean François, the reluctant slave emancipator of Saint Domingue defeated by Toussaint Louverture's rise to power, into "Juan Francisco," an admiral that served at the orders of the black "King Christophe." "Juan Francisco" may have even represented the black King. Free black Salvador Ternero claimed that Aponte "assured" him "that he knew the black King, and had seen him in Havana many years ago."[74] Aponte may have been referring to the "many years ago" when Jean François had briefly stayed in Havana. Reports of aid from "Juan Francisco" to execute the orders of Haitian king Henri Christophe literally took on a life of their own. Jean François had died in Cádiz, Spain, in 1805. His resurrection, however, as "Juan Francisco" in the minds of Cuba's slave and free people of color population provided another life for the revolutionary from Haiti.[75]

The arrival in Havana and subsequent arrest of several soldiers who had more than ten years earlier served under Jean François provided further credibility to the reports of Haitian assistance for the Aponte Rebellion. At the end of December 1811, "twenty blacks from the island of Santo Domingo with six heads of family" arrived in Havana. Captain General Someruelos housed the blacks from Saint Domingue at the military fort Casa Blanca, provided a "ration in specie of silver" to buy goods and supplies owing to their previous service to the Spanish Crown, and allowed them to stay in Havana while they prepared to return to Hispaniola.[76] During their stay at Casa Blanca, Gil Narciso and others made several requests to cross the harbor to hear mass, wash clothes, and receive medical treatment in Havana.[77] Sometime before 24 March 1812, colonial officials detained Gil Narciso and three of his aides,

Juan Luis Santillán, José Gaston, and Isidro Plutton, for suspected involvement in the rebellions. Santillán explained that it was not the first time he and the others had been to Havana: "We came in a boat from Bayajá [Fort Dauphin] when Juan Francisco had also come, and after staying awhile, we went with Gil Narciso to the Kingdom of Guatemala."[78] Narciso told authorities that while in Guatemala, he had learned of a royal order from Cádiz "for all of the migrants of said island [Hispaniola] to return to their origin." Jean François' former soldiers explained that they had only stopped in Havana en route to Santo Domingo.[79]

Cuban authorities did not ask questions specifically related to their possible involvement in the rebellion but only whether they had contact with blacks from Havana. Narciso admitted he had visited the free people of color and slave neighborhoods located outside the city walls of Havana. Greeted by various people of color, mulattos as well as blacks, Narciso had been "asked from where he had come and where he was headed."[80] José Gaston told authorities that several blacks and mulattos "on various occasions, asked if it was true that among him and his companions there was a Brigadier." Gaston noted that he was asked by slaves that the brigadier "be shown in a uniform."[81] The interest expressed in seeing the "brigadier" may refer to Gil Narciso's military rank while fighting under Jean François in the service of the Spanish Crown.[82] Likewise, the "people of color in the neighborhoods outside the city walls," showed an interest in the military uniform of Isidro Plutton.[83] Just one day after questioning Narciso, Santillán, Gaston, and Plutton for the first time, Captain General Someruelos ordered that "the blacks who are imprisoned at Casa Blanca should leave today for Santo Domingo," and they left the island.[84]

The brief questioning, prompt release, and unspecified dates of detention in Havana, make it difficult to establish the relationship of Jean François' former soldiers to the Aponte Rebellion. Someruelos may have decided to release the prisoners in the belief that Gil Narciso and those under his command intended to aid the rebellion; thus, by sending them to Santo Domingo, he followed the familiar policy of isolating Cuba from the contagion of radical insurgents. On the other hand, the captain general may have believed that while unconnected to the rebellion, the soldiers' presence in Havana and the interest shown by people of color in their uniforms fanned the flames of an already insurrectionary situation by legitimizing the rumors of Haitian assistance. It is also possible that Narciso and the others had intended to join the rebellion but, after learning of its quick suppression, opted to continue on to Santo Domingo. Gil Narciso may have been a man in search of a revolution. The same year Narciso arrived in Santo Domingo, he participated in a slave revolt.[85] At the very least, the presence of Gil Narciso and his troops served to

Vanquish the Arrogance

substantiate rumors of "Juan Francisco's" participation in the revolt, if not provide the inspiration for such reports.

While it is unclear if Jean François' former soldiers planned to participate in the rebellion, several free people of color and slaves sought them out to ask them why they had come to Havana. Isidro Plutton noted—as had Gil Narciso and José Fantacia Gaston—that several people "had come to visit him and his companions."[86] Among those who wanted to see and talk with the troops of Gil Narciso was Salvador Ternero. He testified that he crossed Havana's harbor and went to the small military fort of Casa Blanca that quartered the former soldiers of Jean François "to see them and ask if they were Brigadiers as it had been said."[87] Ternero reported that there he spoke with three of the soldiers but did "not see the French general that Aponte told him" about.[88] The free black Juan Barbier also went to Casa Blanca to see the soldiers.[89] According to Clemente Chacón, Barbier told several at a meeting at Aponte's house that "the blacks at Casa Blanca are his people and they have come to conquer this land for the people of color as they had done numerous times."[90] The leaders of the Aponte Rebellion seized upon the opportunity provided by the presence of former soldiers of Jean François to build support and enthusiasm for their own movement. As an artist accustomed to working with images and representations, Aponte used the medium of Haiti to craft a powerful movement supported by the only independent black country in the Western Hemisphere born from the liberating destruction of a slave revolution.

In addition to stories of Haitian assistance and the presence of Saint Domingue veterans in Cuba, the rebels creatively invoked the military uniforms of the Haitian Revolution as a recruitment strategy in planning the insurrection. After the military quashed the rebellion, a slave named Joaquín owned by José Domingo Pérez told the mayor of San Antonio Abad that, at the time of the revolt, he had seen a "black with a uniform from Guarico [Haiti]."[91] Unless Joaquín was from Haiti, somebody must have influenced his ideas of what a "uniform from Guarico" looked like. Clemente Chacón reported to authorities that he had been introduced to Juan Francisco, who was "dressed in a blue military jacket demonstrating he was a great subject, indicated by his line of gold buttons on his jacket, some with the image of an anchor and an eagle."[92] Gold buttons may have caught the attention of Chacón because they were often included in wills of free people of color.[93] Further, French traveler Julian Mellet reported that "buttons of gold" served as a form of currency in Cuba.[94]

For Juan Barbier to convincingly assume the identity of Juan Francisco as an admiral that served at the orders of Haitian emperor Henri Chrsitophe required an elaborate uniform to project status and authority. Estanislao Aguilar testified that when he traveled to the plantations to recruit slaves for the rebellion, "Juan Francisco . . . entered a slave hut and returned dressed in a blue military jacket and military pants, taking off the clothes he had worn."[95] Several other rebels questioned about the revolts provided similar descriptions of soldiers in uniform.[96] Soldiers in the free men of color militia could have obtained military uniforms relatively easily. When authorities searched Aponte's house, they found his "blue military jacket" in a closet.[97] The success of the Haitian Revolution added new meaning to the familiar sight of people of African ancestry in military uniforms throughout the Caribbean. In recruiting others to their cause, the leaders of the Aponte Rebellion refashioned their own military experience in Cuba to wed it with the imagery of the Haitian Revolution.[98]

In addition to emancipation decrees by Henri Christophe, the arrival of Jean François' former troops, and the wearing of military uniforms, Aponte's drawings of Haitian revolutionary leaders added yet another layer of Haitian connections to the Aponte Rebellion. The most fascinating document to emerge from the Aponte Rebellion was Aponte's book of drawings. As mentioned in the introduction, the book of drawings has yet to be found by scholars, but what does exist is the testimony in which for three days Aponte explained the significance of the book to authorities.[99] Colonial officials demanded that Aponte elaborate on where he obtained the images of the black revolutionaries that once filled the pages of his book. Aponte explained that the portraits of Louverture, Dessalines, and Jean François "were copied by myself from many other engravings acquired when the Campaign of Ballajá came to Havana."[100] The "campaign of Ballajá" refers to the exodus of the Spanish-allied black Saint Domingue troops from the city of Fort Dauphin in 1795. Aponte told judicial officials that he "had copied the portrait of Enrique the First [Henri Christophe] from another owned by a black who worked on the docks." Melchor Chirinos, one of the many suspected conspirators, told authorities that Aponte had drawn the portrait from a copy owned by black militia captain Fernando Núñez.[101] When asked about the portraits' location, Aponte explained that "he had burnt them for having heard . . . they were banned illustrations."[102] Apparently, Aponte and Núñez were not the only people who owned portraits of Haitian revolutionary figures. After the colonial government suppressed the rebellion and captured the principal leaders, another portrait surfaced when soldier Domingo Calderón "found in the street a portrait of the king Enrique."[103]

Many of the captured rebels stated that Aponte had shown them drawings of Haitian leaders in what probably amounted to lessons in the history of the Haitian Revolution. Melchor Chirinos told officials that "many asked" to see "the black King José Antonio Aponte had painted."[104] Salvador Ternero reported that Aponte "showed [him] a book that had three figures painted . . .

Vanquish the Arrogance

one a black King and two generals of the same color."[105] Free black militiamen Francisco Javier Pacheco and José del Carmen Peñalver stated that "Aponte showed them the portrait of the black king of Haiti named Henrique Cristóbal, informing us of his coronation and recognition by the King of England and the King of Spain."[106] According to the testimony of accused rebel Clemente Chacón, Aponte's portrait of "Cristóval Henriques" contained the inscription: "Execute what is ordered."[107] Authorities concluded that "following the examples and events of those of the same class in the neighboring colony of Haiti, Aponte kept a portrait of Enrique Cristóbal, the first king of Haiti, to show the slaves."[108] Aponte and other people involved in the rebellion were not unique in displaying a fascination with Haiti. People of African ancestry throughout the Americas held great admiration for revolutionary leaders from Haiti. Only a year after Haitian independence, slaves as far away as Rio de Janeiro wore necklaces bearing the image of Dessalines.[109] The Haitian Revolution provided powerful images of a black king and military generals that inspired Aponte and others. The rebels' particular fascination with Haiti perhaps had as much to do with its successful example of slave revolution as with its status as an independent black country. While there is no documentation or reported pronouncements that Aponte and other excluded mulattos or other races from their movement, of the known racial characteristics among the arrested rebels, 96 percent were black.[110] In crafting their own ideology of insurrection, they interwove emancipation decrees and powerful black Haitian imagery to create a political and cultural tapestry to resist their subordinate position demanded by a society based upon racial hierarchy.

REBELLIOUS ROYALISM

The widespread circulation of emancipation rumors stemming from diverse monarchical figures in 1812 Cuba confirms the important role of royalist ideology, or what other scholars have labeled "naïve monarchism," in shaping movements of resistance by slaves, peasants, and other subaltern groups. Only by the end of the eighteenth century and throughout the nineteenth century did a concerted action to limit and eventually abolish monarchical forms of governments sweep through the Atlantic world. Similar to serfs in nineteenth century Russia, slaves utilized the rhetoric of the benevolent monarch that would deliver them from bondage. As scholar James Scott has observed, it was common for peasants to rebel "on behalf of reforms in serfdom, or its abolition, which had been decreed by the czar but concealed from them by cruel officials." In what Scott describes as a "symbolic jujitsu," slaves and peasants could transform an apparently conservative myth counseling loyalty to the king into a legitimizing basis for violent insurrection.[111]

As part of the legitimizing process in planning the insurrection, Cuban slaves made constant references to edicts that king-given rights had been denied them.[112] Several slaves reported that the order issued by the king had been hidden in an effort to usurp their rights. In response, they planned to go to Havana to demand its promulgation.[113] Similarly, twenty years earlier in Saint Domingue, slaves reported that the king and National Assembly in Paris issued decrees abolishing the whip and providing three free days a week to work on their own. Their masters, however, would not enact the new laws.[114] Roughly occurring at the same time as the Aponte Rebellion of 1812, but in a different context, historian Eric Van Young noted that during the War for Mexican Independence, the use of documents or references to edicts "were often seen as essential to legitimate community collective action."[115] Undoubtedly, the three centuries of employing written documentation in dealing with the Spanish colonial state served to reinforce the centrality of edicts, papers, and orders in shaping protest behaviors. The importance of documentation may have acquired additional importance in slave societies such as Cuba in legitimating struggles for freedom because ultimately it was a written document that reduced individuals to enslavement and a written document that could free them.[116]

The Aponte Rebellion of 1812 shares certain similarities with other protest movements by slaves and peasants in its appeal to royalist ideology or "naïve monarchism," but the divergent discourses of the emancipating ruler in the form of the kings of Spain, England, Haiti, and the Kongo powerfully illustrate the different cultural and political influences in Cuba. In Mexico or Russia, for example, Native Americans and serfs constructed their "naïve monarchism" around the authority of a single and apparently widely recognized monarch. In Cuba, however, the divergent backgrounds of slaves and free people of color, coupled with the changing politics of the era that began to question slavery as an institution for the first time, often determined which monarch the rebels ascribed with emancipatory powers. The competing ideologies of monarchical authority in Cuba testified to how rebels and slaves could transform rumors to resonate with their own concepts of legitimate authority, which were not constructed through the Spanish colonial context alone. The appeal to royalist authority in the form of the kings of Spain, Britain, Haiti, and Kongo represented a political counterweight that Cuban rebels attempted to swing against their masters and the institutions they controlled.

SITUATING THE APONTE REBELLION in its multiple Caribbean, Latin American, African, and Atlantic contexts, the different monarchial decrees from the kings of Spain, England, Haiti, and the Kongo offered a reflection of the diverse backgrounds and experiences of the population of African descent on the island. Consequently, applying Van Young's suggestion for Mexico, it is enlightening to think of the Aponte Rebellion not as an appeal to "naïve monarchism" in terms of "false consciousness," where slaves and free people of color could only construct a movement through the hegemonic authority of monarchical power, but rather as a ritualized aspect of planning the insurrection. The repeated references to monarchical authority indicate a widely recognized and widely shared political script. The rebel leaders incorporated references to royalist authority to catalyze their movement. Slaves and free people of color involved in the Aponte Rebellion legitimated their actions through royalist power that would aid them in their battle against the colonial elite.[117]

The ideology of a benevolent king interceding on behalf of loyal subjects did not prevent rebellion by slaves in early nineteenth-century Cuba. Just the opposite occurred. References to Cuban masters and government officials usurping monarchical authority served to frame and justify the argument for insurrection in the widely recognized political idiom of the day. That this rebellious royalism operating in Cuba could be bent, twisted, and refashioned to include the kings of Spain, England, Haiti, and the Kongo to sanctify insurrection testifies to the effectiveness of slaves and free people of color in crafting their own ideology of liberation to reflect their own specific circumstances.

# Plaques of Loyalty

The crowd of spectators did not leave after they "applauded" the punishments meted out to the rebels.[1] When the executions and whippings of the insurgents came to an end, an encore performance began. Colonial authorities had to address the rebels' strong desires for freedom that inspired their motivations for revolt. Executing the leaders served as a deadly warning of the consequences awaiting anyone who attempted to achieve their own independence by rebellion, but it did not address whether their hopes and aspirations for liberation were wrong. The Puerto Príncipe town council recognized that chopping off the heads of twelve leaders would not kill their goals for individual liberty: "Who is capable of believing that after the contamination" of the slaves with rebellion "they will return to their duties because we have killed ten or twelve of the principle leaders?"[2] The captivated crowd present at the execution provided the opportunity for colonial officials to publicly offer freedom to loyal slaves and rewards to free people of color who denounced the movement and assisted in its suppression. By executing the rebels and awarding freedom to the loyalists during the same ceremony, the colonial government attempted to persuade people of African ancestry that the most effective strategy for gaining freedom was not armed rebellion but allegiance to masters and the Spanish Empire.

As soon as word of the insurrection reached colonial authorities, and even before lawyers ended the investigation, government officials decided on execution as punishment for the leaders. Likewise, long before magistrates questioned all the rebels to discover the complete details of the rebellion, they decided to provide rewards to slaves and free people of color who denounced the movement and aided the suppression of the insurrection. The Havana town council called an emergency meeting to discuss the punishments and the investigation of the rebellion. They decided that "in the good interest of the people, they will promptly punish the insurrectionaries of the Peñas-Altas plantation, and, at the same time, reward with publicity and distinction the slave driver and slaves that suppressed the [rebels] at the Santa Ana plantation."[3] Havana's town council encouraged judicial officials to "make it known without delay . . . by the appropriate method of awarding and distinguishing those that deserve it [for their loyalty], to make them notorious in every corner of the island."[4] Council members Joaquín Herrera, Luis Hidalgo, and José María Saenz wrote to the Spanish Cortes at Cádiz a week after the revolts erupted to inform them of the rebellion's suppression. They agreed that the loyalists would be "awarded with publicity and distinction."[5] Colonial officials throughout the island decided to single out slaves and free people of color who betrayed the rebellion in order to offer examples of the benefits and rewards for allegiance to the existing order.

Shortly after the militia, the standing army, and armed citizens subdued the revolts in Puerto Príncipe, the town council decided to purchase the freedom of slaves who had denounced the rebellion. Town council members called for "a voluntary subscription" among Puerto Príncipe residents to collect money for the manumission of slaves Rafael Medrano and Francisco Adan.[6] Local resident José de Jesús Fuentes recommended buying the freedom of loyal slaves, because it "will serve as a stimulus and example to the well-behaved, just as punishments have done for the wicked."[7] Only several days after the town council called for donations to buy the freedom of loyal slaves, 254 residents had contributed a combined total of 677 pesos. Most donations varied between one and four pesos. Included on the list of the 254 donors were the names of ten women, one black, and one mulatto; the remaining 242 were all white males.[8] The voluntary contributions to the manumission fund by more than 250 local residents demonstrated that the local population believed ending the rebellion required not only swift punishments for the guilty but generous rewards to prevent future movements.

While masters and colonial officials agreed that offering freedom to loyal slaves would serve as a powerful example to encourage conformity, they differed on how to assess the monetary value of fidelity. Even though slaves' actions had most likely saved their masters' lives, slaveowners would not free their bound servants without recompense. Even in the life and death situation of rebellion, greed trumped gratitude. Loyalty carried no discount for a slave's price of freedom; masters demanded the market value and even higher for freeing their slaves. For many, the slaves' loyalty only served to increase their value. Given that many slaves participated in the revolts once they erupted on plantations, masters had a strong incentive to retain the loyal laborers they owned. Judicial officials in Puerto Príncipe agreed to pay Don

José Fernando Perdomo 400 pesos for the freedom of his black slave Pedro. The local magistrate assessed Pedro's value based upon his "fidelity . . . and by virtue of his agility in the countryside, sound health, and being without defects."[9] The governor of Puerto Príncipe, Francisco Sedano, paid Don Ramón Adan the above market price of 500 pesos for the freedom of his slave Francisco. Sedano announced Francisco's emancipation to the crowd gathered to witness the executions and the awards of freedom. He presented him with a plaque to commemorate the ceremony that declared in clear letters " 'Loyalty Rewarded.' "[10] In Bayamo, the town council "redeemed from slavery in compensation for his loyalty" Antonio José, who informed his master of the planned uprising.[11] The ceremony of punishments and freedom forcefully represented both life and death. The spectacle provided a powerful image of liberation and a new life for slaves after emancipation, while the executions ended the earthly existence of the insurgents.

Judicial officials and colonial authorities in Havana also decided to buy the freedom of slaves who informed authorities about the rebellion. However, they did not intend to pay masters the full market price for emancipating the slaves. The Havana town council paid Antonio Bustamante 600 pesos for the freedom of his two slaves, José María Mandinga and Joaquín Karabali. The two slaves had warned the overseer of the rebels' plans to spread the insurrection to their plantation.[12] According to the town council, the price had been determined below the market "because the master received, in part, the benefit of their service" in denouncing the movement.[13] The town council decided it would not pay Bustamante the full value of his slaves because he owed his life to their loyalty.

The Havana town council called José María and Joaquín to their chambers and gave them documents attesting to their emancipation. The captain general told them to "take these documents that justice has conceded to you as a reward for your loyalty." He announced that José María and Joaquín "are free Spaniards," instructing them to "show these [documents] to your friends and associates so that they can see how we reward good men such as yourselves, loyal to the king and the nation."[14] Judicial officials then decided to announce the emancipation of José María and Joaquín to "their *compañeros* as an example . . . to learn the notable difference between those who behave and those who misplace their loyalty to their country and their masters."[15] The colonial government had gone to considerable lengths to single out and focus on the traitors because it provided a comforting image of division among the ranks of free people of color and slaves. By emphasizing the divisions among the rebels, they hoped to provide an example that loyalty could result in freedom.

Did the government succeed in deterring rebellion by awarding freedom and benefits for those who broke ranks with the insurgents? The brutality of the punishments offered a grim warning to prevent revolutionary activities. The executions culminated in placing decapitated heads on pikes at entrances to plantations and in free people of color neighborhoods to remind would-be insurgents of the deadly costs of rebellion. Nearly seven months after colonial officials executed the leaders of the Havana rebellion, the severed head of free black Clemente Chacón remained on display inside a cage at the entrance to his Guadalupe neighborhood.[16] At the conclusion of the criminal investigation, the colonial state ended thirty-four lives by execution, ripped open the backs of seventy-eight people by public whippings that collectively totaled 4,725 lashes, and sentenced 170 individuals to jails throughout the Spanish empire that collectively added up to 1,279 years of hard prison labor.[17] The execution of the leaders and the punishments of their followers provided tangible reasons to think twice about joining the risky, overwhelmingly unsuccessful, and brutally suppressed insurrectionary movements.

Some free people of color and slaves, however, proved more difficult to convince. Colonial officials later arrested several slaves and free people of color for involvement in conspiratorial activities and personal acts of resistance who may have acquired vital training and experience from the Aponte Rebellion. In 1835, an uprising erupted in Havana led by the free and enslaved Lucumies organized by *cabildo* associations.[18] According to historian Philip Howard, the "goals of the rebellion were the same as those of Aponte's—the destruction of the institution of slavery and the overthrow of the government."[19] In 1839, the government investigated "certain clandestine meetings of blacks in this capital to discover their plans and tendencies." Authorities believed several people involved in these secret meetings had been questioned "for their involvement many years ago in the investigation of Aponte, Lisundia, and others for planning a conspiracy against the whites."[20] Militia captain León Monzón organized the secretive meetings through militia and *cabildo* networks in a manner similar to the Aponte Rebellion twenty years earlier. According to judicial officials, Monzón had planned the rebellion with the goal of ending slavery and destroying Spanish colonialism. Free black Pilar Borrego played a leading role in the movement organized by Monzón.[21] Borrego most certainly drew upon his personal experience with conspiratorial activities acquired while participating in the Aponte Rebellion. In 1812, colonial officials arrested, questioned, and sentenced Borrego to a four-year prison term in Puerto Rico for his involvement in the Aponte Rebellion.[22] Apparently, the imprisonment did not deter Borrego. He returned to Cuba and took up the cause to end slavery and Spanish colonialism again in 1839.

Colonial officials suspected revolutionaries from Aponte's movement became involved in another elaborately planned rebellion aimed at ending slavery and colonial rule in 1844. The event is gruesomely known in Cuban history as the *Escalera* Conspiracy after the Spanish term for "ladder" (*escalera*). During the course of the investigation, military officials tied thousands of slaves and free people of color to ladders and brutally whipped them. Many had their lives painfully ended by the deadly lashes that landed on their backs.[23] Judicial officers investigating the *Escalera* Conspiracy studied the trial testimony and the court records from the Aponte Rebellion for over a year during 1844 and 1845 to examine the similarities of the two movements.[24]

In particular, officials suspected that free black José Herrera put his first-hand knowledge of the Aponte Rebellion to use in the *Escalera* Conspiracy.[25] More that thirty years earlier, Juan Ignacio Rendón had questioned Herrera for his suspected role in planning the Havana revolts. Rendón believed Herrera used his militia contacts to gather arms and ammunition for the Aponte Rebellion. While Herrera denied any involvement in the Aponte Rebellion, his admitted personal associations with Aponte, Chacón, and others only contributed to colonial officials' suspicions that he participated in the insurrection.[26] Drawing upon his militia connections and *fuero* rights, he wrote to the captain general requesting his release from prison because "there is not any merit to continuing the proceedings . . . because there are no witnesses to verify [my involvement]."[27] Herrera made an important legal point that likely saved his life. By the time judicial officials questioned Herrera in December of 1812, every person who provided testimony against him had died. Authorities originally sentenced Herrera to four years in prison, but then released him for unspecified reasons after eight months of incarceration.[28] As for his association with the 1844 *Escalera* Conspiracy, judicial officials suspected he joined the rebellion and played an important part in organizing the movement. Herrera's specific role in the *Escalera* Conspiracy, however, cannot be known for certain until scholars comb through the more than 10,000 folios of trial testimony located in the Cuban National Archive.[29] Herrera, Borrego, and others apparently did not learn the didactic lesson that colonial officials attempted to teach by juxtaposing execution for rebellion with freedom for loyalty.

The most attentive pupils to the lessons of death for rebellion and rewards for loyalty to the Spanish Crown were the white Creoles. The Aponte Rebellion served to dilute whatever aspirations white Cubans had of creating an independent country. Unlike their fellow British, French, Portuguese, and Spanish colonists throughout the Americas, white Cubans did not join the independence movements sweeping the Atlantic world. Slavery acted as a powerfully conservative force on the thoughts and actions of white Cuban Creoles. The expansion of Cuban slavery during the Age of Revolution chained masters and elites ever more firmly to the protection of the Spanish Crown. Cuban slaveowners reached the conclusion that an anticolonial movement that could possibly lead to slaves and free people of color foment-ing a revolution beyond their control was not worth the risk. Contemporaries and historians have long recognized that the fear of slave and free people of color insurrection delayed independence until 1898.[30]

The Aponte Rebellion offered a clear lesson to masters that the dramatic increase in the slave population could result in their own demise. Pedro Juan de Erice, one of Cuba's wealthiest residents who financed the expansion of slavery and sugar production, urgently wrote to the Spanish Cortes after the Aponte Rebellion. He requested immediate assistance from Spain "about the occurrences at Peñas-Altas" to provide for the "salvation and security of this important province."[31] Cuban slaveowners and elites readily admitted they remained dependent on Spain for protection against their "domestic ene-mies." In the immediate aftermath of the rebellion, some residents called for an end to slavery.[32] An unidentified male citizen from the town of Guana-bacoa, near the location of the Peñas-Altas revolt, wrote to Captain Gen-eral Someruelos urging him to take preventive measures to deter future re-bellions. He called for the "immediate suppression of the risky trading in slaves."[33] The Aponte Rebellion illustrated in bold strokes the dangers of expanding slavery and plantation agriculture throughout the island.

Fear, as with gratitude, seldom overcomes greed. Masters and colonial officials decided to impose stricter regulations on slaves and free people of color to monitor their activities and extinguish their revolutionary aspira-tions. In Puerto Príncipe, the government prevented slaves and free people of color from traveling for the purpose of seeking contract labor. After the rebellion, all contract labor between slaves and free people of color and their employers had to be prearranged before the job began.[34] In Havana, local authorities decided to prevent public gatherings at bars and other locations because they had provided opportunities for planning and organizing the Aponte Rebellion. An unnamed Havana resident complained to the town council that "slaves of both sexes and people among the lowest plebes" gathered in taverns to cause "disorders."[35] The Cuban representatives to the Spanish Cortes authorized the formation of additional military units to "pro-vide extraordinary vigilance" to prevent insurrectionary movements in "the cities as well as in the countryside."[36] Historian Larry Jensen argues the Aponte Rebellion "reminded the white population that . . . political innova-tions, such as the free press . . . might not be appropriate for a society based upon slavery."[37] White Cuban Creoles sacrificed their own control over local affairs by calling upon Spanish military assistance and subjecting themselves to self-censorship. The dependence of white Cubans on assistance from Spain in suppressing the Aponte Rebellion served to strengthen their ties with the mother country and undercut their desires for independence. Cuba would survive the Age of Revolution, which brought independence to all the mainland colonies of Spanish America, with the well-earned title of the "ever faithful island."

Historians of Cuba have perhaps focused too much scholarly attention on explaining the "non-event" of Cuban independence for the early nineteenth century. Counterfactual historical methodology can provide important insights to focus analysis, but historians need to first explain what happened before they can understand what did not happen. Almost all of the scholarly accounts that explain the absence of an independence movement in Cuba for the early 1800s are implicitly restricted to the white Creole population.[38] The Aponte Rebellion demonstrates that greater attention needs to be given to the anticolonial ideas and actions of slaves and free people of color during the early nineteenth century. Aponte, after all, dictated Cuba's first declaration of independence and ordered it nailed to the captain general's residence. The anomaly of Cuban independence only appears abnormal when compared to the mainland European colonies of North and South America. When Cuba is studied and situated in its multiple Caribbean, Latin American, and Atlantic contexts, rather than only its Latin American setting, the "non-event" of independence resembles the same experiences of the British, Dutch, French, and Spanish islands of the Caribbean. The only independent Caribbean country born during the Age of Revolution was Haiti. This fact, alone, should persuade scholars to focus more squarely on the thoughts, plans, and aspirations of slaves and free people of color.

THE APONTE REBELLION IN A HEMISPHERIC CONTEXT

Before moving to a conclusion and summary of the individual chapters and findings of this study, it is important to situate briefly the Aponte Rebellion in an Atlantic context of slave revolts during the Age of Revolution. This will serve to focus analysis on both the shared and specific characteristics of the Aponte Rebellion in comparison with other movements throughout the hemisphere. During the Age of Revolution the number of slave revolts throughout the hemisphere dramatically increased.[39] As mentioned in the introduction, scholars continue to debate what force or forces most powerfully account for the dramatic spike in rebellions during the Age of Revolution. Clearly, the era was a time of ideological conflict over natural rights and freedom, which transformed governments on both sides of the Atlantic. In this heated political climate, rumors of emancipation, hearsay decrees of abolition, news of toppling regimes, and reports of transfers in power, served as catalytic forces to spark insurrection. Historical explanations that move from simply identifying the widespread presence of liberating thoughts floating around in the ideological stratosphere to attributing to those ideas causal force, however, requires "intensive research," according to historian Eugene Genovese.[40] The difficult task facing scholars of slave revolts is to document how these political notions circulated and became appropriated by slave insurgents.[41]

The Cuban novelist Alejo Carpentier captured the challenge facing historians in his historical novel *Explosion in the Cathedral* (*El sigilo de la luces*), on slave insurrection in the Caribbean during the era of the French Revolution. In the novel, the Swiss planter Sieger tells the young radical Esteban that the French Revolution did not cause slave revolts but merely changed their political meaning. " 'All the French Revolution has achieved in America is to legalise the Great Escape which has been going on since the sixteenth century. The blacks didn't wait for you, they've proclaimed themselves free a countless number of times . . . You can see,' concluded Sieger, 'that the famous Pluvoise Decree didn't bring anything new into this continent; it was just one more reason for proceeding with the everlasting Great Escape.' "[42] In analyzing the Aponte Rebellion within the context of Carpentier's "everlasting Great Escape," comparisons will be made with the Haitian Revolution (1791–1804), Gabriel's Conspiracy in Virginia (1800), the Demerara Rebellion (1823), the Jamaican Baptist War (1831), and the Malê Rebellion in Bahia, Brazil (1835).

The Haitian Revolution began with a massive slave revolt in August 1791 that would culminate in 1804 with the only independent black republic in the Western Hemisphere. Haiti's historical starting point represents a singular event of human accomplishment. The Haitian Revolution offers the only example of a rebellion in human history where slaves overthrew their masters, expelled them from their territory, and created their own independent country. Similar to the Aponte Rebellion, political conflict in the imperial capital provided an opportunity to begin the insurrection. The 1789 French Revolution created an opening that the slaves would take control of and make their own. Just as the debate over slavery in the Spanish Cortes resulted in emancipation rumors circulating in Cuba, stories of emancipation decrees issued by the French king and the National Assembly circulated widely in Haiti. The African background of the slaves also influenced the course of events in Haiti. Among the slaves drawn from various locations within Africa, some from the Kingdom of Kongo looked back to their place of origin as they legitimated and organized their struggle in Haiti. A few slaves claimed loyalty to the king of the Kongo and believed he would send troops to aid their cause. Likewise, they also blended African and European political traditions by drawing inspiration from the *Declaration of the Rights of Man and Citizen* and carrying African amulets for protection in battle. Just as the militia played an important role in the Aponte Rebellion, some of the leaders of the Haitian

Conclusion

Revolution had previously served in the French colonial militia based in the Caribbean. The most striking difference between the Haitian Revolution and the Aponte Rebellion rests with the size of the slave population. At the time of the insurrection, slaves outnumbered whites in Haiti by a ratio of at least 10:1, whereas in Cuba, whites outnumbered slaves. In 1790, Haitian slaveowners imported over 40,000 slaves and then suffered the deadly consequences. Culturally, in terms of the ideas that informed slaves and free people of color to rise in rebellion, many similarities, from emancipation rumors, to monarchical degrees, to royalist ideology, and to claiming natural political rights can be drawn between the Aponte Rebellion and the Haitian Revolution. Structurally, and more specifically demographically, the Haitian rebels had the numbers on their side to build a slave army that no European power could defeat, despite numerous attempts.[43]

In 1800, reports rocked Richmond, Virginia, that slaves planned to revolt and take the capital city. Before the rebellion occurred, authorities foiled the insurgents' conspiracy led by the slave Gabriel, owned by Thomas Prosser. Virginia officials quickly arrested the suspected rebels, had them questioned, and then punished them for what would subsequently become known as Garbriel's Conspiracy. While both the Aponte Rebellion and Gabriel's Conspiracy's foremost goal was freedom for slaves, how the rebels made sense of what that freedom meant and legitimated their cause points to important differences in the cultural and social dynamics of slave societies in the Atlantic world. By the mid-eighteenth century, Virginia possessed a Creole slave population which grew by natural increase. While tied to a larger world, being born and raised in Virginia created a different sense of community for Gabriel and his followers than in Cuba where African origins and ethnicity figured prominently in everyday social interactions. At a religious level, slaves forged the beliefs of evangelical Christianity that swept through the Anglo-Protestant world into a weapon to attack master dominion. By comparison, there are few equivalents from the Catholic French, Spanish, or Portuguese slave societies of the Americas where biblical inspiration from the Old Testament and mastery of the religious world of Christianity served such a powerful role in building violent antislavery movements. In terms of the background of the rebels, urban artisans dominated the leadership ranks of both the Aponte Rebellion and Gabriel's Conspiracy. Moreover, in both movements, literacy and mastery of the written word served as an organizing tool, not only for providing logistics and planning, such as forged passes, but court testimony from Virginia and Cuba makes clear that writing held special emancipatory powers and often served as a criterion for leadership roles. At the political level, similar to Aponte and his followers, slaves in Virginia may have taken courage to rebel from what they perceived as a division among elites over the bitter presidential campaign of 1800 that pitted John Adams against Thomas Jefferson. In terms of planning, as in the Aponte Rebellion, Gabriel's Conspiracy called for seizing the armory to gather weapons and ammunition to expand the insurrection. In summary, evangelical Christianity and the Creole background of Virginia's slaves mark significant cultural differences with the Aponte Rebellion, while the urban world of artisans in planning and organizing their insurrections points to important similarities.[44]

The British Caribbean experienced a cycle of slave insurrection after 1800 that hammered the final nails into slavery's coffin. After twenty years of debate, the British Parliament abolished the trans-Atlantic slave trade in 1807. Slowly, the overwhelmingly African background of the eighteenth-century British Caribbean slave populations began to include significant percentages of Creoles. Cuba's slave population would undergo a similar demographic shift, but not until the second half of the nineteenth century with the final abolition of the trans-Atlantic slave trade in 1867. As news and stories of parliamentary debates and the formation of abolitionist societies crisscrossed the Atlantic, slaves in the British Caribbean learned that they had a few allies in London. In response, they increased their resistance to bring about total emancipation by 1838. Historian Michel Craton has identified more than two dozen revolts and conspiracies that erupted in the British Caribbean after 1800. Two of the biggest rebellions occurred in the colonies of Demerara in 1823 and Jamaica in 1831.[45]

The British had only acquired Demerara (present-day Guyana) from the Dutch at the very end of the eighteenth century. Similar to the Aponte Rebellion, which followed a rapid increase in Cuban sugar production, Demeraran plantation owners switched from cotton to sugar to capitalize on the economic opening in the world market produced by the Haitian Revolution. The twenty-five-mile east coast of Demerara was home to some of the most exploitative sugar plantations in the New World. At the time of the insurrection in 1823, the slave population numbered 77,000, while the white population numbered only 2,500. Africans represented 54 percent of the slave population, drawn predominantly from Gold Coast Akan-speakers collectively identified as Coromantees. In contrast, the enslaved Creoles made up 46 percent of this population. As a concession to British abolitionists, masters allowed missionaries to minister to the slaves. Similar to how Aponte and his followers crafted their own ideology of liberation from disparate sources that resonated with their local and Atlantic backgrounds, Demeraran slaves appropriated the missionaries' evangelical language and symbols and turned Sunday church services, which brought enslaved laborers together from various plantations, into organizational opportunities for the rebellion. When the rebellion broke out in August 1823, in a matter of weeks the slave army numbered 10,000 to 12,000 and controlled nearly sixty plantations. Comparable to the Aponte Rebellion, Demeraran slaves believed the king and British Parliament had granted them various rights that local officials had usurped. When the colonial governor asked why the slaves revolted, in an attempt to end the rebellion through negotiation, they boldly demanded " 'Our rights.' " The governor recognized how the slaves had wed the radical beliefs of Christianity, emphasizing equality of all men before God, with abolition rumors. The slaves told the governor that " 'God had made them of the same flesh and blood as the whites; they were tired of being slaves; their good King has sent orders that they should be free, and they would not work any more.' "[46] After making it clear that they would not return to slavery, the British colonial state brought to bear its full military force and violently subdued the insurgents.[47]

The Demerara Rebellion served as a prelude to the largest slave revolt in the British Caribbean eight years later. Erupting in Jamaica on Christmas Day in 1831, the slave revolt included 20,000 to 30,000 slaves, who blanketed the western end of the island leaving torched canefields and smoldering plantations in their path. The rebellion subsequently became known as the "Baptist War" in an act of historical revisionism to put the blame on Baptist missionaries who actively evangelized in the region, rather than recognizing the slaves' strike for freedom. Similar to Demerara, the slaves appropriated the missionaries' teachings and refashioned them as tools to resist their enslavement. As part of their missionary strategy to have the converted do the converting, the Baptists encouraged free people of color and slaves to run their own church services. Similar to the security *cabildo* houses provided the Aponte Rebellion, inside church services, Jamaican slaves began to plot their rebellion as early as April 1831. The leader of the rebellion, Deacon Samuel "Daddy" Sharpe, used his religious position to move from plantation to plantation, ministering to his flock and spreading plans of insurrection. Emancipation rumors, once again, demonstrated slaves' yearning for freedom and how they reformulated news and hearsay of abolition politics into monarchical and parliamentary decrees to justify insurrection. Several slaves testified that Sharpe told them that the king had declared them free, but their masters and colonial officials would not recognize the order. Just as Aponte and others had used the relative freedom of Christmas and Easter to make their final revolutionary preparations, Sharpe and his followers spread the news that they had been declared free during the holidays leading up to Christmas. They made a pact and vowed not to work as slaves after 25 December. The next day, the revolt began, and it quickly spread throughout the western part of the island by New Year's Day 1832. Only after several months of bitter fighting did Jamaican authorities subdue the insurrection. The repression that followed resulted in the execution of more than 300 rebels, with thousands questioned and punished. The Jamaican Baptist War sent masters, the Jamaican Assembly, and the British Parliament a powerful message of the huge costs required for maintaining slavery as a system of human domination. In the aftermath of the rebellion, the need to reform slavery and place it on the peaceful road to gradual abolition with compensation for masters, as opposed to immediate emancipation by the slaves' own hands, now seemed more urgent than ever. In 1838, slavery, under the guise of a four-year apprenticeship system, came to an end in the British Caribbean.[48]

Similar to the British Caribbean, Bahia, Brazil, witnessed an elevated commitment by Africans to end slavery by violent insurrection during the first decades of the nineteenth century. From 1807–35, more than twenty revolts, plantation uprisings, maroon rebellions, and foiled conspiracies occurred in Bahia and the surrounding plantation hinterland called the Recôncavo. The largest insurrection, the Malê Rebellion, occurred in 1835. Unlike Cuba where a single ethnicity did not predominate among the enslaved population of African descent, the marked increase in Bahian slave resistance partially reflected the migratory patterns of the trans-Atlantic slave trade. As a result of reviving and expanding plantation agriculture in northeastern Brazil, combined with the rapid decline of the Oyo Empire in West Africa due to incessant warfare, ethnic Yorubas, known in Brazil as Nagôs, arrived in Bahia by the thousands. Their common West African background and origins provided a degree of cultural homogeneity and unity among the rebels, which gave the Malê Rebellion pronounced Yoruba characteristics. In addition, many of the rebels shared a diasporic Muslim culture, and they continued practicing their Islamic faith in Brazil. The plans of the Bahian rebels showed several similarities to the Aponte Rebellion. The start of the rebellion coincided with the religious fete of Our Lady of Guidance (quite appropriately), which allowed for greater freedom of movement in the city and countryside. The rebels planned to take over the police barracks and gain arms before moving on to the plantations. Islam, however, represents the single most distinguishing feature of the Malê Rebellion. When Africans went into battle to end their enslavement, they wore amulets that contained folded Koranic verses written in Arabic containing fiery and revolutionary messages. Moreover, Muslims figured prominently among the rebels' leadership. Like the Aponte Rebellion and Gabriel's Conspiracy, mastery of the written word and the power of literacy served to structure the movement. And as in Cuba, free and enslaved urban artisans played a prominent role in the 1835 Malê Rebellion. In summary, the overwhelming African background of the rebellion, and in particular its identity as Muslim, displayed the specific Atlantic cultural dynamics of the Bahian revolt, while the methods slaves and free people of color utilized in the urban environment to resist slavery highlighted how they drew upon local circumstances in executing their plans.[49]

The establishment of racial slavery throughout the New World and the ubiquitous resistance to that institution throughout the hemisphere has long provided historians with a topic for comparative history. Regardless of the variances and similarities across place and time, however, it is worth remembering historian Herbert Aptheker's simple but important reminder that the "cause" of slave rebellion was first and foremost slavery.[50] Slave revolts represented dramatic and often desperate attempts by slaves, sometimes in alliance with free people of color, to take justice into their own hands by violent insurrection. In formulating their ideas, building alliances, justifying and legitimating their actions, catalyzing their movements, and carrying out their plans, rebels pulled from an Atlantic world historical landscape that spread from Europe and Africa to the Americas. At the same time and just as important, they gave concrete meaning to their culturally specific notions of freedom in deeply layered local settings. As the buying and selling of human chattel provided the initial thrust for the creation of an interconnected Atlantic world linking Europe, Africa, and the Americas in the fifteenth century, it is only natural that understanding the courageous actions by slaves and free people of color, such as Aponte and his followers, to end that system requires placing their story within both an Atlantic and local setting.

THIS STUDY HAS SITUATED the Aponte Rebellion within the overlapping contexts of Cuban, Caribbean, Latin American, and Atlantic history. Cuba served as a colony for more than three centuries prior to the Aponte Rebellion of 1812, but only after most Latin American countries gained their independence did the island become the prized possession of the Spanish Crown. Similarly, slavery had existed for over 300 years, but Cuba only became strongly linked with Africa and dependent on slave labor in the nineteenth century. Cuba had long played an important role in the complex interactions that brought Europeans, Africans, and Americans into contact with each other, but it was only in the nineteenth century that Atlantic connections decisively shaped Cuban history. The rebels looked to both their immediate surroundings and the larger Atlantic world as they planned their rebellion and made sense of their role in history. Several of the leaders such as Aponte and Barbier had traveled throughout the Caribbean and found inspiration from political actions in other regions of the Atlantic. Africans continued to identify with their places of origin on the other side of the Atlantic and formed associations to reinforce ancestral, linguistic, and cultural ties that the middle passage had attempted to sever.

Cuba's links to an Atlantic world chained together by slavery occurred at the precise moment the system began to break apart. The Age of Revolution that inspired radical political changes in Europe and wars for independence in the Americas ushered in the beginning of the end for Atlantic slavery. Cuban masters were not impervious to the global trends in slavery and attempted to insulate the island from the radical ideas crisscrossing the Atlantic as a strategy of self-preservation. Slaves, and free people of color as well, were not ignorant of the larger transformations operating outside of Cuba and the possibility for radical changes. The Aponte Rebellion of 1812 confirmed masters' fears of the external influences of the Age of Revolution, and most especially the Haitian Revolution, in catalyzing slave and free people of color insurrection. As an island, Cuba has always been tied to forces greater than its own history. Consequently, any history of Cuba will have to tell a story beyond the narrow confines of the nation-state.

The Aponte Rebellion occurred during one of the most formative periods in the Cuban past: the emergence of plantation society structured on sugar and slavery. The epicenter of New World sugar production moved from Brazil to Barbados to Jamaica to Saint Domingue before Cuba commanded the world market in the nineteenth century.[51] With the transition to plantation agriculture worked by slave labor and tied to Atlantic commerce, Cuban society became racialized. In the relatively short span of thirty years from 1790 to 1820, Cuba imported more than 300,000 slaves, amazingly tripling the entire volume of the trans-Atlantic slave trade for the previous three centuries. The massive importation of slaves and the expansion of plantation agriculture transformed Cuba into a racialized plantation society. Racial identity ever more rigidly defined the barriers of inclusion for the white population of European ancestry and exclusion for the black population of African ancestry.

The racial plantation society, however, did not immediately eclipse the past society that allowed for a free population of color to exist on the island. Free people of color and slaves made sure that the circles of inclusion and exclusion that separated the white and black populations overlapped. They used their existing and longstanding limited rights and privileges to gain freedom and manipulated institutions to protect their free status. Through incredible ingenuity, hard work, and years of saving, slaves purchased their own freedom through the practice of *coartación*. Freedom from a master, however, did not provide equality in Cuban society. The rise of the racialized plantation economy in the 1790s corroded the special niche and limited privileges free men and women of color had previously enjoyed in Cuba's hierarchical society. But just as slaves did not accept their subordinate position, free people of color gave concrete meaning to their liberty through work, family relations, and above all independence from master control.

While Cuba developed relatively late as a plantation colony, the divisions between urban and rural society were not as rigid as argued in the existing historiography. The investigation by colonial officials into the Aponte Rebellion discovered an extensive network of trade routes, communication networks, and familial ties that linked the rural and urban areas together as one coherent and integrated system of production. Slaves arrived at Havana from the middle passage and were then sold to the plantations. Sugar had to be shipped from the countryside to port cities for the international market. Wage laborers often contracted their services out to the countryside. And plantation slaves sold goods and crafts in urban markets on the weekends. While material conditions undoubtedly differed between rural and urban areas, the two areas shared much more in common than our modern perspective on town and country has recognized.

This study has also argued that the free men of color militia provided a crucial institution for social advancement. The militia created a leadership structure that extended far beyond the military. The changing reactions to militiamen of African ancestry at the end of the eighteenth century and the beginning of the nineteenth century reflected the larger transformation of Cuban society by race. Tracing its origins to the sixteenth century, the militia had long served as a distinct corporate body that provided social mobility for free men of color. The dramatic increase in slave labor and the expansion of plantation agriculture beginning in the 1790s, however, served to dilute the distinctions and privileges of militia service. During the preplantation era, the black and mulatto militia defended the island against foreign attacks and maintained domestic stability. In the racialized plantation society of the late eighteenth and nineteenth centuries, however, the militia came under attack as a possible ally for slaves. More than ever, free people of color represented a contradiction in Cuba's slave society. Aponte and others decided to turn their military training in the service of Spanish colonialism into a weapon to destroy it. The militia provided crucial access to the arms and weapons necessary for the rebellion to be a success. The camaraderie of militiamen and their elevated social and economic position within their own community presented them as leaders to unite the free and enslaved populations in the Aponte Rebellion.

My analysis of the Aponte Rebellion supports the revisionist trends in diaspora studies that argues greater attention must be given to African ethnicity. Africans in Cuba arrived with their own sense of history, culture, and identity that cannot be ignored. Africans in Cuba often expressed their Old World identity and ethnicity through *cabildo* associations to define themselves in cooperation with others who shared a similar ancestry rooted in West and Central Africa. In this sense, they show the importance of understanding that

Africans in the Americas did not immediately or exclusively adopt a racialized identity of blackness. Although notions of blackness and whiteness undoubtedly represent the most important legacy of slavery in the New World, it cannot be considered the single defining characteristic for slavery from the very beginning, or even as late as the nineteenth century. The African population in Cuba defined itself, and became defined by others, through cultural, geographic, and linguistic criteria that tended to militate against a broad racial identity. At meetings inside *cabildo* houses when the societies discussed the needs of their members, they addressed the problems their organizations faced of existing in a society based upon a racial hierarchy that privileged the European over the African. Although the functions of *cabildos* did not concentrate exclusively on attacking racial inequalities, the organizations sought to remedy, in one way or another, the grossly unequal position of their members. By providing a network of alliances and an institutional structure that offered a limited sense of familiarity for Africans in Cuba, *cabildos* helped their members survive in a society based upon racial oppression. The process by which *cabildos* could address the specific needs of their own organization and also serve the common interests of all people of African ancestry became apparent in the Aponte Rebellion. *Cabildo* houses offered security to organize and plan the revolts. The Aponte Rebellion revealed the flexibility and innovative nature of African identity in Cuba. Africans in Cuba could define themselves by simultaneously emphasizing both their Old World ethnicity and their New World racial identity.

While manuscript sources related to the Aponte Rebellion have been consulted from Cuban, Spanish, British, and United States archives, it still remains unclear (and perhaps unknowable with any degree of certainty) if the revolts and conspiracies in Puerto Príncipe, Bayamo, Holguín, and Havana represented one coordinated plan of revolution or several separate rebellions. This study has argued that José Antonio Aponte served as only *one* of the many leaders of the rebellion that bears his name. By focusing on the other participants, such as *cabildo* members, militia soldiers, slaves, and free people of color, the Aponte Rebellion offers a window through which to examine in detail the larger social, cultural, political, and economic changes in Cuba during the early nineteenth century. Whether the Aponte Rebellion represented one unified revolution of four distinct movements should not detract from its important role in Cuba's history. As with other protest movements by the dispossessed and downtrodden throughout history, the greatest legacy of the Aponte Rebellion rests with the powerful reminder of the ability to imagine a better world and the courage, regardless of the odds, to bring these dreams to fruition.

# Biographical Database
# of the Aponte Rebels

During the course of my investigation of the Aponte Rebellion, I collected biographical data on any identifiable individual arrested, questioned, punished, imprisoned, or the executed for involvement in the insurrections that erupted in Puerto Príncipe, Bayamo, Holguín, and Havana. I originally intended to construct a database with the goal of quantifying biographical criteria such as profession, literacy, marital status, African ethnicity, and other qualities to provide a statistical profile of the rebels similar to João José Reis's analysis of the 1835 Malê Rebellion.[1] Unlike censuses or notary records that have a standard formulaic representation and somewhat regular consistency, which allows scholars to skillfully overcome some of the particular irregularities of individual census takers and notaries, the expediency of the investigations conducted in four different cities with four different judicial teams produced considerable obstacles to converting qualitative data into quantitative arguments. Moreover, the quick punishments and imprisonments of slave and free people of color involved in the rebellion produced a wide variance in the quality of the documentary record, as described in chapter 4. The detail of biographical data on any particular individual arrested varied widely, from court testimony (generally the most detailed) to simple lists of prisoners to even just a nameless total of the number of executions. Consequently, the database constructed using the Statistical Package for the Social Sciences (SPSS) on 381 individuals has numerous variable gaps, as revealed in the table below.[2] The inconsistencies in the data caused me to hesitate from making any definitive statistical arguments and clearly revealed that the documentary record most naturally lent itself to a cultural-narrative interpretation of the Aponte Rebellion.

Despite these reservations, several trends are revealed by the data that deserve brief mention. Of the known juridical status of 329 individuals, 78 percent were slaves and 22 percent were free people of color. Thus, despite judicial officials' attention on José Antonio Aponte, Clemente Chacón, Salvador Ternero, and the free people of color leadership, the Aponte Rebellion was a majority slave movement. Similarly, while Creoles could be found among the leadership, 71 percent of the arrested were African-born *bozales*.[3] Even more numerically significant is the fact that it was overwhelmingly a black movement. Of the known racial identity among 281 rebels, 96 percent were black, with mulattos noticeably absent. As described in chapter 5, the dominant black racial characteristics of the movement combined with the particular fascination with Haiti provide every reason to think of the Aponte Rebellion as an early nineteenth-century variant on what would be labeled in the twentieth century as a Black Power movement. While the rebellions erupted on rural plantations, 34 percent of the arrested had their primary residence in urban areas. As chapters 2, 3, and 4 explained, although Cuba became transformed into an agrarian plantation society, rural and urban areas remained linked together in important ways that facilitated unity and coordination for the Aponte Rebellion. In regard to sex among the arrested, 92 percent were male. In summary, the data displays completely typical and unsurprising conclusions for Caribbean slave insurrections. The statistical evidence provides a broad outline of a movement whose participants were in the majority African-born, black male slaves who labored on rural plantations. If our analysis of the Aponte Rebellion were only to focus on these static statistical profiles and ignore the detailed transcribed spoken words from the court testimony, we would not know why they rose in rebellion, what they planned to accomplish, or how they made sense of the changing world they lived in.

Slaves and Free People of Color Arrested and/or Punished for Involvement in the Aponte Rebellion of 1812

| Name | Physical Punishment | Prison Term | Rebellion Location[a] | Sex (M/F) | Slave/ Free | Race[b] | Creole/ Bozal[c] | African Ethnicity | Rural/ Urban | Profession | Literate (Y/N)[d] | Marital Status[e] | Militia |
|---|---|---|---|---|---|---|---|---|---|---|---|---|---|
| Joaquín Peñalver | Execution | n/a | Havana | M | S | | | | | | | | |
| Tomas Peñalver | Execution | n/a | Havana | M | S | | | | | | | | |
| Esteban Peñalver | Execution | n/a | Havana | M | S | B | B | | | | | | |
| Antonio Cao | Execution | n/a | Havana | M | S | B | | | Both | | | | |
| Baltasar Peñalver | Execution | n/a | Havana | M | S | B | | | R | | | | |
| Gabriel Peñalver | Execution | n/a | Havana | M | S | B | B | Karabali | R | | | | |
| Tiburcio Peñalver | Execution | n/a | Havana | M | S | B | | | Both | | | | |
| Juan Barbier | Execution | n/a | Havana | M | F | B | B | | U | | No | | |
| Salvador Ternero | Execution | n/a | Havana | M | F | B | B | Mina | U | Artisan | No | Mar | Y |
| Clemente Chacón | Execution | n/a | Havana | M | F | B | C | | U | Artisan | Yes | Mar | Y |
| José Antonio Aponte | Execution | n/a | Havana | M | F | B | C | | U | Artisan | Yes | Mar | Y |
| Juan Bautista Lisundia | Execution | n/a | Havana | M | F | B | B | Kongo | Both | | | | |
| José del Carmen Peñalver | Execution | n/a | Havana | M | F | B | C | | U | | Yes | Mar | Y |
| Francisco Xavier Pacheco | Execution | n/a | Havana | M | F | B | C | | U | Artisan | Yes | Sing | Y |
| Estanislao Aguilar | Execution | n/a | Havana | M | F | M | C | | U | | Yes | | |
| Unknown | Execution | n/a | Prto Prin | M | | | | | | | | | |
| Unknown | Execution | n/a | Prto Prin | M | | | | | | | | | |
| Unknown | Execution | n/a | Prto Prin | M | | | | | | | | | |
| Unknown | Execution | n/a | Prto Prin | M | | | | | | | | | |
| Unknown | Execution | n/a | Prto Prin | M | | | | | | | | | |
| Unknown | Execution | n/a | Prto Prin | M | | | | | | | | | |
| Unknown | Execution | n/a | Prto Prin | M | | | | | | | | | |
| Unknown | Execution | n/a | Prto Prin | M | | | | | | | | | |
| Unknown | Execution | n/a | Prto Prin | M | | | | | | | | | |

Slaves and Free People of Color Arrested and/or Punished for Involvement in the Aponte Rebellion of 1812 (continued)

| Name | Physical Punishment | Prison Term | Rebellion Location[a] | Sex (M/F) | Slave/Free | Race[b] | Creole/Bozal[c] | African Ethnicity | Rural/Urban | Profession | Literate (Y/N)[d] | Marital Status[e] | Militia |
|---|---|---|---|---|---|---|---|---|---|---|---|---|---|
| Unknown | Execution | n/a | Prto Prin | M | | | | | | | | | |
| Unknown | Execution | n/a | Prto Prin | M | | | | | | | | | |
| Calixto Gutiérrez | Execution | n/a | Prto Prin | M | S | B | B | Karabali | R | Artisan | Yes | Mar | |
| Rafael Antonio Arango | Execution | n/a | Prto Prin | M | S | B | B | Kongo | R | | No | | |
| José Miguel González | Execution | n/a | Prto Prin | M | S | B | | | U | | | | |
| Blas Tamayo | Execution | n/a | Bayamo | M | | B | | | | | | | |
| Antonio José Barriaga | Execution | n/a | Bayamo | M | S | B | B | Kongo | R | | | | |
| Juan Tamayo | Execution | n/a | Bayamo | M | F | B | | | | | | | |
| Caridad Echevaria | Execution | n/a | Bayamo | F | F | B | C | | U | | Yes | | |
| Juan Nepomuceno | Execution | n/a | Holguin | M | S | B | B | Kongo | | | | Sing | |
| Lorenzo Rengil | 25 lashes | 10 yrs | Havana | M | S | B | | | | | | | |
| Andres Mandinga Santa Cruz | 50 lashes | Shackles | Havana | M | S | B | B | Mandinga | R | Slave driver | | | |
| Nepomuceno | 50 lashes | Shackles | Prto Prin | M | | | | | | | | | |
| Francisco | 50 lashes | Shackles | Prto Prin | M | | B | B | Kongo | R | Laborer | No | Sing | |
| Miguel | 50 lashes | Shackles | Prto Prin | M | S | | | | | | | | |
| Nepomuceno | 50 lashes | Shackles | Prto Prin | M | S | | | | | | | | |
| Miguel | 50 lashes | Shackles | Prto Prin | M | S | B | B | Kongo | | | | | |
| Rafael | 50 lashes | Shackles | Prto Prin | M | S | B | B | Kongo | R | | No | Mar | |
| José Antonio | 50 lashes | Shackles | Prto Prin | M | S | B | B | Kongo | R | Laborer | No | Sing | |
| Rafael | 50 lashes | Shackles | Prto Prin | M | S | B | B | Kongo | R | Laborer | No | Sing | |
| Nepomuceno | 50 lashes | Shackles | Prto Prin | M | S | B | B | Kongo | | | | | |
| Raymundo Peñalver | 50 lashes | n/a | Havana | M | S | B | | | R | | | | |
| Cosme Peñalver | 50 lashes | n/a | Havana | M | S | B | | | R | | | | |

| | | | | | | | | | Domestic | | |
|---|---|---|---|---|---|---|---|---|---|---|---|
| Pedro Francisco Guerra | 50 lashes | n/a | Prto Prin | M | | B | | R | Laborer | No | |
| Pasqual | 50 lashes | n/a | Prto Prin | M | S | B | | R | | No | Sing |
| José Maria | 50 lashes | n/a | Prto Prin | M | S | B | Kongo | | | | |
| Tadeo Peñalver | 100 lashes | 5 yrs | Havana | M | S | B | | R | | | |
| Alfonso Santa Cruz | 100 lashes | 6 yrs | Havana | M | S | B | Kongo | R | | | |
| Bernardo Santa Cruz, alias Briche | 100 lashes | 6 yrs | Havana | M | S | B | | R | | | |
| Antonio Alonso | 100 lashes | 6 yrs | Havana | M | S | B | | R | | | |
| Francisco González | 100 lashes | 10 yrs | Havana | M | S | B | Kongo | R | Laborer | No | Sing |
| Carlos de Aguilar | 100 lashes | 10 yrs | Havana | M | S | C | | R | | No | |
| José Antonio Alarcon | 100 lashes | n/a | Prto Prin | M | S | B | Kongo | | | | |
| Francisco | 100 lashes | n/a | Prto Prin | M | S | B | Kongo | | | No | Mar |
| Tomas Infante | 150 lashes | 6 yrs | Bayamo | M | | | | | | | |
| José Isidro Petion | 150 lashes | 6 yrs | Bayamo | M | | | | | | | |
| Mateo Tamayo | 150 lashes | 6 yrs | Bayamo | M | S | B | | | | | |
| Juan Trelles | 150 lashes | 6 yrs | Bayamo | M | S | B | | R | | | |
| Antonio José Sanchez | 150 lashes | 6 yrs | Bayamo | M | S | B | | R | Laborer | | |
| Francisco, alias el Emeperador | 150 lashes | 6 yrs | Bayamo | M | F | B | | U | | | Mar |
| Simón Antunes | 150 lashes | 6 yrs | Bayamo | M | F | B | | R | | | Mar |
| Miguel Ramón de Cespedes | 150 lashes | 6 yrs | Bayamo | M | F | B | Karabali | | | | Mar |
| José Caridad Perera | 150 lashes | 6 yrs | Bayamo | M | F | B | Karabali | U | | | Mar |
| Isabel Infante | 150 lashes | 6 yrs | Bayamo | F | | | | | | | |
| Diomicio Cespedes | 150 lashes | | Bayamo | M | | | | | | | |
| Juan Sacatecas | 150 lashes | | Bayamo | M | | | | | | | |
| Manuel Hechevarria | 150 lashes | | Bayamo | M | | | | | | | |
| Rafael Ramos | 150 lashes | | Bayamo | M | | | | | | | |

Slaves and Free People of Color Arrested and/or Punished for Involvement in the Aponte Rebellion of 1812 (continued)

| Name | Physical Punishment | Prison Term | Rebellion Location[a] | Sex (M/F) | Slave/Free | Race[b] | Creole/Bozal[c] | African Ethnicity | Rural/Urban | Profession | Literate (Y/N)[d] | Marital Status[e] | Militia |
|---|---|---|---|---|---|---|---|---|---|---|---|---|---|
| Bernaro Manzano | 150 lashes | | Bayamo | M | | | | | | | | | |
| Salvador Sacatecas | 150 lashes | | Bayamo | M | | | | | | | | | |
| Juana Villegas | 150 lashes | | Bayamo | F | F | B | C | | U | | No | | |
| Antonio Betancourt | 200 lashes | 4 yrs | Prto Prin | M | S | B | B | Kongo | R | | Yes | | |
| Antonio | 200 lashes | 6 yrs | Prto Prin | M | S | B | B | Kongo | R | | No | | |
| Antonio Roque | 200 lashes | 6 yrs | Prto Prin | M | S | B | B | Kongo | R | Laborer | No | | |
| Federico | Unspecified | Unspecified | Holguín | M | | B | | | | | | | |
| Mateo | Unspecified | Unspecified | Holguín | M | | B | | | | | | | |
| Antonio | Unspecified | Unspecified | Holguín | M | | B | | | | | | | |
| Miguel | Unspecified | Unspecified | Holguín | M | | B | | | | | | | |
| Manuel | Unspecified | Unspecified | Holguín | M | | B | | | | | | | |
| Desiderio Malagamba | | 0–3 mos | Havana | M | S | B | B | Mina | R | Slave driver | Yes | Mar | |
| Juan de Mesa | | 4–6 mos | Havana | M | | B | B | | U | | | | |
| Juan de Dios Pacheco | | 4–6 mos | Havana | M | S | B | B | Karabali | U | Artisan | No | Sing | |
| José Maria Santa Cruz | | 4–6 mos | Havana | M | S | B | C | | R | | | | |
| Modesto Santa Cruz | | 4–6 mos | Havana | M | S | B | B | Karabali | R | | | | |
| José de la Trinidad Santa Cruz | | 4–6 mos | Havana | M | S | B | B | Mandinga | R | Artisan | | | |
| Rufino Santa Cruz | | 4–6 mos | Havana | M | S | B | B | Ganga | R | | | | |
| Antonio Maria Santa Cruz | | 4–6 mos | Havana | M | S | B | B | Macau | R | | | | |
| Roberto Beltran | | 4–6 mos | Havana | M | F | B | | | U | Artisan | Yes | Mar | Y |
| José Melendez | | 1 yr | Havana | M | F | B | C | | U | Artisan | Yes | Cohab | Y |
| José Menedez | | 1 yr | Havana | M | F | B | C | | U | Artisan | Yes | Mar | Y |
| José Guadalupe | | 1 yr | Prto Prim | M | S | B | | | R | | | | |

| Name | Yrs | City | Sex | Cond. | Color | Origin | Nation | Res. | Occup. | Lit. | Marital | |
|---|---|---|---|---|---|---|---|---|---|---|---|---|
| Francisco Ximenes | 1 yr | Prto Prin | M | S | B | B | Mina | R | Artisan | No | Sing | |
| José de la Cruz | 4 yrs | Havana | M | S | B | C | | R | Artisan | Yes | Sing | Y |
| Pilar Borrego | 4 yrs | Havana | M | F | B | | | U | Artisan | Yes | Sing | Y |
| José Sendinga | 4 yrs | Havana | M | F | B | C | | U | Artisan | Yes | | |
| José Herrera, alias Bonaparte | 4 yrs | Havana | M | F | B | C | | U | Artisan | Yes | Mar | Y |
| Francisco Andrade | 4 yrs | Havana | M | F | B | C | | U | Artisan | No | Widow | Y |
| José Perfecto y Barbusea | 4 yrs | Havana | M | F | B | C | | U | Artisan | Yes | Mar | |
| Antonio Benito y Barbusea | 4 yrs | Havana | M | F | B | C | | U | Artisan | | Sing | |
| Francisco Barbusea | 4 yrs | Havana | M | F | B | C | | U | Artisan | | Mar | |
| Alexandro de Estrada | 4 yrs | Havana | M | F | B | C | | U | Artisan | No | Mar | Y |
| Hilario Santa Cruz | 4 yrs | Havana | M | F | B | C | | U | Artisan | Yes | Mar | Y |
| Felipe Chamiso | 4 yrs | Havana | M | F | B | C | | U | Artisan | Yes | Widow | |
| Cristobal Barbusea | 4 yrs | Havana | M | F | B | C | | U | Artisan | No | Sing | |
| Marcelo Cantos | 4 yrs | Havana | M | F | B | C | | U | Artisan | | Sing | Y |
| Melchor Chirinos | 4 yrs | Havana | M | F | C | C | | U | Artisan | No | Mar | Y |
| Joaquin Belaguer | 4 yrs | Prto Prin | M | F | B | B | Kongo | R | | Yes | | |
| Maria Merced Llanes | 4 yrs | Prto Prin | F | F | B | | | R | | No | | |
| Francisco Maroto | 6 yrs | Havana | M | | | | | | | | | |
| Pedro Betancourt Cartagena | 6 yrs | Prto Prin | M | | | | | | | | | Y |
| Antonio Karabali | 6 yrs | Prto Prin | M | S | | | | | | | | |
| Pablo José Valdez | 10 yrs | Havana | M | S | B | | | U | | | | |
| Martin Betancourt | 10 yrs | Prto Prin | M | | | | | | | | | |
| Francisco Osorio | 10 yrs | Prto Prin | M | | | | | | | | | |
| Santiago Betancourt | 10 yrs | Prto Prin | M | | | | | | | | | |
| Manuel Maria Betancourt | 10 yrs | Prto Prin | M | | | | | | | | | |
| Rafael Miguel Cisneros | 10 yrs | Prto Prin | M | | B | | | | | | | |

Slaves and Free People of Color Arrested and/or Punished for Involvement in the Aponte Rebellion of 1812 (continued)

| Name | Physical Punishment | Prison Term | Rebellion Location[a] | Sex (M/F) | Slave/Free | Race[b] | Creole/Bozal[c] | African Ethnicity | Rural/Urban | Profession | Literate (Y/N)[d] | Marital Status[e] | Militia |
|---|---|---|---|---|---|---|---|---|---|---|---|---|---|
| Mauricio Cisneros | | 10 yrs | Prto Prin | M | | B | | | | | | | |
| Juan de Dios Pelaez | | 10 yrs | Prto Prin | M | S | | | | R | | No | | |
| José Miguel | | 10 yrs | Prto Prin | M | S | | | | | | No | | |
| Simón Cisneros | | 10 yrs | Prto Prin | M | S | | | | | | No | Mar | |
| José le los Reyes, aka Capitan | | 10 yrs | Prto Prin | M | S | | | | | | No | | |
| Antonio Arias | | 10 yrs | Prto Prin | M | S | | | | | | | | |
| José Cisneros | | 10 yrs | Prto Prin | M | S | | | | | | | | |
| Mariano Cisneros | | 10 yrs | Prto Prin | M | S | | | | | | | | |
| José Napoles | | 10 yrs | Prto Prin | M | S | | | | | | | | |
| Ant Miguel Chiquito | | 10 yrs | Prto Prin | M | S | | | | | | | | |
| Carlos Escobar | | 10 yrs | Prto Prin | M | S | | | | | | | | |
| Felipe Lescano | | 10 yrs | Prto Prin | M | S | | | | | | | | |
| Manuel Moya | | 10 yrs | Prto Prin | M | S | | | | | | | | |
| Pablo Socarrais | | 10 yrs | Prto Prin | M | S | | | | | | | | |
| Raman Napoles | | 10 yrs | Prto Prin | M | S | | | | | | | | |
| José Antonio Barraso | | 10 yrs | Prto Prin | M | S | | | | | | | | |
| José Antonio Tapias | | 10 yrs | Prto Prin | M | S | | | | | | | | |
| Pomuseno Rabelo | | 10 yrs | Prto Prin | M | S | | | | | | | | |
| Antonio Rabelo | | 10 yrs | Prto Prin | M | S | | | | | | | | |
| Rafael Rabelo | | 10 yrs | Prto Prin | M | S | | | | | | | | |
| Miguel Castellanos | | 10 yrs | Prto Prin | M | S | | | | | | | | |
| Xavier Castellanos | | 10 yrs | Prto Prin | M | S | | | | | | | | |
| Nicolas Castellanos | | 10 yrs | Prto Prin | M | S | | | | | | | | |

| | | | | | |
|---|---|---|---|---|---|
| Juan Bautista Castellanos | 10 yrs | Prto Prin | M | S | |
| Francisco Alonso Castellanos | 10 yrs | Prto Prin | M | S | |
| José de los Santos Plasares | 10 yrs | Prto Prin | M | S | C |
| Luis Plasares | 10 yrs | Prto Prin | M | S | |
| Antonio Plasares | 10 yrs | Prto Prin | M | S | |
| Miguel Lazo | 10 yrs | Prto Prin | M | S | |
| José Maria Lazo | 10 yrs | Prto Prin | M | S | |
| Antonio Lazo | 10 yrs | Prto Prin | M | S | |
| Antonio Maria Lazo | 10 yrs | Prto Prin | M | S | |
| Francisco | 10 yrs | Prto Prin | M | S | |
| José Maria | 10 yrs | Prto Prin | M | S | |
| Miguel | 10 yrs | Prto Prin | M | S | |
| Joaquin | 10 yrs | Prto Prin | M | S | |
| José | 10 yrs | Prto Prin | M | S | |
| José del Rosario | 10 yrs | Prto Prin | M | S | |
| Manuel Cabo | 10 yrs | Prto Prin | M | S | |
| Tadeo | 10 yrs | Prto Prin | M | S | |
| José | 10 yrs | Prto Prin | M | S | |
| Juan de Dios | 10 yrs | Prto Prin | M | S | |
| Francisco Antonio Conga | 10 yrs | Prto Prin | M | S | |
| Joaquin | 10 yrs | Prto Prin | M | S | |
| Abrosio | 10 yrs | Prto Prin | M | S | |
| Pepe Castallanos | 10 yrs | Prto Prin | M | S | |
| Volasco Castellanos | 10 yrs | Prto Prin | M | S | |
| José Maria Castellanos | 10 yrs | Prto Prin | M | S | |
| Juan de Dios Castellanos | 10 yrs | Prto Prin | M | S | |
| José Maria Basulto | 10 yrs | Prto Prin | M | S | |

Slaves and Free People of Color Arrested and / or Punished for Involvement in the Aponte Rebellion of 1812 (continued)

| Name | Physical Punishment | Prison Term | Rebellion Location[a] | Sex (M/F) | Slave/Free | Race[b] | Creole/Bozal[c] | African Ethnicity | Rural/Urban | Profession | Literate (Y/N)[d] | Marital Status[e] | Militia |
|---|---|---|---|---|---|---|---|---|---|---|---|---|---|
| José Basulto | | 10 yrs | Prto Prin | M | S | | | | | | | | |
| Miguel Basulto | | 10 yrs | Prto Prin | M | S | | | | | | | | |
| Francisco Basulto | | 10 yrs | Prto Prin | M | S | | | | | | | | |
| Antonio Basulto | | 10 yrs | Prto Prin | M | S | | | | | | | | |
| Isidro Aguilar | | 10 yrs | Prto Prin | M | S | | | | | | | | |
| Gergorio | | 10 yrs | Prto Prin | M | S | | | | | | | | |
| Luis | | 10 yrs | Prto Prin | M | S | B | B | Kongo | R | Laborer | | | |
| Manuel Maria Betancourt | | 10 yrs | Prto Prin | M | S | B | B | Mandinga | R | Laborer | No | | |
| Francisco Adan | | 10 yrs | Prto Prin | M | S | B | B | Mandinga | | | | | |
| Cristobal Castellanos | | 10 yrs | Prto Prin | M | S | B | | | R | Laborer | | | |
| Manuel Castellanos | | 10 yrs | Prto Prin | M | S | B | B | Kongo | R | Laborer | | | |
| Juan Aguilar | | 10 yrs | Prto Prin | M | S | B | B | Karabali | R | | No | | |
| Gaspar Gonzales | | 10 yrs | Prto Prin | M | S | B | | | | | | | |
| José Antonio | | 10 yrs | Prto Prin | M | S | B | | | | | No | | |
| José Antonio Adan | | 10 yrs | Prto Prin | M | S | B | B | Kongo | | | No | | |
| Juan de Dios Recio | | 10 yrs | Prto Prin | M | S | B | | | | | | | |
| Francisco Xavier Arias | | 10 yrs | Prto Prin | M | S | B | B | Mandinga | | | No | | |
| Juan de Dios Arias | | 10 yrs | Prto Prin | M | S | B | B | Kongo | R | Laborer | No | | |
| José Joaquin Arias | | 10 yrs | Prto Prin | M | S | B | B | Karabali | R | Laborer | No | | |
| Tiburcio Recio | | 10 yrs | Prto Prin | M | S | B | B | | R | Laborer | No | Sing | |
| Roman Recio | | 10 yrs | Prto Prin | M | S | B | B | Mandinga | R | Laborer | No | Mar | |
| José [Frutroso] | | 10 yrs | Prto Prin | M | S | B | B | Mina | | | No | | |
| Prudencio Gonzales | | 10 yrs | Prto Prin | M | S | B | | | | | No | | |
| Miguel Gonzales | | 10 yrs | Prto Prin | M | S | B | | | | | No | | |

| Name | Term | Place | Sex | Status | B | B | Nation | R | Laborer | No | Sing |
|---|---|---|---|---|---|---|---|---|---|---|---|
| Percio González | 10 yrs | Prto Prin | M | S | B | | | | | | |
| José Miguel Socarrais | 10 yrs | Prto Prin | M | S | B | | | | | | |
| Francisco Socarrais | 10 yrs | Prto Prin | M | S | B | | | | | | |
| Pedro Rodríguez | 10 yrs | Prto Prin | M | S | B | | | | | | |
| Luis Cisneros | 10 yrs | Prto Prin | M | S | B | | | | | | |
| Alfonso Lescano | 10 yrs | Prto Prin | M | S | B | | | | | | |
| Miguel Guati | 10 yrs | Prto Prin | M | S | B | | | | | | |
| Juan de Dios Saldivar | 10 yrs | Prto Prin | M | S | B | B | Kongo | | | | |
| Francisco Saldivar | 10 yrs | Prto Prin | M | S | B | B | Kongo | | | | |
| Miguel Saldivar | 10 yrs | Prto Prin | M | S | B | B | Kongo | | | | |
| Manuel José Saldivar | 10 yrs | Prto Prin | M | S | B | B | Kongo | | | | |
| Juan Bautista | 10 yrs | Prto Prin | M | S | B | B | Mandinga | | | | |
| Gabriel de Pablo | 10 yrs | Prto Prin | M | S | B | B | Mandinga | | | | |
| José Manuel Plasares | 10 yrs | Prto Prin | M | S | B | B | Kongo | | | | |
| José Antonio Plasares | 10 yrs | Prto Prin | M | S | B | B | Kongo | | | | |
| Antonio Plasares | 10 yrs | Prto Prin | M | S | B | B | Kongo | | | | |
| Francisco Plasares | 10 yrs | Prto Prin | M | S | B | B | Kongo | | | | |
| Juan Lazo | 10 yrs | Prto Prin | M | S | B | B | Kongo | | | | |
| Santiago | 10 yrs | Prto Prin | M | S | B | B | Karabali | | | | |
| Fernando | 10 yrs | Prto Prin | M | S | B | B | Mina | | | | |
| Francisco Antonio | 10 yrs | Prto Prin | M | S | B | B | Ganga | | | | |
| Juan Bautista | 10 yrs | Prto Prin | M | S | B | B | Karabali | | | | |
| Fransisco Karabali | 10 yrs | Prto Prin | M | S | B | B | Karabali | | | | |
| Rafael Napoles | 10 yrs | Prto Prin | M | S | B | | | | | | |
| Pablo Lescano | 10 yrs | Prto Prin | M | S | B | | | | | | |
| Cristobal Betancourt | 10 yrs | Prto Prin | M | S | B | | | | | | |
| Narcisco | Shackles | Havana | M | S | B | B | Ganga | R | Laborer | No | Sing |
| José Mauricio | Life | Holguín | M | | B | | | | | | |

Slaves and Free People of Color Arrested and / or Punished for Involvement in the Aponte Rebellion of 1812 (continued)

| Name | Physical Punishment | Prison Term | Rebellion Location[a] | Sex (M/F) | Slave/Free | Race[b] | Creole/Bozal[c] | African Ethnicity | Rural/Urban | Profession | Literate (Y/N)[d] | Marital Status[e] | Militia |
|---|---|---|---|---|---|---|---|---|---|---|---|---|---|
| Tomas Gomez | | | Havana | M | | | C | | U | Artisan | Yes | Mar | |
| Antonio Abad | | | Havana | M | S | | | | | | | Mar | |
| [Name not given] | | | Havana | M | S | | B | | R | Driver | No | Mar | |
| Matias Santa Cruz | | | Havana | M | S | | | | R | Artisan | | | |
| Cristobal | | | Havana | M | S | B | C | | U | | | | |
| Benito | | | Havana | M | S | B | B | Kongo | U | Domestic | | Sing | |
| José Lorenzo | | | Havana | M | S | B | B | Karabali | U | | | | |
| Juan Brinas | | | Havana | M | S | B | B | | R | | No | Sing | |
| Francisco Colina | | | Havana | M | S | B | B | | R | | No | Sing | |
| Leon | | | Havana | M | S | B | B | Karabali | U | | No | Sing | |
| Antonio Kongo | | | Havana | M | S | B | B | Kongo | R | | | | |
| Pedro Martin Santa Cruz | | | Havana | M | S | B | | | | | | | |
| Damato | | | Havana | M | S | B | B | Mina | R | | No | | |
| José Antonio | | | Havana | M | S | B | B | Lucumi | R | | No | | |
| Gabriel | | | Havana | M | S | B | | | R | | No | | |
| Joaquin | | | Havana | M | S | B | B | | R | | No | | |
| Juan Reganifieros | | | Havana | M | S | B | B | | R | | No | | |
| José Joaquin Machado | | | Havana | M | S | B | B | Macau | R | Artisan | No | Sing | |
| Andres Santa Cruz | | | Havana | M | S | B | | | R | | | | |
| Estanislao Santa Cruz | | | Havana | M | S | B | | | R | | | | |
| Pantaleon Santa Cruz | | | Havana | M | S | B | | | R | | | | |
| José Juilian Santa Cruz | | | Havana | M | S | B | B | Karabali | R | | | | |
| Rafael Santa Cruz | | | Havana | M | S | B | B | Lucumi | R | Artisan | | | |
| Antonio Santa Cruz | | | Havana | M | S | B | B | Mandinga | R | | | | |

| | | | | | | | Mar |
|---|---|---|---|---|---|---|---|
| Mariano Santa Cruz | Havana | M | S | B | Kongo | R | |
| Joaquin Santa Cruz | Havana | M | S | B | Kongo | R | |
| Florentino Santa Cruz | Havana | M | S | B | Karabali | R | |
| Ziprian Santa Cruz | Havana | M | S | B | Karabali | R | |
| Martin Santa Cruz | Havana | M | S | B | Mandinga | R | |
| Cayetano Santa Cruz | Havana | M | S | B | Kongo | R | |
| Gaspar Santa Cruz | Havana | M | S | B | Karabali | R | |
| Fermin Santa Cruz | Havana | M | S | B | Kongo | R | |
| Jazinto Santa Cruz | Havana | M | S | B | Kongo | R | |
| Teodoro Santa Cruz | Havana | M | S | B | Mandinga | R | |
| José Luciano Santa Cruz | Havana | M | S | C | | R | |
| Angel Santa Cruz | Havana | M | S | B | Karabali | R | |
| Benito Santa Cruz | Havana | M | S | B | Karabali | R | |
| Diego Santa Cruz | Havana | M | S | B | Kongo | R | |
| Mariano Santa Cruz | Havana | M | S | B | Karabali | R | |
| Roque Santa Cruz | Havana | M | S | B | Karabali | R | |
| Ramón Santa Cruz | Havana | M | S | B | Karabali | R | |
| Felix Santa Cruz | Havana | M | S | B | Karabali | R | |
| Antonio José Santa Cruz | Havana | M | S | B | Karabali | R | |
| José Alvino Santa Cruz | Havana | M | S | B | Karabali | R | |
| José del Rosario Santa Cruz | Havana | M | S | B | Karabali | R | |
| José de la Trinidad Santa Cruz | Havana | M | S | B | Karabali | R | |
| José de Jesus Santa Cruz | Havana | M | S | B | Kongo | R | |
| José Elias Santa Cruz | Havana | M | S | B | Kongo | R | |
| Francisco Santa Cruz | Havana | M | S | B | Macau | R | |
| José Apolinario Santa Cruz | Havana | M | S | B | Karabali | R | |

Slaves and Free People of Color Arrested and / or Punished for Involvement in the Aponte Rebellion of 1812 (continued)

| Name | Physical Punishment | Prison Term | Rebellion Location[a] | Sex (M/F) | Slave/ Free | Race[b] | Creole/ Bozal[c] | African Ethnicity | Rural/ Urban | Profession | Literate (Y/N)[d] | Marital Status[e] | Militia |
|---|---|---|---|---|---|---|---|---|---|---|---|---|---|
| Lino Santa Cruz | | | Havana | M | S | B | B | Mandinga | R | | | | |
| Felipe Santa Cruz | | | Havana | M | S | B | B | Ganga | R | | | | |
| Nicolas Santa Cruz | | | Havana | M | S | B | B | Karabali | R | | | | |
| José Guillermo Santa Cruz | | | Havana | M | S | B | C | | R | | | | |
| Chino Ubaldo | | | Havana | M | S | M | C | | R | | No | Sing | |
| Juan Luis Santillan | | | Havana | M | F | | C | | | Militia | Yes | Mar | Y |
| Luis | | | Havana | M | F | B | B | Mandinga | | Artisan | | Mar | |
| Mauricio Guiteras | | | Havana | M | F | B | | | U | Artisan | | Mar | |
| Gil Narciso | | | Havana | M | F | B | C | | | Militia | Yes | Mar | Y |
| José Fantacia Gaston | | | Havana | M | F | B | C | | U | Militia | Yes | Mar | Y |
| Isidro Plutton | | | Havana | M | F | B | C | | U | Militia | | | Y |
| José Domingo Bejarano y Escobar | | | Havana | M | F | B | C | | U | Artisan | Yes | Sing | Y |
| Agustin Santa Cruz | | | Havana | M | F | B | C | | U | Artisan | Yes | Sing | |
| José Trinidad Nunez | | | Havana | M | F | B | C | | U | Artisan | Yes | Sing | |
| Ciracao Ulabarro | | | Havana | M | F | B | | | U | Artisan | | Mar | |
| Patricio Arostegui | | | Havana | M | F | B | | | R | Artisan | No | Mar | |
| Pablo Aguilar | | | Havana | M | F | B | C | | U | Artisan | No | Mar | |
| José Maria Espinosa | | | Havana | M | F | B | B | Mandinga | Both | Artisan | No | Mar | |
| Alfonso Ubaldo | | | Havana | M | F | B | C | | U | Artisan | No | Mar | |
| Manuel Pacheco | | | Havana | M | F | B | C | | U | Artisan | No | Mar | |
| José Sendinga | | | Havana | M | F | B | C | | U | Artisan | Yes | | Y |
| Christoval Barbusea | | | Havana | M | F | B | C | | U | Artisan | No | Sing | |
| Esteban Sanchez | | | Havana | M | F | M | C | | U | Artisan | Yes | Mar | Y |

| Name | Birthplace | Sex | | | | Nation | | Occupation | | Status |
|---|---|---|---|---|---|---|---|---|---|---|
| José Manuel Santa Ana | Havana | M | F | M | C | | U | Artisan | No | Sing |
| Ysabel | Havana | F | S | B | C | Mina | R | Laborer | No | Mar |
| Maria Joséfa de la Cruz | Havana | F | S | B | B | | R | Domestic | No | Mar |
| Maria de la Trinidad | Havana | F | S | B | C | | U | | No | Cohab |
| Parda Andrea | Havana | F | S | M | C | | R | | No | Sing |
| Maria de la Luz Sanchez | Havana | F | F | B | B | Kongo | U | Artisan | No | Mar |
| Geronima Urrutia | Havana | F | F | B | | | U | Domestic | No | Sing |
| Liverata Poveda | Havana | F | F | B | C | | U | | No | Sing |
| Maria de la Presentación Poveda | Havana | F | F | B | | | U | Domestic | No | Mar |
| Manuela de la Encarnación Lima | Havana | F | F | B | C | | U | Domestic | No | Cohab |
| Maria Joséfa Perez | Havana | F | F | B | C | | U | Domestic | No | Widow |
| Maria de los Dolores | Havana | F | F | B | C | | U | Domestic | No | Sing |
| Ana del Quino | Havana | F | F | B | B | Ararra | U | Domestic | No | Widow |
| Maria de la Encarnacion | Havana | F | F | B | B | | U | | No | |
| Andres Rodriguez | Prto Prin | M | | | | | R | Overseer | No | |
| Manuel Aguilera | Prto Prin | M | | | | | R | Overseer | Yes | Sing |
| Fermin Rabelo | Prto Prin | M | | | | | | | No | |
| Juan Antonio Abile | Prto Prin | M | | | | | R | Overseer | No | |
| Ramón | Prto Prin | M | S | | | | | | | |
| Manuel de Jesus | Prto Prin | M | S | B | | | R | Laborer | | |
| Francisco Xavier | Prto Prin | M | S | B | B | Mandinga | R | Laborer | | Sing |
| Joaquin | Prto Prin | M | S | B | | | R | | | |
| Juan José Placeres | Prto Prin | M | S | B | | | R | | | |
| José Rafel | Prto Prin | M | S | B | | | | | No | |
| Segundo | Prto Prin | M | S | B | C | Mina | R | | No | |
| Manuel Kongo | Prto Prin | M | S | B | B | Kongo | | | No | |

Slaves and Free People of Color Arrested and / or Punished for Involvement in the Aponte Rebellion of 1812 (continued)

| Name | Physical Punishment | Prison Term | Rebellion Location[a] | Sex (M/F) | Slave/Free | Race[b] | Creole/Bozal[c] | African Ethnicity | Rural/Urban | Profession | Literate (Y/N)[d] | Marital Status[e] | Militia |
|---|---|---|---|---|---|---|---|---|---|---|---|---|---|
| José (conocida Funga) | | | Prto Prin | M | S | B | B | Kongo | | | No | | |
| Bartolo | | | Prto Prin | M | S | B | B | Mandinga | R | Laborer | No | | |
| Antonio [Machado] | | | Prto Prin | M | S | B | B | Ararra | | | No | Sing | |
| Francisco [Machado] | | | Prto Prin | M | S | B | B | Kongo | | | No | | |
| José Joaquin | | | Prto Prin | M | S | B | C | | R | Laborer | No | Mar | |
| José Maria | | | Prto Prin | M | S | B | | | R | | No | | |
| Francisco Borge | | | Prto Prin | M | S | B | B | Karabali | R | | No | | |
| Juan de la Cruz | | | Prto Prin | M | S | B | | | R | Laborer | | | |
| Serapio Arias | | | Prto Prin | M | S | B | | | R | Laborer | | | |
| Antonio | | | Prto Prin | M | S | B | B | Kongo | R | | No | | |
| Antonio José | | | Prto Prin | M | S | B | B | Kongo | R | Domestic | No | Sing | |
| Rafael | | | Prto Prin | M | S | B | B | Karabali | R | | | | |
| Juan | | | Prto Prin | M | S | B | | | R | Laborer | | | |
| Geronimo [Criollo] | | | Prto Prin | M | S | B | C | | | | No | | |
| Francisco Antonio | | | Prto Prin | M | S | B | | | | | | | |
| José Maria | | | Prto Prin | M | S | B | B | Kongo | | | | | |
| Domingo | | | Prto Prin | M | S | B | B | Kongo | | | No | | |
| Liborio [Laborio] | | | Prto Prin | M | S | B | B | Kongo | R | Laborer | No | Sing | |
| Maximo Cisneros | | | Prto Prin | M | S | B | B | Kongo | | | No | | |
| Tomas | | | Prto Prin | M | S | B | B | Mandinga | R | Laborer | No | Mar | |
| Luis Mandinga | | | Prto Prin | M | S | B | B | Mandinga | | | No | | |
| Manuel | | | Prto Prin | M | S | C | | | | | No | | |
| José Rafael | | | Prto Prin | M | F | B | | | | | No | | |
| José Antonio Brinfas | | | Prto Prin | M | F | B | | | | | No | | |

| Name | | | | | | | | | | Cohab |
|---|---|---|---|---|---|---|---|---|---|---|
| Maria Antonia | Prto Prin | F | | B | | | | | | |
| José Miguel Lastre | Prto Prin | F | | B | | | | | | |
| Francisca Antonia Figararoa | Prto Prin | F | | M | | | | | | |
| Maria de la Buena Viaje | Prto Prin | F | S | B | | | R | | | |
| Francisca de las Casas | Prto Prin | F | S | B | C | | | | | |
| Maria Antonia [Antola] | Prto Prin | F | S | B | | | | | No | |
| Maria Belen | Prto Prin | F | S | B | | | | | No | |
| Tomasa | Prto Prin | F | F | B | | | | | No | Mar |
| Paula de Socarrais | Prto Prin | F | F | B | | | | | | |
| Rudesinda [de Aguero] | Prto Prin | F | F | C | | | | | | |
| Patricio | Bayamo | M | | B | | | | | | |
| Joséf Maria Matamuchos | Bayamo | M | | B | | | | | | |
| Juan Bautista Bayllant | Bayamo | M | | B | C | | U | Laborer | | Mar |
| Patricio de Bernardo de Figuerdo | Bayamo | M | S | B | | Karabali | R | | | |
| Antonio Maria Valdez | Bayamo | M | S | B | C | Mandinga | U | | | |
| Felipe Togiro | Bayamo | M | S | B | C | Kongo | U | | | |
| José Maria Aguilera | Bayamo | M | S | B | | Lucumi | R | Laborer | | |
| Manuel | Bayamo | M | S | B | | | | | | |
| José Rafel Infante | Bayamo | M | S | B | | Kongo | U | | | |
| Juan Farrio | Bayamo | M | S | B | | Kongo | | | | |
| José Ramón Borrero | Bayamo | M | S | M | | | R | Laborer | | |
| Aguilera | Bayamo | M | F | B | | Kongo | R | Laborer | | |
| Juan Bautista Valiente, el Cubano | Bayamo | M | F | B | C | Mina | U | | | |
| Antonio Tamayo | Bayamo | M | F | B | | Mandinga | | | | |
| José Maria Tamayo | Bayamo | M | F | B | | Karabali | U | Artisan | | Mar |

Slaves and Free People of Color Arrested and/or Punished for Involvement in the Aponte Rebellion of 1812 (continued)

| Name | Physical Punishment | Prison Term | Rebellion Location[a] | Sex (M/F) | Slave/Free | Race[b] | Creole/Bozal[c] | African Ethnicity | Rural/Urban | Profession | Literate (Y/N)[d] | Marital Status[e] | Militia |
|---|---|---|---|---|---|---|---|---|---|---|---|---|---|
| Blas Tamyo | | | Bayamo | M | F | B | C | Mandinga | | | | Mar | |
| Juan Tamayo, aka el Frances | | | Bayamo | M | F | B | C | | R | Laborer | | Mar | |
| José Caridad Ozorio | | | Bayamo | M | F | M | C | | | | | | |
| Caridad Fontayne | | | Bayamo | F | F | B | B | | | | | | |
| Candelaria | | | Bayamo | F | S | B | B | | U | | | | |
| Dolores | | | Bayamo | F | S | B | B | | | | | | |
| Maria Francisca Barriaga | | | Bayamo | F | S | B | B | Mina | | | | | |
| Gertrudis | | | Bayamo | F | F | B | B | | U | | | | |

Sources: Compiled from court testimony and correspondence found in ANC-AP, leg. 11, no. 37, leg. 12, nos. 9, 11, 13, 14, 16, 17, 18, 20, 21, 23, 25, 26, 27, leg. 13, nos. 1, 15, 18, 38, leg. 14, no. 1, leg. 15, no. 22; ANC-GG, leg. 545, no. 27103; AGI-PC, leg. 1548, 1640, 1649, 1778A, 1780, 1864, 1865A; AGI-UM, leg. 84: AHPC-AC, leg. 27; AHPH-TG, leg. 69, no. 2048; AMPH-Colonial, nos. 76, 191, 717–2.

ªPrto Prin = Puerto Príncipe.

ᵇB = Black; M = Mulatto; C = Chino.

ᶜCreoles are designated by "C" and include all slaves and free people of color born anywhere outside of the African continent. Bozales are designated by "B" and include all African-born slaves and free people of color.

ᵈLiteracy here is determined by whether the deponent could sign his or her own testimony.

ᵉMar = Married; Sing = Single; Cohab = Cohabitation but not married.

# Notes

The following are abbreviations of citations in the notes that include archival collections and libraries. In the cases where a particular collection or archive was only cited a few times, an abbreviation was not used. A complete list of all archival collections consulted can be found in the bibliography.

| ACH | Archivo de la Catedral de San Isidoro de Holguín |
|---|---|
| AGI | Archivo General de Indias, Seville |
| -IG | Indiferente General |
| -PC | Papeles de Cuba |
| -SD | Audiencia de Santo Domingo |
| -UM | Ultramar |
| AGS | Archivo General de Simancas |
| -GM | Guerra Moderna |
| AHMCF | Archivo Histórico del Museo Carlos J. Finlay, Havana |
| -Romay | Tomás Romay |
| AHMSC | Archivo Histórico Municipal de Santiago de Cuba |
| -AC | Actas Capitulares |
| AHN | Archivo Histórico Nacional, Madrid |
| -UM | Ultramar |
| AHPC | Archivo Histórico Provincial de Camagüey |
| -AC | Actas Capitulares |
| -AO | Alcaldía Ordinario |
| -IERH | Intendencia de Ejercito y Real Hacienda |
| -JJC | Jorge Juárez Cano |
| -Protocolos | Protocolos Notariales |
| -TG | Tenencia de Gobierno |

| | |
|---|---|
| AHPG | Archivo Histórico Provincial de Granma, Bayamo |
| -Protocolos | Protocolos Notariales |
| AHPH | Archivo Histórico Provincial de Holguín |
| -AC | Actas Capitulares |
| -Protocolos | Protocolos Notariales |
| -TG | Tenencia de Gobierno |
| AHPSC | Archivo Histórico Provincial de Santiago de Cuba |
| -GP | Gobierno Provincial |
| -JPI | Juzgado de Primera Instancia |
| -Protocolos | Protocolos Notariales |
| AMPH | Archivo del Museo Provincial de Holguín |
| -Colonial | Colección Colonial |
| ANC | Archivo Nacional de Cuba, Havana |
| -AP | Asuntos Políticos |
| -ASC | Audiencia de Santiago de Cuba |
| -ASD | Audiencia de Santo Domingo |
| -CCG | Correspondencia de los Capitanes Generales |
| -CM | Comisión Militar |
| -DR | Donativos y Remisiones |
| -EC | Escribanía de Cabello |
| -ED | Escribanía de Antonio D'aumy |
| -EG | Escribanía de Gobierno |
| -EO | Escribanía de Ortega |
| -EVal | Escribanía de Valerio |
| -EVar | Escribanía de Varios |
| -GG | Gobierno General |
| -GSC | Gobierno Superior Civil |
| -IGH | Intendencia General de Hacienda |
| -RCJF | Real Consulado y Junta de Fomento |
| AOHCH | Archivo de la Oficina del Historiador de la Ciudad, Havana |
| -AC | Actas Capitulares |
| -JLF | José Luciano Franco |
| BNJM | Biblioteca Nacional José Martí, Havana |
| -Arango | Colección Francisco Arango y Parreño |
| -Arredondo | Colección Francisco de Arredondo |
| -Morales | Colección Vidal Morales y Morales |
| -Pérez | Colección Manuel Pérez Beato |
| BNM | Biblioteca Nacional, Madrid |
| -Zaragoza | Colección de Justo Zaragoza |
| CNC | Casa de la Nacionalidad Cubana, Bayamo |
| exp. | Expediente: a file or case to indicate an archival collection |
| HL | Houghton Library, Harvard University, Cambridge Massachusetts |
| -EC | EC |
| -EC-Sup | Escoto Collection, Supplement |

ILL          Biblioteca del Instituto de Literatura y Lingüística, Havana
  -ARSEAP      Actas de la Real Sociedad Económica de Amigos del País
leg.         Legajo: a carton or book containing archival documents
PRO          Public Records Office, Kew, England
  -CO           Colonial Office
  -FO           Foreign Office
USNA         United States National Archives, Washington, D.C.
  -RG 59        Dispatches from Consuls in Cuba, Record Group 59

## INTRODUCTION

1   "Expediente sobre declarar José Antonio Aponte el sentido de las pinturas que se hayan en el Libro que se aprendió en su casa. Conspiración de José Antonio Aponte," 24 Mar. 1812, Archivo Nacional de Cuba, Havana, fondo Asuntos Políticos (ANC-AP), leg. 12, no. 17, fol. 4v.

2   Apodaca to Cano, Havana, 14 Dec. 1812, Archivo General de Indias, Seville, fondo Santo Domingo (AGI-SD), leg. 1284, no. 71, fol. 1v.

3   Sedano to Someruelos, Puerto Príncipe, 4 Feb. and 22 Mar. 1812, Archivo General de Indias, Seville, fondo Papeles de Cuba (AGI-PC), leg. 1640.

4   "Testimonio del quaderno de las confesiones que siguen adherentes al numero: 3," AGI-PC, leg. 1865A, fol. 12; Sedano to Someruelos, Puerto Príncipe, 1 Feb. 1812, AGI-PC, leg. 1640; "Sobre la Conspiración intentada por los negros esclavos para invadir la villa a resultas de la libertad que suponen estarles declaradas por las Cortes Generales y extraordinarias del Reyno de Puerto Príncipe," Jan. 1812, ANC-AP, leg. 11, no. 37, fols. 63v–65; Cabildo Minutes, Puerto Príncipe, 17 Jan.–31 Jan. 1812, Archivo Histórico Provincial de Camgüey, Actas Capitulares (AHPC-AC), leg. 27, fols. 34v–65.

5   Sedano to Someruelos, Puerto Príncipe, 1, 4 Feb. and 22 Mar. 1812, AGI-PC, leg. 1640; Cabildo Minutes, Puerto Príncipe, 17 Jan.–23 Mar. 1812, AHPC-AC, leg. 27, fols. 35–121, passim.

6   Armiñan to [?], Holguín, 17 Feb. 1812, Archivo Histórico Provincial de Holguín, Tenencia de Gobierno (AHPH-TG), leg. 69, exp. 2048.

7   ANC-AP, leg. 12, no. 9, fols. 4, 71; Corral to Urbina, Bayamo, 27 Feb. 1812, AGI-PC, leg. 1548.

8   ANC-AP, leg. 12, no. 9, fol. 14.

9   Ibid., fol. 18.

10  Corral to Someruelos, Bayamo, 16 Feb. 1812, AGI-PC, leg. 1649, no. 66.

11  ANC-AP, leg. 12, no. 9, fols. 101–3.

12  Alvarez to Corral, Bayamo, 15 Feb. 1812, ANC-AP, leg. 12, no. 9, fols. 124–25v.

13  [Armiñan?], Holguín, 14 Feb. 1812, Archivo del Museo Provincial de Holguín, fondo Colonial (AMPH-Colonial), no. 191.

14  Cabildo Minutes, Holguín, 7 Feb. 1812, Archivo Nacional de Cuba, fondo Gobierno General (ANC-GG), leg. 545, no. 27103.

15  Urbina to Governor of Holguín, Santiago, 26 Feb. 1812, AGI-PC, leg. 1548.

16  Armiñan to Urbina, Holguín, 16 Mar. 1812, AGI-PC, leg. 1548; and Armiñan to Urbina, Holguín, 15 Mar. 1812, ANC-GG, leg. 545, no. 27103.

17  Someruelos to Pezuela, Havana, 14 Feb. 1812, Archivo General de Indias, Seville, fondo Ultramar (AGI-UM), leg. 84, no. 343.

18 "Quaderno de los autos formados contra varios negros de aquella ciudad [La Habana] por insurrección," 21 July 1812, ANC-AP, leg. 13, no. 15, fol. 70.

19 ANC-AP, leg. 13, no. 1, fol. 128.

20 ANC-AP, leg. 12, no. 25, fol. 100v, and leg. 13, no. 1, fols. 13, 42v–43.

21 ANC-AP, leg. 12, no. 14, fol. 41.

22 ANC-AP, leg. 12, no. 23, fol. 3, and leg. 13, no. 1, fols. 176–77, 188–89.

23 ANC-AP, leg. 13, no. 1, fols. 103v–4.

24 ANC-AP, leg. 13, no. 15, fol. 70.

25 Hitar to [Rendón?], Havana, 20 Mar. 1812, ANC-AP, leg. 12, no. 14, fol. 33.

26 ANC-AP, leg. 12, no. 17, fols. 3–5, 7–12, 33v–35v. A more systematic search of the house itemizing everything from clothing to sculpting tools to furniture was conducted on 15 Apr. 1812. "Expediente sobre el embargo hecho a la casa de José Antonio Aponte (trunco)," ANC-AP, leg. 12, no. 26. fols. 7–14.

27 ANC-AP, leg. 12, no. 17, fol. 3v.

28 ANC-AP, leg. 12, no. 14, fol. 92, no. 17, and "Documento trunco que trata de una conspiración de negros siendo el cabecilla Juan Bautista Lisundia," 25 Mar. 1812, no. 18, fols. 25, 28. Cuban historian José Luciano Franco has reprinted some, but not all, of Aponte's explanation of the book of drawings in *La conspiración de Aponte*, 66–72, 74–97; Franco, *Las conspiraciones de 1810 y 1812*, 109–63. I would like to thank archivist Jorge Macle for locating ANC-AP, leg. 12, no. 17, which had been declared missing.

29 I have decided to refer to the "Aponte Conspiracy" as the "Aponte Rebellion" to indicate and emphasize that several revolts erupted across the island. Scholars commonly label any insurrection by slave and free people of color a "conspiracy" if authorities foiled the planned movement or somebody denounced the rebellion before it began, whereas, in general, if revolts occurred the events are usually given the title of "rebellion." By using these criteria, it would be difficult to classify the movement led by Aponte as either a conspiracy or a rebellion. In Havana and Puerto Príncipe the rebels burnt plantations and killed whites, while in Bayamo and Holguín the conspirators plotted their insurrection until authorities discovered their plans through informants. In referring to the movement as a whole, I have decided to employ the title "Aponte Rebellion" instead of "Aponte Conspiracy" to draw attention to the revolts. Moreover, contemporaries most frequently referred to the movement as a *levantamiento* (uprising), *insurrección* (insurrection), and *rebelión* (rebellion), and less frequently as a *conspiración* (conspiracy).

30 Rendón to Apodaca, Havana, 30 Nov. 1812, AGI-SD, leg. 1284, no. 71.

31 "Bando del Capitán General de la Isla," Havana, 7 Apr. 1812, ANC-AP, leg. 12, no. 24.

32 Ginzburg, *Clues, Myths, and the Historical Method*, 157.

33 ANC-AP, leg. 13, no. 1, fols. 445v–46.

34 Quoted in Fick, *Making of Haiti*, 111. Similarly, individuals brought before the Spanish Inquisition who confessed their transgressions, by pleading the devil tricked them, often received lighter punishments. See Lewis, *Hall of Mirrors*, 3.

35 Recently scholars have engaged in a heated debate over the existence of the Denmark Vesey conspiracy that rocked Charleston, South Carolina's slave society in 1822, largely because of inconclusive court records. See "Making of a Slave Conspiracy," Parts 1 and 2; Paquette and Egerton, "Of Facts and Fables," 8–48; Paquette, "From Rebellion to Revisionism," 291–334.

36 Boyer, *Lives of the Bigamists*, 10–11 (parentheses in original). My use of criminal records and other testimonial sources has greatly benefited from Calvi, *Histories of a Plague*

*Year*; Cook and Cook, *Good Faith and Truthful Ignorance*; Davis, *Return of Martin Guerre*; Davis, *Fiction in the Archives*; Ginzburg, *Cheese and the Worms*; Gutiérrez, *When Jesus Came, the Corn Mothers Went Away*; Jordan, *Tumult and Silence at Second Creek*; Le Roy Laudrie, *Montaillou*; Lockhart, *Nahuas and Spaniards*; Scott, *Domination and the Arts of Resistance*; Van Young, "Cuautla Lazarus"; Van Young, "Millenium on the Northern Marches"; Van Young, *Other Rebellion*; Lewis, *Hall of Mirrors*, 35–45; and the articles and debates cited in note 35.

37 Palmié, *Wizards and Scientists*, 82.

38 Apodaca to Aguilar, Havana, 20 Apr. 1812, Archivo Nacional de Cuba, fondo Correspondencia de los Capitanes Generales (ANC-CCG), leg. 94, no. 9; Aguilar to Someruelos, Havana, 1 Apr. 1812, ANC-CCG, leg. 94, no. 12; [Aguilar?] to Rl. Comandante del Castillo de Morro, Havana, 7 Apr. 1812, AGI-PC, leg. 1676; Comandante del Castillo de Morro to al Intendente del hospital San Ambrosio, Havana, 26 July 1812, AGI-PC, leg. 1640.

39 Sedano to Someruelos, Puerto Príncipe, 6 Mar. 1812, AGI-PC, leg. 1640, no. 139.

40 Aguilar to Someruelos, Havana, 1 Apr. 1812, ANC-CCG, leg. 94, no. 12.

41 ANC-AP, leg. 12, no. 25, fols. 83v–84.

42 Ibid., fols. 81v–82.

43 Ibid., fols. 80–80v.

44 The 1789 Real Cédula declaring free trade in slaves can be found in Archivo General de Indias, Seville, fondo Indiferente General (AGI-IG), leg. 2823.

45 García, "Importación de esclavos de ambos sexos," 471–73, table 11; Pérez de la Riva, *El Monto de la Inmigración Forzada*, table 3; Eltis, *Economic Growth*, 245.

46 Valdés, *Historia de la isla de Cuba*, 263–64.

47 Villaverde, *Cecilia Valdés*, 114.

48 Ibid., 298.

49 Zaragoza, *Las insurrecciones en Cuba*, 1:254–56.

50 Márquez, "Conspiración de Aponte," 441–54. I would like to thank Robert Paquette for providing me with a copy of this source.

51 Calcagno, *Diccionario biográfico cubano*.

52 Calcagno, *Poetas de Color*.

53 Calcagno, *Aponte*, 9.

54 My understanding of Calcagno's writing on slavery and people of African ancestry has greatly benefited from Labrador-Rodríguez, " 'El miedo al negro,' " 111–28, esp. 122.

55 Ortiz's most succinct statement on "transculturation" can be found in *Cuban Counterpoint*, 97–103.

56 Ortiz, *Los negros brujos*, 38–39; Ortiz, *Los negros esclavos*, 388.

57 Pérez, *Essays on Cuban History*, 145.

58 Kapcia, *Cuba*, 175.

59 Conversations with Daniela Barbaro and her father, who participated in these debates, provided essential information on these well-known discussion groups. Interviews by author, Havana, May 1998–July 1999.

60 Betancourt, *El Negro*, 39–42.

61 Carbonell, *Critica*, esp. 110–11.

62 De la Fuente, *Nation for All*, 4.

63 Augier, "José Antonio Aponte y la conspiración de 1812," 48–49, 64.

64 Franco, *La conspiración de Aponte*.

65 [Carta autobiográfica 1980?], Archivo de la Oficina del Historiador de la Ciudad de

la Havana, fondo José Luciano Franco (AOHCH-JLF), leg. 222, no. 9. The letter had likely been addressed to Julio Le Riverend, who wrote "Homenaje a José Luciano Franco" for the *Revista Santiago*. Le Riverend repeated many of the details in Franco's autobiographical letter.

66   See the unpublished manuscript, located with his personal papers, given the title for classification "Articulo incompleto sobre los problemas raciales," AOHCH-JLF, leg. 218, no. 18.

67   Biographical information from [Carta autobiógraphica 1980?], AOHCH-JLF, leg. 222, no. 9; Franco, "Recorrido autobiográfico"; Le Riverend "Homenaje a José Luciano Franco"; Le Riverend, "José Luciano Franco"; Barreal, "Los aportes etnológicas"; Almondovar Muñoz, "José Luciano Franco."

68   [Carta autobiógraphica 1980?], AOHCH-JLF, leg. 222, no. 9.

69   Franco, *La conspiración de Aponte*, 56.

70   Roberto Fernández Retamar to José Luciano Franco, Havana, 14 Aug. 1963, Año de Organización, AOHCH-JLF, leg. 223, no. 42.

71   Le Riverend et al., *Historia de Cuba*, 30–31.

72   Franco, *Las conspiraciones de 1810 y 1812*.

73   See for example Paquette, *Sugar is Made with Blood*, 123–25; Deschamps Chapeaux, *Los batallones de pardos y morenos libres*, 77–80; Thomas, *Cuba*, 90–91; Delgado de Torres, "Reformulating Nationalism," 27–46; Walker, *No More, No More*, 136–38. A 1952 article that predated Franco's study could be placed with the works that emphasize rebellion, but the title is misleading because it actually deals with international events in the Caribbean at the turn of the nineteenth century, and especially Haitian foreign policy. Lanier, "Cuba et la conspiration d'Apunte [sic] en 1812," 21–30.

74   See for example Kuethe, *Cuba, 1753–1815*, 171; Jensen, *Children of Colonial Despotism*, 38–39; Murray, "Slave Trade, Slavery, and Cuban Independence," 112–13.

75   García, *Conspiraciones y revueltas*, 66–74; Howard, *Changing History*, 73–80; Yacou, "La conspiración de Aponte (1812)," 39–58.

76   Fischer, *Modernity Disavowed*, 41–56.

77   Palmié, *Wizards and Scientists*, 14. For a critique of Palmié's interpretation of the Aponte Rebellion, see Childs, "Expanding Perspectives," 292–95.

78   Davis, "Impact of the French and Haitian Revolutions," 4.

79   Genovese, *From Rebellion to Revolution*.

80   Craton, *Testing the Chains*; Mullin, *Africa in America*.

81   Geggus has made a cottage industry out of examining slave and free people of color revolts during the Age of Revolution. See his following works: "Slave Resistance Studies"; "Enigma of Jamaica"; "Causation of Slave Rebellions"; "French and Haitian Revolutions"; "Slaves and Free Coloreds"; "Slavery, War, and Revolution"; "Slave Resistance in the Spanish Caribbean"; and *Haitian Revolutionary Studies*.

82   Scott, "Common Wind."

83   Paquette, "Social History Update," 683.

84   Mintz, "Slave Life," 8–28.

85   Dubois, *Colony of Citizens*, 28.

86   Harris, "Dilemmas in Teaching," 33–35. Also see similar reservations raised by Kolchin, "American Historians," 87–111, esp. 92–95; Davis, "Looking at Slavery," 452–66; Johnson, "On Agency," 113–24; and Faust, "Trainspotting." In addressing the issue of subaltern agency from a methodological and empirical level, Alan Knight argues that we "arrive at the paradox that subalterns, who are defined precisely by their subordi-

nate and disempowered status, are seen to be calling the shots. The inmates have taken over the asylum. . . . To put it simply, if we overemphasize agency, we no longer have subalterns." Knight, "Subalterns, Signifiers, and Statistics," 142.

87 Aptheker, *American Negro Slave Revolts*, 140–49; Bauer and Bauer, "Day to Day Resistance," 388–419.

88 Scott, *Weapons of the Weak*, esp. xvi. Scott's own scholarly trajectory reflects a noticeable disillusionment with politics that can be observed among other academics who began their careers in the 1960s and 1970s. In 1976, Scott initially expressed a keen interest in peasant insurrection inspired by the Vietnam Revolution; see *Moral Economy of the Peasant*. In *Weapons of the Weak*, xvi, he states that "[i]t is my guess" that the everyday forms of resistance are the most effective, and not political actions such as rebellion. His recent work focuses on the failed political efforts by the state to improve the human condition; see *Seeing like a State*.

89 Eugene Genovese's magnum opus, *Roll, Jordan, Roll*, was driven in many ways by explaining the absence of revolts in the U.S. South compared to other slave societies in the Americas. Genovese, however, deftly used the question to offer one of the most culturally sophisticated and theoretically nuanced treatments of slavery written to date.

90 Thompson, "Moral Economy," 76–136, esp. 77–78. The exact opposite of the "spasmodic" model of rebellion can be found in the work of Robert Dirks. He argues that the preponderance of slave rebellion in the British Caribbean during Christmas can be attributed not only to the ease of travel and relaxed supervision but also to a sudden improvement in diet through holiday feasts. His simplistic observation that "the effect of this nutritional boost and the availability of other fresh sources of nourishment was nothing short of explosive" detracts from an otherwise excellent study. *Black Saturnalia*, 171.

91 Darnton, "It Happened One Night," 60. See also Burke, "History of Events," for similar historiographical analysis.

92 Zanetti, "Realidades y urgencias," 123.

CHAPTER ONE

1 Juan Ruiz de Apodaca to Ignacio de la Pezuela, 19 July 1812, Havana, AGI-SD, leg. 1284, no. 21.

2 *Diario de la Habana*, 10 April 1812.

3 "Primero Incidente de los autos sobre la averiguación de los cómplices en la conspiración de los negros y comprende todo lo obrado para inquirir sí los negros que estaban depositados en Casa Blanca estaban comprendidos en aquella," 24 March 1812, ANC-AP, leg. 12, no. 16, fols. 9–13; "Autos sobre el incendio de Peñas-Altas y conspiración de José Antonio Aponte," 23 May 1812, ANC-AP, leg. 13, no. 1, fols. 116, 183. Stephan Palmié's consultation of only select printed primary sources causes him to fail to mention Barbier's time in Saint Domingue. Moreover, his revisionist interpretation results in him downplaying the revolutionary intentions of the movement and direct association or possible inspiration from Saint Domingue. For reasons that remain unclear, Palmié incorrectly spells Juan Barbier's name throughout the book as "Juán Barbier," which does not reflects orthography particular to the primary sources, the secondary sources, or early nineteenth century Spanish. *Wizards and Scientists*, 132.

4 ANC-AP, leg. 12, no. 16, fol. 18.

5   ANC-AP, leg. 13, no. 1, fol. 190.

6   ANC-AP, leg. 13, no. 1, fol. 178.

7   ANC-AP, leg. 12, no. 26, fol. 45.

8   "5a pieza contra los morenos Cristóbal de Sola, Pablo José Valdés y otros sobre sublevación," 9 March 1812, ANC-AP, leg. 12, no. 13, fols. 30, 33v; ANC-AP, leg. 13, no. 1, fol. 105.

9   "Autos criminales obrados en razón de la insurrección que contra los blancos tenían proyectada en Bayamo los negros vosales," 8 Feb. 1812, ANC-AP, leg. 12, no. 9, fol. 115v.

10  Ferrer, "Noticias de Haití en Cuba," 675–94; Childs, " 'Black French General,' " 135–56.

11  Berlin, *Many Thousands Gone*, 17–28; Bolster, *Black Jacks*, 7–43; Gilroy, *Black Atlantic*, 12–13; Thornton, *Africa and Africans*, 13–21, 33–36.

12  Scott, "Crisscrossing Empires,"128–43.

13  See for example Palmer, *Age of the Democratic Revolution*; Hobsbawm, *Age of Revolution*; Davis, *Problem of Slavery in the Age of Revolution*; Langley, *Americas*; Gaspar and Geggus, *Turbulent Time*; Van Young, "Conclusion," 219–46; Hensel, "Was There an Age of Revolution," 237–49; and several articles in the February 2000 "AHR Forum."

14  Benigno López del Real to Príncipe de la Paz, Madrid, 6 Aug. 1796, Archivo Histórico Nacional, Madrid, fondo Estado (AHN-Estado), leg. 3208, no. 351–1. The same accusations by Spain of Anglo-Saxon imperialism would be repeated one hundred years later in the War of 1898. The Spanish newspaper *El Progresso* editorialized: " 'The absorbing character of the Anglo-Saxon race, the ideals that inspire it and the aspirations that encourage it found complete expression and a definite and clear purpose in Monroe's formula.' " Quoted in Hilton, "U.S. Intervention and Monroeism," 48.

15  Quoted in Knight, "Haitian Revolution," 104.

16  John Adams to Abigail Adams, 14 April 1776, *Familiar Letters*, 155. Fellow American Abiel Abbot, who traveled to Cuba in the 1820s, made the same observation: "The war of the revolution served in some degree to lower the high standard of family discipline in our country; the French revolution gave to it a still heavier shock. The cants and rant of the day was 'Liberty and Equality'; and the thing at once penetrated the sanctuary of private life." Abbot, *Letters*, 166.

17  Pares, *War and Trade*, 563–79, 590–95; Savelle, *Empires to Nations*, 148–49; and especially Kuethe, *Cuba*, 3–23.

18  "Journal of the Siege of Havana, 1762," Public Records Office, Colonial Office, Kew, England (PRO-CO), 117/1.

19  Francisco Lópes to Julian de Arriaga, 21 April 1763, Havana, AGI-SD, leg. 2210; Saco, *Historia de la esclavitud*, 4:318; Thomas, *Cuba*, 49–50, 1532; Moreno Fraginals, *El Ingenio*, 1:35–36; Tornero Tinajero, *Crecimiento económico y transformaciones sociales*, 35; Murray, *Odious Commerce*, 4; Jennings, "State Enslavement," 177–78 n. 6. In a revisionist work Celia María Parcero Torre argues that too much credit has been given to the British occupation for reforms that Spain had already placed in motion prior to the occupation. Her overwhelming reliance on Spanish archival sources without consultation of Cuban and British sources biases her interpretation to overemphasize the active role of Spain. See *La pérdida de la Habana y las reformas borbónicas en Cuba*.

20  "Account of the Blacks and Mulattoes taken from Spaniards, now on board English ships in Havana Harbour," 16 Sept. 1762, PRO-CO, 117/2, fol. 48; for the raising of black troops from other British Caribbean islands for the attack see, Walker, "Colony versus Crown," 74–83. The British commonly awarded freedom to slaves who aided

them during times of war, and they repeated this strategy during the American Revolution under Lord Dunmore. George Washington realized that slaves fighting for their freedom in the service of the British could quickly end the Revolutionary War. He declared that Dunmore's "strength will increase like a snowball running down hill. Success will depend on which side can arm the Negroes faster." Quoted in Blackburn, *Overthrow of Colonial Slavery*, 112; for an account of slaves fighting in the American Revolution for their own freedom, see Frey, *Water from the Rock*.

21  "Los esclavos que ganaron su libertad por acciones de guerra, Aranjuez, 13 May 1763," reprinted in Marrero, *Cuba*, 9:2; "Sobre la libertad de los negros que se distinguieron durante el sitio de la Habana por los ingleses en 1762, Aranjuez, 13 May 1763," reprinted in Garrigó, *Historia documentada de la conspiración de los soles y rayos de Bolívar*, 2:6; "Account of Seamen that were killed and wounded at the Attack on Morro Castle on the 1st July 1762," PRO-CO, 117 / 2, fol. 19.

22  "José de Aponte reclamando su Libertad," 1777, ANC-Escribanía de Gobierno (ANC-EG), leg. 305, no. 11, fols. 2–3.

23  Ibid., fol. 5.

24  ANC-AP, leg. 12, no. 17, fols. 36–36v.

25  Ibid., fol. 37.

26  Ibid., fol. 47v, 50–50v.

27  Entry for "El Capitán de Granaderos Joaquín Aponte" in "Libro de servicios de los oficiales y sargentos del batallón de Morenos libres de la Havana, reglados hasta fin de diciembre de 1775," AGI-PC, leg. 1136-A.

28  Ysidro Moreno to Capitan General, Havana, 22 April 1790, AGI-PC, leg. 1433-B.

29  Kuethe, *Cuba*, xi.

30  Alejandro O'Reilly, "Descripción de la isla de Cuba, ganados, haciendas, frutos y comercio," Havana, 12 April 1764, reprinted in Marrero, *Cuba*, 8:262.

31  Murray, *Odious Commerce*, 308–9, 319; Murray, "Slave Trade," 122–23; Schmidt-Nowara, *Empire and Antislavery*, 134–35; Casanovas, *Bread, or Bullets?* 50; Corwin, *Spain and the Abolition of Slavery*, 222; Martínez Heredia, "Introducción," 17.

32  Hamnett, "Process and Pattern," 279–328; Rodríguez O., *Independence of Spanish America*, 19–35; Brading, *First America*, 467–83.

33  Kuethe, *Cuba*, ix–x; Domínguez, *Insurrection or Loyalty*, 103–6, 125–26, 142, 160–63; Johnson, *Social Transformation*, 6, 11–13, 77–81, 182.

34  The literature on the *sociedad de castas* is extensive; see for example Chance and Taylor, "Estate and Class in a Colonial City," 454–87; Chance and Taylor "Estate and Class: A Reply," 434–42; McCaa, Schwartz, and Grubessich, "Race and Class," 421–33; Anderson, "Race and Social Stratification," 209–44; Kuznesof, "Ethnic and Gender Influences," 153–76; Poot-Herrera, "Los criollos: nota sobre su identidad y cultura," 177–83; Schwartz, "Colonial Identities," 184–201; and Kuznesof, "More Conversation," 129–33. Historian William Taylor has observed that "Bourbon reformers were fond of vertical classifications and graded inequalities, but their standardizing policies . . . strengthened lateral connections and hastened the decline of vertical ones." Taylor, *Magistrates of the Sacred*, 26.

35  Kuethe, *Cuba*, 78–112.

36  ANC-AP, leg. 12, no. 17, fols. 42v–43.

37  Kuethe, *Cuba*, 117.

38  Scott, "Common Wind," 85–86; Genovese, *From Rebellion to Revolution*, 97; Trouillot,

*Silencing the Past*, 38; Garrigus, "Catalyst or Catastrophe?" 109–125. David Geggus states the "muster roll reads like a roll call for future revolutionaries." "Haitian Revolution," 25.

39  Pérotin-Dumon, "Free Colored and Slaves," 268.

40  "Consulta del Consejo de Indias sobre la instancia hecha por el negro Manuel Huevo, esclavo de V.M. solicitando su libertad," Madrid, 26 Sept. 1785, in Konetzke, *Colección de documentos*, vol. 3, tomo 2, pp. 583–85.

41  ANC-AP, leg. 12, no. 17, fol. 77.

42  Kimberly S. Hanger has emphasized that it "is important to highlight free black participation in the American Revolution, because other than the occasional mention of Crispus Attucks and a few blacks who fought in the northern Anglo colonies, little attention has been accorded the service of African Americans in this historic episode." *Bounded Lives, Bounded Places*, 119.

43  For a concise treatment of this process see Freehling, *Reintegration of American History*, 12–33.

44  Francisco Arango y Parreño, "Estado del acrecentamiento y disminución respectivos de esclavos que en los diferentes Estados de la Unión Americana hubo durante los diez años que mediaron entre los censos generales de 1790 y 1800," in Arango y Parreño, *Obras*, 2:206.

45  Stephen Fuller to Henry Dudas, London, 15 Nov. 1791, PRO-CO, 137 / 89, fol. 203v.

46  Blackburn, *Overthrow of Colonial Slavery*, 51, 74–75, 138–40, 208; Davis, *Problem of Slavery in the Age of Revolution*, 32, 46, 95, 115; Hochshild, *Bury the Chains*, 307–9.

47  Domingo de Hernándes to Antonio Valdés, Havana, 19 Dec. 1789, AGI-SD, leg. 2207.

48  "Representación manifestado las ventajas de una absoluta libertad en la introducción de negros y solicitando se amplíe a ocho años la prorroga concedida por dos años," Aranjuez, 10 May 1791, Biblioteca Nacional José Martí, Colección Francisco Arango y Parreño (BNJM-Arango), fol. 40.

49  José Sedano, "Estado que manifiesta el numero de negros bozales, importados en este puerto de Buques extrangeros y Españoles desde 1 de Enero de 1804 hasta fin de Diciembre de 1813," Havana, 16 Aug. 1814, Biblioteca Nacional José Martí, Havana, Colección Vidal Morales y Morales (BNJM-Morales), leg. 78, no. 45, fol. 603.

50  Francisco Arango y Parreño to Someruelos, Havana, 17 Oct. 1809, ANC-Gobierno Superior Civil (ANC-GSC), leg. 1021, no. 95998, fols. 2–2v.

51  Duke of Infantado to Marquis of Wellesley, London, 15 Oct. 1811, PRO-Foreign Office (PRO-FO), 72 / 119, fol. 57; James Meeks to Lord Keith, London, 25 Jan. 1812, PRO-FO, 72 / 137, fol. 199–199v; Archivo Histórico Provincial de Santiago de Cuba, fondo, Juzgado de Primera Instancia (AHPSC-JPI), leg. 376, no. 4, fols. 8, 13.

52  Conde de Santa Maria de Loreto to Someruelos, Havana, 5 July 1810, ANC-GSC, leg. 1021, exp. 95998, fols. 11–12v, Antonio del Valle Hernández to Someruelos, Havana, 5 July 1810, fol. 13; "Expediente relativo á la formación de una compañía nacional para emprender el comercio directo de esclavos de la costa de Africa," 216–31.

53  Castellanos and Castellanos, *Cultura afrocubana*, 1:25.

54  France, National Assembly, *Proceedings*, 5.

55  Ibid., 9.

56  Antillon, *Disertación sobre origen de la esclavitud de los negros*, 76–77.

57  Consulado de la Habana to Someruelos, Havana, 29 Oct. 1802, BNJM-Morales, leg. 79, no. 61, fol. 220v.

58  Arango y Parreño, "Representación hecha a su S. M con motivo de la sublevación de

esclavos en los dominios francés de la Ysla de Santo Domingo," San Lorenzo, 22 Nov. 1791, BNJM-Arango, fol. 56.

59 ANC-AP, leg. 12, no. 17, fol. 77.

60 Bolívar, "Decree," 65–66; Bolívar, "Address," in *Selected Writings*, 1:194.

61 For a discussion of the role of slavery in the wars for Spanish American independence see Blackburn, *Overthrow of Colonial Slavery*, 331–79; Rout, *African Experience*, 162–82; Lynch, *Spanish American Revolutions*, 347; Mellafe, *Negro Slavery*, 133; Mintz, "Models of Emancipation," 14–15; and Blanchard, "Language of Liberation," 499–523.

62 Rene Cordero to Someruelos, Castillo de Morro, Havana, 22 July 1802, AGI-PC, leg. 1752.

63 AHPC-AC, Jan. 1810, leg. 26, fol. 206v.

64 Cabildo Minutes, 5 Mar. 1812, Archivo de la Oficina del Historiador de la Ciudad, Havana, fondo Actas Capitulares (AOHCH-AC), leg. 83, fols. 55–55v.

65 Andrés Jáuregui to Ayuntamiento de la Havana, Cádiz, 9 July 1811, BNJM-Morales, leg. 79, no. 67, fol. 280.

66 Consulado to Lardizbal y Uribe, Havana, 16 Aug. 1814, BNJM-Morales, leg. 78, no. 45, fol. 596; Jameson, *Letters from the Havana*, 52–53; H. U. Addington to George Canning, Washington, D.C., 21 May 1825, in *Britain and the Independence of Latin America*, 2:519; Abbot, *Letters*, 131; Cornelius P. Van Ness to John Forsyth, 10 Dec. 1836, in Manning, *Diplomatic Correspondence*, 11:303; Bremmer, *Homes of the New World*, 2:437; Paquette, *Sugar Is Made with Blood*, 84, 115, 180, 211, 242; Jensen, *Children of Colonial Despotism*, 30, 38–39; Ferrer, "Social Aspects of Cuban Nationalism," 43; Ferrer, *Insurgent Cuba*, 2, 48; Helg, *Our Rightful Share*, 17, 78–80; Knight, "Haitian Revolution," 114; Oquendo, "Las rebeldías de los esclavos en Cuba," 53. Fidel Castro remarked "esta clase social, aunque interesada en superar las trabas coloniales que estorban el desarrollo de la economía y su acceso al poder político, no podía prescindir de la fuerza militar de la metrópoli para mantener Cuba de la heroica historia de Haití y supeditaba, sin vacilación, la cuestión de la independencia nacional a su interese de clase esclavista." Castro, *Informe central del primero congreso del Partido Comunista de Cuba*, 7.

67 Thornton, *Kingdom of Congo*; Thornton, *Africa and Africans*, 304–17; Lovejoy, *Transformations in Slavery*, 46, 66–67, 74; Klein, *Atlantic Slave Trade*, 117–18.

68 Law, *Oyo Empire*, 217–28, 245–99; Eltis, *Economic Growth*, 169; Lovejoy, "Yoruba Factor," 40–55.

69 Ajayi Crowther, "Narrative of Samuel Ajayi Crowther," in Curtin, *Africa Remembered*, 301.

70 Thornton, "African Dimensions," 1108–13; Thornton, "African Soldiers," 50–80; Lovejoy, "Background to Rebellion," 151–80.

71 Eltis, *Rise of African Slavery*, 253. Various scholars have remarked on the impact of Yoruban culture in Cuba; see for example Ortiz, *Los Negros Esclavos*, 50; Castellanos, *Cultura Afrocubana*, 1:35; and Howard, *Changing History*, 22, 24, 57, 60, 63.

72 Consulado to Miguel de Lardizbal y Uribe, 16 Aug. 1814, Havana, BNJM-Morales, leg. 78, no. 45, fol. 578v–79 [emphasis in original].

73 "Papel sobre los negros esclavos por un religioso de la isla de Cuba con ocasión de los urgentes debates habidos públicamente en ocasión de los cortes extraordinarias españolas de 2 de Abril de 1811," BNJM-Morales, leg. 79, no. 107, fols. 384.

74 Seed, *Ceremonies of Possession*, 180–84; Pagden, *Lords of All the World*, 11–28.

75 "Informe del Sor. Zavedra sobre esclavos," 1792, BNJM-Morales, leg. 80, no. 12, fol. 157.

76 Ibid., fol. 160.

77 Ibid., fol. 163.

78 Juan Baptista Valiente to Diego de Gardogui, 7 Feb. 1792, Santiago de Cuba, AGI-IG, leg. 2822.

79 "Copia de las noticias sobre el estado de su jurisdicción [Bayamo] por un anomino en 1795," BNJM-Morales, leg. 80, no. 21, fol. 357.

80 Joseph Coppingeros to Someruelos, 30 May 1802, Bayamo, AGI-PC, leg. 1649, no. 111; "Expediente instruido por el consulado de la Habana, sobre los medios que convenga proponer para sacar la agricultura y comercio de esta Isla," Havana, 1808, AGI-SD, leg. 1157.

81 Juan Batista Valiente to Consejo de Indias, 13 July 1794, Havana, AGI-SD, leg. 2236. The discursive link between Cuban slavery, sugar, and blood would be repeated throughout the nineteenth century; see Paquette, *Sugar Is Made with Blood*, 56.

82 Arango ". . . sublevación de esclavos en los dominios francés," BNJM-Arango, fol. 60.

83 Arango, "Discurso sobre la agricultura de la Havana y medio de fomentarla," 24 Jan. 1792, in Arango, *Obras*, 1:122; Oquendo "las rebeldías de los esclavos," 52.

84 Tomas Romay, "Discurso sobre los obstáculos que han impedido progresen la colmenas en la Isla de Cuba y los médicos de Fomentarlas," 1796, Havana, Archivo Histórico del Museo Carlos J. Finlay, Havana, fondo Tomas Romay (AHMCF-Romay), MS C-2390.

85 Joaquin Obispo de Cuba, 30 Nov. 1794, Havana, AGI-SD, leg. 2236.

86 See for example Genovese's classic treatment on the subject, *Roll, Jordan, Roll*, 49–70.

87 "Real cédula de su magestad sobre la educación, trato y occupaciones de los esclavos, en todos sus dominios de indias, e islas filipinas baxo las reglas que expresan," Aranjuez, 31 May 1789, BNJM-Morales, leg. 79, no. 3. The 1789 Código Negro can also be found in ANC-Real Consulado y Junta de Fomento (RCJF), leg. 150, exp. 7405, fols. 1–9; "Real Cédula de su magestad sobre la educación, trato y ocupaciones de los esclavos"; Ortiz, *Los negros esclavos*, 408–15; Lucena Salmoral, *Los códigos negros de la América Española*, 95–124, 279–284; Barcia Paz, *Con el látigo de la ira*, 85–94.

88 The clearest refutation of the legislation in shaping slave life can be found in Knight, *Slave Society*, 36; and Hall, *Social Control*, 111–12, which address the optimistic conclusions of Tannenbaum, *Slave and Citizen*; Elkins, *Slavery*, 63–80; and Klein, *Slavery in the Americas*, 77–85.

89 For a notable, albeit brief exception, see de la Torre, "Posiciones y actitudes en torno a la esclavitud en Cuba," 74.

90 "Representación le extendió D. Diego Miguel de Moya y que se elevó al Rey, firmado por casi todos los amos de Ingenios de esta Jurisdicción," Havana, 19 Jan. 1790, ANC-RCJF, leg. 150, exp. 7405, fol. 10. For a transcription of the document, see García *La esclavitud desde la esclavitud*, 62–79.

91 "Informe del Sor. Zavedra sobre esclavos," 1792, BNJM-Morales, leg. 80, no. 12, fol. 174.

92 Ibid., fol. 155.

93 BNJM-Morales, leg. 79, no. 3., fol. 8.

94 Joaquin Obispo de Cuba, Havana, 30 Nov. 1794, AGI-SD, leg. 2236.

95 ANC-RCJF, leg. 150, exp. 7405, fols. 18v–19. Future events in Brazil and Cuba in the 1870s and 1880s as the state began to limit punishments during the last years of slavery would verify masters' fears; see for example, Scott, *Slave Emancipation in Cuba*, 178–84; and Dean, *Rio Claro*, 126–34.

96 Contemporary Jamaican planter and politician Bryan Edwards protested any attempts that would undermine the coercive authority necessary for slavery: "'In countries where slavery is established, the leading principle on which the government is supported is fear: or a sense of that absolute coercive necessity which, leaving no choice of action, supersedes all questions of right. It is vain to deny that such actually is, and necessarily must be, the case in all countries where slavery is allowed.'" Quoted in Dayan, *Haiti, History, and the Gods*, 207.

97 BNJM-Morales, leg 79, no. 3, fol. 6v.

98 ANC-RCJF, leg. 150, exp. 7405, fol. 13v.

99 "Informe del Sor. Zavedra sobre esclavos," 1792, BNJM-Morales, leg. 80, no. 12, fol. 177.

100 Arango, "Representación hecha a su S. M con motivo de la sublevación de esclavos...," BNJM-Arango, fols. 57–58.

101 Consulado de la Habana to Someruelos, Havana, 29 Oct. 1802, BNJM-Morales, leg. 79, no. 61, fol. 221.

102 Hall, *Social Control*, 81–112.

103 Ignacio Maria de Alava to Consulado, Havana, 17 July 1811, ANC-RCJF, leg. 150, exp. 7409, fols. 3–3v.

104 Tomas Romay to Consulado, Havana, 12 July 1811, ANC-RCJF, leg. 150, exp. 7409, fol. 6. Part of Romay's report to the Havana Conuslado is reprinted in Romay, *Obras Completas*, 1:245–48.

105 Eltis, *Rise of African Slavery*, 232.

106 Tomas Romay to Consulado, Havana, 12 July 1811, ANC-RCJF, leg. 150, exp. 7409, fol. 6v.

107 Conde de Santo Maria de Loreto to Someruelos, Havana, 5 July 1810, ANC-GSC, leg. 1021, exp. 95998, fol. 12; Mathias de la Cantura to Consulado, Havana, 10 Jan. 1815, ANC-RCJF, leg. 150, exp. 7409, fol. 24.

108 "Agregada a la Rl. Cédula reservada," 22 Apr. 1804, ANC-RCJF, leg. 150, exp. 7405, fol. 47–47v.

109 Cabildo Minutes of Havana, 15 Sept. 1809, AOHCH-AC, leg. 77, fol. 658.

110 "Instrucciones que ha dexado un mayoral de azucarera a sus herederos"; "Premio de dos mil pesos al que componga el mejor estado sobre el gobierno económico de los ingenios de azúcar en la isla de Cuba," 1799, BNJM-Morales, leg. 79, no. 6, fol. 23v.

111 Moreno Fraginals identifies this uncertainty as a "crisis in the superstructure." *El Ingenio*, 1:105–33.

112 Francisco Sánchez to Juan Baptista Valliant, Bayamo, 3 Jan. 1795, ANC-GG, leg. 540, no. 27096; Franco, *Ensayos históricos*, 95.

113 Francisco Sánchez to Juan Baptista Valliant, Bayamo, 16 May 1795, ANC-GG, leg. 540, no. 27096; Cabildo Minutes, Puerto Príncipe, 18 Aug. 1808, AHPC-AC, leg. 25, fol. 6v.

114 Stephen Fuller to Henry Dudas, Southampton, 30 Oct. 1791, PRO-CO, 137/89, fol. 196 [emphasis in original].

115 Someruelos to [?], Havana, 27 Jan. 1800, AHN-Estado, leg. 6366, caja 1, exp. 2; "Circular Prohibiendo desembarquen en esta isla, los negros insurrectos de la Guadalupe," Havana, 13 Sept. 1802, 356–58; Coppingeros to Someruelos, 10 Apr. 1801, Bayamo, AGI-PC, leg. 1649, no. 70.

116 AHPC-AC, 30 March 1796, leg. 23, fol. 22.

117 Humboldt, *Ensayo político sobre la isla de Cuba*, 211.

118 Someruelos to [?], Havana, 27 Jan. 1800, AHN-Estado, leg. 6366, caja 1, exp. 2.

119 "Bando del General Salvador José de Muro y Salazar, Marques de Someruelos, Gobernador y Capitán General de la Isla, sobre que ninguna persona nacional o extranjera
se embarque sin pasaporte del gobierno . . . ," Havana, 18 Feb. 1803, 398–99.

120 Someruelos to [?], Havana, 27 Jan. 1800, AHN-Estado, leg. 6366, caja 1, exp. 2.

121 See Geggus, *Impact of the Haitian Revolution*, esp. chaps. 13, 14, and 15.

122 AHPSC-JPI, leg. 376, no. 2, fol. 2; AHPSC-Protocolos, leg. 241, fols. 49v, 108, leg. 242,
fol. 86, leg. 357, fol. 331v, leg. 358, fol. 92v; AHPH-Protocolos, Escribano Rodríguez,
año 1810, fol. 66v, Escribano Fuentes, año 1809, fol. 40, año 1810, fol. 20v; AHPC-
Protocolos, Escribano Mora, año 1810, fol. 171v; Murrilo to Someruelos, Baracoa, 2
July 1804, and Murrilo to Someruelos, Havana, 22 Aug. 1806, AGI-PC, leg. 1785; Suares
de Urbina to Apodaca, Santiago, 15 June 1812, AGI-PC, 1702; "Noticia de los francés
existentes en el Barrio de Guadalupe," 1809, AGI-SD, 1284, no. 330; Someruelos to
Ignacio de la Pezuela, Havana, 8 Jan. 1812, AGI-SD, 1284; "Expediente de al Escribanía
de Real Hacienda de Matanzas por el remate de los barracones para las familias
emigradas de Santo Domingo," Matanzas, 2 July 1797, Houghton Library, Harvard
University, Escoto Collection (HL-EC), box 7, no. 8; "Documentos sobre la evacuación de la Isla de Santo Domingo."

123 For French émigrés in Cuba, see Lux, "French Colonization in Cuba," 57–61; Yacou,
"Esclaves et libres français a Cuba," 163–98; Yacou, "La présence française dans
la parte occidentale," 149–88; Debien, "Les colons de Saint-Domingue réfugiés à
Cuba"; Childs, " 'Black French General,' " 138–39.

124 Arango, "Representación hecha a su S. M. con motivo de la sublevación de esclavos . . . ," BNJM-Arango, fol. 60; AHPC-AC, 24 Jan. 1812, no. 27, fol. 55v.

125 Murrilo to Someruelos, Baracoa, 2 July 1804, AGI-PC, leg. 1648.

126 Entry for 20 Mar. 1804, in Nugent, *Lady Nugent's Journal*, 199.

127 Someruelos to [?], Havana, 31 Jan. 1804, AHN-Estado leg. 6366, caja 1, exp. 4; Juan de
Dios Zayas, "Resumen general de los moradores franceses que comprehende la
ciudad de Cuba," Santiago de Cuba, 27 July 1808, ANC-AP, leg. 142, no. 86. Nearly
thirty years ago Bohumil Badura corrected, with archival sources, the often repeated
incorrect estimate of 30,000 French refugees in Santiago by Ramiro Guerra that
continues to be cited. "Los Franceses en Santiago de Cuba," 157–60.

128 Adam Williamson to Duke of Portland, King's House, Jamaica, 5 March 1795, no. 2,
PRO-CO, 137 / 94, fols. 103–4.

129 AHPH-Tenencia de Gobierno (TG), leg. 68, no. 2007; AMPH-Colonial, no. 103;
AHPC-AC, 15 April 1809, no. 25, fols. 190–90v, 3 Jan. 1810, leg., 26, fol. 155; *Calendario
manual y guía de forasteros de la isla de Cuba*, 113; Lachance, "Repercussion of the
Haitian Revolution," 213–14.

130 AHPSC-JPI, leg. 375, no. 4; AMPH-Colonial, no. 649.

131 Arambarri to Someruelos, Guarico [Le Cap François], 19 Feb. 1800, AHN-Estado, leg.
6366, caja 1, exp. 3, no. 3.

132 Someruelos to Arambarri, Havana, 28 Feb. 1800, AHN-Estado, leg. 6366, caja 1, exp. 3,
no. 3.

133 Someruelos to [?], Havana, 12 Aug. 1800, AHN-Estado, leg. 6366, caja 1, exp. 16, no. 2.

134 For an account of the conflict between Rigaud and Louverture, see Dubois, *Avengers
of the New World*, 231–36.

135 Linebaugh and Rediker, *Many-Headed Hydra*, 177; Egerton, *He Shall Go Out Free*, 224.

136 "Branches under the Charge of the Royal Officers of Havana, 1762," PRO-CO, 117 / 1,
fols. 262–65.

137  BNJM-Arango, "Papel sobre el comercio de negros," Madrid, 29 Dec. 1811, fol. 4.

138  Tomás de Acosta to Governor of Jamaica, Jan. 1812, Santa Marta, and Edward Morrison to the Earl of Liverpool, King's House, Jamaica, 21 Feb. 1812, PRO-CO, 137/134, fols. 26–27, 91.

139  Le General Ferrand to Mon. Someruelos, 22 July 1807, AGI-PC, leg. 1648.

140  Francisco Arango to Rochambeau, Abordo del Bergantin de Guerra Español, 10 April 1803, HL-EC, box 9, no. 5.

141  Duke of Infantado to Marquis of Wellesley, London, 15 Oct. 1811, PRO-FO, 72/119, fol. 27, Marquis of Wellesley to Duke del Infantado, 25 Feb., 1812, Draft, 72/134, fol. 99.

142  Humboldt, Ensayo Político, 211 n. 2.

143  Dallas, History of the Maroons, 2:35.

144  Earl of Balcarres to the Duke of Portland, Near Maroon Town, Jamaica, 29 Dec. 1795, no. 3, PRO-CO, 137/96, fol. 58–58v.

145  Dayan, Haiti, History, and the Gods, 152, 155.

146  Oquendo, "Las rebeldías de los esclavos," 55; Ortiz, Los negros brujos, 37.

147  Louis A. Pérez's observation on the interdependence between Cuba and the United States could apply equally to the European powers of the Caribbean who defended each other's slave institutions. According to Pérez, "Cubans and North Americans discovered early that colonists even of rival empires often had more in common with one another than they did with the authorities that governed them. They developed needs that each was uniquely qualified to meet, or perhaps it was the other way around: they developed those needs precisely because they could be so well met by the other. Proximity and accessibility promoted affinity, which joined them in a relationship that was simultaneously reciprocal and inexorable. Geography made these connections possible and convenient circumstances made them practical and necessary." On Becoming Cuban, 17.

148  "Testimonio de las diligencias obradas sobre la profugación de los seis negros venidos de esta Ciudad de la Colonia Bretanica en solicitud de la Cristiandad como de ellos mas bien consta," 1789, in PRO-CO, 137/89, fol. 59v.

149  Thornton, "African Dimensions," 1102, 1105; Smith, "Remembering Mary," 513–34.

150  Consulta del Consejo de Indias, 5 Aug. 1789, Madrid, AGI-SD, leg. 1142; Landers, Black Society in Spanish Florida, 24–28, 76–79, 87; Marrero, Cuba, 9:21–22.

151  PRO-CO, 137/89, fol. 60.

152  Alfred Clarke to Lord Lyndsey, 30 May 1789, Jamaica, PRO-CO, 137/88, no. 104, fol. 13.

153  "Testimonio de las diligencias obradas sobre la profugación de los seis negros venidos de esta Ciudad de la Colonia Bretanica en solicitud de la Cristiandad como de ellos mas bien consta," 1789, PRO-CO, 137/89, fols. 55v–56v.

154  Alfred Clarke to José de Ezpuleta [sic], 9 March 1789, Jamaica, PRO-CO, 137/88, fols. 23–24

155  José de Espeleta to Governor Clarke, 25 March 1789, Havana, PRO-CO, 137/88, fol. 25.

156  Mellet, Viajes por el interior de la América meridional, 386; also see Christelow, "Contraband Trade."

157  ANC-AP, leg. 12, no. 9, fol. 54.

158  Scott, "Common Wind," 92, 95–103. The flow of English slaves seeking refuge in Cuba would later be reversed when the English Caribbean began its gradual transition to free labor. In 1831, Francisco Monitt, a slave cook belonging to Don Manuel Monitt, escaped from a Spanish schooner anchored in Nassau Harbor in the Bahamas. British officials, perhaps remembering the hundreds of slaves who sought refuge

in Spanish Catholic lands, declared Francisco Monitt a "free man" and refused to turn him over to the Cuban merchant despite repeated requests; see Johnson, *Race Relations in the Bahamas*, 160–61.

159 Francisco Sánchez to Juan Baptista Valliant, 18 May 1795, Bayamo, ANC-GG, leg. 540, no. 27096.

160 Felix Corral to Sebastián Kindleman, 30 April 1810, Bayamo, ANC-AP, leg. 212, no. 26, 179.

161 Vice Admiral Mosley to Governor of Bayamo, 24 July 1810, Port Royal, Jamaica, ANC-AP, leg. 212, no. 26.

162 Joseph Ignacio Nuñez to Kindleman, 29 March 1809, Santiago de Cuba, ANC-CCG, leg. 82, no. 7; Someruelos to Gobernador de Cuba, 9 Feb. 1811, Havana, ANC-AP, leg. 212, no. 174.

163 Kuethe, *Cuba*, 139–46.

164 ANC-AP, leg. 12, no. 9, fols. 52, 54, 65, 68v.

165 Ibid., fols. 88v–89v.

166 Felix del Corral to Someruelos, 18 March 1812, Bayamo, AOHCH-AC, leg. 84, fol. 269.

167 Franklin Knight observed the same problem: "Here was a society which had a very long tradition of slavery, among the oldest in the Americas. Yet it was only when most other societies were turning away from slavery as an economic system and a form of labor organization that the Cubans became involved in the agricultural revolution that had entered the Caribbean Sea in the early seventeenth century." *Slave Society*, xvi.

168 Cabildo Minutes, Puerto Príncipe, 18 June 1811, AHPC-AC, leg. 26, fol. 314v.


CHAPTER TWO

1 ANC-AP, leg. 13, no. 1, fols. 192–94.

2 Ibid., fols. 195–96.

3 Fick, *Making of Haiti*, 171.

4 Gómez de Avellaneda y Arteaga, *Sab and Autobiography*, 47, 68.

5 Martín Aróstegui to Someruelos, Ingenio Soledad, 4 Apr. 1812, in "Criminales contra José de la Cruz y Narciso Tabuada negros esclavos del L. D. Nicolas Tabuada sobre sospechas de complicidad en la Conspiración de José Antonio Aponte," 5 Apr. 1812, ANC-AP, leg, 12, no. 23, fol. 3.

6 Rendón to Apodaca, La Cabaña, 16 Apr. 1812, in "8a pieza de la 2a Conspiración de José Ant° Aponte," 15 Apr. 1812, ANC-AP, leg. 12, no. 25, fol. 5v.

7 ANC-AP, leg, 13, no. 1, fol. 190; Rendón to Apodaca, Havana, 12 June 1812, AGI-SD, leg. 1284, no. 21.

8 "Quaderno de los autos formados contra varios negros de aquella ciudad por insurrección," 21 July 1812, ANC-AP, leg. 13, no. 15, fol. 6v.

9 "Expediente formado para tratar sobre el cobro de las costas causadas en los autos que contra José Antonio Aponte y otros por la conspiración que tramaban," 10 Nov. 1812, ANC-AP, leg. 13, no. 38, fol. 6v.

10 ANC-AP, leg. 13, no. 1, fols. 328v–29v; *Diario de la Habana*, 22 Oct. 1812.

11 For the *asiento* see Aimes, *History of Slavery in Cuba*, 7–24, 30–31, 46–49; Murray, *Odious Commerce*, 2–11; Franco, *Comercio clandestino de esclavos*, 2–13; Palmer, *Human Cargoes*, 59–82; Tornero Tinajero, *Crecimiento económico y transformaciones sociales*, 34–44; "De la Esclavitud a la Negritud: Documentos," insert, p. 1.

12 Pierson, "Institutional History of the Intendencia," 74–133; Kuethe, *Cuba*, 70–71, 94; Torres-Cuevas, "De la ilustración reformista al reformismo liberal," 315–19; Góngora, *Studies*, 168, 173–75.

13 The 1789 Real Cédula declaring free trade in slaves can be found in AGI-IG, leg. 2823.

14 Johnson, "Rise and Fall of Creole Participation," 52–75.

15 Arango y Parreño, "Representación manifestado las ventajas de una absoluta libertad en la introducción de negros y solicitando se amplíe a ocho la prórroga concedida por dos años," in his *Obras*, 1:98.

16 Las Casas to Pedro Herrera, Havana, 2 May 1791, AGI-IG, leg. 2822; "Comunicaciones, oficios, etc. del superintendente de la Isla, al intendente de ejercito y Rl. Hacienda de la provincia para que este envié a las subdelegaciones con puertos Rl. cédula de 20 de Abril de 1804, donde se manda ampliar el comercio de Negros Bozales," Archivo Histórico Provincial de Camagüey, fondo Intendencia de Ejercito y Real Hacienda de la Provincia de Puerto Príncipe (AHPC-IERH), leg. 1, no. 5, fols. 1–5; BNJM-Morales, tomo 79, no. 181; Murray, *Odious Commerce*, 11–13.

17 The original customs house returns can be found in AGI-SD, leg. 2207. For a discussion of Humboldt's figures see Klein, *Middle Passage*, 212; Eltis, "Nineteenth-Century Transatlantic Slave Trade," 120–21; Murray, *Odious Commerce*, 18–19; García, "Importación de esclavos de ambos sexos por varios puertos de Cuba," 471–73, table 11; Pérez de la Riva, *El Monto de la Inmigración Forzada en el siglo xix*, table 3; Eltis, *Economic Growth*, 245.

18 Thomas, "Narrative of William Thomas," 22–23.

19 Ibid.

20 Ibid.

21 As Herbert S. Klein has noted regarding the Atlantic slave trade, "There are few recorded experiences of the slave trade itself." *Atlantic Slave Trade*, 221.

22 Dorsey, *Slave Traffic*, chaps. 4 and 5.

23 Cabellos to Antonio Valdéz, Havana, 3 Feb. 1791, AGI-IG, leg. 2822; Coppingeros to Someruelos, Bayamo, 10 Apr. 1801, AGI-PC, leg. 1649, no. 70; Someruelos, 31 Jan. 1804, Havana, AHN-Estado, leg. 6366, caja 1, exp. 66, no. 1; Joseph Murrillo to Someruelos, Baracoa, 2 July 1804, AGI-PC, leg. 1648; Mellet, *Viajes por el interior de la América meridional*, 401.

24 Ruíz de Azúa to Apodaca, Havana, 24 Mar. 1814, ANC-RCJF, leg. 150, exp. 7409.

25 "Real Orden aboliendo la practica de marcar a los negros esclavos en el rostro o espalda," San Lorenzo, 4 Nov. 1784, AGI-IG, leg. 2822.

26 Apodaca to Figueroa, Havana, 17 Nov. 1812, Habana, AGI-SD, leg. 1284, no. 62.

27 Someruelos, "Reglamento para el enterramiento a los cadáveres de los infieles," 9 Aug. 1809, San Lázaro, Havana, AGI-PC, leg. 1680.

28 *Barracones* is a term with distinct meanings in Cuban slave society depending on geographic location. In urban centers, *barracones* indicated the housing-pens for recently arrived Africans where they would be fed, cleaned, and inspected before being sold. On plantations, *barracones* represented the slave quarters. See Pérez de la Riva, *El Barracón*, 21; Johnson, "Rise and Fall of Creole Participation," 60–61.

29 José Aguilar to Someruelos, San Lázaro, Havana, 2 Oct. 1802, AGI-PC, leg. 1691; José Agustín Jurco to Someruelos, 17 May 1808, San Lázaro, Havana, AGI-PC, leg. 1680.

30 "Depositions of the Cuban Slaves: Lorenzo Clarke," 234.

31 "Depositions of the Cuban Slaves: Miguel Marino," 235.

32 Lovejoy, "Identifying Enslaved Africans," 2

33 Tomás Romay, "Memoria sobre la introducción y progresos de la vacuna en la isla de Cuba, leída en juntas generales celebradas por la Sociedad Económica de la Havana el 12 de Diciembre de 1804," (Havana: Imprenta de la Capitanía General, 1805), AHMCF-Romay, MS C-739.

34 Someruelos to Gobernador de Cuba, Havana, 15 July 1808, no. 29, ANC-AP, leg. 213, no. 108.

35 Cabildo Minutes, Havana, 22 May 1812, AOHCH-AC, leg. 83, fol. 121v.

36 De Madrid, "Memoria sobre la disentería en general, y en particular sobre la disentería de los barracones," published by Biblioteca del Instituto de Literatura y Lingüística, Havana, Actas de la Real Sociedad Económica de Amigos del País, 1817.

37 ANC-AP, leg. 12, no. 17, fol. 28.

38 For a discussion of the interpretations of the 1792 and 1817 censuses, including summary tables and figures by other scholars, see Kiple, *Blacks in Colonial Cuba*, 28–30, 34–38.

39 De la Sagra, *Historia económico*, 3–10.

40 "Cálculos de aproximación sobre la población de la Habana y su jurisdicción," 1799, BNJM-Morales, 79, no. 4. fol. 16.

41 Calculated from de la Sagra, *Historia económico*, 3–10.

42 Francisco Barrera y Domingo, "Reflexiones histórico fisco naturales medico quirúrgicas . . ." Havana, 23 July 1798, Biblioteca Nacional José Martí, Colección Manuel Pérez Beato (BNJM-Pérez), no. 801, fol. 27. An incomplete transcription of the manuscript was published as *Reflexiones*.

43 See for example the numerous census tables and scattered manuscript census returns in AGI-PC, leg. 1680 and 1689.

44 "Cálcuclos de aproximación sobre la población de la Havana y su jurisdicción," 1799, BNJM-Morales, 79, no. 4. fol. 17.

45 Humboldt, *Ensayo politico*, 69.

46 This problem would continue throughout nineteenth-century Cuban history and reach a peak during the debates over censuses in the 1840s; see Paquette, *Sugar Is Made with Blood*, 298 n. 43. For the politics of the United States census, see Anderson and Fienberg, *Who Counts?* esp. 2–3, 214–24.

47 "Holguín, padrón de 1775," Antonio Luque, Holguín, 4 May 1775, ANC-GG, leg. 490, no. 25132; "Holguín, padrón de 1803," Felix Corral, Holguín, 3 Jan. 1803, ANC-CCG, leg. 471, no. 3. I would like to thanks José Novoa for directing me to these sources.

48 Kuethe, *Cuba*, 41. Bruce A. Castleman has labeled a similar process of fluctuating racial categories for late eighteenth-century Mexico as "racial drift." See Castleman, "Social Climbers," 229–49.

49 "Quaderno Sobre la denuncia que hiso la Negra María Antonia Antola contra El Negro José Wilson esclabo de Rafael Wilson," Feb. 1812, AGI-PC, leg. 1865-A, fol. 4v.

50 ANC-AP, leg. 12, no. 13, fol. 21.

51 Ibid., no. 21, fol. 16.

52 Joaquin Obispo de Cuba, Havana, 30 Nov. 1794, AGI-SD, leg. 2236. Unfortunately, these stereotypes continue to be evoked today. Historian Hugh Thomas is only the most recent scholar to repeat racial stereotypes that Europeans used to justify not performing manual labor in tropical climates. According to Thomas: "The reason why the Atlantic slave trade lasted so long is that, in the Americas, the Africans proved to be admirable workers, strong enough to survive the heat and hard work on sugar, coffee, or cotton plantations or in mines, in building fortresses or merely

acting as servants; and, at the same time, they were good-natured and easily docile. . . . Both indigenous Indians and Europeans seemed feeble compared with them." *Slave Trade*, 792.

53 "Copia de un oficio de D. Luis de Las Casas al Sor Gov. del Consulado de Indias," BNJM-Morales, leg. 79, no. 13, fol. 38v. Canary Islanders throughout the Spanish Empire were often assumed to be "black" because of their racial complexion. In 1620, Thomas de Rizo from the Canary Islands complained of his arrest in Mexico for carrying a weapon because of the presumption that he was black. He stated in his petition for the right to carry a weapon that " '[a]ll Spaniards born in that land are dark. . . . Coming to these lands and others they are not taken to be Spaniards because they do not know the Canary Islands and their people.' " Quoted in Lewis, *Hall of Mirrors*, 77–78.

54 Avellaneda, *Sab and Autobiography*, 73.

55 Felix del Corral to Someruelos, Bayamo, 2 Dec. 1808, AGI-PC, leg. 1649, no. 66.

56 Jurrco to Someruelos, Jesús del Monte, Havana, 12 Sept. 1809, AGI-PC, leg. 1680.

57 Apodaca to José de Limonata, Havana, 4 April, 1814, AGI-UM, leg. 85, no. 287.

58 Alexander, *Transatlantic Sketches*, 201.

59 Childs, " 'Sewing' Civilization," 83–107.

60 "Acuerdo de la junta consular de 1° de Agosto de 1798 en que ofrecieron D. Nicolás Calvo y D. Francisco de Arango contribuir al establecimiento de una escuela gratuita de primeras letras en el pueblo de Guines," Havana, 21 Apr. 1799, BNJM-Morales, leg. 79, no. 9, fol. 29.

61 See Abbot, *Letters*, 55; Bremmer, *Homes of the New World*, 2:401–2; Jameson, *Letters from the Havana*, 44–46; Mellet, *Viajes por el interior de la América meridional*, 383–84; Villaverde, *Cecila Valdés*, 90; Thompson, "Narrative of James Thompson," 71; Castañeda, "Female Slave in Cuba," 145–46; and Paquette, *Sugar Is Made with Blood*, 71.

62 BNJM-Pérez, leg. 801, tomo 2, fol. 145.

63 ANC-RCJF, leg. 150, no. 7405, fol. 12.

64 See the poignant comments by David Eltis on the fallacy of economic rationality in shaping the slave trade, "Atlantic History in Global Perspective," 141–61, esp. 156.

65 Abbot, *Letters*, 55.

66 Mellet, *Viajes por el interior de la América meridional*, 383–84.

67 "Diligencia promovidas por el sindico procurador general contra Luis Gerbet, por el castigo que dio a su esclava Luisa Montaño," 1811, Archivo Nacional de Cuba, fondo Audiencia de Santiago de Cuba (ANC-ASC), leg. 606, no. 13897, fols. 2v–5v.

68 Juan Ruíz de Apodaca to Antonio Cano Manuel, Havana, 12 Nov. 1812, AGI-SD, leg. 1284.

69 Somereulos to Havana Ayuntamiento, Havana, 21 Apr. 1809, AOHCH-AC, leg. 76, fol. 209.

70 Somereulos to Havana Ayuntamiento, Havana, 4 Aug. 1809, AOHCH-AC, leg. 77, fol. 597.

71 José María Escobar and José María Jiménez to Havana Ayuntamiento, Havana, 15 Sept. 1809, AOHCH-AC, leg. 77, fols. 661–64. Someruelos apparently had no knowledge of or simply ignored the Spanish crown's ruling in 1794 that the Council of the Indies would not publish or enforce the rules of the *Código Negro*. See "Consulta del Consejo de las Indias sobre el reglamento expedido en 31 de Mayo de 1789 para la mejor educación, buen trato y ocupación de los negros esclavos de América."

72 Pedro López de la Vega to Someruelos, Jesús Monte, 3 Mar. 1809, AGI-PC, leg. 1680.

73  See for example Francisco Jurco to Someruelos, Jesús Monte, 10 Nov. 1809, and 24 Oct. 1811, AGI-PC, leg. 1680.

74  Torres to Aguilar, Havana, 3 Jan. 1812, ANC-CCG, leg. 93, no. 12; Jurrco to Someruelos, Jesús Monte, 6 May 1808, Antonio de Arcilas to Someruelos, 7 Nov. 1810, Horcón, Havana, AGI-PC, leg. 1680; "Diario de la Rl. Audiencia de la Ysla de Cuba de los procesos criminales despachados en el primer semestre del año de 1812," AGI-UM, leg. 96, fol. 19; Abbot, *Letters*, 44; Bremmer, *Homes of the New World*, 2:332, 437.

75  Ortiz, *Cuban Counterpoint*, 86.

76  Paquette, *Sugar Is Made with Blood*, 71–72; Knight, *Slave Society*, 78; Hall *Social Control*, 20–23, 49–50. Pérez, *To Die in Cuba*, chap. 1.

77  Humboldt, *Ensayo político*, 109–10.

78  Apodaca to Lardizabal y Uribe, 3 Oct. 1814, Havana, AGI-SD, leg. 1287.

79  Thomas, "Narrative of William Thomas," 23.

80  "Depositions of the Cuban Slaves: Margarita Cabrera," 235.

81  "Depositions of the Cuban Slaves: Agustin Acosta," 238.

82  Tornero, *Crecimiento económico*, 225.

83  Mintz, "Caribbean Region," 60.

84  "Documento trunco que trata de una conspiración de negros siendo el cabecilla Juan Bautista Lisundia," 25 Mar. 1812, ANC-AP, leg. 12, no. 18. fol. 29v.

85  ANC-AP, leg. 12, no. 13, fol. 41

86  Ibid., no. 14, fol. 89, no. 16, fol. 13; Juan Ruíz de Apodaca to Ignacio de la Pezuela, 19 July 1812, Havana, AGI-SD, leg. 1284, no. 21.

87  ANC-AP, leg. 13, no. 1, fol. 95.

88  Ibid., fols. 190–95.

89  ANC-AP, leg. 12, no. 14, fol. 12v.

90  Ibid., fols. 27v, 72, no. 13, fols. 41–42.

91  Ibid., no. 16, fols. 11–12.

92  ANC-AP, leg. 13, no. 1, fol. 22.

93  Ibid., no. 15, fols. 19v–20, no. 1, fol. 193.

94  The classic statements can be found in Tannenbaum, *Slave and Citizen*; Elkins, *Slavery*, 63–80; and Klein, *Slavery in the Americas*, 77–85. For early refutations of these conclusions see Knight, *Slave Society*; and Hall, *Social Control*. For recent interpretations of the Tannenbaum thesis for Cuba, see de la Fuente, "Slave Law and Claims-Making," 339–70; Díaz, "Beyond Tannenbaum," 371–76; Schmidt-Nowara, "Still Continents," 377–82; and de la Fuente, "Slavery and the Law," 383–88.

95  Humboldt, *Ensayo político*, 88–89, 213.

96  Historian Eugene Genovese trenchantly observed more than thirty years ago that the slave society to emerge in Cuba after 1790 was really two slave societies: "The rise of the sugar plantations meant the rise of a new regime. Cuban slavery became simultaneously the mildest and harshest of slave systems; it yielded to and yet effectively opposed the old institutional restraints; it did and did not transform itself under the pressure of commercialization. Two systems, in short, had arisen side by side. The new regime for the most part grew alongside of, not out of, the old and was the creation of a new class." *World the Slaveholders Made*, 69.

97  Mörner, *Race Mixture*, 116; Klein, *Slavery in the Americas*, 196–200; Klein, *African Slavery*, 220–29; Lucena Salmoral, *Los codigos negros de la America Española*.

98  Bowser, "Free Person of Color," 344.

99  "R. C. al Gobernador de la Habana ordenándole haga observar el método y reglas

que se expresan, en la exacción del derecho de alcabala de la venta de los negros esclavos coartados de aquella isla"; "R. C. al Gobernador de la Habana previéndole que deben considerarse y según la misma regla que se dio para los esclavos enteros la de los coartados." For an overview see Lucena Salmoral, "El derecho de coartación del esclavo en la América Española," 357–74.

100 Jameson, *Letters from the Havana*, 38, 42.

101 "Quaderno de escrituras de negros del Rey," 1800–1801, Archivo Nacional de Cuba, Havana, fondo Intendencia General de Hacienda (ANC-IGH), leg. 18, no. 7, fol. 2, and also see fols. 8, 12, 16 for other examples.

102 Jameson, *Letters from the Havana*, 44; Humboldt, *Ensayo político*, 213; Ortiz, *Los Negros Esclavos*, 290; Paquette, *Sugar Is Made with Blood*, 63; Johnson, "'Honor Is Life,'" 120; Howard, *Changing History*, 11–12. The British *Anti-Slavery Reporter* noticed the difference between rural and urban access to freedom in Cuba: "Now, although the Spanish slave-law posses many humane features, and the rights of the slaves under it are guaranteed by a public opinion greatly in advance of any that ever prevailed in our own colonies, or that now exists in America, yet in the provinces it is by no means easy for the slaves employed on estates to assert their rights and claim their privileges owing to their being so remote from any local authority. Thus the humane provisions of the law are rendered almost inoperative." "Cuban Slaves in England," 239.

103 Bergad, Garcia, and del Carmen Barcia, *Cuban Slave Market*, 128. In contrast to Cuban historiography, Brazilian scholars have carried out numerous quantitative studies of manumission; see Schwartz, "Manumission of Slaves," 603–35; Queirós Mattoso, "A propósito de cartas de alforria na Bahia," 23–55; Karasch, *Slave Life*, 335–69; Slenes, "Demography and Economics," 484–574; Ramos, "Community, Control and Acculturation," 419–51; Eisenberg, "Ficando livre," 175–216; and Nishida, "Manumission and Ethnicity," 361–91.

104 For a discussion of this process and the customary and legal definitions of *coartación*, see Lucena Salmoral, "El derecho de coartación," 357–74.

105 "Quaderno sobre la denuncia que hiso la negra María Antonia Antola contra el negro José Wilson esclavo de Rafael Wilson," Archivo General de Indias, Seville, fondo Papeles de Cuba (hereafter AGI-PC), leg. 1865-A, fol. 9.

106 See for example Archivo Histórico Provincial de Camagüey, fondo Protocolos (AHPC-Protocolos), Diego Antonio Urra, 1809–12, fols. 50, 101, 209, 325, Andrés Antonio Rodríguez, 1810, fol. 46, Salvador Fuentes, 1809, fol. 95v; Archivo Histórico Provincial de Santiago de Cuba, fondo, Protocolos (AHPSC-Protocolos), leg. 63, fol. 59, leg. 241, fol. 108, leg. 356, fol. 171v, leg. 357, fols. 253, 379v, leg. 358, fols. 153, 248, leg 359, fol. 374. James Thompson purchased his freedom after trading for seven years in "hides and wax." Thompson, "Narrative of James Thompson," 71. We can only expect that other informal arrangements of how payments would be made and over what time were worked out between master and slave, but not always detailed in the notarial registers.

107 Archivo Histórico de la Provincia de Granma, Bayamo, fondo Protocolos (AHPG-Protocolos), leg. 11, libro 3, (1812), fol. 4v.

108 "Real Cédula sobre coartación de hijo de madres coartadas," Havana, 21 April 1789, AGI-PC, leg. 1433-B, fols. 1–3; "Consulta del consejo de las Indias sobre la coartación de los esclavos en beneficio de su libertad"; Lucena Salmoral, "El derecho de coartación," 367–70.

109 AHPG-Protocolos, leg. 4, libro 2, 1795, fol. 84.

110   "Real Cédula sobre coartación de hijo de madres coartadas," Havana, 21 April 1789, AGI-PC, leg. 1433-B, fols. 1–3; also see the discussion in Lucena Salmoral, "El derecho de coartación," 367–70.

111   Klein, *African Slavery*, 93; Paquette, *Sugar Is Made with Blood*, 29; Knight, *Slave Society*, 31–38; Zanetti and García, *Sugar and Railroads*, 33.

112   José Antonio de la Ossa to Juan de Aguilar, Havana, 30 Nov. 1812, ANC-CCG, leg. 97, no. 4. According to Klein, "The lack of a large white immigration for the first two-hundred years and the wholesale abandonment of the artisanal occupations to the negroes, slave and free, set a pattern of unchallengable Negro power in the Cuban labor market. Because of this the Negro came to be employed in almost every branch of industry and commerce on the island." Klein, *Slavery in the Americas*, 144; also see Bremmer, *Homes of the New World*, 2:280; and Villaverde, *Cecila Valdés*, 486.

113   "Quaderno Sobre la denuncia que hiso la negra María Antonia Antola . . . ," 1812, AGI-PC, 1865-A. For the importance of African ethnicity and marketing practices in the Americas, see Reis, " 'Revolution of the Ganhadores,' " 355–94.

114   "R. C. para el remedio de los esclavos en el servicio de los esclavos negros."

115   Ferrer, "Cuba en 1798," 311.

116   Puerto Príncipe, 6 Mar. 1812, AHPC-AC, leg. 27, fol. 96. A contemporary copy of the town council report sent to Spain can be found in AGI-PC, leg. 1640.

117   Havana, 31 Jan. 1809, AOHCH-AC, leg. 76, fols. 56–57, 24 Apr. 1812, leg. 83, fol. 99v.

118   Leonardo Del Monte to Apodaca, Havana, 15 June 1812, Havana, AGI-PC, leg. 1640.

119   Juan de Dios Molina y Gato to Someruelos, 14 Feb. 1810, Guadalupe, Havana, AGI-PC, leg. 1679.

120   Roca to Sor. Dn. Pedro Terrón, 13 Feb. 1810, La Cabaña, Havana, AGI-PC, leg. 1679.

121   For other examples see, Apodaca to Havana Ayuntamiento, Havana, 11 June 1812, AOHCH-AC, leg. 84, fol. 204; Jameson, *Letters from the Havana*, 38, 71–73; Tylden, "La isla de Cuba en el siglo xix" 94; Howard, *Changing History*, 11–12.

122   AHPC-Protocolos Quesada, 1812, fol. 457; for other examples see Juan de Mesa to Someruelos, 27 Feb. 1809, Jesús María, Havana, AGI-PC, leg. 1679; "Instancias, certificaciones, etc. del expediente heridas hechas José Sánchez en Puerto Príncipe, 1811," Archivo Histórico Provincial de Camgüey, fondo Alcaldía Ordinario (AHPC-AO), leg. 38, no. 427, fol. 10; ANC-AP, leg. 12, no. 13, fol. 37v, no. 17, fol. 94; "Diligencia promovidas por el sindico procurador general contra Luis Gerbet, por el castigo que dio a su esclava Luisa Montaño," 1811, ANC-ASC, leg. 606, no. 13897, fol. 5; "Testimonio de la diligencias practicadas por María Francisca, parda libre, sobre haber suministrado el dinero a la negra Rosa Govert para comprar a la negra Felicite esclava que fue de Magdalena Chavin, mujer legitima de Francisco Sales Badillo, Santiago de Cuba, 1801," Archivo Nacional de Cuba, fondo Audiencia de Santo Domingo (ANC-ASD), leg. 130, no. 1, fol. 5.

123   AHPC-AO, leg. 52, no. 741.

124   ANC-ASC, leg. 606, no 13897, fol. 12.

125   Jurco to Someruelos, 12 Mar. 1805, Jesús Monte, Havana, AGI-PC, leg. 1680.

126   Cohen and Greene, *Neither Slave nor Free*; Berlin, *Slaves without Masters*. As historian Stuart Schwartz has observed for Brazil: "Here in the heart of a sugar economy was a sector of workers that by its very existence validated the system of slavery on which the industry was based by providing examples of mobility and advantage to those enslaved." Schwartz, *Sugar Plantations*, 313

127   ANC-AP, leg. 12, no. 17, fol. 15v.

128 Deschamps Chapeaux, *El negro en la economía habanera del siglo xix*, 47–86; Duharte, *El negro en la sociedad colonial*, 91–115; Díaz, *Virgin,*, 179–98.

129 "Certificaciones, autos, etc., por la parda María Ramona Cabrera contra moreno José María por lesiones producidos con un cuchillo," Puerto Príncipe, 1821, AHPC-AO, leg. 55, no. 806.

130 Trouillot, *Silencing the Past*, 74–83.

131 Juan Ruíz de Apodaca to Stephen Kingston, Havana, 3 July 1812, United States National Archives, Record Group 59, General Records of the Department of State, Dispatches from United States Consuls in Havana, 1783–1906, roll 2, vol. 2, 11 Jan. 1808–12 Sept. 1812.

132 Deschamps Chapeaux, *El negro en la economía habanera*; Deschamps Chapeaux, *Los cimarrones urbanos*; Paquette, *Sugar Is Made with Blood*; Casanovas, *Bread, or Bullets!* 41.

133 Arango y Parreño, "Sobre la población de Cuba," 20 June 1811, in his *Obras*, 2:215; Knight, *Slave Society*, 94.

134 Antonio del Valle Hernández, "Relación de los libertos a los esclavos en algunos países extranjeros y en la isla de Cuba," Havana, 20 July 1813, in Arango y Parreño, *Obras*, 2:205.

135 Sherry Johnson's study of the militia through Spanish institutional sources found little interaction with the slave population as it would not be revealed in military sources. Consequently, she deduces from sources written about (but not by) the free people of color population that they "thought of themselves as privileged because of the unique status they enjoyed" and the "free colored population of Cuba distanced itself from the slave population." *Social Transformation*, 9. Phillip Howard's work, in contrast, found militia leaders actively involved with the slave population through *cabildos de nación. Changing History*, 30–36.

136 Jurco to Someruelos, 16 Oct. 1805, Jesús Monte, Havana, AGI-PC, leg. 1680.

137 Jurco to Someruelos, 24 Oct. 1805, Jesús Monte, Havana, AGI-PC, leg. 1680. In order to distinguish free people of color from slaves a Frenchman from Saint Domingue proposed "branding them on their two cheeks with an 'L' which will mean Libre." Quoted in Dayan, *Haiti, History, and the Gods*, 187.

138 Juan de Mesa to Someruelos, 24 Oct. 1811, Havana, AGI-PC, leg. 1679.

139 Tomás Aguilar to Urbina, Santiago de Cuba, 23 Dec. 1811, ANC-CCG, leg. 93, no. 5.

140 Pedro López de la Vega to Someruelos, 15 Nov. 1808, Jesús Monte, Havana, AGI-PC, leg. 1680.

141 "Noticia de los Individuos destinados a la obra de la Alameda de esta [Havana] ciudad," 1807, AGI-PC, leg. 1667; Jurco to Someruelos, 30 Sept. 1807, Jesús Monte, Havana, AGI-PC, leg. 1680.

142 Navarro, "Bando sobre prohibir el uso de armas"; "Oficio contra el moreno Rafael Pérez, Polinario Valdés, y Juan Guerra por haberlos cogido con machetes, Juez el Sor Presidente, Gobernador, y Capitán General," 1807, AGI-PC, leg. 1780.

143 Diego Miguel de Moya to His Majesty, Havana, 19 Jan. 1790, ANC-RCJF, leg. 150, no. 7405, fol. 12v.

144 Information on professions for free people of color in 1812 can be found in ANC-AP, leg. 12, nos. 9, 13, 14, 16, 17, 18, 20, 23, 25, 27, leg. 13, nos. 1, 15, 38, and leg. 14, no. 1. For accounts of the skilled labor performed by free people of color in Cuba, see Deschamps Chapeaux, *El negro en la economía habanera*; Duharte, *El negro en la sociedad colonial*, 11–30, 91–115; Rodríguez Ochoa, "Situación socioeconómica de la población libre de color"; Paquette, *Sugar Is Made with Blood*, 39–40, 80, 106–7, 119; Knight,

"Cuba," 278–308, esp. 289–95; Knight, "Free Colored Population in Cuba," 224–47, esp. 232–36; Knight, *Slave Society*, 94; Klein, *Slavery in the Americas*, 204–9.

145 ANC-AP, leg. 13, no. 1, fols. 419v–21v, 425v–26v, leg. 14, no. 1, fols. 5–6, 30v–38.

146 Rudesindo de los Olivos to Someruelos, 7 July 1800, Jesús María, Havana, AGI-PC, leg. 1679.

147 Stolcke, *Marriage, Class and Colour*, 12–13, 42–57.

148 Someruelos to Gobernador of Santiago de Cuba, Havana, 29 July 1811, ANC-AP, leg. 213, no. 118.

149 Someruelos to Gobernador of Santiago de Cuba, Havana, 28 Mar. 1810, ANC-AP, leg. 211, no. 70.

150 Apodaca to Gobernador of Santiago de Cuba, Havana, 18 Nov. 1812, ANC-CCG, leg. 97, no. 5. For interracial couples living conjugally, see Teniente del Partido de Jesús María, 19 May 1800, Jesús María, Havana, AGI-PC, leg. 1679.

151 Antonio Vaillant, Santiago de Cuba, 11 Apr. 1810, ANC-AP, leg. 211, no. 83, fol. 6.

152 Manuel Velásquez to Gobernador, Santiago de Cuba, 26 Mar. 1810, ANC-AP, leg. 211, no. 83, fol. 5.

153 Ibid., fols. 1, 3

154 Ibid., fol. 9.

155 Ibid., fols. 4, 7.

156 Antonio Vaillant, Santiago de Cuba, 11 Apr. 1810, ANC-AP, leg. 211, no. 83, fol. 7. The case may have been more common than recognized in the Spanish colonial world. Christon Archer discovered in Mexico that "on some occasions, one brother might be enlisted in the pardo unit and another in a provincial unit [that] were open in theory only to whites, castizos, and mestizos." *Army in Bourbon Mexico*, 224.

157 Antonio Vaillant, Santiago de Cuba, 11 Apr. 1810, ANC-AP, leg. 211, no. 83.

158 Governor of Holguín, Holguín, 28 Junio 1810, AGI-PC, leg. 1648; Don Diego Antonio del Castillo, Puerto Príncipe, 18 Sept. 1812, AGI-PC, leg. 1820; "Establecimiento, progresos, y actual estado de la casa de beneficencia, extramuros de la Habana," 1813, AGI-UM, leg. 85; González-Ripoll Navarro, *Cuba, la isla de los ensayos*, 172–74. For numerous examples of the arrest of vagrants, see AGI-PC, leg. 1679, 1680. Teresita Martínez-Vergne provides an excellent treatment of the subject in Puerto Rico; see *Shaping the Discourse on Space*.

159 See for example "Vista de los partidos de Arroyo Arenas, Guataco, y Guajabal," 1791, AGI-PC, leg. 1498-B.

160 José Agustín Hernández to Someruelos, 24 Sept. 1804, Jesús María, Havana, AGI-PC, leg. 1679.

161 Juan de Mesa to Someruelos, 27 Feb. 1809, Jesús María, Havana, AGI-PC, leg. 1679.

162 Alexander, *Transatlantic Sketches*, 196.

163 Mariano de la Guardia to Someruelos, 9 Mar. 1808, Arroyo Naranjo, Havana, AGI-PC, leg. 1680; "Autos de Juegos Prohibidos," AGI-PC, leg. 1498-B.

164 Someruelos to Urbina, Habana, 6 Dec. 1811, ANC-CCG, leg. 93, no. 4. Also see the additional examples in ANC-CCG, leg. 94, no. 10. Suares de Urbina to Rl. Audiencia, Santiago de Cuba, 8 Abril 1812, Juan de Dios Hernández to Someruelos, 13 May 1810, Jesús María, Havana, Juan José González to Someruelos, 25 June 1808, Jesús María, Havana, Juan José González to Someruelos, 22 June 1808, Jesús María, Havana, AGI-PC, leg. 1679; Miguel de Chavez to Someruelos, 28 Oct. 1799, Horcón, Havana, AGI-PC, leg. 1680.

165 "Actas diligencias, etc. promovido por Miguel de Céspedes y Carlos de Quesada

contra Vicente Cañizares soldado de la cuarta compania de las milicias provisionales por utilizar esclavos bajo promesa de libertad para asaltar diferente haciendas en beneficios propios," Puerto Príncipe, Nov. 1821, AHPC-AO, leg. 52, no. 745.

166 Puerto Príncipe, Cabildo Minutes, 15 Apr. 1809, AHPC-AC, leg. 25, fol. 189v.

167 ANC-AP, leg. 12, no. 25, fol. 137; AGI-PC, 1865A; AHPC-AO, leg. 52, no. 741, fols. 3v–4.

168 ANC-AP, leg. 12, no. 20, fols. 10–11.

169 "2 testimonios y dos cartas sobre la herida de Francisca Ximénez, 1807," AGI-PC, leg. 1667. For fighting, see the numerous examples in AGI-PC, leg. 1679, 1680.

170 Teniente Gobernador to Someruelos, Holguín, 29 Nov. 1804, AGI-PC, leg. 1648.

171 Tomas Aguilar to Urbina, Santiago de Cuba, 23 Dec. 1811, ANC-CCG, leg. 93, no. 5.

172 ANC-AP, leg. 12, no. 27, fol. 9.

173 "Sumario contra el moreno José Gordillo esclavo de Dn. Pedro Gordillo acusado de haver hecho resistencia a la guardia de Puerta de Tierra y herido al comandante de la segunda puerta," April 1811, AGI-PC, leg. 1774-A.

174 Sedano to Apodaca, 11 July 1812, Puerto Príncipe, AGI-PC, leg. 1820, no. 214; also see José Coppingenros to Someruelos, 16 Mar. 1808, Bayamo, AGI-PC, leg. 1649, no. 226.

175 Jurco to Someruelos, 29 Dec. 1809, Jesús del Monte, Havana, AGI-PC, leg. 1680; "Instancias, certificaciones, etc. del expediente heridas hecha a José Sánchez en Puerto Príncipe," 1811, AHPC-AO, leg. 38, no. 427.

176 James, *Black Jacobins*, 11.


CHAPTER THREE

1 ANC-AP, leg. 13, no. 1, fols. 192–94.

2 ANC-AP, leg. 12, no. 25, fols. 39–39v.

3 ANC-AP, leg. 12, no. 14, fol. 27v.

4 ANC-AP, leg. 12, no. 13, fols. 28, 41, leg. 12, no. 14, fols. 4v, 27v, 28v, no. 17, fol. 72, no. 18, fols. 3v, 5, no. 25, fols. 88–89v.

5 ANC-AP, leg. 12, no. 25, fol. 13v.

6 ANC-AP, leg. 12, no. 17, fol. 13. The size of Chacón's building as an ideal location for meetings is indicated by the authorities' belief that he employed several clerks who worked in the tavern and grocery. ANC-AP, leg. 12, no. 25, fols. 55v–56.

7 Juan José González to Someruelos, 22 June 1808, Jesús María, Havana, AGI-PC, leg. 1679; ANC-AP, leg. 13, no. 1, fols. 443–43v.

8 ANC-AP, leg. 12, no. 14, fol. 15.

9 Ibid., no. 25, fol. 14.

10 ANC-AP, leg. 13, no. 1, fols. 5, 7.

11 ANC-AP, leg. 12, no. 25, fols. 44v–45.

12 Ibid., no. 14, fol. 92, leg. 12, no. 18, fols. 25v–26.

13 ANC-AP, leg. 12, no. 17, fols. 13–13v.

14 Ibid., fol. 14.

15 Ibid., fols. 14v–15.

16 Ibid., fols. 17v–18.

17 Ibid., fols. 16–16v.

18 Klein, "Colored Militia of Cuba," 20–21; Kuethe, *Cuba*, 38; Deschamps Chapeaux, *Los batallones*, 39.

19 ANC-AP, leg. 12, no. 17, fol. 16v.

20 Kuethe, *Cuba*, 75.

21 Kuethe, "Status of the Free Pardo," 113–15. In Saint Domingue the American Mary Hassal also noticed the resentment blacks expressed for "failing to take off [their] hat before a White meant lack of respect for a superior." Dayan, *Haiti, History, and the Gods*, 158.

22 ANC-AP, leg. 12, no. 17, fol. 46 [parentheses in original].

23 Service record for Antonio Soledad in "Libro de servicios de los oficiales y sargentos de la batallón de morenos libres de la Havana," 1791, AGI-PC, leg. 1491A.

24 *Calendario manual y guía de forasteros de la isla de Cuba par el año de 1795*, 119, located at P. K. Yonge Library Special Collections, University of Florida, Gainesville, Florida.

25 ANC-AP, leg. 12, no. 17, fol. 46.

26 Stephan Palmié's analysis of Aponte's militia service explores the issues of pride and self-esteem, but since his reading of Aponte's book ahistorically divorces the document from the movement that bears Aponte's name, Palmié only naturally cautions against regarding these images as signs of insurrection. Palmié, *Wizards and Scientists*, 100–103.

27 For a discussion of the militia in colonial Spanish America, see Kuethe, "Status of the Free Pardo"; Andrews, "Afro-Argentine Officers of Buenos Aires," 85–100; Vinson, "Race and Badge," 471–96; Vinson, *Bearing Arms for His Majesty*; McAlister, '*Fuero Militar*', 43–54; Archer, "Pardos, Indians, and the Army," 231–55; Booker, "Needed but Unwanted," 259–76; Hanger, *Bounded Lives*, 109–35; Helg, "Limits of Equality," 14–15; Sánchez, "African Freedmen and the Fuero Militar," 165–84; Landers, *Black Society in Spanish Florida*, 202–28; Marchena Fernández, *Ejército y milicias*, 119–24; and Vinson and King, "'New' African Diasporic Military History."

28 Deschamps Chapeaux, *Los batallones*, 18–40; Kuethe, *Cuba*, 38–42; Klein, "Colored Militia," 18–21.

29 "La nación lucumí contra Dn. Manuel Blanco y otros sobre propiedad del terreno en que se halla fundado el cavildo de nación," 1777–81, ANC, fondo Escribanía Cabello (ANC-EC), leg. 147, no. 1, fols. 41–42.

30 Sánchez, "African Freedmen and the Fuero Militar," 183–84.

31 Marchena Fernández, *Ejército y milicias*, 106–7; Kuethe, "Status of the Free Pardo," 106, 108; Hanger, *Bounded Lives*, 112.

32 Manuel Atraso to Someruelos, Havana, 22 Dec. 1809, AGI-PC, leg. 1668.

33 "3 documentos para el plan de establecimiento de Batallón de Morenos en Stgo.," 1810, and "Informe sobre la formación de Batallón de Morenos en la Jurisdicción de Havana," 1810, both in AGI-PC, leg. 1668; "Formulario de defensa: Ideas generales para ella aplicables en todos tiempos a un caso de invasión contra esta plasa, Santiago de Cuba," 1811, AGI-PC, leg. 1786-A.

34 "Documento que se refiere al estado, fecha Santiago de Cuba, 31 de Agosto de 1810, de las companias de milicias urbanas de Infantería y caballería, Blancos y morenos del partido de aquella ciudad," ANC-AP, leg. 212, no. 37; Francisco Sánchez to Urbina, Santiago, 6 Mar. 1812, AGI-PC, leg. 1548.

35 "R. C. sobre preemencias de oficiales y soldados milicianos"; "Reglamento para las milicias y infantería y caballería de la isla de Cuba"; Navarro, "Bando sobre prohibir el uso de armas," Havana, 4 May 1779, 103–4; Deschamps Chapeaux, *Los batallones*, 21–22, 41; Klein, "Colored Militia of Cuba," 17.

36 McAlister, "*Fuero Militar*", 44, 51; Sánchez, "African Freedmen and the Fuero Militar," 166.

37 See the retirement lists for the mulatto and black battalion of Havana in AGI-PC, leg. 1667.

38 Deschamps Chapeaux, *Los Batallones*, 42; Klein, "Colored Militia of Cuba," 19. While recognizing differences between the mulatto and black militia in New Orleans, Hanger does not explore in detail the divisions, concluding that the "distinctions made between pardos and morenos in Louisiana and Cuba did not materially affect free black soldiers." *Bounded Lives*, 112. Similarly, Allan Kuethe recognizes the difference in pay but concludes "militia officials commonly ignored such fine distinctions and referred to all of them as 'pardos.'" Kuethe, "Status of the Free Pardo," 109.

39 Ysidro Moreno to Capitán General, Havana, 22 Apr. 1790, AGI-PC, leg. 1433-B.

40 Hanger, *Bounded Lives*, 127.

41 Vinson, "Race and Badge," 486–87.

42 Someruelos to Urbina, Havana, 14 Dec. 1811, ANC-CCG, leg. 93, no. 3.

43 ANC-AP, leg. 12, no. 17, fols. 8, 12v.

44 Marchena, *Ejército y milicias*, 109; Sánchez, "African Freedmen and the Fuero Militar," 167.

45 "Relación de los individuos de dho. Batallón que quedaron enteramente excluydos por orden que paso el Señor conde de Mopox Brigadier de los Rl exércitos y sub-inspector Gral. de las tropas de la Isla de Cuba el día 29 de Diciembre de 1800 mediante hallarse accidentados o cansados con 20 años cumplidos o mas de servicio por cuya razón son acreedores a fuero militar," Antonio Seidel, Havana, 15 Jan. 1801, AGI-PC, leg. 1667. Various historians have repeated José Luciano Franco's incorrect statement that Aponte had been forced to retire in 1810, not 1800. *Conspiración de Aponte*, 19, 24.

46 ANC-AP, leg. 12, no. 17, fol. 19.

47 Ibid., fols. 75–75v. Franco incorrectly gives Escobar's name as "José Domingo Escobal" in the documents he edited. Franco, *Las conspiraciones de 1810 y 1812*, 168–69.

48 ANC-AP, leg. 12, no. 17, fols. 95–95v.

49 Ibid., fol. 75v.

50 Ibid., fols. 96–97v.

51 Juan de Dios Hernández to Someruelos, 29 Sept. 1809, Jesús María, Havana, AGI-PC, leg. 1679.

52 Juan de Dios Hitar to Someruelos, 10 Oct. 1811, Guadalupe, Havana, AGI-PC, leg. 1679.

53 ANC-AP, leg. 12, no. 14, fol. 33, leg. 13, no. 1, fols. 25–29, 226, leg. 14, no. 1, fols. 8, 11v; Francisco de Campos to Someruelos, Havana, 17 Dec. 1801, Havana, AGI-PC, leg. 1667; Rudesindo de los Olivos to Someruelos, 7 July 1800, and Juan de Dios Hernández to Someruelos, 5 Mar. 1810, Jesús María, Havana, AGI-PC, leg. 1679.

54 ANC-AP, leg. 12, no. 14, fols. 8, 11v; Sánchez, "African Freedmen and the Fuero Militar," 166–67.

55 Juan de Mesa to Someruelos, 29 Apr. 1808, 27 July 1809, Jesús María, Havana, AGI-PC, leg. 1679. In Mexico, blacks not enlisted in the militia often attempted to claim special rights reserved only for soldiers. As a result, Viceroy Croix required militiamen of color to always wear a distinguishing belt or cap to prevent slaves from impersonating soldiers. Vinson, "Race and Badge," 483, 489; Sánchez, "African Freedmen and the Fuero Militar," 169.

56 ANC-AP, leg. 12, no. 25, fol. 3v, leg. 14, no. 1, fols. 27, 47.

57  Urbina to Someruelos, Santiago, 9 Mar. 1812, AGI-PC, leg. 1548.

58  Manzano, *Autobiography of a Slave*, 53.

59  Francisco de Campos to Someruelos, 9 Jan. 1801, Havana, AGI-PC, leg. 1667.

60  ANC-AP, leg. 12, no. 26, fol. 9; *Calendario manual y guía de forateros de la isla de Cuba para el año de 1809*, 177; Deschamps Chapeaux, *Los batallones*, 43–44.

61  Marrero, *Cuba*, 13:135.

62  See the service records for commanding officers in AGI-PC, leg, 1136-A, 1491-A, 1491-B, 1492-B, 1493-A, 1493-B, 1770-A, 1771-B, and 1773-A. Also see Kuethe, *Cuba*, 74; and Deschamps Chapeaux, *El negro en la economía habanera*, 61–62.

63  Domingo Quintero to Juan de Aguilar, Havana, 24 Mar. 1809, ANC-CCG, leg. 82, no. 5. Hanger observed the same phenomenon of a close tie between carpenters and the militia when she commented that a soldier named "Enrique learned the craft of carpentry, like so many other free blacks, and followed his father into militia service." *Bounded Lives*, 130. Also see Landers for the important role played by militia soldiers in the artisan trades, *Black Society in Spanish Florida*, 88–89.

64  See the examples in ANC-AP, leg, 12, nos. 14, 16, 17, 18, 25, 26; ANC-AP, leg. 13, nos. 1, 15, 38; and ANC-AP, leg. 14, no. 1.

65  ANC-AP, leg. 12, no. 25, fol. 73v.

66  Hanger, *Bounded Lives*, 119, 126; Bowser, "Colonial Spanish America," 46, 52, 58; Archer, "Pardos, Indians, and the Army," 239–40; Helg, "Limits of Equality," 14–15.

67  Apodaca to José Vásquez Figueroa, Havana, 17 Nov. 1812, AGI-SD, leg. 1284, no. 62.

68  Hanger, *Bounded Lives*, 119, 121–22; Voelz, *Slave and Soldier*, 333–37; Helg, "Limits of Equality," 15–16, 19.

69  "Nuevo reglamento y arancel que debe gobernar en la captura de esclavos cimarrones, aprobado por S. M. en real orden expedida en San Lorenzo con fecha de veinte de diciembre de 1797," AGI-PC, leg. 1515-B; Lampros, "Merchant-Planter Cooperation and Conflict" 217–85; La Rosa Corzo, *Los cimarrones de Cuba*, 34–49.

70  For numerous documents on runaway slave communities and efforts to conquer them around Santiago, see AGI-SD, leg. 2210; see also Danger Roll, *Los cimarrones de el Frijol*, 33–72; and La Rosa Corzo, *Runaway Slave Settlements*, chaps. 2 and 3.

71  Julian Francisco Marquez de Campos to Someruelos, Havana, 11 Oct. 1809, AGI-PC, leg. 1548.

72  Antonio Vaillant, Santiago de Cuba, 22 June 1805, AGI-PC, Leg. 1548.

73  "3 documentos para el plan de establecimiento de Batallón de Morenos en Stgo," 1810, AGI-PC, leg. 1668; "Formulario de Defensa: Ideas Generales para ella aplicables en todos tiempos a un caso de invasión contra esta plasa, Santiago de Cuba," 1811, AGI-PC, leg. 1786-A; "Documento que se refiere al estado, fecha Santiago de Cuba, 31 de Agosto de 1810, de las compañías de milicias urbanas de Infantería y caballería, Blancos y morenos del partido de aquella ciudad," ANC-AP, leg. 212, no. 37.

74  "Batallón de morenos de la Habana, relación de los individuos que de orden de Excmo. Sor. Pres. Gob. y Cap. Gral. se pusieron al sueldo para buscar barios reos criminales," Havana, 12 May 1812, AGI-PC, leg. 1803; ANC-AP, leg. 13, no. 15, fol. 73v, leg. 14, no. 1, fols. 84v–85.

75  Cuban historian Pedro Deschamps Chapeaux incorrectly states that the free men of color militia "was never utilized against the numerous runaway communities in the diverse regions of Cuba" and they were "never employed on the island to crush slave insurrections." *Los batallones*, 11, 25.

76  Hanger, *Bounded Lives*, 126.

77  Deschamps Chapeaux, *El negro en la economía habanera*, 47–86; also see Duharte Jimenez, *El negro en la sociedad colonial*, 91–115.

78  Juan de Dios Hernández to Someruelos, 29 Sept. 1809, Jesús María, Havana, AGI-PC, leg. 1679.

79  AHPG-Protocolos, leg. 8, libro 2 (1805), fol. 238.

80  Deschamps Chapeaux, *El negro en la economía habanera*, 65–86.

81  "Dos cartas sobre la herida de Francisca Ximenez, 1807," AGI-PC, leg. 1667.

82  José Andrili to Capitán General, Havana, 25 June 1787, AGI-PC, leg. 1433-B.

83  ANC-AP, leg. 12, no. 25, fol. 13v.

84  AHPG-Protocolos, leg. 11, libro 3 (1812), fol. 77. For a similar dynamic in Saint Augustine, see Landers, *Black Society in Spanish Florida*, 127–28.

85  Arango y Parreño, "Discurso sobre la agricultura de la Habana y medios de fometarla," Arango y Parreño, *De la factoría a la Colonia*, 88–89. The term "Guarico" referred to the port of Le Cap François, but also more broadly to the colony of Saint Domingue and the independent republic of Haiti.

86  Ibid., 90–91.

87  Ibid., 88–91.

88  Kuethe, *Cuba*, 167.

89  "Representación dirigida por el Real Consulado de la Habana al ministro de Hacienda en 10 de Julio de 1799," reprinted in Saco, *Historia de la esclavitud*, 5:136–37.

90  Someruelos to Sor. Comandante de las Armas en Trinidad, Havana, 29 Mar. 1808, Habana, AGI-PC, leg. 1667.

91  Vinson, "Race and Badge," 490–91.

92  Consider for example the arrests of Mexican deserters in the Jesús Maria neighborhood of Havana; see Juan Jose Gonzalez to Someruelos, 17 Oct. 1806, Juan de Mesa to Someruelos, 20 Sept. 1809, and Juan de Dios Hernandez to Someruelos, 29 Jan. 1810, AGI-PC, leg. 1679.

93  ANC-AP, leg. 12, no. 17, fols. 41v–42.

94  "Noticia de los Individuos destinados a la obra de la Alameda de esta ciudad [Havana], 1807," AGI-PC, leg. 1667.

95  Someruelos to Juan de Aguilar, Havana, 6 Feb. 1812, ANC-CCG, leg. 94, no. 1.

96  Pedro López de la Vega to Someruelos, 15 Nov. 1808, Jesús del Monte, Havana, and Benito Conderos to Someruelos, 14 Nov. 1806, Bauta, AGI-PC, leg. 1680.

97  Montes de Oca y Fajardo, *Sermón de Santiago*, 11–12, P. K. Yonge Library Special Collections, University of Florida, Gainesville, Florida.

98  Kuethe, *Cuba*, 123, 126, 176; Hanger, *Bounded Lives*, 112, 126–27.

99  Someruelos to Gobernador de Cuba, Havana, 10 Mar. 1812, ANC-CCG, leg. 94, no. 6.

100  Someruelos to Gobernador de Cuba, Havana, 14 June 1811, ANC-AP, leg. 213, no. 72.

101  Someruelos to Juan José Blas, Havana, 14 June 1811, ANC-AP, leg. 213, no. 72; Pedro Suarez de Urbina to Apodaca, Santiago, 6 June 1812, AGI-PC, leg. 1785, no. 587; Cabildo Minutes, Santiago de Cuba, 6 Apr. 1812, Archivo Histórico Municipal de Santiago de Cuba, fondo Actas Capitulares (AHMSC-AC). I would like to thank John-Marshall Klein for directing me to this last source.

102  AOHCH-AC, 4 Dec. 1795, leg. 54, fols. 204v–5; García to Príncipe de la Paz, Santo Domingo, 3 Mar. 1796, no. 48, in Rodríguez Demorizi, *Cesión de Santo Domingo a Francia*, 75. According to Cuban historian José Luciano Franco, Aponte planned to participate in the festivities welcoming Jean François. José Franco, *La conspiración de Aponte*, 9. I could find no sources to document Franco's statement.

103 Landers, "Rebellion and Royalism," 163–70; Landers, *Black Society in Spanish Florida*, 209–217; Houdaille, "Negros Franceses en América Central a fines del siglo xviii," 65–67; Fernández Repetto and Negroe Sierra, *Una población perdida en la memoria*, 55; Vinson, "Race and Badge," 491.

104 Someruelos to [?], Havana, 27 Jan. 1800, AHN-Estado, leg. 6366, caja 1, exp. 2.

105 Someruelos to Bardari y Azara, Havana, 10 Feb. 1811, AGI-SD, leg. 2210.

106 AHPG-Protocolos, leg. 8, libro 1 (1804), fol. 110.

107 Carlos de Ayala to Someruelos, 23 Dec. 1800, Jesús María, Havana, AGI-PC, leg. 1679.

108 ANC-AP, leg. 13, no. 1, fols. 5, 30, 204, 322, 403–5, 410v, leg. 14, no. 1, fols. 19v–21.

109 ANC-AP, leg. 12, no. 14, fol. 75.

110 ANC-AP, leg. 12, no 18, fol. 28, leg. 13, no. 1, fol. 44v.

111 ANC-AP, leg. 12, no. 14, fols. 4–4v, 90.

112 Ibid., leg. 13, no. 1, fol. 167; "Bando del Capitán General de la Isla," Havana, 7 Apr. 1812, ANC-AP, leg. 12, no. 24; ANC-AP, leg. 13, no. 38, fol. 3v.

113 José Augustino Jurco to Someruelos, San Lázaro, Havana, 21 Nov. 1808, AGI-PC, leg. 1680.

114 ANC-AP, leg. 12, no. 18, fol. 32.

115 I have relied on the following sources for identifying African ethnicity: Nuñez, *Dictionary of Afro-Latin American Civilization*; Thornton, *Africa and Africans*, x–xxvi; Curtin, *Atlantic Slave Trade*, esp. 291–98; Castellanos and Castellanos, *Cultura Afrocubana*, 1:28–43; Castellanos and Castellanos, "Geographic, Ethnologic, and Linguistic Roots," 95–110; Ortiz, *Los negros brujos*, 22–26; Ortiz, *Los negros esclavos*, 40–59; Deschamps Chapeaux, *El negro en la economía habanera*, 31–46; Deschamps Chapeaux "Cabildos," 50–51; Deschamps Chapeaux, *Los cimarrones urbanos*, 42–47; Andrews, *Afro-Argentines*, 233–34; Bowser, *African Slave*, 346.

116 For a discussion of the terms "nation" and "ethnicity" as they apply to identity in the early modern world and the African Diaspora in particular, see Eltis, *Rise of African Slavery*, 244–57; Gómez, *Exchanging Our Country Marks*, 2–8; Gómez, "African Identity and Slavery," 111–20; Law, "Ethnicity and the Slave Trade," 205–19; Lovejoy, "Identifying Enslaved Africans," 1–29; Thornton, "Coromantees," 161–78; Thornton, *Africa and Africans*, 183–205.

117 Bell, "Unbearable Lightness of Being French," 1218–19.

118 Miller, "History and Africa / Africa and History," 14–16.

119 In his pioneering study of the *cabildos* historian Philip A. Howard states the societies were "known as *cabildos de naciones de afrocubanos.*" *Changing History*, xiv. I only found the societies described as "*cabildos de nación*" in documents from the 1790s to 1820s.

120 Mina Guagni to Capitán General, Havana, 29 Apr. 1794, "La nación mina guagni contra Salvador Ternero sobre que de cuentas del producido del *cabildo* de la misma nación," 1794, ANC, fondo Escribanía Ortega, (ANC-EO), leg. 65, no. 11, fols. 1–1v.

121 "La nación mina contra Juana de Mesa," 1797, ANC, fondo Escribanía Antonio D'aumy (ANC-ED), leg. 673, no. 9.

122 "La nación mina guagni contra Salvador Ternero sobre cuentas," 1794–97, ANC-ED, leg. 893, no. 4, fol. [?]. (It is not possible to cite all the specific folios of this document and others in the fondo Escribanía because the pagination has been destroyed by deterioration.)

123 Francisco Ferrer to Capitán General, Havana, 24 Jan. 1794, ANC-EO, leg. 65, no. 11, fol. 5.

124 ANC-ED, leg. 893, no. 4; ANC-EO, leg. 65, no. 11, fol. 55.

125   Entry for "Dn. Antonio Seidel" in "Libro de los veteranos que componen la plana mayor de blancos agregada por S. M. al batallón de Morenos libres de la Havana, arreglados hasta fin de diciembre de 1795," Archivo General de Simancas, fondo Guerra Moderna, leg. 7262. (Microfilm copy consulted at Howard-Tilton Memorial Library, Tulane University.) The 1795 Havana city index listed Antonio Seidel as the highest-ranking official supervising the black battalion. See *Calendario manual y guía de forasteros de la isla de Cuba par el año de 1795*, 119, P. K. Yonge Library, Special Collections, University of Florida, Gainesville.

126   ANC-ED, leg. 893, no. 4.

127   Salvador Ternero to Capitán General, Havana, 4 June 1794, ANC-EO, leg. 65, no. 11, fol. 40.

128   ANC-EO, leg. 65, no. 11, fols. 65v, 123v.

129   ANC-ED, leg. 893, no. 4, fols. 143–44 (parentheses in original).

130   Ibid., fol. 51v.

131   Ibid., fol. 52–53.

132   Ibid., fol. [?].

133   Ibid., fol. [?]. Scholar Stephan Palmié hastily concluded, with only consulting a handful of published sources, that for Ternero "we will, of course, never know what precisely these ostensibly ethnic identity referents mean in the historical context in which these men deployed them." Historians interested in Ternero's own words, however, can certainly gain critical insights into his own ideas behind such terms, how he created degrees of Mina Guagni ethnicity depending on African or Cuban birth, and the historical setting in which he used these terms by consulting the sources. Palmié, *Wizards and Scientists*, 143.

134   ANC-EO, leg, 65, no. 11, fol. 72.

135   ANC-ED, leg. 893, no. 4, fol. 61v.

136   Ibid., fol. [?]. Morales may have sided with Vásquez in the hope that, should Ternero be removed as *capataz*, he would be rewarded by the new leader buying his freedom.

137   Jameson, *Letters from the Havana*, 21.

138   See Gómez, "African Identity and Slavery," 118; and Thornton, "Coromantees," 161.

139   Eltis, *Rise of African Slavery*, 244.

140   For the emphasis on the heterogeneity of the slave population see in particular, Mintz, "Caribbean as a Socio-Cultural Area," 912–37; Mintz and Price, *Birth of African-American Culture*; and Morgan, "Cultural Implications," 122–45. For the revisionist emphasis on African ethnicity and culture, see Lovejoy, "Identifying Enslaved," 1–29; Thornton, *Africa and Africans*, 183–205; Eltis, *Rise of African Slavery*, 224–57; and Gómez, "African Identity and Slavery,"111–20.

141   For references to African "nations" in Anglo-America, see Ligon, *True and Exact History*, 55; Eltis, *Rise of African Slavery*, 230; Thornton, *Africa and Africans*, 195; Thornton, "Coromantees," 161, 173; Linebaugh and Rediker, *Many-Headed Hydra*, 152; Craton, *Testing the Chains*, 108–10, 125–39; Gaspar, *Bondsmen and Rebels*; Sheridan, "Jamaican Slave Insurrection Scare," 303. While scholars continue to debate whether there actually was a slave conspiracy led by Denmark Vesey in 1822 Charleston, South Carolina, contemporaries believed it was quite plausible that an ethnically organized Igbo column led by Monday Gell from the Bight of Biafra played a leading role in planning the rebellion; see "Trial of Peter, 21 June 1822," in Pearson, *Designs against Charleston*, 176; Egerton, *He Shall Go Out Free*, 133; and Gómez, *Exchanging Our Country Marks*, 3. For the debate on the veracity of the Vesey Conspiracy, see Johnson, "Den-

mark Vesey and His Co-Conspirators," 915–76; the responses by various authors in the forum titled "Making of a Slave Conspiracy," part 2; Paquette and Egerton, "Of Facts and Fables," 8–48; and Paquette, "From Rebellion to Revisionism," 291–334.

142 As historian Linda M. Heywood has argued, "African folk Christianity" thrived among Lisbon's black population of the sixteenth century and in the Portuguese colonies of Africa and Brazil because, in part, the church honored petitions to establish ethnic-based confraternities. "Angolan-Afro-Brazilian Cultural Connections," 10.

143 Heywood, "Angolan-Afro-Brazilian Cultural Connections," 19; Kiddy, "Ethnic and Racial Identity," 238–43; Reis, *Slave Rebellion in Brazil*, 149–51, 153; Reis, "Différences et résistances," 19, 21; Mulvey, "Slave Confraternities in Brazil," 46, 49; Russell-Wood, "Black and Mulatto Brotherhoods," 582–83; Karasch, *Slave Life*, 84–85, 358–59; Carvalho Soares, *Devotos da cor*; Mello e Souza, *Reis negros no Brasil escravista*.

144 See the numerous documents on an Angolan brotherhood reprinted inSmith, "Manuscritos da igreja de Nossa Senhora do Rosario"; and Smith, "Décadas do Rosário dos pretos."

145 St. John d'el Rey Mining Company, *Circular to the Proprietors*, 39, in St. John d'el Rey Mining Company Archive, Nettie Lee Benson Latin American Collection, University of Texas at Austin. In 1849 the superintendent of the same gold mine told the House of Lords that masters grouped Africans by nations "for the purpose of preserving peace on the establishment. [Otherwise t]hey would be able to league together." Great Britain, House of Lords, "Report from the Select Committee," vol. 9, par. 2493, p. 171.

146 Pike, "Sevillan Society," 344–46.

147 Bowser, *African Slave in Colonial Peru*, 249–50, 339.

148 See the numerous petitions in *Indice del Archivo del Departamento General de Policía*. For a broader discussion see Chamosa, " 'To Honor the Ashes,' " 347–78; and Andrews, *Afro-Argentines of Buenos-Aires*, 142–51.

149 Ortiz, *Los cabildos*, 6; Montejo-Arrechea, *Sociedades*, 14–16.

150 Landers, *Black Society in Spanish Florida*, 109.

151 Morell de Santa Cruz, "El Obispo Morell de Santa Cruz oficializa los *cabildos*," 8:159.

152 Ibid.

153 Ibid., 159–60.

154 Ibid., 159.

155 "Diligencias sobre cuentos del *cabildo* de la nación Induri pos su capataz Nicolas Veitia," 1800, ANC-ED, leg. 398, no. 23, fols. 1–5.

156 This date is earlier than Howard's, who argues that by "the beginning of the nineteenth century, cabildos . . . outnumber[ed] cofradías." *Changing History*, 26–7.

157 Bachiller y Morales, *Los Negros*, 114–15. Ortiz, *Los cabildos*, 4–6; Montejo-Arrechea, *Sociedades*, 12–13; Deschamps Chapeaux, "Cabildos," 51; Deschamps Chapeaux, "Sociedades," 54; Howard, *Changing History*, 21–25.

158 Lovejoy and Richardson, "Trust, Pawnship, and Atlantic History," 347–49; also see the discussion in Sparks, *Two Princes of Calabar*, esp. 59–60.

159 Lovejoy, "Identifying Enslaved Africans," 8; Howard, *Changing History*, 48, 53, 68–69, 109–10. The classic treatment of the Abakuá in Cuba remains Cabrera, *La Sociedad Secreta Abakuá*.

160 Morton-Williams, "Yoruba Ogboni Cult in Oyo," 362–74; Atanda, "Yoruba Ogboni Cult," 365–72; Law, *Oyo Empire*, 61. For Yoruba imports into Cuba, see Eltis, "Diaspora of Yoruba Speakers," 17–39.

161 Thornton, "Coromantees," 163, 169.

162 Falola and Akanmu, *Culture, Politics, and Money*, 131–39.

163 Eltis et al., *Trans-Atlantic Slave Trade*.

164 Eltis, *Rise of African Slavery*, 251–54. A growing body of scholarship is linking specific ports of exportation in Africa with specific ports of importation in the Americas. For historiographical and methodological approaches, see Mann, "Shifting Paradigms," 3–21; Heywood, "Introduction," 2–8, and Childs and Falola, "Yoruba Diaspora," 1–14.

165 For an emphasis on the methodological problems, see Alleyne, "Linguistics and the Oral Tradition," 19–45, esp. 31; and Morgan, "Cultural Implications," 122–45.

166 Eltis, Richardson, and Behrendt, "Patterns," 30. Preliminary data from an updated version of the transatlantic slave trade database indicates that Angola provided the largest percentage of forced migrants with 29 percent. Personal communication from David Eltis by e-mail, 22 May 2005.

167 Eltis, *Rise of African Slavery*, 253 n. 104.

168 ANC-ED, leg. 893, no. 4, fol. [?].

169 "La nación lucumi contra Dn. Manuel Blanco y otros sobre propiedad del terreno en que se halla fundado el cavildo de nación," 1777–81, ANC-EC, leg. 147, no. 1, fols. 50–53v.

170 Bishop of Cuba to His Majesty, Havana, 6 Dec. 1753, in Ortiz, *Los negros curros*, 212–13.

171 Estimate derived from documentation found in the following: ANC-EC, leg. 6, no. 6, leg. 47, no. 1; ANC-ED, leg. 336, no. 1, leg. 398, no. 23, leg. 439, no. 16, leg. 548, no. 11, leg. 583, no. 5, leg. 610, no. 15, leg. 660, no. 8, leg. 673, no. 9, leg. 893, no. 4; ANC-Escribanía de Gobierno (hereafter ANC-EG), leg. 28, no. 4, leg. 123, no. 15, leg. 123, no. 15-A, leg. 125, no. 3, leg. 277, no. 5; ANC-EO, leg. 3, no. 8, leg. 6, no. 1, leg. 65, no. 11, leg. 494, no. 2; ANC-Escribanía de Valerio (ANC-EVal), leg. 671, no. 9873; ANC-Escribanía de Varios (ANC-EVar), leg. 211, no. 3114; ANC-AP, leg. 11, no. 37, leg. 12, nos. 9, 14, 17, 27, leg. 13, no. 1, leg. 14, no. 1; ANC-Donativos y Remisiones (ANC-DR), leg. 542, no. 29; AGI-PC, leg. 1433-B, 1667. There is no documentation in various secondary sources or primary sources that would support Fannie Theresa Rushing's very conservative estimate that in "1801, there were thirteen *cabildos de nación* in Havana" or her statement that by 1827 "there were twenty-one *cabildos de nación* in Havana." Rushing, "Afro-Cuban Social Organization," 181. For the city of Matanzas alone, historian Israel Moliner Castañeda has identified seventeen *cabildo* houses in 1816. *Los Cabildos*, 83–84.

172 ANC-EC, leg. 147, no. 1, fol. 53v.

173 Thornton, *Africa and Africans*, 190; also see Law, "Ethnicity and the Slave Trade," 207, 209.

174 "Pedro José Santa Cruz solicitando nombramiento de Capataz al *Cabildo* de la nación Congos Musolongos," 1806, ANC-ED, leg. 660, no. 8, fols. 1–4.

175 "La nación Caravali Umugini sobre división con la Osso y con la misma Umugini, y liquidación de cuentas con el capitán Pedro Nolasco Eligió," 1805–6, ANC-EG, leg. 123, no. 15-A, fol. 9.

176 "Real cédula de su magestad sobre la educación, trato y ocupaciones de los esclavos, en todos sus dominios de indias, e islas filipinas baxo las reglas que expresan," Aranjuez, 31 May 1789, BNJM-Morales, leg. 79, no. 3, fol. 7.

177 Diego Miguel de Moya to His Majesty, Havana, 19 Jan. 1790, ANC-RCJF, leg. 150, no. 7405, fol. 11.

178 Ibid., fol. 18v.

179 AOHCH-AC, leg. 76, Cabildo Minutes, Havana, 2 Mar. 1809, fol. 73v.

180 For a detailed discussion of the slave family and the role of *cabildos* related to family structure, see Barcia Zequeira, *La otra familia*, 121–36.

181 ANC-AP, leg. 12, no. 9, fol. 9v.

182 Ibid., fol. 22v.

183 Ibid., fol. 30v. In Brazil, Africans who shared a similar ethnic bond also used the Portuguese term for relative, "parente," to refer to each other. See Reis and Galloti Mamigonian, "Nagô and Mina," 81.

184 "Expediente seguido por Cristoval Govin, capataz de la nación Oquella contra Lázaro Rodríguez, capataz del la Agro, sobre cuentas," 1799, ANC-EO, leg. 6, no. 1, fol. 62.

185 ANC-AP, leg. 12, no. 9, fol. 23v.

186 Francisco Alonzo de Morazan to Someruelos, Havana, 28 June 1811, AGI-PC, leg. 1667.

187 ANC-AP, leg. 12, no. 9, fols. 86–87.

188 "Cabildo musolongo sobre nombramientos de Capataz," 1806, ANC-ED, leg. 548, no. 11, fols. 15v–16.

189 ANC-ED, leg. 893, no. 4, fol. [?].

190 ANC-AP, leg. 12, no. 14, fol. 12.

191 ANC-AP, leg. 14, no. 1, fols. 182v–83v. According to contemporary J. M. Pérez, the minuet was the most popular dance in 1800. "Siglo XIX: Costumbres de Cuba en 1800 por J. M. Pérez," AOHCH-JLF, leg. 214, no. 31.

192 ANC-AP, leg. 12, no. 9. fol. 109.

193 ANC-ED, leg. 893, no. 4, fol. 46; "La nación Caravali Induri sobre nombramiento de capataz del cavildo del Santo Cristo de Buen Viaje," 1802–6, ANC-EG, leg. 125, no. 3, fol. [?]; ANC-EO, leg. 65, no. 11, fol. 72.

194 "Juan Nepomuceno Montiel y Rafael Arostegui como apoderados en la nación Lucumi Llane contra Agustina Zaraza y Antonio Ribero sobre la extracción de pesos que hicieron de la caja de la nación," 1807–10, ANC-EC, leg. 64, no. 6, fols. 13–15.

195 ANC-EO, leg. 6, no. 1, fol. 59.

196 ANC-ED, leg. 893, no. 4, fol. [?].

197 ANC-EG, leg. 123, no. 15-A, fol. 21.

198 Howard, *Changing History*, 48.

199 "José Antonio Diepa, capataz del cabildo nación Congo, sobre que se recojía los memoriales que promovió Cayetano García y socios para despojarlo del encargo de capataz del cabildo nación Congo Macamba," 1808–9, ANC-ED, leg. 439, no. 16, fol. 51v.

200 ANC-AP, leg. 12, no. 9, fols. 68v–69v.

201 Ibid., fols. 13, 44v.

202 ANC-EG, leg. 125, no. 3, fols. 106–15.

203 ANC-ED, leg. 893, no. 4, fol. 47.

204 "José Xavier Mirabal y consortes contra Domingo Acosta y socios sobre pesos, trata del cabildo de Apapa," 1808–30, ANC-ED, leg. 583, no. 5, fols. 82–82v (emphasis in original).

205 ANC-EC, leg. 147, no. 1, fol. 54v.

206 "Tomás Poveda, Clemente Andrade, Antonio de Prucia, Joaquín de Soto y Antonio María Lisundia contra el moreno José Arostegui sobre que cuentas de caja del cavildo," 1805, ANC-ED, leg. 336, no. 1, fol. 40. Joao José Reis has identified a similar

process of how the Yoruba in Bahia, Brazil, began to forge a common Nagô identity: "The Yoruba of the Oyo, Ehba, Ijebu, Ilesha and Ketu kingdoms became Nagôs in Bahia through complex exchanges and convergences of cultural signs with the help of a common language, similar divinities (Orishas), the unification of many under Islam, long experience as subjects of the Oyo *alafins* (kings), Yoruba urban traditions and, obviously, a life of slavery in Bahia." " 'Revolution of the *Ganhadores*,' " 361.

207  ANC-EO, leg. 6, no. 1, fol. 60v.

208  "Expediente relativo a la renovación de cargos de un cabildo de nación ante las autoridades en la ciudad de Matanzas," ANC-DR, leg. 542, no. 29, fol. 1. Some of the documentation for the Matanzas Karabali cabildo is published in "Constitución de un cabildo Carabali en 1814."

209  ANC-AP, leg. 12, no. 9, fols. 45, 68v, 73.

210  Ibid., fols. 36v, leg. 13, no. 1, fol. 101.

211  ANC-EG, leg. 125, no. 3, fol. 115–15v.

212  Pedro Alonso to [?], Havana, 10 Oct. 1759, published in Ortiz, *Los negros curros*, 214.

213  ANC-AP, leg. 12, no. 9, fol. 30v.

214  Ibid., no. 27, fol. 12v.

215  Thornton, " 'I Am the Subject,' " 186–98.

216  ANC-EC, leg. 147, no. 1, fols. 41–42.

217  "Tomás Poveda, capataz de los cabildos Carabali Osso solicitando nombramiento de otra capataz," 1806, ANC-ED, leg. 610, no. 15.

218  "La nación Caravali Umugini sobre división con la Oso y con la misma Umugini, y liquidación de cuentas con el capitán Pedro Nolasco Eligio," 1805–6, ANC-EG, leg. 123, no. 15A.

219  "Salvador Flores y demás individuos de la nación Carabali Ibo sobre que se suspenda capataz a José María Pimenta y que de cuentas," 1814, ANC-EG, leg. 123, no. 15; "Cabildo musolongo sobre nombramientos de Capataz," 1806, ANC-ED, leg. 548, no. 11; "La nación mina guagni contra Salvador Ternero sobre que de cuentas del producido del cabildo de la misma nación," 1794, ANC-EO, leg. 65, no. 11; "La nación mina contra Juana de Mesa," 1797, ANC-ED, leg. 673, no. 9; "La nación mina guagni contra Salvador Ternero sobre cuentas," 1794–97, ANC-ED, leg. 893, no. 4; also see Howard's detailed treatment in *Changing History*, 31–36.

220  Kuethe, "Status of the Free Pardo," 109.

221  ANC-ED, leg. 583, no. 5, fol. 24.

222  ANC-EO, leg. 65, no. 11, fol. 55.

223  ANC-EC, leg. 147, no. 1, fol. 41; also see Howard for the link between militia soldiers and *cabildo* activities, *Changing History*, 31–36.

224  Kimberly S. Hanger discovered that in New Orleans the town council often rejected petitions by blacks to hold dances, "but when the free black militia, represented by four officers, submitted its request in 1800," authorities approved it. *Bounded Lives*, 132.

225  "Expediente seguido por los de la nación Caravali Oquella sobre nombramiento de segundo y tercero capataces," 1804, ANC-EV, leg. 211, no. 3114, fols. 9v–12.

226  ANC-ED, leg. 439, no. 16, fol. [?].

227  ANC-EG, leg. 125, no. 3, fol. 108v.

228  Ibid., fol. 115.

229  ANC-EO, leg, 6, no. 1, fol. 60v–61.

230  ANC-ED. leg. 336, no. 1, fol. [?].

231 ANC-ED, leg. 439, no. 16, fol. [?].

232 See for example *Diario de la Habana*, 3 Feb. 1812, 3; for an analysis of newspaper slave sales, see Núnez Jiménez, *Los esclavos negros*, 79–148.

233 ANC-ED, leg. 336, no. 1, fol. 38v.

234 "Expediente de cuentas que produce Tomás Betancourt de las cantidades que han entrado en su poder del cavildo Caravali Oquella," 1804, ANC-EO, leg. 3, no. 8, fol. 7v.

235 Ibid., fol. 6v; ANC-EO, leg. 6. no. 1, fol. 8v; for a discussion of the Spanish coffer, see Bushnell, *King's Coffer*, 1, 36, 45.

236 ANC-ED, leg. 398, no. 23, fol. 3.

237 ANC-ED, leg. 439, no. 16, fol. [?].

238 Ibid., no. 16, fol. [?].

239 ANC-EO, leg. 6, no. 1, fol. 33.

240 Ibid., fol. 30v.

241 Howard, *Changing History*, 40–42.

242 ANC-ED, leg. 660, no. 8, fol. 4.

243 ANC-ED, leg. 583, no. 5, fol. 100.

244 "Sobre la conspiración intentada por los negros esclavos para invadir la villa a resultas de la libertad que suponen estarles declaradas por las Cortes Generales y estraor-dinarias del Retno de Puerto Príncipe," Jan. 1812, ANC-AP, leg. 11, no. 37, fol. 58.

245 ANC-ED, leg. 398, no. 23, fol. 1; ANC-EO, leg. 6, no. 1, fol. 1v.

246 ANC-EO leg. 3, no. 8, fol. 3v; ANC-EC, leg. 64, no. 6, fol. 60; ANC-ED, leg. 439, no. 16, fol. 51v.

247 ANC-EG, leg. 123, no. 15A, fol. 6.

248 ANC-ED, leg. 336, no. 1, fol. 22v.

249 ANC-EG, leg. 125, no. 3, fol. 167.

250 ANC-ED, leg. 336, no. 1 fol. 22, leg. 610, no. 15, fol. 2; ANC-EO, leg, 3, no. 8, fol. 7.

251 ANC-AP, leg. 12, no. 9, fols. 68v–69.

252 Jameson, *Letters from the Havana*, 21–22; Walker, *No More, No More*, 1–18.

253 ANC-AP, leg. 12, no. 9, fol. 23.

254 ANC, fondo Comisión Militar, leg. 11, no. 1, fols. 456v–458. I would like to thank Gloria García for directing me to this source.

255 ANC-ED, leg. 893, no. 5, fols. 51–51v.

256 Jameson, *Letters from the Havana*, 21–22; Bremmer, *Homes of the New World*, 2:379–83.

257 ANC-EC, leg. 64, no. 6, fol. 60.

258 "Tomás Povea, capataz de los cabildos Carabali Osso solicitando nombramiento de otra capataz," 1806, ANC-ED, leg. 610, no. 15, fol. 2.

259 Howard identifies the same process whereby "members of these organizations mani-fested a 'consciousness of kind': an identity that mitigated, to a certain degree, differences of language, ethnicity, and customs, an identity that allowed them to discern the common problems all people of color confronted on a daily basis." *Changing History*, xvii.

260 ANC-AP, leg. 12, no. 14, fols. 4–4v, 90.

CHAPTER FOUR

1 ANC-AP, leg. 12, no. 24, leg. 13, no. 38, fol. 4.

2 ANC-AP, leg. 12, no. 14, fols. 11, 25, no. 17, fol. 20, no. 18, fol. 6.

3 ANC-AP, leg. 12, no. 26, fols. 3–14.

4 ANC-AP, leg. 13, no. 1, fol. 42.
5 ANC-AP, leg. 12, no. 16, fols. 11–12.
6 Ibid., no. 18, fols. 4–5.
7 Ibid., no. 14, fol. 89, no. 25, fols. 39–39v.
8 Ibid., no. 25, fols. 35v–36.
9 ANC-AP, leg. 13, no. 1, fol. 12v.
10 ANC-AP, leg. 12, no. 18, fol. 8.
11 ANC-AP, leg. 13, no. 1, fol. 181.
12 ANC-AP, leg. 12, no. 18, fol. 8.
13 ANC-AP, leg. 13, no. 15, fols. 19v–20 (emphasis in original).
14 ANC-AP, leg. 13, no. 1, fols. 42v–43.
15 Ibid; ANC-AP, leg. 12, no. 25, fol. 100v.
16 ANC-AP, leg. 13, no. 1, fols. 35v–36.
17 ANC-AP, leg. 12, no. 18, fols. 5, 36.
18 Juan Ruíz de Apodaca to Stephen Kingston, Havana, 3 July 1812, USNA-RG, 59. Figures were most likely taken from 1810 census.
19 "3 cartas sobre negros Franceses en Pto. Pre," Sept. and Oct. 1795, AGI-PC, leg. 1463-B; "Relación de los acontecimientos políticos ocurridos en el Camagüey," 1903, Biblioteca Nacional José Martí, Colección Arredondo (BNJM-Arredondo), no. 8; Oquendo, "Las rebeldías de los esclavos en Cuba," 68; "Noticias acaecidas en la villa de Puerto Príncipe el día 12 de Junio de 1798," AOHCH-JLF, leg. 224, exp. 14; Cabildo Minutes, Puerto Príncipe, 13 Feb. 1805, AHPC-AC, leg. 24 (1801–05), fol. 433; Coppingeros to Kindelan, Bayamo, 9 Mar. 1805, Urbina to Coppingeros, Santiago, 30 Aug. 1805, ANC-GSC, leg. 1099, no. 40586; Ada Ferrer, "Noticias de Haití en Cuba," 683. The record of Cuban slave rebellions in the 1790s and 1800s does not support Sherry Johnson's conclusion that the island "experienced relatively little unrest in the black population." *Social Transformation*, 8.
20 Sedano to Apodaca, Havana, 29 July 1812, AGI-PC, leg. 1640.
21 Someruelos to Pezuela, Havana, 5 Mar. 1812, AGI-UM, leg. 84. no. 348.
22 Sedano to Someruelos, Puerto Príncipe, 4 Feb. and 22 Mar. 1812, AGI-PC, leg. 1640.
23 "Testimonio del quaderno de las confesiones que sieguen adherentes al numero: 3," AGI-PC, leg. 1865A, fol. 12; Sedano to Someruelos, Puerto Príncipe, 1 Feb. 1812, AGI-PC, leg. 1640; ANC-AP, leg. 11, no. 37, fols. 63v–65; Cabildo Minutes, Puerto Príncipe, AHPC-AC, leg. 27, 17–31 Jan. 1812, fols. 34v–65.
24 "Autos de la insurrección de negros en la villa de Puerto Príncipe," AGI-PC, leg. 1865A, fol. 5.
25 Ibid., fol. 6.
26 ANC-AP, leg. 11, no. 37, fols. 25, 34, leg. 12, no. 27, fols. 8–15; Sedano to Someruelos, Puerto Príncipe, 19 Jan. 1812, AGI-PC, leg. 1640; "Respecto a haberse presentado Dn. Fernado del Monte natural de la Ciudad de Santiago de los Cavalleros de esta villa a hacer denuncia de nueva ocurrencia sobre la insurrección intentada por los negros esclavos en razón de libertad, previno su merced se examinando en la forma debida por los particulares que contienense su denuncia," AGI-PC, leg. 1865A, fols. 1v–6.
27 "Autos de la insurrección de negros en la villa de Puerto Príncipe," AGI-PC, leg. 1865A, fols. 3v, 6v–8.
28 ANC-AP, leg. 11, no. 37, fol. 65; "1a Pieza. De los autos seguidos sobre sublevación de negros esclabos de la villa de Puerto Príncipe," 20 Jan 1812, AGI-PC, leg. 1780, fols. 17, 20, 31v, 34, 37, 57.

29 ANC-AP, leg. 11, no. 37, fol. 34.

30 Ibid., fols. 49–50.

31 ANC-AP, leg. 12, no. 27, fols. 8–16v.

32 ANC-AP, leg. 11, no. 37, fols. 57–58.

33 "Sublevación de un cafetal, 1812," AGI-PC, leg. 1779, fol. 1v.

34 Ibid., fol. 4.

35 Ibid., fol. 4v.

36 Ibid., fol. 6v.

37 Ibid., fol. 10.

38 Ibid., fol. 14.

39 Cabildo Minutes, Puerto Príncipe, 18 Jan. 1812, AHPC-AC, leg. 27, fol. 40v. Notarized copies of the original cabildo minutes made in 1812 and sent to Spain can be found in AGI-PC, leg. 1640; copies sent to Havana can be found in ANC-AP, leg. 124, no. 33.

40 Sedano to Someruelos, Puerto Príncipe, 19 Jan., 3 and 17 Feb., 11 Apr 1812, AGI-PC, leg. 1640; Someruelos to Aguilar, Havana, 13 Mar. 1812, ANC-CCG, leg. 94, no. 8; Cabildo Minutes, Puerto Príncipe, 31 Jan. 1812, AHPC-AC, leg. 27, fol. 65.

41 "Testimonio del quaderno de las confesiones que sieguen adherentes al numero: 3," AGI-PC, leg. 1865A, fol. 12v.

42 Someruelos to Pezuela, Havana, 5 Mar. 1812, AGI-UM, leg. 84. no. 348; Someruelos to Ministerio de Gracia y Justicia, Havana, 5 Mar, 1812, AGI-PC, leg. 1752.

43 Sedano to Someruelos, Puerto Príncipe, 18 Feb. 1812, AGI-PC, leg. 1640.

44 Cabildo Minutes, Puerto Príncipe, 18 June 1811, AHPC-AC, leg. 26, fol. 314v; Sedano to Someruelos, Puerto Príncipe, 1 Feb. 1812, AGI-PC, leg. 1640.

45 Cabildo Minutes, Puerto Príncipe, 21 and 23 Jan. 1812, AHPC-AC, leg. 27, fols. 46, 50v.

46 Someruelos to Pezuela, Havana, 14 Feb. 1812, AGI-SD, leg. 1284, no. 343.

47 Sedano to Someruelos, Puerto Príncipe, 1 and 4 Feb. 1812, AGI-PC, leg. 1640; Cabildo Minutes, Puerto Príncipe, 21 Mar. 1812, AHPC-AC, leg. 27, fol. 121.

48 Apodaca to Pezuela, Havana, 22 May 1812, AGI-UM, leg. 84, no. 13.

49 Sedano to Someruelos, Puerto Príncipe, 22 Mar. 1812, AGI-PC, leg. 1640, no. 147.

50 Punishments listed in AGI-PC, leg. 1640, 1865A

51 ANC-AP, leg. 12, no. 27, fols. 16–16v.

52 Cabildo Minutes, Puerto Príncipe, 24 Jan. 1812, AHPC-AC, leg. 27, fols. 55–55v.

53 Juan Ruíz de Apodaca to Stephen Kingston, Havana, 3 July 1812, USNA-RG, 59. Figures are most likely taken from the 1810 census.

54 Francisco Sánchez, "Precauciones que el Capn. de Infantería Dn. Francisco Sánchez Grinan subinspector del Batallón de Milicias disciplinadas de Cuba y villa de Bayamo, y Teniente de Gobernador en esta juzga conveniente tomar para que no llegue a padecer las desgracia que le preparaba la conmoción premeditada por Nicolás Morales Pardo Libre, y natural de ella, por otra semejante que pueda subsistirse," Bayamo, 24 Sept. 1795, ANC-GG, leg. 540, no. 27096; "Testimonio contra Nicolás Morales por el levantamiento que intentaba," Bayamo, 1795, AGI-PC, leg. 1498-B. Paquette, *Sugar Is Made with Blood*, 124–25, mistakenly dates the planned rebellion to 1796; see Franco, *Ensayos históricos*, 93–100, for a discussion of the event.

55 "Testimonio de la criminalidad seguida de oficios contra el negro Miguel, Juan Bautista, y José Antonio, sobre la conjuración que intentaban contra el Pueblo, y sus moradores, Juez, El Sor Teniente Gobernador," Bayamo, 25 Aug. 1805, AGI-PC, leg. 1649; Franklin, "Gender and Slave Rebellion."

56 ANC-AP, leg. 12, no. 9, fols. 4, 71; Corral to Urbina, Bayamo, 27 Feb. 1812, AGI-PC, leg. 1548.

57 ANC-AP, leg. 12, no. 9, fol. 6v.

58 Ibid., fol. 62.

59 AHPG-Protocolos, leg. 11, libro 3 (1812), fols. 108v–9; ANC-AP, leg. 12, no. 9, fols. 9–10v, 12–12v, 62v–64.

60 ANC-AP, leg. 12, no. 9, fol. 14.

61 Ibid., fol. 18.

62 Ibid., fol. 22v, 34v, 38–42, 98–99v.

63 Ibid., fol. 58v.

64 Corral to Someruelos, Bayamo, 16 Feb. 1812, AGI-PC, leg. 1649, no. 66.

65 ANC-AP, leg. 12, no. 9, fols. 101–3.

66 Ibid., fol. 68v.

67 Ibid., fol. 7v.

68 Ibid., fols. 8–8v, 13, 22v–23, 30v, 44v, 65.

69 For a general discussion of Candelaria as a Catholic holiday, see Smith, "Candlemas," 3:23. I have been unable to find a contemporary description of the festival in Bayamo other than the brief references from the court testimony in ANC-AP, leg. 12, no. 9. I would like to thank Onoria Céspedes Argote and Angel Lagio Vieito of the Casa de la Nacionalidad Cubana in Bayamo for researching the holiday.

70 ANC-AP, leg. 12, no. 9, fol. 16 (emphasis in original).

71 Ibid. The person asked to explain the significance of the chant cannot be identified because the document has been partially destroyed by deterioration.

72 Ibid., fol. 50.

73 PRO-CO, 705/108, fols. 66–67, available at "Songs of Resistance," <http://www.nationalarchives.gov.uk/pathways/blackhistory/africa_caribbean/caribbean_resistence.htm (accessed 14 April 2005).

74 Darnton, "Early Information Society," 19.

75 ANC-AP, leg. 12, no. 9, fol. 8v.

76 Ibid., fol. 28.

77 Ibid., fol. 36v.

78 Ibid., fol. 65.

79 Ibid., fols. 44v–45, 48v.

80 Ibid., fol. 102.

81 Ibid., fols. 9–9v.

82 Ibid., fols. 5–5v.

83 Ibid., fol. 21v.

84 Ibid., fol. 33.

85 "Testimonio de la criminalidad seguida de oficios contra el negro Miguel, Juan Bautista, y José Antonio, sobre la conjuración que intentaban contra el Pueblo, y sus moradores, Juez, El Sor Teniente Gobernador," Bayamo, 25 Aug. 1805, AGI-PC, leg. 1649, fol. 47v; Franklin, "Gender and Slave Rebellion," 107–11.

86 According to historian Robert Darnton, if we emphasize the eighteenth-century understanding of cosmopolitan, which stressed polyglot skills, the term is even more appropriate to refer to the multilingualism and varied backgrounds of the slave population. Even more fitting, Darnton writes that cosmopolitanism also indicated a sense of "nationlessness" and the "term could be used pejoratively, as indicated by the

dictionary of *Académie Française*: 'COSMOPOLITAN. Someone who does not adopt any fatherland. A cosmopolitan is not a good citizen.' Even the *Encyclopédie* noted that 'One sometimes uses the term in joking, to signify a man who has no fixed abode or a man who is not a foreigner anywhere.' " Darnton, "Euro State of Mind," 30.

87  ANC-AP, leg. 12, no. 9, fols. 36–36v.

88  Ibid., fol. 50.

89  Ibid., fol. 52.

90  Ibid., fol. 115v.

91  Ibid., fols. 34, 44v–45, 54, 68v–69, 86v–87, 88v, 89v, 110, 123.

92  Corral to Someruelos, Bayamo, 18 Mar. 1812, AOHCH-AC, leg. 84, fols. 269–69v.

93  Corral to Someruelos, Bayamo, 16 Mar. 1812, AGI-PC, leg. 1649.

94  Corral to Someruelos, Bayamo, 23 Apr. 1812, AGI-PC, leg. 1824.

95  Urbina to Someruelos, Santiago, 21 and 28 Feb., 6 Mar. 1812, Corral to Urbina, Bayamo, 27 Feb. 1812, AGI-PC, leg. 1548; Someruelos to Urbina, Havana, 4 Mar. 1812, ANC-AP, leg. 214, no. 65; Someruelos to the Governor of Santiago, Havana, 6 Apr. 1812, ANC-AP, leg. 214, no. 96; Juan Francisco Solas to Urbina, Santiago, 19 Feb. 1812, ANC-CCG, leg. 93, no. 14; Antonio Alonzo de la Torres to Urbina, Santiago, 16 Feb. 1812, Antonio Vaillant to Urbina, Santiago, 16 Feb. 1812, and Urbina to Subinspector de Pardos, Santiago, 26 Feb. 1812, ANC-CCG, leg. 93, no. 15.

96  Cabildo Ordinario, Santa Clara, 13 Feb. 1812, Diego Gómez to Someruelos, Santa Clara, 18 Feb. 1812, AGI-PC, leg. 1631.

97  ANC-AP, leg. 12, no. 9, fols. 62v–64.

98  Someruelos to Governor of Santiago, Havana, 23 Mar. 1812, ANC-AP, leg. 214, no. 81; Urbina to Alcaldes del Pueblo de Jiguaní, Santiago, 17 Feb. 1812, Urbina to Some-ruelos, Santiago, 23 Feb. and 4 Mar. 1812, AGI-PC, leg. 1548.

99  ANC-AP, leg. 12, no. 9, fols. 21v–22; Governor of Santiago to Ayuntamiento, Santi-ago, 23 Mar. 1812, ANC-AP, leg. 214, no. 82; Cabildo Minutes, Santiago, 6 Apr. 1812, AHMSC-AC. (I would like to thank John-Marshall Klein for directing me to this source.)

100  Francisco Curado to John Cunningham, Montego Bay, Jamaica, 9 Feb. 1812, PRO-CO, 137 / 134, fols. 48–48v.

101  Edward Morrison to the Earl of Liverpool, King's House, Jamaica, 21 Feb. 1812, PRO-CO, 137 / 134, fol. 46.

102  Someruelos to Pezuela, Havana, 14 Feb. 1812, AGI-SD, leg. 1284, no. 343; Someruelos to Pezuela, Havana, 14 Feb. 1812, AGI-UM, leg. 84.

103  Gray to Monroe, Havana, 14 Apr. 1812, USNA-RG, 59. For the Gabriel Conspiracy of 1800 in Virginia and Monroe's active role in the investigation, see Sidbury, *Plough-shares into Swords*, 118–28; Egerton, *Gabriel's Rebellion*, 74–76, 103–4, 107, 112–13.

104  Scott, "Common Wind," chaps. 4 and 5.

105  Sedano to Armiñán, Puerto Príncipe, 1 Feb. 1812, ANC-GG, leg. 545, no. 27103. The letter has been reprinted in Gálvez and Novoa, *1812*, 38. They mistakenly date the letter to 10 Feb. 1812.

106  Francisco Curado to John Cunningham, Montego Bay, Jamaica, 9 Feb. 1812, PRO-CO, 137 / 134, fol. 48.

107  Alvarez to Corral, Bayamo, 15 Feb. 1812, ANC-AP, leg. 12, no. 9, fols. 124–25v.

108  [Armiñan ?], Holguín, 14 Feb. 1812, AMPH-Colonial, no. 191.

109  Cabildo Minutes, Holguín, 7 Feb. 1812, ANC-GG, leg. 545, no. 27103.

110  Armiñan to Urbina, Holguín, 8 Feb. 1812, ANC-GG, leg. 545, no. 27103.

111 Urbina to Armiñan, Santaigo, 12 Feb. 1812, ANC-GG, leg. 545, no. 27103. Gálvez and Novoa incorrectly read *patética* (pathetic) as *potencia* (power, strength, force). *1812*, 42.

112 Urbina to Comandante de Artillería, Santiago, 12 Feb. 1812, ANC-CCG, leg. 93, no. 4.

113 Armiñan, Holguín, 17 Feb. 1812, AHPH-TG, leg. 69, no. 2048; Cabildo Minutes, Holguín, 16 Feb. 1812, AHPH-AC, leg. 64, no. 1936, fols. 9v–10; Urbina to Someruelos, Santiago, 15 Feb. 1812, AGI-PC, leg. 1548, no. 456.

114 Cabildo Minutes, Holguín, 1 Aug. 1808, AHPH-AC, leg. 63, no. 1933, fol. 36v.

115 [Governor of Holguín, 1809 ?], AHPH-TG, leg. 68, no. 2007.

116 Urbina to Navia, Santiago, 20 Sept. 1810, Urbina to Governor of Holguín, Santiago, 2 Nov. 1810, Juan Salvadar to Francisco de Zayas, Gibara, 9 Oct. 1823, AMPH-Colonial, nos. 77, 78, and 619.

117 Cabildo Minutes, Holguín, 7 Feb. 1812, ANC-GG, leg. 545, no. 27103.

118 Armiñan to Urbina, Holguín, 20 Feb. 1812, ANC-GG, leg. 545, no. 27103.

119 Cabildo Minutes, Holguín, 7 Feb. 1812, ANC-GG, leg. 545, no. 27103.

120 Cabildo Minutes, Holguín, 16 Feb. 1812, AHPH-AC, leg. 64, no. 1936, fols. 9v–10; Armiñan, Holguín, 17 Feb. 1812, AHPH-TG, leg. 69, no. 2048.

121 Armiñan to Urbina, [private correspondence], Holguín, 15 Mar. 1812, ANC-GG, leg. 545, no. 27103.

122 Urbina to Governor of Holguín, Santiago, 26 Feb. 1812, AGI-PC, leg. 1548.

123 Armiñan to Urbina, Holguín, 16 Mar. 1812, AGI-PC, leg. 1548; Armiñan to Urbina, Holguín, 15 Mar. 1812, ANC-GG, leg. 545, no. 27103.

124 Urbina to Governor of Holguín, Santaigo, 20 Mar. 1812, AGI-PC, leg. 1548; and the rough draft of the same letter with no changes, [Urbina] to [Armiñan], Santiago, 20 Mar. 1812, ANC-GG, leg. 545, no. 27103.

125 Santiago Márquez to Governor of Holguín, Puerto Príncipe, 25 Mar 1812, AMPH-Colonial, no. 717–2. The colonial collection at the AMPH was created by local historian José García Castañeda, who selectively chose documents that had been abandoned and were most likely going to be destroyed. It is possible that he may have decided to save the cover letter but not the court records. I did not find any copies of the testimony or any mention of the court records in municipal, regional, specialized, national, or colonial archives in Cuba, Spain, England, or the United States. I would like to thank Angeles Aguilera at the AMPH, José Abreu, historian of the Cuban Communist Party in Holguín, and José Novoa, director of the Casa de Iberoamérica, for their efforts to locate the court records and long discussions about their possible location and disappearance.

126 Armiñan to Urbina, Holguín, 15 Mar. 1812, ANC-GG, leg. 545, no. 27103; Armiñan to Urbina, Holguín, 16 Mar. 1812, AGI-PC, leg. 1548.

127 Armiñan to Urbina, Holguín, 15 Mar. 1812, ANC-GG, leg. 545, no. 27103.

128 Urbina to Armiñan, Santiago, 14 Feb. 1812, ANC-GG, leg. 545, no. 27103.

129 Slaves and free people of color, of course, had every incentive to state they had no knowledge of the revolts as it would be an admission of guilt. However, since many confessed that they did have knowledge of the rebellion, there must be some truth to the fact that numerous individuals claimed the first time they heard of the revolts was when they had been questioned about them. See the examples in ANC-AP, leg. 12, no. 9, fols. 8v, 64, 113v; no. 13, fol. 32, no. 14, fol. 29v; no. 17, fols. 73v, 88v, no. 18, fol. 12v, no. 23, fol. 17, no. 25, fols. 7v, 8, 14, 44v–45, 79, leg. 13, no. 1, fols. 426v, 428, 438, 441v, leg. 14, no. 1, fols. 5v, 7, 13v, 17–17v, 29–30, 131–31v.

130 Urbina to Armiñan, Santiago, 20 Mar. 1812, AGI-PC, leg. 1548.

131 Armiñan to Ayuntamiento of Holguín, Holguín, 2 Apr. 1812, AMPH-Colonial, no. 76.

132 Armiñan to Urbina, Holguín, 5 Apr. 1812, ANC-GG, leg. 545, no. 27103. Francisco de Zayas would later play an influential role in Holguín society and politics; see Abreu Cardet, "Francisco de Zayas," 503–8.

133 Archivo Histórico Provincial de Holguín, fondo Protocolos, Rodríguez, 1807–10, fol. 10v.

134 "303, Juan Nepomuceno," 3 Apr. 1812, in Libro de Defunciones de Pardos, vol. 1, 1783–1856, in Archivo de la Catedral de San Isidoro de Holguín. I would like to thank José Novoa for directing me to this source.

135 Ortiz, *Carta al Rey*, 131–57.

136 Armiñan to Urbina, Holguín, 5 Apr. 1812, ANC-GG, leg. 545, no. 27103.

137 On the acquisition of surnames as a marker of freedom for free people of color, see Díaz, *Virgin*, 42.

138 Urbina to Armiñan, Santiago, 11 and 26 Apr. 1812, ANC-GG, leg. 545, no. 27103.

139 Armiñan to Urbina, Holguín, 16 Mar. 1812, Urbina to Armiñan, Santiago, 20 Mar. 1812, ANC-GG, leg. 545, no. 27103.

140 Cabildo Minutes, Havana, 5 Mar. 1812, AOHCH-AC, leg. 83, fols. 57–58.

141 ANC-AP, leg. 12, no. 18, fol. 12, no. 20, fols. 1–9.

142 ANC-AP, leg. 12, no. 13, fols. 3–3v.

143 Ibid., fol. 18.

144 ANC-AP, leg. 12, no. 14, fol. 98.

145 Humboldt, *Ensayo político*, 205; Manzano, *Autobiography of a Slave*, 77–83.

146 ANC-AP, leg. 12, no. 20, fol. 10, no. 25, fols. 10, 35v–36, 48–56.

147 ANC-AP, leg. 12, no. 18, fols. 3, 5, no. 26, fols. 36, 45, leg. 13, no. 1, fols. 51–52, 192–95.

148 ANC-AP, leg. 12, no. 21, fol. 27.

149 Ibid., no. 14, fol. 89, no. 18, fols. 33–37, no. 21, fol. 11, no. 25, fol. 65.

150 Ibid., no. 14, fol. 44, no. 18, fol. 20.

151 ANC-AP, leg. 12, no. 18, fol. 3, leg. 13, no. 1, fols. 52, 95–98, 192–95.

152 ANC-AP, leg. 12, no. 23, fols. 5–5v, 13–13v.

153 Ibid., no. 13, fol. 4

154 Ibid., fol. 4v.

155 Ibid., fol. 5.

156 Ibid., fol. 6v.

157 Ibid., fol. 15.

158 ANC-AP, leg. 12, no. 18, fols. 5–11, 33–37, no. 21, fol. 17, no. 25, fols. 48, 53v–54, 114v–16.

159 ANC-AP, leg. 13, no. 1, fol. 42.

160 ANC-AP, leg. 12, no. 13, fols. 40v–42v.

161 ANC-AP, leg. 12, no. 21, fol. 12, no. 23, fols. 7v–9, leg. 13, no. 1, fols. 111–13, 176–83.

162 ANC-AP, leg. 12, no. 13, fols. 9v–10.

163 ANC-AP, leg. 13, no. 1, fol. 80.

164 Juan de Santa Cruz to Sor. Intendente de Ejercito y Rl. Hacienda, Havana, 30 Nov. 1811, Archivo Nacional de Cuba, Havana, fondo Realengos (ANC-Realengos), leg. 50, no. 8.

165 Joaquín de Lastra to Somereulos, Guanabo, 6 Dec. 1811, ANC-Realengos, leg. 50, no. 8.

166 Masters and colonial officials constantly complained about the presence of outsiders on plantations. In 1838, Captain General Miguel Tacón stated that it "appears impossible" to prevent interactions "that could cause insubordination among the slaves and

introduce into our midst confusion and disorder." Quoted in Pérez, *On Becoming Cuban*, 21.

167  ANC-AP, leg. 13, no. 1, fol. 128.
168  Ibid., fols. 100, 183, 180v–81, 191.
169  ANC-AP, leg. 12, no. 25, fol. 100v, leg. 13, no. 1, fols. 13, 42v–43.
170  ANC-AP, leg. 13, no. 1, fol. 100.
171  ANC-AP, leg. 12, no. 14, fol. 41.
172  Ibid., no. 23, fol. 3, leg. 13, no. 1, fols. 176–77, 188–89.
173  ANC-AP, leg. 12, no. 23, fols. 6v, 7v, 8.
174  Ibid., fol. 8.
175  ANC-AP, leg. 13, no. 1, fols. 103v–4.
176  ANC-AP, leg. 12, no. 14, fol. 28v.
177  Ibid., fols. 73–85, leg. 13, no. 1, fols. 44–52.
178  ANC-AP, leg. 13, no. 1, fol. 44.
179  ANC-AP, leg. 12, no. 14, fol. 74.
180  Ibid., fol. 92.
181  ANC-AP, leg. 13, no. 1, fol. 43.
182  ANC-AP, leg. 12, no. 25, fols. 88–90, leg. 13, no. 1, fols. 95–98.
183  ANC-AP, leg. 12, no. 14, fols. 79v–80.
184  Palmié, *Wizards and Scientists*, 82.
185  ANC-AP, leg. 12, no. 14, fols. 3, 9v, 10, no. 25, fols. 39, 69, leg. 13, no. 1, fols. 18, 193.
186  ANC-AP, leg. 12, no. 25, fols. 13–14.
187  Ibid., no. 14, fol. 27v.
188  ANC-AP, leg. 13, no. 1, fols. 97–98, 193.
189  ANC-AP, leg. 12, no. 14, fols. 4–4v.
190  Ibid., fols. 25v–26.
191  Ibid., fol. 90.
192  ANC-AP, leg. 13, no. 1, fol. 168.
193  ANC-AP, leg. 12, no. 14, fol. 12.
194  Ibid., fols. 3, 28, no. 25, fols. 12–12v, 15v–16, 16v–17, 17v–18.
195  Franco, *La conspiración de Aponte*, 25; Franco, *Las conspiraciones de 1810 y 1812*, 13; see Paquette, *Sugar is Made with Blood*, 123–25; and Howard, *Changing History*, 73–78, among numerous others who have followed Franco's study.
196  Morton-Williams, "Yoruba Ogboni Cult in Oyo," 362–74;. Atanda, "Yoruba Ogboni Cult," 365–72; Law, *Oyo Empire*, 61.
197  ANC-AP, leg. 12, no. 14, fols. 25v–26.
198  Ibid., no. 21, fols. 13, 21, leg. 13, no. 1, fol. 319.
199  ANC-AP, leg. 12, no. 14, fols. 8–9, 13, 16, 92, no. 18, fol. 26.
200  ANC-AP, leg. 12, no. 14, fol. 90, no. 18, fols. 31–32.
201  ANC-AP, leg. 12, no. 25, fol. 8, leg. 13, no. 1, fols. 222–25.
202  ANC-AP, leg. 12, no. 18, fol. 31.
203  Ibid., fol. 35.
204  ANC-AP, leg. 12, no. 13, fol. 5.
205  ANC-AP, leg. 13, no. 15, fol. 19v. Also see the other references to slaves being seduced by free people of color to fight for their liberation in ANC-AP, leg. 12, no. 21, fols. 7, 26, leg. 13, no. 1, fol. 80, and no. 15, fols. 43, 49v.
206  Hitar to Someruelos, Havana, Guadalupe, 20 Mar. 1812, ANC-AP, leg. 12, no. 14, fol. 33. See chapter 3 for his previous arrests and use of the *fuero*.

207 ANC-AP, leg. 12, no. 14, fols. 33, 48, no. 25, fols. 37–37v, 105; Someruelos to Aguilar, Havana, 23 Mar. 1812, ANC-AP, leg. 214, no. 80; Someruelos to Aguilar, Havana, 17 Mar. 1812, Aguilar to Somereulos, Havana, 18 and 19 Mar. 1812, Quintero to Aguilar, Havana, 24 Mar. 1812, ANC-CCG, leg. 94, no. 6; Aguilar to Somereulos, Havana, 21 and 22 Mar. 1812, ANC-CCG, leg. 94, no. 7; Aguilar to Someruelos, Havana, 14 Apr. 1812, ANC-CCG, leg. 94, no. 13.

208 ANC-AP, leg. 12, no. 25, fols. 37–37v; Someruelos to Aguilar, Havana, 17 Mar. 1812, Aguilar to Somereulos, Havana, 18 Mar. 1812, ANC-CCG, leg. 94, no. 6; Aguilar to Someruelos, Havana, 24 Mar. 1812, ANC-CCG, leg. 94, no. 7; Roca to Someruelos, La Cabaña, Havana, 7 Apr. 1812, AGI-PC, leg. 1676; Cabildo Minutes, Havana, 18 Mar. 1812, AOHCH-AC, leg. 83, fols. 62v–67v; leg. 84, fol. 273.

209 Somereulos to Ayuntamiento, Havana, 23 Mar. 1812, AOHCH-AC, leg. 84, fols. 273–73v. This represented an enormous sum, given that the prices for slaves in Havana newspapers usually ranged from 300 to 500 pesos. See for example *Diario de la Habana*, 3 Feb. 1812, 3.

210 Cabildo Minutes, Havana, 18 Mar. 1812, AOHCH-AC, leg. 83, fols. 65–65v.

211 Cabildo Minutes, Extraordinary Meeting, Havana, 23 Mar. 1812, AOHCH-AC, leg. 83, fols. 67v–68.

212 Apodaca to Caro Manuel, Havana, 3 Sept. 1812, AGI-SD, leg. 1284, no. 39.

213 The punishments for the Havana rebels can be found in AGI-SD, leg. 1284; AGI-UM, leg. 84, 96; ANC-AP, leg. 12, nos. 13, 14, 16, 17, 18, 21, 23, 24, 25, leg. 13, nos. 1, 15, 38, leg. 14, no. 1, leg. 214, no. 56; ANC-CCG, leg. 94, nos. 12, 13; ANC-DR, leg. 562, no. 7; and AOHCH-AC, leg. 83, leg. 84.

214 "Memorial de los diputados de la Habana sobre una insurrección de esclavos en el ingenio Peñas-Altas," Cádiz, 23 May 1812, BNJM-Morales, 79, no. 72, fols. 287–92.

215 "Bando de Capitán General Someruelos sobre la Conspiración de José Ant° Aponte," Havana, 9 Apr. 1812, ANC-AP, leg. 12, no. 24. A copy of the document can also be found in AGI-SD, leg. 1286. Franco reprints the document in *Las conspiraciones de 1810 y 1812*, 213–20.

216 ANC-AP, leg. 12, no. 9, fol. 102.

217 Ibid., fol. 62.

218 ANC-AP, leg. 12, no. 9, fols. 4, 6v–7, no. 27, fol. 3; Francisco Curado to John Cunningham, Montego Bay, Jamaica, 9 Feb. 1812, PRO-CO, 137/134, fol. 48; Someruelos to Ministerio de Gracia y Justicia, Havana, 5 Mar. 1812, AGI-PC, leg. 1752, no. 348.

219 Urbina to Someruelos, Santiago, 15 Feb. 1812, AGI-PC, leg. 1548, no. 456; [Armiñan?], Holguín, 14 Feb. 1812, AMPH-Colonial, no. 191; Francisco Curado to John Cunningham, Montego Bay, Jamaica, 9 Feb. 1812, PRO-CO, 137/134, fol. 48; Alvarez to Corral, Bayamo, 15 Feb. 1812, ANC-AP, leg. 12, no. 9, fols. 124–24v; Armiñan to Urbina, Holguín, 1 and 8 Feb. 1812, ANC-GG, leg. 545, no. 27103.

220 Alvarez to Corral, Bayamo, 13 Feb. 1812, ANC-AP, leg. 12, no. 9, fols. 124–24v.

221 Urbina to Armiñan, 26 Feb. 1812, Santiago, AGI-PC, leg. 1548

222 Armiñan to Urbina, Holguín, 15 Mar. 1812, ANC-GG, leg. 545, no. 27103.

223 Urbina to Falcón, Santiago, 10 Apr. 1812, ANC-CCG, leg. 94, no. 10.

224 Cabildo Minutes, Puerto Príncipe, 15 Apr. 1809, AHPC-AC, leg. 25, fols. 189–89v

225 AHPG-Protocolos, leg. 11, libro 3, 18 Mar. 1812, fols. 108v–9.

226 Urbina to los Alcaldes de Jiguaní, Santiago, 26 Nov. 1811, ANC-CCG, leg. 93, no. 2; Rudesindo de los Olivos to Someruelos, 24 Dec. 1799, Havana, AGI-PC, leg. 1679; Sedano to Someruelos, 1 and 8 Mar. 1812, Puerto Príncipe, AGI-PC, leg. 1640; Urbina

to Someruelos, Santiago, 23 Feb. 1812, AGI-PC, leg. 1548, no. 463; Urbina to los Alcaldes de Jiguani, Santiago, 17 Feb. 1812, AGI-PC, leg. 1548; ANC-AP, leg. 12, no. 9, fols. 62v–64.

227 Hitar to Somreuelos, Havana, 17 Dec. 1810, AGI-PC, leg. 1679; ANC-AP, leg. 12, no. 9, fol. 22.

228 Sedano to Urbina, Puerto Príncipe, 23 Feb. 1812, ANC-AP, leg. 214, no. 46, fols. 1–2.

229 Urbina to Gobernador Político Interno de Santo Domingo, Santiago, 29 Feb. 1812, ANC-AP, leg. 214, no. 55.

230 Sedano to Urbina, Puerto Príncipe, 23 Feb. 1812, ANC-AP, leg. 214, no. 46, fols. 1–2.

231 Urbina to [?], Santiago, 29 Feb. 1812, ANC-AP, leg. 214, no. 54; Urbina to Gobernador Político Interno de Santo Domingo, Santiago, 29 Feb. 1812, ANC-AP, leg. 214, no. 55; Buenaventura to Urbina, Santiago, 1 Mar. 1812, ANC-AP, leg. 214, no. 56; Urbina to Teniente Gobernador de Holguín, Santiago, 29 Feb. 1812, AHPH-TG, no. 71; Urbina to Sedano, Santiago, 1 Mar. 1812, ANC-CCG, leg. 94, no. 7.

232 Sedano to Urbina, Puerto Príncipe, 23 Feb. 1812, ANC-AP, leg. 214, no. 46; Corral to Alcalde Ordinario, Bayamo, 29 Feb. 1812, ANC-CCG, leg. 94, no. 4; ANC-CCG, [Feb. 1812?], leg. 94, no. 3.

233 Corral to Alcalde Ordinario, Bayamo, 29 Feb. 1812, ANC-CCG, leg. 94, no. 4.

234 ANC-AP, leg. 12, no. 14, fol. 86.

235 Franco, *La conspiración de Aponte*, 31–33. I could find no sources in Spanish or Cuban archives, or Franco's personal papers housed at the AOHCH, to document his statements. Nonetheless, Franco may have been correct to suggest a possible link to Haitian military aid. At the time of the search for Herrera, Holguin Governor Armiñan reported the arrival of a "French corsair." Armiñan to Urbina, Holguín, 5 Apr. 1812, ANC-GG, leg. 545, no. 27103. Gálvez and Novoa omitted this important section of the letter that they reprinted as a document in *1812*, 66.

236 [Urbina?] to Gobernador del Puerto Príncipe, Santiago, 3 Mar. 1812, ANC-AP, leg. 214, no. 61; [Urbina?] to Governador de Santo Domingo, Santiago, 3 Mar. 1812, ANC-AP, leg. 214, no. 60.

237 Franco, *La conspiración de Aponte*, 31; Geggus, "Slavery, War, and Revolution," 42 n. 115; Méndez Capote, *4 conspiraciones*, 38.

238 Valdés, *Historia de la isla de Cuba*, 263–64.

239 ANC-AP, leg. 12, no. 17, fols. 3–5.

240 Ibid., fols. 17v–18.

241 ANC-AP, leg. 13, no. 15, fols. 6v–50v.

242 Rendón to Peñalver, Havana, 10 June 1812, ANC-AP, leg. 12, no. 25, fols. 130–31.

243 Apodaca to Pezuela, Havana, 15 Apr. 1812, AGI-SD, leg. 1284, no. 1; Apodaca to Ayuntamiento, Havana, 24 Apr. 1812, AOHCH-AC, leg. 84, fols. 198–99v.

244 Filomeno, *Elogio del excelentísimo Señor Don Salvador de Muro y Salazar, Marques de Someruelos*, 21–22, P. K. Yonge Library Special Collections, University of Florida, Gainesville, Florida.

245 Antonio Cano Manuel to Juan Madrid Davila, Cádiz, 17 Feb. 1813, AGI-UM, leg. 98.

246 ANC-AP, leg. 12, no. 25, fol. 74v; Estanislao Godino y Muñoz, Cádiz, 26 Nov. 1812, AGI-UM, leg. 98.

247 ANC-AP, leg. 12, no. 25, fols. 88–89v, leg. 13, no. 1, fols. 42, 51–52, 95–98.

248 ANC-AP, leg. 12, no. 14, fol. 71 (emphasis in original).

249 Ibid., fols. 73v–75, leg. 13, no. 1, fol. 44.

250 Jordan, *Tumult and Silence*.

251 See the numerous examples in ANC-AP, leg. 12, nos. 9, 13, 14, 16, 17, 18, 25, leg. 13, nos. 1, 38, leg. 14, no. 1.

252 ANC-AP, leg. 12, no. 18, fol. 29.

253 Ibid., no. 14, fol. 79.

254 Ibid.; ANC-AP, leg. 13, no. 1, fols. 98, 170.

255 ANC-AP, leg. 13, no. 1, fol. 224.

256 Ibid., fol. 170.

257 Huerta to Apodaca, Havana, 24 Oct. 1812, ANC-AP, leg. 13, no. 1, fol. 335 (emphasis in original).

258 Juan de Velasco to Captain General, Havana, 13 Dec. 1839, ANC-AP, leg. 40, no. 33.

259 [?] to Captain General, Havana, 6 Apr. 1844, Eugenio Solas to Pedro Vidal Rodríguez, Havana, 28 May 1845, ANC-AP, leg. 40, no. 33.

CHAPTER FIVE

1 ANC-AP, leg. 12, no. 25, fol. 48, leg. 13, no. 1, fols. 42, 314, leg. 13, no. 38, fol. 4.

2 ANC-AP, leg. 12, no. 25, fols. 5v, 36–37; Hernández to Rendón, Havana, 7 May 1812, ANC-AP, leg. 12, no. 25, fol. 47; Apodaca to Pezuela, Havana, 19 July 1812, AGI-SD, leg. 1284, no. 21.

3 ANC-AP, leg. 13, no. 18, fols. 5v–6; Apodaca to Antonio Caro Manuel, Havana, 3 Sept. 1812, AGI-SD, leg. 1284, no. 39.

4 Apodaca to Antonio Caro Manuel, Havana, 28 Oct. 1812, AGI-SD, leg. 1284, no. 60; the same letter can be found in Apodaca to Antonio Caro Manuel, Havana, 28 Oct. 1812, AGI-SD, leg. 1286.

5 Juan de Dios Corona to [Apodaca], Havana, 23 Oct. 1812, ANC-AP, leg. 13, no. 1, fols. 329v–30.

6 ANC-AP, leg. 13, no. 1, fols. 438–38v.

7 ANC-AP, leg. 13, no. 15, fol. 73v, leg. 12, no. 25, fol. 53v.

8 ANC-AP, leg. 12, no. 17, fols. 13v, 70v.

9 ANC-AP, leg. 12, no. 25, fols. 54–55v, leg. 13, no. 15, fol. 73v.

10 ANC-AP, leg. 12, no. 25, fols. 68v, 75v.

11 Ibid., fols. 89–90.

12 The original proclamation nailed to the captain general's residence can be found in ANC-AP, leg. 12, no. 14, fol. 35. For reasons the remain unclear, Stephan Palmié did not consult Franco's more widely known book on the Aponte Rebellion that would have qualified some of his conclusions about the historiography. Instead, Palmié consulted Franco's *Las conspiraciones de 1810 y 1812*, a very brief twenty-four-page introduction to the document collection that only has two footnotes, as it was intended for a general and not a scholarly audience. Palmié writes: "Franco makes rather vague references to what he thinks may have been prior seditious activities on the part of Aponte. He thus claims that Aponte dictated an inflammatory proclamation that was posted in Havana in early March 1812 but fails to cite any evidence." *Wizards and Scientists*, 80–81. Had Palmié consulted the more detailed 1963 study, he would have found that not only did Franco cite evidence of the proclamation for the rebellion, he also provided a facsimile of the document that Aponte dictated. See Franco, *La conspiración de Aponte*, between pp. 20–21.

13 Cabildo Minutes, Havana, 18 Mar. 1812, AOHCH-AC, leg. 83, fols. 65–65v.

14  ANC-AP, leg. 12, no. 14, fol. 77. Reportedly, Aponte repeated the same statement in his last confession, which is not included in the extant trial record. ANC-AP, leg. 13, no. 1, fol. 49.

15  ANC-AP, leg. 13, no. 1, fol. 49, leg. 12, no. 14, fol. 82.

16  ANC-AP, leg. 13, no. 1, fol. 48.

17  ANC-AP, leg. 11, no. 37, fol. 58.

18  Ibid, fol. 59v.

19  Ibid., fols. 63v–64.

20  ANC-AP, leg, 12, no. 9, fol. 7v.

21  Ibid., no. 13, fol. 18.

22  Ibid., no. 21, fol. 8.

23  Ibid., fol. 13.

24  Ibid., fol. 26.

25  "Proposiciones del Sr. don José Miguel Guridi Alcocer," Cádiz, 26 March 1811, in Spain, Cortes, *Documentos*, 87. For an account of the issue of slavery in the Cortes debates, see King, "Colored Castes," 29–34; Franco, *Las conspiraciones de 1810 y 1812*, 15–16; Tornero, *Crecimiento económico* 80–89; and Yacou "La conspiración de Aponte (1812)," 48–49.

26  "Representación que el Capitán General de la isla de Cuba, Marques de Someruelos, elevó a las Cortes," Havana, 27 May 1811, in Spain, Cortes, *Documentos*, 102–3.

27  Andres de Jáuregui to Ayuntamineto de la Ciudad de la Habana, Cádiz, 2 Apr. 1811, ANC-DR, leg. 561, no. 8, fol. 1.

28  "Correspondencia del Sor. Don Andrés de Jáuregui diputado á Cortes con el Ayuntamiento de esta ciudad, 1811 a 1813," ANC-GSC, leg. 11000, no. 40589.

29  "Copias de la Junta del Real Consulado y Sociedad Patriótica, sobre las proposiciones relativas a la manumisión de los esclavos y los graves peligros que podrían resultar a esta Isla," Habana, 23 May 1811, HL-EC, box 19, no. 18, fol. 13.

30  Cabildo Minutes, Puerto Príncipe, 18 June 1811, AHPC-AC, no. 26, fol. 314v.

31  "Documentos que se refiere al acta del cabildo celebrado por el Ayuntamiento, fecha Santiago de Cuba 25 de Junio de 1811, en que se trató del proyecto presentado a las Cortes sobre la abolición de la esclavitud," ANC-AP, leg. 213, no. 81, fol. 8.

32  Shaler to Smith, Havana, 14 June 1811, USNA-RG, 59.

33  "Bando del Capitán General de la Isla D. Salvador José de Muro y Salazar, fecha Habana 7 de Abril de 1812, acerca de las medidas acordadas con motivo de la alternación del orden . . ." ANC-AP, leg. 12, no. 24.

34  ANC-AP, leg. 12, no. 9, fol. 7v; also see ANC-AP, leg. 13, no. 15, fols. 42–43; and AHPC-AC, no. 27, fol. 35, for additional comments.

35  ANC-AP, leg. 12, no. 9, fol. 110.

36  ANC-AP, leg. 13, no. 15, fol. 43v.

37  Ibid., no. 1, fols. 315–16.

38  ANC-AP, leg. 12, no. 21, fol. 15v–16.

39  Someruelos to Ignacio de la Pezuela, Havana, 5 Mar. 1812, AGI-UM, leg. 84, no. 348.

40  Francisco Sánchez to Juan Baptista Valliant, 16 May and 29 Oct. 1795, Bayamo, ANC-GG, leg. 540, no. 27096; for Jamaican slaves in Cuba see Alfred Clarke to José de Ezpuleta (*sic*), 9 March 1789, Jamaica, PRO-CO, 137 / 88, fols. 23–24; "Testimonio de las diligencias obradas sobre la profugación de los seis negros venidos de esta Ciudad de la Colonia Bretanica en solicitud de la Cristiandad como de ellos mas bien consta,"

1789, in PRO-CO, 137 / 89, fols. 55v–56v; Julian Mellet, *Viajes por el interior de la América meridional*, 386; Kindleman to Corral, Santiago de Cuba, 9 May 1810, ANC-AP, leg. 212, no. 26.

41  AHPG-Protocolos, leg. 4, libro 1, fols. 6v, 7v, 10, libro 2, fols. 15, 20, 30, 60v, 73, 122, 163, 179, 206, 211, 228, leg. 11, libro 3, fol. 13; Cabildo Minutes, Puerto Príncipe, 26 Aug. 1808, AHPC-AC, leg. 25, fols. 81–85.

42  ANC-AP, leg. 12, no. 9, fol. 54.

43  Franklin, "Gender and Slave Rebellion," 107–11.

44  Thompson, "Narrative of James Thompson," 71.

45  "Quaderno sobre la denuncia que hiso la Negra María Antonio Atola contra el Negro José Wilson eslavo de Rafael Wilson," Puerto Príncipe, 1812, AGI-PC, leg. 1865A, fol. 4.

46  Ibid. fol. 5.

47  Ibid. fol. 7v.

48  African ethnicity through self-identification by slaves and free people of color (as opposed to identification by masters and government officials, who often incorrectly labeled African origins and ethnicity, as evidenced in census and notarial records) among those questioned for involvement in the Aponte Rebellion is taken from testimony found in ANC-AP, leg. 11, no. 37, leg. 12, nos. 9, 11, 13, 14, 16, 17, 18, 20, 21, 23, 25, 26, 27, leg. 13, nos. 1, 15, 18, 38, leg. 14, no. 1, leg. 15, no. 22; AGI-PC, leg. 1640, 1778-A, 1780, 1864, 1865A.

49  Grandío Moráguez, "African Origins of Slaves."

50  Thornton, " 'I Am the Subject,' " 181–214.

51  Geggus, "Slaves and Free Coloreds," 284. French and British officials in the second half of the eighteenth century wrote "Angola" to designate people from the Congo.

52  ANC-AP, leg. 12, no. 14, fols. 9, 19–24, 34, 70.

53  ANC-AP, leg. 12, no. 26, fol. 34.

54  Ibid., fol. 36.

55  ANC-AP, leg. 12, no. 27, fols. 13v–14v.

56  Apodaca to Ministro de Guerra, Havana, 29 Oct. 1812, AGI-PC, leg. 1849, no. 184.

57  "Informe presentado al cabildo los Sres. D. Joaquín Herrera, D. Luis Hidalgo Gato y Dor. D. José María Saenz, sindico procurado general relativo a la moción de la Cortes para abolir al trafico de negros," Havana, 23 Mar. 1812, BNJM-Morales, leg. 78, no. 8, fol. 90.

58  Andres de Jáuregui and Juan Bernardo O'Gavan, "Memorial de los diputados de la Habana sobre una insurreción de esclavos en el ingenio de Peñas-Altas," Cádiz, 23 May 1812, BNJM-Morales, leg. 79, no. 72, fol. 292.

59  Salvador Meléndez to Secretario de Estado, Puerto Rico, 30 Jan. 1812, in Morales Carrión, *El proceso abolicionista en Puerto Rico*, 1:117; Baralt, *Esclavos rebeldes*, 27.

60  ANC-AP, leg. 12, no. 18, fol. 6.

61  Ibid., no. 16, fol. 12.

62  ANC-AP, leg. 13, no. 1, fol. 49.

63  Ibid., fol. 70. Aponte denied Chacón's assertion that Juan Francisco was his confidant and that he told others the Haitian admiral was on the island to serve at the orders of Henri Christophe. Instead, he countered that "one morning Chacón and Juan Lisundia appeared at his [Aponte's] house." According to Aponte, Chacón told him that "Juan Francisco had gone to the countryside . . . to carry out . . . the orders of his King." ANC-AP, leg. 12, no. 18, fol. 29v–30.

64  James, *Black Jacobins*, 94.

65  ANC-AP, leg. 12, no. 16, fol. 13.

66  ANC-AP, leg. 12, no. 14, fol. 73, no. 16, fols. 4–5, 13–14, no. 18, fols. 8–9, 34v, leg. 13, no. 1, fols, 83v–84, no. 15, fol. 18v. Invoking the Haitian Revolution through assuming the name of revolutionary figures also occurred in the Curaçao rebellion of 1795. Among the leaders executed by Dutch authorities, one called himself Toussaint, and another was known by the nickname Rigaud. Scott, "Common Wind," 264.

67  Someruelos to Ministro de Estado, Havana, 1 Sept. 1800, AHN-Estado, leg. 6366, caja 1, exp. 20, no. 1, fols. 2v–3; Luis de Las Casas to [?], Havana, 13 Jan. 1796, AGI-Estado, leg. 5-A, no. 28.

68  AOHCH-AC, 4 Dec. 1795, fols. 204v–5; García to Príncipe de la Paz, Santo Domingo, 3 Mar. 1796, no. 48, in Rodríguez Demorizi, *Cesión de Santo Domingo a Francia*, 75.

69  Luis de Las Casas to Paz, Havana, 16 Dec. 1795, AGI-Estado, leg. 5, no. 176. I would like to thank David Geggus for directing me to this source. According to Cuban historian José Luciano Franco, Aponte's *cabildo* planned to participate in the festivities welcoming Jean François. I could find no sources to confirm this statement. Franco, *La conspiración de Aponte*, 9.

70  Childs, " 'Black French General,' " 144–48.

71  Rey, "Les Garifunas"; Victoria Ojeda, "Jean François," 26–48; Geggus, *Haitian Revolutionary Studies*, 179–203; Landers, "Rebellion and Royalism," 163–70; Houdaille, "Negros Franceses en América Central," 65–67; Fernández Repetto and Negroe Sierra, *Una población perdida en la memoria*, 55; Vinson, "Race and Badge," 491; Cáceres Gómez, "Los esclavos del rey."

72  Someruelos to [?], Havana, 27 Jan. 1800, AHN-Estado, leg. 6366, caja 1, exp. 2; Someruelos to [?], Havana, 31 July 1804, AGI-PC, leg. 1778-B; Someruelos to Bardari y Azara, Havana, 10 Feb. 1811, AGI-SD, leg. 2210.

73  "Testimonio de la criminalidad seguida de oficios contra el negro Miguel, Juan Bautista, y José Antonio, sobre la conjuración que intentaban contra el Pueblo, y sus moradores, Juez, El Sor Teniente Gobernador," Bayamo, 25 Aug. 1805, AGI-PC, leg. 1649, fol. 46.

74  ANC-AP, leg. 12, no. 14, fol. 93.

75  Geggus, *Haitian Revolutionary Studies*, 199–200, esp. note 103.

76  ANC-AP, leg. 214, no. 28, fols. 2–3v.

77  Gil Narciso, Josef Fantacia, Juan Luis Santillan, and Ysidro Plutton to Someruelos, Casablanca, Habana, 10 Jan. 1812, Joseph Antonio de la Ossa to Someruelos, Havana, 21 Jan. 1812, ANC-CCG, leg. 93, no. 8; Juan Antonio Lopez to [Someruelos?], Havana, 28 Dec. 1811, ANC-CCG, leg. 93, no. 13; Aguilar to Cristóbal Solas, Havana, 2 Mar. 1812, ANC-CCG, leg. 94, no. 8.

78  ANC-AP, leg. 12, no. 16, fol. 6.

79  Ibid., fol. 4.

80  Ibid., fol. 4.

81  Ibid., fol. 8v.

82  Luis de Las Casas to [?], Havana, 13 Jan. 1796, AGI-Estado, leg. 5-A, no. 28.

83  ANC-AP, leg. 12, no. 16, fol. 10.

84  Ibid., fol. 22.

85  Franco, *La conspiración de Aponte*, 33; Geggus, "Slavery, War, and Revolution," 15; Méndez Capote, *4 conspiraciones*, 38.

86  ANC-AP, leg. 12, no. 16, fol. 10.

87   ANC-AP, leg. 12, no. 14, fol. 91. The military fort Casa Blanca would later provide the name for the neighborhood that grew around the building.

88   ANC-AP, leg. 12, no. 14, fol. 92.

89   Ibid., fol. 88.

90   ANC-AP, leg. 12, no. 16, fol. 18.

91   Ibid., no. 26, fol. 30.

92   Ibid., no. 14, fol. 73.

93   AHPSC-Protocolos, leg. 63, fol. 26v, leg. 64, fol. 156, leg. 243, fol. 118; AHPG-Protocolos, leg. 11, libro 3, fol. 52.

94   Mellet, *Viajes por el interior de la América meridional*, 403.

95   ANC-AP, leg. 12, no. 18, fols. 9, 34v.

96   Ibid., no. 13, fols. 21v–23v, 31, 36–37, no. 17, fol. 72.

97   Ibid., no. 26, fols. 7–14. For a description of Cuban militia uniforms in 1809, see *Calendario manual y guía de forasteros de la isla de Cuba par el año de 1809*, 177, 179, P. K. Yonge Library Special Collections, University of Florida, Gainesville, Florida.

98   In attempting to make sense of the proliferation of Haitian imagery, and in particular the widely reported role of Juan Barbier assuming the identity of "Juan Francisco," Stephan Palmié writes that it "is tempting to rationalize Barbier's posing as a Haitian revolutionary hero as a strategy to mobilize popular support," but he dismisses such interpretations because they "will necessarily remain guesswork of a dangerously teleological character." In terms of critiquing historical teleologies of radical revolution, Juan Barbier posing as "Juan Francisco" most accurately illustrates the antiteleological vision Aponte and others had of history. If historians are to use revolutionary teleological terminology, "Jean François," the historical figure, was a "reactionary royalist" of the Haitian Revolution who did not embrace full emancipation for all the slaves or the conversion of them into "revolutionary citizens" of the French Republic. The proclamations, statements, and actions by the Aponte rebels make it clear that they manipulated Haitian imagery and converted the historical figure of "Jean François" into "Juan Francisco" for their own political goals. To dismiss such actions as merely latter day inventions of historians caught in teleological traps reveals a condescending academic understanding of the past. Palmié, *Wizards and Scientists*, 133, 135.

99   Most, but not all, of Aponte's testimony discussing the book of drawings with authorities is found in "Expediente sobre declara José Antonio Aponte el sentido de las pinturas que se hallan en el libro que se le aprehendido en su casa," ANC-AP, leg. 12, no. 17.

100  ANC-AP, leg. 12, no. 17, fol. 78v. Stephan Palmié incorrectly states that the images "were not of Aponte's making." *Wizards and Scientists*, 99.

101  ANC-AP, leg. 12, no. 18, fols. 27–28.

102  Ibid., no. 17, fol. 80.

103  Ibid., no. 18, fol. 41.

104  Ibid., fol. 25.

105  ANC-AP, leg. 12, no. 14, fol. 92.

106  ANC-AP, leg. 13, no. 1, fol. 316.

107  ANC-AP, leg. 12, no. 17, fol. 16.

108  ANC-AP, leg. 13, no. 15, fol. 18v. Guarico was used in Spanish to refer to the city of Le Cap François, but also generically to Saint Domingue and Haiti.

109  Reis, *Slave Rebellion in Brazil*, 48.

110  Data taken from ANC-AP, leg. 11, no. 37, leg. 12, nos. 9, 11, 13, 14, 16, 17, 18, 20, 21, 23, 25,

26, 27, leg. 13, nos. 1, 15, 18, 38, leg. 14, no. 1, leg. 15, no. 22; ANC-GG, leg. 545, no. 27103; AGI-PC, leg. 1640, 1649, 1778A, 1780, 1864, 1865A; AGI-UM, leg. 84; AHPC-AC, leg. 27.

111 Scott, *Domination*, 98.

112 See the discussion of the important role of these edicts for shaping slave identity in Díaz, *Virgin*, 303–4.

113 ANC-AP, leg. 11, no. 37, fols. 63v–64, leg. 12, no. 9, fols. 7v, 110, leg. 12, no. 13, fol. 18, leg. 12, no. 21, fols. 8, 15v–16,, leg. 12, no. 26, fol. 44, leg. 13, no. 1 fols. 315–16; AGI-PC, leg. 1865A, fol. 4.

114 Dubois, " 'Our Three Colors,' " 87, 92.

115 Van Young, *Other Rebellion*, 488.

116 For the importance of literacy and written documents for slaves, see Gates, *Figures in Black*, 3–28. For the cultural importance of literacy and written documents in slave insurrection, see Sidbury, *Ploughshares into Swords*, 73–82; Reis, *Slave Rebellion in Brazil*, 96–104; and Goody, "Writing, Religion, and Revolt," 318–43.

117 Van Young, *Other Rebellion*, 464–65.

## CONCLUSION

1 Apodaca to Pezuela, 19 July 1812, Havana, AGI-SD, leg. 1284, no. 21; Apodaca to Antonio Caro Manuel, Havana, 28 Oct. 1812, AGI-SD, leg. 1284, no. 60; this same letter can be found in AGI-SD, leg. 1286.

2 Cabildo Minutes, Puerto Príncipe, 24 Jan. 1812, AHPC-AC, leg. 27, fols. 55–55v.

3 Cabildo Minutes, Havana, 23 Mar. 1812, Extraordinary Meeting, AOHCH-AC, leg. 83, fol. 67v.

4 Ibid.

5 "Informe presentado al cabildo por los Sres. D. Joaquín Herrera, D. Luis Hidalgo Gato, y Dor. D. José María Saenz, síndico procurador general relativo a la moción de las Cortes para abolir al trafico de negros," Havana, 23 Mar. 1812, BNJM-Morales, leg. 78, no. 8, fols. 94v–95.

6 Cabildo Minutes, Puerto Príncipe, 27 Jan. 1812, AHPC-AC, leg. 27, fol. 58.

7 "Testimonio del quaderno de las confecciones que siguen adherentes al numero: 3," Feb. 1812, AGI-PC, leg. 1865A.

8 Cabildo Minutes, Puerto Príncipe, 27 Jan. 1812, AHPC-AC, leg. 27, fols. 60–64.

9 Testimonio del quaderno de las confecciones que siguen adherentes al numero: 3," Feb. 1812, AGI-PC, leg. 1865A.

10 Ibid. (emphasis in original)

11 Urbina to Someruelos, Santiago, 15 Feb. 1812, AGI-PC, leg. 1548, no. 456; ANC-AP, leg. 12, no. 9, fol. 14.

12 ANC-AP, leg. 13, no. 15, fols. 68–69.

13 Cabildo Minutes, Havana, 7 Nov. 1812, AOHCH-AC, leg. 83, fol. 233v.

14 Ibid., fols. 227–27v.

15 ANC-AP, leg. 13, no. 15, fol. 69v.

16 ANC-AP, leg. 13, no. 1, fols. 427a–28.

17 Punishments taken from ANC-AP, leg. 11, no. 37, leg. 12, nos. 9, 11, 13, 14, 16, 17, 18, 20, 21, 23, 25, 26, 27, leg. 13, nos. 1, 15, 18, 38, leg. 14, no. 1, leg. 15, no. 22; ANC-GG, leg. 545, no. 27103; AGI-PC, leg. 1640, 1649, 1778A, 1780, 1864, 1865A; AGI-UM, leg. 84; AHPC-AC, leg. 27.

18  Deschamps Chapeaux, *El negro en la economía habanera*, 43–44; Deschamps Chapeaux, "La Habana de intra y extramuros y los Cabildos de los negros de nación," 20.

19  Howard, *Changing History*, 79.

20  Juan de Velasco to Captain General, Havana, 13 Dec. 1839, ANC-AP, leg. 40, no. 33.

21  Deschamps Chapeaux, "Margarito Blanco 'Ocongo de Ultan,' " 97–109, esp. 98, 102, and 104 for Borrego's role in the Monzón Conspiracy.

22  ANC-AP, leg. 12, no. 17, fol. 86, no. 25, fols. 6–9v, leg. 13, no. 1, fols. 222–35, no. 38, fol. 4.

23  The most complete accounts of the Escalera Conspiracy can be found in Paquette, *Sugar Is Made with Blood*; García Rodríguez, *Conspiraciones y revueltas*, 114–32; and Howard, *Changing History*, 89–96.

24  Eugenio Solas to Pedro Vidal Rodríguez, Havana, 28 May 1845, ANC-AP, leg. 40, no. 33.

25  [?] to Captain General, Havana, 6 Apr. 1844, ANC-AP, leg. 40, no. 33.

26  ANC-AP, leg. 13, no. 1, fols. 337–40v, 405–8.

27  Herrera to Apodaca, Havana, 15 Dec. 1812, ANC-AP, leg. 14, no. 1, fols. 13v–14.

28  ANC-AP, leg. 14, no. 1, fols. 50–50v, 184.

29  [?] to Captain General, Havana, 6 Apr. 1844, ANC-AP, leg. 40, no. 33.

30  Consulado to Lardizbal y Uribe, Havana, 16 Aug. 1814, BNJM-Morales, leg. 78, no. 45, fol. 596; Jameson, *Letters from the Havana*, 52–53; H. U. Addington to George Canning, Washington, D.C., 21 May 1825, in Webster, *Britain and the Independence of Latin America*, 2:519; Abbot, *Letters*, 131; Cornelius P. Van Ness to John Forsyth, 10 December 1836, in Manning, *Diplomatic Correspondence*, 11:303; Bremmer, *Homes of the New World*, 2:437; Paquette, *Sugar Is Made with Blood*, 84, 115, 180, 211, 242; Jensen, *Children of Colonial Despotism*, 30, 38–39; Ferrer, "Social Aspects of Cuban Nationalism," 43; Ferrer, *Insurgent Cuba*, 2, 48; Helg, *Our Rightful Share*, 17, 78–80; Knight, "Haitian Revolution," 114; Oquendo, "Las rebeldías de los esclavos en Cuba," 53; Castro, *Informe central del primero congreso del Partido Comunista de Cuba*, 7.

31  Erice to Jáuregui, Havana, 21 Apr. 1812, ANC-GSC, leg. 1100, no. 40589.

32  See, for example, Cabildo Minutes, Puerto Príncipe, 7 Feb. 1812, AHPC-AC, leg. 27, fols. 74–80v; Bosniemel to Someruelos, Havana, 10 Apr. 1812, ANC-DR, leg. 562, no. 35.

33  [?] to Someruelos, Havana, 8 Apr. 1812, AOHCH-AC, leg. 84, fol. 225.

34  Sedano, Puerto Príncipe, 4 Feb. 1812, Sedano to Someruelos, Puerto Príncipe, 21 Mar. 1812, AGI-PC, leg. 1640; ANC-AP, leg. 12, no. 27, fol. 34.

35  [?] to Havana Town Council, Havana, 20 Apr. 1812, AOHCH-AC, leg. 84, fol. 319.

36  "Memorial de los diputados de la Havana sobre una insurrección de esclavos en el ingenio de Peñas-Altas," Cádiz, 23 May 1812, BNJM-Morales, leg. 79, no. 72, fol. 289.

37  Jensen, *Children of Colonial Despotism*, 38.

38  This problem has been remedied for the study of Cuban independence during the second half of the nineteenth century by the excellent work of Helg, *Our Rightful Share*; and Ferrer, *Insurgent Cuba*.

39  For works that catalog slave insurrections during the Age of Revolution, see Geggus, "Slavery, War, and Revolution," 1–50, esp. 46–49; and Craton, *Testing the Chains*, 335–39. Historian John Coatsworth, in a survey of the historical literature on maroon wars, slave insurrections, and plantation uprisings from 1700–1899, found that out of a total of 142 such events during two centuries, ninety corresponded to the years 1770–1850. Of the 104 plantation uprisings identified by Coatsworth, only sixteen occurred prior to 1770. Coatsworth, "Patterns of Rural Rebellion," tables 2.4 and 2.5, 40–41.

40 Genovese, *Rebellion to Revolution*, xx.

41 Dubois, *Colony of Citizens* is an outstanding example of how slaves in Guadeloupe appropriated the ideology of the French Revolution and made it their own as "citizens" of the French Republic.

42 Carpentier, *Explosion in the Cathedral*, 231–32.

43 My account of the Haitian Revolution is drawn from James, *Black Jacobins*; Fick, *Making of Haiti*; Dubois, *Avengers of the New World*; Dubois, "Our Three Colors"; Trouillot, *Silencing the Past*; Geggus, *Slavery, War, and Revolution*; Geggus, *Haitian Revolutionary Studies*; Geggus "Haitian Revolution"; Thornton, "African Soldiers"; and Thornton, " 'I Am the Subject.' "

44 For Gabriel's Conspiracy, see Sidbury, *Ploughshares into Swords*; Sidbury, "Saint Domingue in Virginia"; Egerton, *Gabriel's Rebellion*; Mullin, *Flight and Rebellion*, 140–63.

45 Craton, *Testing the Chains*, esp. 335–39; Blackburn, *Overthrow of Colonial Slavery*, chaps. 4, 6, 8, and 11.

46 Quoted in Viotti da Costa, *Crowns of Glory, Tears of Blood*, 216.

47 For an analysis of the Demerara Rebellion see Viotti da Costa, *Crowns of Glory*; Craton, *Testing the Chains*, 267–90; Blackburn, *Overthrow of Colonial Slavery*, 428–31; Mullin, *Africa in America*, 249–53.

48 Craton, *Testing the Chains*, 291–321; Blackburn, *Overthrow of Colonial Slavery*, 432–68; Mullin, *Africa in America*, 253–60.

49 My analysis of the 1835 Malê Rebellion is drawn from Reis, *Rebelião escravo no Brasil*; Reis, *Slave Rebellion in Brazil*; Reis, "Slave Resistance in Brazil"; Schwartz, *Sugar Plantations*, 468–88; Kent, "African Revolt in Bahia"; Lovejoy, "Background to Rebellion"; and Goody, "Writing, Religion, and Revolt."

50 Aptheker, *American Negro Slave Revolts*. For Aptheker's influence on slave historiography, see Okihiro, *In Resistance*.

51 Schwartz, *Tropical Babylons*.

## APPENDIX

1 See Reis, *Slave Rebellion*, tables 5–13.

2 Sarah Franklin greatly assisted converting my ad hoc qualitative "database" to skillfully manipulated SPSS.

3 The percentage of *bozal* participation was likely much higher than 71 percent because most of the data for slaves arrested on plantations in Puerto Príncipe did not record place of birth, which most likely would have been Africa, given the increase in imports on the eve of the rebellion.

# Bibliography

ARCHIVAL SOURCES

## Cuba

BAYAMO
Archivo Histórico Provincial de Granma
    Protocolos
Casa de la Nacionalidad Cubana

CAMAGÜEY
Archivo Histórico Provincial de Camagüey
    Actas Capitulares
    Alcaldía Ordinario
    Intendencia de Ejercito y Real Hacienda
    Jorge Juárez Cano
    Protocolos
    Tenencia de Gobierno

HAVANA
Archivo de la Oficina del Historiador de la Ciudad, Havana
    Actas Capitulares
    José Luciano Franco
Archivo Histórico del Museo Carlos J. Finlay
    Tomás Romay
Archivo Nacional de Cuba
    Asuntos Políticos
    Audiencia de Santiago de Cuba
    Audiencia de Santo Domingo
    Comisión Militar
    Correspondencia de los Capitanes Generales
    Donativos y Remisiones
    Escribanía de Cabello

Escribanía de Antonio D'aumy
Escribanía de Gobierno
Escribanía de Ortega
Escribanía de Valerio
Escribanía de Varios
Gobierno General
Gobierno Superior Civil
Intendencia General de Hacienda
Real Consulado y Junta de Fomento
Realengos
Biblioteca del Instituto de Literatura y Lingüística, Havana
    Actas de la Real Sociedad Económica de Amigos del País
Biblioteca Nacional José Martí, Havana
    Colección Francisco Arango y Parreño
    Colección Francisco de Arredondo
    Colección Manuel Pérez Beato
    Colección Vidal Morales y Morales

HOLGUÍN

Archivo de la Catedral de San Isidoro de Holguín
    Libro de Defunciones de Pardos
Archivo del Museo Provincial de Holguín
    Colonial
Archivo Histórico Provincial de Holguín
    Actas Capitulares
    Protocolos
    Tenencia de Gobierno

SANTIAGO

Archivo Histórico Municipal de Santiago de Cuba
    Actas Capitulares
Archivo Histórico Provincial de Santiago de Cuba
    Gobierno Provincial
    Juzgado de Primera Instancia
    Protocolos

## Spain

MADRID

Archivo Histórico Nacional
    Estado
    Ultramar
Biblioteca Nacional
    Colección de Justo Zaragoza

SEVILLE

Archivo General de Indias
    Audiencia de Santo Domingo
    Estado
    Indiferente General

Papeles de Cuba
Ultramar

SIMANCAS
Archivo General de Simancas
Guerra Moderna

## United Kingdom

Public Records Office, Kew, England
Colonial Office
Foreign Office

## United States

Houghton Library, Harvard University, Cambridge, Massachusetts
Escoto Collection
Escoto Collection, Supplement
Howard-Tilton Memorial Library, Tulane University, New Orleans, Louisiana
Rare Book Collection
National Archives, Washington, D.C.
Dispatches from Consuls in Cuba, Record Group 59
Nettie Lee Benson Latin American Collection, University of Texas, Austin, Texas
Rare Book Collection
P. K. Yonge Library Special Collections, University of Florida, Gainesville, Florida
Rare Book Collection

PRINTED PRIMARY SOURCES

Abbot, Abiel. *Letters Written in the Interior of Cuba, between the Mountains of Arcana, to the East, and of Cusco, to the West, in the Months of February, March, April, and May 1828.* 1829. Reprint, Freeport, New York: Books for Libraries, 1971.

Adams, John, and Abigail Adams. *Familiar Letters of John Adams and His Wife Abigail Adams, during the Revolution.* 1875. Reprint, Freeport, New York: Books for Libraries, 1970.

Ajayi Crowther, Samuel. "The Narrative of Samuel Ajayi Crowther." In *Africa Remembered: Narratives by West Africans from the Era of the Slave Trade*, edited by Philip D. Curtin, 289–316. Madison: University of Wisconsin Press, 1967.

Alexander, James Edward. *Transatlantic Sketches, Comprising Visits to the Most Interesting Scenes in North and South America, and the West Indies. With Notes on Negro Slavery and Canadian Emigration.* Philadelphia: Key and Biddle, 1833.

Antillon, Isidoro. *Disertación sobre origen de la esclavitud de los negros: motivos que la han perpetuado, ventajas que se le atribuyen y medios que podrían adoptarse para hacer prosperar nuestras colonias sin la esclavitud de los negros. Leída en la Real Academia Matritense de decreto español y publicó, el día 2 de abril 1802.* Mallorca: Imprenta de Miguel Domingo, 1811.

Arango y Parreño, Francisco. *De la factoría a la Colonia.* 1792. Reprint, Havana: Publicaciones de la Secretaría de Educación, 1936.

——. *Obras.* 2 vols. Havana: Dirección de Cultura, Ministerio de Educación, 1952.

*Aurora: Correo politico-economico de la Habana.* 1808–10.

Bachiller y Morales, Antonio. *Los Negros*. Barcelona: Gorgas y compañía, 1887.

"Bando del General Salvador José de Muro y Salazar, Marques de Someruelos, Gobernador y Capitán General de la Isla, sobre que ninguna persona nacional o extranjera se embarque sin pasaporte del gobierno. . . ." Havana, 18 Feb. 1803. *Boletín del Archivo Nacional* (Habana) 50 (Jan–Dec. 1951): 398–99.

Barrera y Domingo, Francisco. *Reflexiones: histórico físico naturales, médico, quirúrgicas; prácticos y especulativos entretenimientos acerca de la vida, usos, costumbres, alimentos, bestidos, color y enfermedades a que propenden los negros de África, venidos a las Américas.* Havana: Ediciones C. R., 1953.

Bolívar, Simón. "Address Delivered at the Inauguration of the Second National Congress of Venezuela in Angostura." 15 Feb. 1819. In *Selected Writings of Bolivar*, edited by Harold A. Bierck, 1:173–97. New York: Colonial, 1951.

———. "A Decree for the Emancipation of Slaves." 2 June 1816. In *The Liberator, Simón Bolívar: Man and Image*, edited by David Bushnell, 65–66. New York: Alfred A. Knopf, 1970.

Bremmer, Frederika. *The Homes of the New World: Impressions of America.* 2 vols. 1853. Reprint, translated by Mary Howitt. New York: Johnson Reprint, 1968.

*Calendario manual y guía de forasteros de la isla de Cuba para el año de 1795.* Havana: En la Imprenta de la Capitanía General, 1795.

*Calendario manual y guía de forasteros de la isla de Cuba para el año de 1809.* Havana: En la Imprenta de la Capitanía General, 1809.

"Circular Prohibiendo desembarquen en esta isla, los negros insurrectos de la Guadalupe." Havana, 13 Sept. 1802. In *Boletín del Archivo Nacional* (Havana) 15, no. 6 (Nov.–Dec. 1916): 356–58.

"Constitución de un cabildo Carabali en 1814." *Archivos del folklore cubano* 1, no. 3 (1925): 281–83.

"Consulta del Consejo de las Indias sobre el reglamento expedido en 31 de Mayo de 1789 para la mejor educación, buen trato y ocupación de los negros esclavos de América." Madrid, 17 Mar. 1794. In *Colección de documentos para la historia de la formación social de Hispanoamérica, 1493–1810*, edited by Richard Konetzke, vol. 3, tomo 2, pp. 726–32. Madrid: Consejo Superior de Investigaciones Científicas, 1962.

"Consulta del Consejo de las Indias sobre la coartación de los esclavos en beneficio de su libertad." Madrid, 5 Dec. 1788. In *Colección de documentos para la historia de la formación social de Hispanoamérica, 1493–1810*, edited by Richard Konetzke, vol. 3, tomo 2, pp. 631–35. Madrid: Consejo Superior de Investigaciones Científicas, 1962.

"Consulta del Consejo de las Indias sobre la instancia hecha por el negro Manuel Huevo, esclavo de V. M. solicitando su libertad." Madrid, 26 Sept. 1785. In *Colección de documentos para la historia de la formación social de Hispanoamérica, 1493–1810*, edited by Richard Konetzke, vol. 3, tomo 2, pp. 583–85. Madrid: Consejo Superior de Investigaciones Científicas, 1962.

"Cuban Slaves in England." *Anti-Slavery Reporter* 2, no. 10 (2 Oct. 1854): 234.

Dallas, R. C. *The History of the Maroons, from Their Origin to the Establishment of Their Chief Tribe at Sierra Leone: Including the Expedition to Cuba, for the Purpose of Procuring Spanish Chasseurs.* 2 vols. London: A. Strahan, 1803.

"De la Esclavitud a la Negritud: Documentos." *Revista de la Universidad de México* 25, no. 2 (October 1970): insert.

de la Sagra, Ramón. *Historia económico, político y estadística de la isla de Cuba.* Havana: Imprenta de las Viudas de Azora y Soler, 1831.

[del Valle Hernández, Antonio.] "Sucinta noticia de la situación presente de esta colonia." Havana, 16 May 1800. *Boletín del Archivo Nacional* (Havana) 17:2–3 (Mar.–Jun. 1918): 171–216.

de Madrid, J. L. F. "Memoria sobre la disentería en general, y en particular sobre la disentería de los barracones." *Memorias de la Real Sociedad Económica de la Habana* 11 (30 Nov. 1817): 381–89.

"Depositions of the Cuban Slaves." *Anti-Slavery Reporter* 2, no. 10 (2 Oct. 1854): 234–39.

*Diario de la Habana*. 1812.

"Documentos: Los esclavos que ganaron su libertad por acciones de guerra." Aranjuez, 13 May 1763. In *Cuba: Economía y sociedad, azúcar, ilustración y conciencia (1763–1868)*, edited by Levi Marrero, 9:2. Madrid: Editorial Playor, 1983.

"Documentos sobre la conspiración de Don Ramón de la Luz." *Boletín del Archivo Nacional* (Havana) 63 ( July–Dec. 1963): 53–88.

"Documentos sobre la evacuación de la Isla de Santo Domingo." *Boletín del Archivo Nacional* (Havana) 48:1–6 ( Jan.–Dec. 1949): 178–81.

Eltis, David, David Richardson, Stephen D. Behrendt, and Herbert S. Klein, eds. *The Trans-Atlantic Slave Trade: A Database on CD-ROM*. Cambridge: Cambridge University Press, 1999.

"Expediente No. 1° sobre establecimiento del Consulado en esta Isla conforme a la Rl. Cedula de 4 de abril de 1794." *Boletín del Archivo Nacional* (Habana) 29:1–6 ( Jan–Dec. 1930): 33–86.

"Expediente relativo á la formación de una compañía nacional para emprender el comercio directo de esclavos de la costa de Africa." Havana, 8 May 1804. *Boletín del Archivo Nacional* (Havana) 49:1–6 ( Jan.–Dec. 1950): 216–31.

Ferrer, Pascual. "Cuba en 1798." *Revista de Cuba* 2 (1877): 310–21.

Filomeno, Francisco. *Elogio del excelentismo Señor Don Salvador de Muro y Salazar, Marques de Someruelos, Teniente General de los Reales Exércitos, Capitán General de la isla de Cuba, Gobernador militar y político de la ciudad de la Habana, presidente de su real sociedad económica socio honorario de ella, &c...* Madrid: Imprenta de Don Miguel de Burgos, 1815.

France. National Assembly. *Proceedings of the National Assembly of France, upon the Proposed Abolition of the Slave Trade in that Kingdom*. London: n.p., 1790.

Franco, José Luciano. *Documentos para la historia de Haití en el Archivo Nacional*. Havana: Publicaciones del Archivo Nacional, 1954.

*Gaceta Diaria*. 1812.

Gálvez, Gisela, and José Novoa, eds. *1812: Conspiración antiesclavista*. Holguín: Ediciones Holguín, 1993.

García Rodríguez, Gloria, ed. *La esclavitud desde la esclavitud: La visión de los siervos*. 2nd ed. Havana: Editorial de Ciencias Sociales, 2003.

Gómez de Avellaneda y Arteaga, Gertrudis. *Sab and Autobiography*. 1841. Reprint, translated and edited by Nina M. Scott. Austin: University of Texas Press, 1993.

Great Britain. House of Lords. "Report from the Select Committee of the House of Lords, Appointed to Consider the Best Means Which Great Britain Can Adopt for the Final Extinction of the African Slave Trade." *Sessional Papers, 1849–50, Slave Trade*, 24 May 1849.

Holliday, John. *A short account of the origin, symptoms, and most approved method of treating the putrid bilious yellow fever, vulgarly called the black vomit: which appeared in the city of Havanna, with the utmost violence, in the months of June, July, and part of August, 1794*. Boston: Manning and Loring, 1796.

Humboldt, Alexander von. *Ensayo político sobre la isla de Cuba.* 1826. Reprint, with an introduction by Fernando Ortiz. Havana: Fundación Fernando Ortiz, 1998.

*Indice del Archivo del Departamento General de Policía desde el año de 1812.* Buenos Aires: Imprenta del Gobierno, 1858–60.

"Instrucciones que ha dexado un mayoral de azucarera a sus herederos." *Papel Periódico de la Havana,* 24–25 July 1791. Reprinted in *Revista Bimestre Cubana* 15:1 (Jan–June 1920): 27–31.

Jameson, Robert Francis. *Letters from the Havana during the Year 1820; Containing an Account of the Present State of the Island of Cuba and Observations on the Slave Trade.* London: John Miller, 1821.

Ligon, Richard. *A True and Exact History of the Island of Barbadoes.* 1657. Reprint, London: Frank Cass, 1970.

Manning, William R., ed. *Diplomatic Correspondence of the United States: Inter-American Affairs, 1831–1860.* 12 vols. Washington: Publications of the Carnegie Endowment for International Peace, 1932–39.

Manzano, Juan Francisco. *Autobiography of a Slave.* 1840. Reprint, introduction by Ivan A Schulman, translated by Evelyn Picon Garfield. Detroit: Wayne State University Press, 1996.

———. *Obras.* 1840. Reprint, Havana: Instituto Cubano del Libro, 1972.

Mellet, Julian. *Viajes por el interior de la América meridional.* 1824. Reprint, Santiago de Chile: Imprenta Universitaria, 1908.

Montes de Oca y Fajardo, Alvaro. *Sermón de Santiago que en la parroquial mayor de Puerto Príncipe predico el 25 de Julio de 1824, uno de sus curas rectores el Dr. D. Alvaro Montes de Oca y Fajardo, en la fiesta que anualmente hacen los Morenos libres al Santo Apóstol.* Puerto Príncipe: Oficina a cargo de D. Francisco Maria Santos, 1824.

Morales Carrión, Arturo, comp. *El proceso abolicionista en Puerto Rico: Documentos para su estudio.* 2 vols. San Juan: Instituto de cultura puertorriqueña, 1974.

Morell de Santa Cruz. "El Obispo Morell de Santa Cruz oficializa los cabildos africanos donde nació la santería, convirtiéndolos en ermitas." Havana, 6 Dec. 1755. In *Cuba: Economía y sociedad, del monopolio hacia la libertad comercial (1701–1763),* edited by Levi Marrero, 8:159–61. Madrid: Editorial Playor, 1980.

Navarro, Diego José. "Bando sobre prohibir el uso de armas y capas a negros y mulatos." Havana, 4 May 1779. In *Boletín del Archivo Nacional* (Havana), 28:1–6 (Jan.–Dec. 1929): 103–4.

Ney, Eugene. *Cuba en 1830: Diario de viaje de un hijo del Mariscal Ney.* 1831. Reprint, introduction by Jorge J. Beato Núñez, translation by Miguel F. Garrido. Miami: Ediciones Universal, 1973.

Nugent, Lady Maria. *Lady Nugent's Journal of Her Residence in Jamaica from 1801 to 1805.* Edited by Philip Wright. Foreword by Verene A Shepherd. Mona: University of West Indies Press, 2002.

O'Gavan, Juan Bernardo. *Observaciones sobre la suerte de los negros de Africa, considerado en su propia patria y transplantados á las Antillas Españolas.* Madrid: Imprenta Universal, 1821.

O'Reilly, Alejandro. "Descripción de la isla de Cuba, ganados, haciendas, frutos y comercio." Havana, 12 April 1764. In *Cuba: Economía y sociedad: Del monopolio hacia la libertad comercial (1701–1763),* edited by Levi Marrero, 8:262–67. Madrid: Editorial Playor, 1980.

Pearson, Edward A., ed. *Designs against Charleston: The Trial Record of the Denmark Vesey Slave Conspiracy of 1822.* Chapel Hill: University of North Carolina Press, 1999.

Pérez de la Riva, Juan. "Documentos para la historia de las gentes sin historia." *Revista de la Biblioteca Nacional José Martí*. 3rd ser., 6, no. 1 (Jan.–Mar. 1964): 27–52.

"R. C. al Gobernador de la Habana ordenándole haga observar el método y reglas que se expresan, en la exacción del derecho de alcabala de la venta de los negros esclavos coartados de aquella isla." Aranjuez, 21 June 1768. In *Colección de documentos para la historia de la formación social de Hispanoamérica, 1493–1810*, edited by Richard Konetzke, vol. 3, tomo 1, pp. 337–40. Madrid: Consejo Superior de Investigaciones Científicas, 1962.

"R. C. al Gobernador de la Habana previéndole que deben considerarse y según la misma regla que se dio para los esclavos enteros la de los coartados." San Ildefonso, 27 Sept. 1769. In *Colección de documentos para la historia de la formación social de Hispanoamérica, 1493–1810*, edited by Richard Konetzke, vol. 3, tomo 1, pp. 360–61. Madrid: Consejo Superior de Investigaciones Científicas, 1962.

"R. C. para el remedio de los esclavos en el servicio de los esclavos negros." Aranjuez, 29 Apr. 1752. In *Colección de documentos para la historia de la formación social de Hispanoamérica, 1493–1810*, edited by Richard Konetzke, vol. 3, tomo 1, pp. 260–61. Madrid: Consejo Superior de Investigaciones Científicas, 1962.

"R. C. sobre preeminencias de oficiales y soldados milicianos." Buen Retiro, 16 Sept. 1708. In *Colección de documentos para la historia de la formación social de Hispanoamérica, 1493–1810*, edited by Richard Konetzke, vol. 3, tomo 1, p. 80. Madrid: Consejo Superior de Investigaciones Científicas, 1962.

"Real cédula de su magestad sobre la educación, trato y ocupaciones de los esclavos." *Revista de Historia de América* (Mexico) 3 (Sept. 1938): 50–59.

"Reglamento para las milicias y infantería y caballería de la isla de Cuba." El Pardo, 19 Jan. 1769. In *Colección de documentos para la historia de la formación social de Hispanoamérica, 1493–1810*, edited by Richard Konetzke, vol. 3, tomo 1, pp. 351–58. Madrid: Consejo Superior de Investigaciones Científicas, 1962.

"Representación a S. M. en 19 de enero de 1790, sobre el régimen de los esclavos." *Revista Bimestre Cubana* 8, no. 1 (Jan.–Feb. 1913): 57–75.

"Representación dirigida por el Real Consulado de la Habana al ministro de Hacienda en 10 de Julio de 1799." In *Historia de la esclavitud: Desde los tiempos mas remotos hasta nuestros días*. 1879. Reprint, edited by José Antonio Saco, 5:131–49. Havana: Editorial "Alfa," 1937.

Rico, Gaspar. *Proyecto relativo al comercio, suerte, y servidumbre de los esclavos, inclinado a su transición oportuna a libre, durante el tiempo que debe continuar la introducción en territorios españoles*. Cádiz: Imprenta Tormentaria, 1813.

Rodríguez de la Vera, Gaspar Antonio. "Diario de operaciones de un rancheador militar en vuelta abajo, 22 de julio de 28 de noviembre, 1820." Introduction by Jorge Freedy Ramírez Pérez and Sergio Luis Márquez Jacaa. *Alcance a la Revista de la Biblioteca Nacional José Martí* 2, no. 2 (1988): 59–82.

Rodríguez Demorizi, Emilio, ed. *Cesión de Santo Domingo a Francia: Correspondencia de Godoy, García, Roume, Hedouville, Louverture, Rigaud, y otros, 1795–1802*. Trujillo: Impresora Dominicana, 1958.

Romay Chacón, Tomás. *Obras Completas*. 2 vols. Compiled by José López Sánchez. Havana: Academia de Ciencias de la República de Cuba, 1965.

Smith, Robert C. "Décadas do Rosario dos pretos: Documemtos da irmandade." *Arquivos* (Recife) 4–10, nos. 7–20 (Dec. 1951): 143–70.

———. "Manuscritos da igreja de Nossa Senhora do Rosario dos homens pretos do Recife." *Arquivos* (Recife) 4–10, nos. 7–20 (Dec. 1951): 53–120.

"Sobre la libertad de los negros que se distinguieron durante el sitio de la Habana por los ingleses en 1762." Aranjuez, 13 May 1763. In *Historia documentada de la conspiración de los soles y rayos de Bolívar*, edited by Roque E. Garrigó, 6. Havana: Academia de la Historia de Cuba, 1929.

Spain. Cortes. *Documentos de que hasta ahora se compone el expediente que principiaron las Cortes Extraordinarias sobre el trafico y esclavitud de los negros*. Madrid: Imprenta de Repulles, 1814.

St. John d'el Rey Mining Company. *Circular to the Proprietors of the St. John d'el Rey Mining Company*. London: R. Clay, 1850.

Thomas, William. "Narrative of William Thomas, a Native of Africa, Twice Rescued from Slavery." *The Anti-Slavery Reporter* 4, no. 3 (8 Feb. 1843): 22–23.

Thompson, James. "Narrative of James Thompson, a British Subject, Twenty-One Years a Cuban Slave." *The Anti-Slavery Reporter* 4, no. 9 (3 May 1843): 71–72.

Tylden, Sir John Maxwell. "La isla de Cuba en el siglo xix vista por los extranjeros: La Habana en 1814–15 según Sir John Maxwell Tylden." *Revista de la Biblioteca Nacional José Martí*. 3rd ser., 14 (May–Aug. 1972): 81–94.

Valdés, Antonio J. *Historia de la isla de Cuba, y en especial de la Habana*. Habana: Oficina de la cena, 1813.

Villaverde, Cirilo. *Cecilia Valdés or Angel's Hill*. 1839. Reprint, translated by Sydney G. Gest. New York: Vantage, 1962.

Webster, C. K., ed. *Britain and the Independence of Latin America, 1812–1830: Select Documents from the Foreign Office Archives*. 2 vols. New York: Octagon Books, 1970.

SECONDARY SOURCES

Abreu Cardet, José "Francisco de Zayas: El Camino Inconcluso entre Cuba y España." *Real Sociedad Bascongada de los Amigos del País* 54, no. 2 (1998): 503–8.

"AHR Forum: Revolutions in the Americas," *American Historical Review* 105, no. 1 (Feb. 2000): 93–152.

Aimes, Hubert H. S. *A History of Slavery in Cuba, 1511 to 1868*. 1907. Reprint, New York: Octagon Books, 1967.

Alleyne, Mervyn C. "Linguistics and the Oral Tradition." In *Methodology and Historiography of the Caribbean*. Vol. 6 of *General History of the Caribbean*, edited by B. W. Higman, 19–45. London: UNESCO, 1999.

Almondovar Muñoz, Carmen. "José Luciano Franco: Ejemplo de saber modesto y profundo." *Boletín del Archivo Nacional* (Havana) 4 (1990): 64–69.

Anderson, Margo J., and Stephen E. Fienberg. *Who Counts? The Politics of Census-Taking in Contemporary America*. New York: Russell Sage Foundation, 1999.

Anderson, Rodney D. "Race and Social Stratification in Guadalajara in 1821." *Hispanic American Historical Review* 68, no. 2 (May 1988): 209–44.

Andrews, George Reid. "The Afro-Argentine Officers of Buenos Aires Province, 1800–1860." *Journal of Negro History* 64, no. 2 (Spring 1979): 85–100.

——. *The Afro-Argentines of Buenos Aires, 1800–1900*. Madison: University of Wisconsin Press, 1980.

Aptheker, Herbert. *American Negro Slave Revolts*. New York: Columbia University Press, 1943.

Archer, Christon I. *The Army in Bourbon Mexico, 1760–1810*. Albuquerque: University of New Mexico Press, 1977.

———. "Pardos, Indians, and the Army of New Spain: Inter-Relationships and Conflicts, 1780–1810." *Journal of Latin American Studies* 6, no. 2 (1974): 231–55.

Atanda, J. A. "The Yoruba Ogboni Cult: Did it Exist in Old Oyo?" *Journal of the Historical Society of Nigeria* 6, no. 4 (1973): 365–72.

Augier, Angel. "José Antonio Aponte y la conspiración de 1812." *Bohemia* 54, no. 15 (13 Apr. 1962): 48–9, 64.

Badura, Bohumil. "Los Franceses en Santiago de Cuba a mediados del año de 1808." *Ibero-Americana Pragensia* (Prague) 5 (1971): 157–60.

Baralt, Guillermo A. *Esclavos rebeldes: Conspiraciones y sublevaciones de esclavos en Puerto Rico (1795–1873)*. Río Piedras: Ediciones Huracán, 1982.

Barcia Paz, Manuel. *"A Colossus on the Sand": The Guamacaro Slave Revolt of 1825 and the Atlantic World*. Tuscaloosa: University of Alabama Press, forthcoming.

———. *Con el látigo de la ira: Legislación, represión y control en las plantaciones cubanas*. Havana: Editorial de Ciencias Sociales, 2000.

———. "Herencia y racionalidad: Acerca de la doble moral de los propietarios cubanos de esclavos." *Debates Americanos* 9 ( Jan.–June 2000): 20–26.

———. *La resistencia esclava en las plantaciones cubanas (1790–1870)*. Pinar del Río, Cuba: Ediciones Vitral, 1998.

Barcia Zequeira, María de Carmen. *La otra familia: Parientes, redes y descendencia de los esclavos en Cuba*. Havana: Fondo Editorial Casa de las Américas, 2003.

Barnet, Miguel. *Biografía de un cimarrón*. 1963. Reprint, Havana: Editorial Academia, 1996.

Barreal, Issac. "Los aportes etnólogicas en la obra de José Luciano Franco." *Boletín del Archivo Nacional* (Havana) 4 (1990): 70–78.

Bauer, Raymond A., and Alice H. Bauer. "Day to Day Resistance to Slavery." *Journal of Negro History* 27, no. 4 (Oct. 1942): 388–419.

Bell, David A. "The Unbearable Lightness of Being French: Law, Republicanism, and National Identity at the End of the Old Regime." *American Historical Review* 106, no. 4 (Oct. 2001): 1215–35.

Bennett, Herman L. *Africans in Colonial Mexico: Absolutism, Christianity, and Afro-Creole Consciousness, 1570–1640*. Bloomington: Indiana University Press, 2003.

Bergad, Laird W. *Cuban Rural Society in the Nineteenth Century: The Social and Economic History of Monoculture in Matanzas*. Princeton, N.J.: Princeton University Press, 1990.

Bergad, Laird W., Fe Iglesias García, and María del Carmen Barcia. *The Cuban Slave Market, 1790–1880*. Cambridge: Cambridge University Press, 1995.

Berlin, Ira. *Many Thousands Gone: The First Two Centuries of Slavery in North America*. Cambridge, Mass.: Harvard University Press, 1998.

———. *Slaves without Masters: The Free Negro in the Antebellum South*. New York: Pantheon Books, 1974.

Betancourt, Juan René. *El Negro: Ciudadano del Futuro: O todos somos felices, o nadie podrá ser feliz*. Havana: Talleres Tipográficas de Cárdenas y Cia., 1959.

Bettelheim, Judith, ed. *Cuban Festivals: An Illustrated Anthology*. New York: Garland, 1993.

Biernacki, Richard. "Method and Metaphor after the New Cultural History." In *Beyond the Cultural Turn: New Directions in the Study of Society and Culture*, edited by Victoria E. Bonnell and Lynn Hunt, 62–92. Berkeley: University of California Press, 1999.

Blackburn, Robin. *The Making of New World Slavery: From the Baroque to the Modern, 1492–1800*. London: Verso, 1997.

———. *The Overthrow of Colonial Slavery, 1776–1848*. London: Verso, 1988.

Blanchard, Peter. "The Language of Liberation: Slave Voices in the Wars of Independence." *Hispanic American Historical Review* 82, no. 3 (August 2002): 499–523.

Bolster, W. Jeffrey. *Black Jacks: African American Seamen in the Age of Sail.* Cambridge, Mass.: Harvard University Press, 1997.

Booker, Jackie R. "Needed but Unwanted: Black Militiamen in Veracruz, Mexico, 1760–1810." *Historian* 55, no. 2 (Winter 1993): 259–76

Bowser, Frederick P. *The African Slave in Colonial Peru, 1524–1650.* Stanford, Calif.: Stanford University Press, 1974.

——. "Colonial Spanish America." In *Neither Slave nor Free: The Freedmen of African Descent in the Slave Societies of the New World,* edited by David W. Cohen and Jack P. Greene, 19–58. Baltimore: Johns Hopkins University Press, 1972.

——. "The Free Person of Color in Mexico and Lima: Manumission and Opportunity, 1580–1650." In *Race and Slavery in the Western Hemisphere: Quantitative Studies,* edited by Stanley Engerman and Eugene D. Genovese, 331–68. Princeton, N.J.: Princeton University Press, 1975.

Boyer, Richard. *Lives of the Bigamists: Marriage, Family, and Community in Colonial Mexico.* Albuquerque: University of New Mexico Press, 1995.

Brading, D. A. *The First America: The Spanish Monarchy, Creole Patriots, and the Liberal State, 1492–1867.* Cambridge: Cambridge University Press, 1991.

Burke, Peter. "History of Events and the Revival of Narrative." In *New Perspectives on Historical Writing,* 2nd ed., edited by Peter Burke, 283–300. University Park: Pennsylvania State University Press, 2001.

Bushnell, Amy. *The King's Coffer: Proprietors of the Spanish Florida Treasury,1565–1702.* Gainesville: University Presses of Florida, 1981.

Cabrera, Lydia. *La Sociedad Secreta Abakuá, narrada por viejos adeptos.* Havana: Ediciones, C. R., 1959.

Cáceres Gómez, Rina. "Los esclavos del rey: Omoa, Honduras y la historia afrocentroamericana." Paper presented at the XXIV Latin American Studies Association International Congress, Dallas, Tex., March 27–29, 2003.

Calcagno, Francisco. *Aponte.* Barcelona: Tipografía de Francisco Costa, 1901.

——. *Diccionario biográfico cubano.* New York: Imprenta y Librería de N. Ponce de León, 1878.

——. *Poetas de Color: Plácido, Manzano, Rodríguez, Echemendía, Silveira, Medina.* Havana: Imprenta Mercantil de los Herederos de S. S. Spencer, 1887.

Calvi, Giulia. *Histories of a Plague Year: The Social and the Imaginary in Baroque Florence.* Translated by Dario Biocca and Bryant T. Ragan Jr. Berkeley: University of California Press, 1989.

Carbonell, Walterio. *Crítica: Cómo surgió la cultura nacional.* Havana: Ediciones Yaka, 1961.

Carpentier, Alejo. *Explosion in the Cathedral.* Translated by John Sturrock. New York: Harper and Row, 1962.

——. *El reino de este mundo.* Havana: Editorial Pueblo y Educación, 1979.

——. *El siglo de las Luces.* Barcelona: Seix Barral, 1962.

Carretta, Vincent. "Olaudah Equiano or Gustavus Vassa? New Light on an Eighteenth-Century Question of Identity." *Slavery and Abolition* 20, no. 3 (1999): 96–105.

——. "Three West Indian Writers of the 1780s Revisited and Revised." *Research in African Literatures* 29, no. 4 (Winter 1998): 73–87.

Casanovas Codina, Joan. *Bread, or Bullets!: Urban Labor and Spanish Colonialism in Cuba, 1850–1898.* Pittsburgh: University of Pittsburgh Press, 1998.

Castañeda, Digna. "The Female Slave in Cuba during the First Half of the Nineteenth Century." In *Engendering History: Caribbean Women in Historical Perspective*, edited by Verene Shepherd, Bridget Brereton, and Barbara Bailey, 141–54. London: James Currey, 1995.

Castellanos, Jorge, and Isabel Castellanos. *Cultura afrocubana: (El negro en Cuba, 1492–1844)*. 4 vols. Miami: Ediciones Universal, 1988–94.

——. "The Geographic, Ethnologic, and Linguistic Roots of Cuban Blacks." *Cuban Studies* 17 (1987): 95–110.

Castleman, Bruce A. "Social Climbers in a Colonial Mexican City: Individual Mobility with the Sistema de Castas in Orizaba, 1777–1791." *Colonial Latin American Review* 10, no. 2 (Dec. 2001): 229–49.

Castro, Fidel. *Informe central del primero congreso del Partido Comunista de Cuba*. Buenos Aires: Editorial Anteo, 1976.

Cepero Bonilla, Raúl. *Azúcar y abolición*. Havana: Editorial de Ciencias Sociales, 1971.

Chamosa, Oscar. " 'To Honor the Ashes of Their Forebears': The Rise and Crisis of African Nations in the Post-Independence State of Buenos Aires, 1820–1860." *Americas* 59, no. 3 (Jan. 2003): 347–78.

Chance, John K., and William B. Taylor. "Estate and Class: A Reply." *Comparative Studies in Society and History* 21, no. 3 (1979): 434–42.

——. "Estate and Class in a Colonial City, Oaxaca in 1792." *Comparative Studies in Society and History* 19, no. 3 (1977): 454–87.

Childs, Matt D. " 'A Black French General Arrived to Conquer the Island': Images of the Haitian Revolution in Cuba's 1812 Aponte Rebellion." In *The Impact of the Haitian Revolution in the Atlantic World*, edited by David Patrick Geggus, 135–56. Columbia: University of South Carolina Press, 2001.

——. "Expanding Perspectives on Race, Nation, and Culture in Cuban History." *Latin American Research Review* 39, no. 1 (Spring 2004): 285–301.

——. " 'Sewing' Civilization: Cuban Female Education in the Context of Africanization, 1800–1860." *Americas* 54, no. 1 (July 1997): 83–107.

Childs, Matt D., and Toyin Falola. "The Yoruba Diaspora in the Atlantic World: Methodology and Research." In *The Yoruba Diaspora in the Atlantic World*, edited by Toyin Falola and Matt D. Childs, 1–14. Bloomington: Indiana University Press, 2004.

Christelow, Allen. "Contraband Trade between Jamaica and the Spanish Main, and the Free Port Act of 1766." *Hispanic American Historical Review*, 22, no. 2 (May 1942): 309–43.

Coatsworth, John. "Patterns of Rural Rebellion in Latin America: Mexico in Comparative Perspective." In *Riot, Rebellion, and Revolution: Rural Social Conflict in Mexico*, edited by Frierdrich Katz, 21–62. Princeton, N.J.: Princeton University Press, 1988.

Cohen, David W., and Jack P. Greene, eds. *Neither Slave nor Free: The Freedman of African Descent in the Slave Societies of the New World*. Baltimore: Johns Hopkins University Press, 1972.

Cook, Alexandra Parma, and David Noble Cook. *Good Faith and Truthful Ignorance: A Case of Transatlantic Bigamy*. Durham, N.C.: Duke University Press, 1991.

Corwin, Arthur F. *Spain and the Abolition of Slavery in Cuba, 1817–1886*. Austin: University of Texas Press, 1967.

Craton, Michael. *Empire, Enslavement, and Freedom in the Caribbean*. Kingston: Ian Randle, 1997.

——. *Testing the Chains: Resistance to Slavery in the British West Indies*. Ithaca, N.Y.: Cornell University Press, 1982.

Curtin, Philip D. *The Atlantic Slave Trade: A Census*. Madison: University of Wisconsin Press, 1969.

Danger Roll, Zoila. *Los cimarrones de el Frijol*. Santiago: Editorial Oriente, 1977.

Darnton, Robert. "An Early Information Society: News and the Media in Eighteenth-Century Paris." *American Historical Review* 105, no. 1 (Feb. 2000): 1–36.

——. "A Euro State of Mind." *New York Review of Books*, 28 Feb. 2002, 30–32.

——. "It Happened One Night." *New York Review of Books*, 24 June 2004, 60–64.

Davis, David Brion. "Impact of the French and Haitian Revolutions." In *The Impact of the Haitian Revolution in the Atlantic World*, edited by David Patrick Geggus, 3–9. Columbia: University of South Carolina Press, 2001.

——. "Looking at Slavery from Broader Perspectives." *American Historical Review* 105, no. 2 (April 2000): 452–66.

——. *The Problem of Slavery in the Age of Revolution, 1770–1823*. Ithaca, N.Y.: Cornell University Press, 1975.

Davis, Natalie Zemon. *Fiction in the Archives: Pardon Tales and Their Tellers in Sixteenth-Century France*. Stanford, Calif.: Stanford University Press, 1987.

——. *The Return of Martin Guerre*. Cambridge, Mass.: Harvard University Press, 1983.

Dayan, Joan. *Haiti, History, and the Gods*. Berkeley: University of California Press, 1995.

Dean, Warren. *Rio Calro: A Brazilian Plantation System, 1820–1920*. Stanford, Calif.: Stanford University Press, 1976.

Debien, Gabriel. "Les colons de Saint-Domingue réfugiés à Cuba (1793–1815)." Pts. 1 and 2. *Revista de Indias* 13 (1953): 559–606; 14 (1954): 11–36.

de Carvalho Soares, Mariza. *Devotos da cor: Identidade étnica, religiosidade e escravidao no Rio de Janeiro, século XVIII*. Rio de Janeiro: Civilizaçao Brasileira, 2000.

de la Fuente, Alejandro. "Esclavos africanos en La Habana: Zonas de Procedencia y denominaciones étnicas, 1570–1699." *Revista Española de Antropología Americana* 20 (1990): 135–60.

——. *A Nation for All: Race, Inequality, and Politics in Twentieth-Century Cuba*. Chapel Hill: University of North Carolina Press, 2001.

——. "Slave Law and Claims-Making in Cuba: The Tannenbaum Debate Revisited." *Law and History Review* 22, no. 2 (Summer 2004): 339–70.

——. "Slavery and the Law: A Reply." *Law and History Review* 22, no. 2 (Summer 2004): 383–88.

de la Torre, Mildred. "Posiciones y actitudes en torno a la esclavitud en Cuba." In *Temas acerca de la esclavitud*, 71–95. Havana: Editorial de Ciencias Sociales, 1988.

Delgado de Torres, Lena. "Reformulating Nationalism in the African Diaspora: The Aponte Rebellion of 1812." *CR: The New Centennial Review* 3, no. 3 (Fall 2003): 27–46.

de Mello e Souza, Marina. *Reis negros no Brasil escravista: história da festa de coroação de rei congo*. Belo Horizonte: Editora da UFMG, 2002.

Deschamps Chapeaux, Pedro. *Los batallones de pardos y morenos libres*. Havana: Instituto Cubano del Libro, 1976.

——. "Cabildos: Solo para esclavos." *Cuba* 7, no. 69 (Jan. 1968): 50–51.

——. *Los cimarrones urbanos*. Havana: Editorial de Ciencias Sociales, 1983.

——. "La Habana de intra y extramuros y los Cabildos de los negros de nación." In *Historia*, 19–25. Havana: Comisión de Activistas de Historia Regional 10 de Octubre, 1972.

——. "Margarito Blanco 'Ocongo de Ultan.'" *Boletín de Instituto de Historia y del Archivo Nacional* (Havana) 65 (July–Dec. 1964): 97–109.

——. *El negro en la economía habanera del siglo XIX*. Havana: Unión de Escritores y Artistas de Cuba, 1971.

——. "Sociedades: La integración de pardos y morenos." *Cuba* 7, no. 71 (Mar. 1968):54–55.

——. "Testamentaria de pardos y morenos libres en la Habana del siglo xix." *Revista de la Biblioteca Nacional José Martí* 14, no. 2 (May–Aug. 1972): 45–54.

Díaz, María Elena. "Beyond Tannenbaum," *Law and History Review* 22, no. 2 (Summer 2004): 371–76.

——. *The Virgin, the King, and the Royal Slaves of El Cobre: Negotiating Freedom in Colonial Cuba, 1670–1780*. Stanford, Calif.: Stanford University Press, 2000.

Dirks, Robert. *The Black Saturnalia: Conflict and Its Ritual Expression on British West Indian Slave Plantations*. Gainesville: University Presses of Florida, 1987.

Domínguez, Jorge I. *Cuba: Order and Revolution*. Cambridge, Mass.: Harvard University Press, 1978.

——. *Insurrection or Loyalty: The Breakdown of the Spanish American Empire*. Cambridge, Mass.: Harvard University Press, 1980.

Dorsey, Joseph C. *Slave Traffic in the Age of Abolition: Puerto Rico, West Africa, and the Non-Hispanic Caribbean, 1815–1859*. Gainesville: University Press of Florida, 2003.

Dubois, Laurent. *Avengers of the New World: The Story of the Haitian Revolution*. Cambridge, Mass.: Harvard University Press, 2004.

——. *A Colony of Citizens: Revolution and Slave Emancipation in the French Caribbean, 1787–1804*. Chapel Hill: University of North Carolina Press, 2004.

—— " 'Our Three Colors': The King, the Republic and the Political Culture of Slave Revolution in Saint-Domingue." *Historical Reflections* 29, no. 1 (2003): 83–102.

Duharte Jiménez, Rafael. *El negro en la sociedad colonial*. Santiago: Editorial Oriente, 1988.

Egerton, Douglas R. "Black Independence Struggles and the Tale of Two Revolutions: A Review Essay." *Journal of Southern History* 64, no. 1 (Feb. 1998): 95–116.

——. *Gabriel's Rebellion: The Virginia Slave Conspiracies of 1800 and 1802*. Chapel Hill: University of North Carolina Press, 1993.

——. *He Shall Go Out Free: The Lives of Denmark Vesey*. Madison, Wis.: Madison House, 1999.

Eisenberg, Peter L. "Ficando livre: As alforrias en Campinas no século xix." *Estudos econômicos* 17, no. 2 (May–Aug. 1987): 175–216.

Elkins, Stanley M. *Slavery: A Problem in American Institutional and Intellectual Life*. Chicago: University of Chicago Press, 1959.

Eltis, David. "Atlantic History in Global Perspective." *Itinerario* 23, no. 2 (1999): 141–61.

——. "The Diaspora of Yoruba Speakers, 1650–1865: Dimensions and Implications." In *The Yoruba Diaspora in the Atlantic World*, edited by Toyin Falola and Matt D. Childs, 17–39. Bloomington: Indiana University Press, 2004.

——. *Economic Growth and the Ending of the Transatlantic Slave Trade*. Oxford: Oxford University Press, 1987.

——. "The Nineteenth-Century Transatlantic Slave Trade: An Annual Time Series of Imports into the Americas Broken Down by Region." *Hispanic American Historical Review* 67, no. 1 (Feb. 1987): 109–38.

——. *The Rise of African Slavery in the Americas*. Cambridge: Cambridge University Press, 2000.

Eltis, David, David Richardson, and Stephen D. Behrendt. "Patterns in the Transatlantic Slave Trade, 1662–1867: New Indications of African Origins of Slaves Arriving in the Americas." In *Black Imagination and the Middle Passage*, edited by Maria Diedrich, Henry Louis Gates Jr., and Carl Pedersen, 21–32. Oxford: Oxford University Press, 1999.

Falola, Toyin and Adebayo Akanmu. *Culture, Politics, & Money Among the Yoruba*. New Brunswick: Transaction, 2000.

Faust, Drew. "Trainspotting." *Nation*, 23 May 2005, 46–49.

Fernández Repetto, Francisco and Genny Negroe Sierra. *Una población perdida en la memoria: Los negros de Yucatán*. Mérida, Yucatán: Universidad Autónoma de Yucatán, 1995.

Ferrer, Ada. *Insurgent Cuba: Race, Nation, and Revolution, 1868–1898*. Chapel Hill: University of North Carolina Press, 1999.

———. "Noticias de Haití en Cuba." *Revista de Indias* 63, no. 229 (2003): 675–94.

———. "Social Aspects of Cuban Nationalism: Race, Slavery, and the Guerra Chiquita, 1879–1880." *Cuban Studies* 21 (1991): 37–56.

———. "Thinking Through Haiti: Cuban Slave Society and the Haitian Revolution." Paper presented at the University of Texas at Austin, Nov. 2000.

Fick, Carolyn, E. *The Making of Haiti: The Saint Domingue Revolution from Below*. Knoxville: University of Tennessee Press, 1990.

Fields, Barbara J. "Ideology and Race in American History." In *Region, Race, and Reconstruction: Essays in Honor of C. Vann Woodward*, edited by J. Morgan Kousser and James M. McPherson, 143–77. New York: Oxford University Press, 1982.

Fischer, Sibylle. *Modernity Disavowed: Haiti and the Cultures of Slavery in the Age of Revolution*. Durham, N.C.: Duke University Press, 2004.

Franco, José Luciano. *Antonio Maceo: Apuntes para una historia de su vida*. 3 vols. Havana: Editorial de Ciencias Sociales, 1975.

———. *Comercio clandestino de esclavos*. Havana: Editorial de Ciencias Sociales, 1996.

———. *La conspiración de Aponte*. Havana: Publicaciones del Archivo Nacional, 1963.

———. *Las conspiraciones de 1810 y 1812*. Havana: Editorial de Ciencias Sociales, 1977.

———. *La diáspora africana en el nuevo mundo*. Havana: Editorial de Ciencias Sociales, 1975.

———. *Ensayos históricos*. Havana: Editorial de Ciencias Sociales, 1974.

———. *Folklore criollo y Afrocubano*. Havana: Publicaciones de la Junta Nacional de Arqueóloga y Etnología, 1959.

———. *La gesta heroica del triunvirato*. Havana: Editorial de Ciencias Sociales, 1978.

———. *Las minas de Santiago del Prado y la rebelión de los cobreros, 1530–1800*. Havana: Editorial de Ciencias Sociales, 1975.

———. *Los palenques de los negros cimarrones*. Havana: Departamento de Orientación Revolucionaria del Comité Central del Partido Comunista de Cuba, 1973.

———. *Placido: Una polémica que tiene cien años y otros ensayos*. Havana: Ediciones UNEAC, 1964.

———. "Recorrido autobiográfico de un historiador." *Revista de la Biblioteca Nacional José Martí*, 3rd ser., vol. 20, no. 3 (Sept–Dec. 1978): 17–31.

———. *Revoluciones y conflictos internacionales en el caribe, 1789–1854*. Havana: Academia de Ciencias, 1965.

Franklin, Sarah Louise. "Gender and Slave Rebellion in Colonial Cuba: The Bayamo Conspiracy of 1805." Master's thesis, Florida State University, 2003.

Freehling, William W. *The Reintegration of American History: Slavery and the Civil War*. New York: Oxford University Press, 1994.

Frey, Sylvia R. *Water from the Rock: Black Resistance in a Revolutionary Age*. Princeton, N.J.: Princeton University Press, 1991.

García Rodríguez, Gloria. *Conspiraciones y revueltas : la actividad política de los negros en Cuba (1790–1845)*. Santiago: Editorial Oriente, 2003.

——. "Importación de esclavos de ambos sexos por varios puertos de Cuba, 1763–1820." In *Historia de Cuba: La colonia, evolución socioeconómica y formación nacional de los origines hasta 1867,* edited by María del Carmen Barcia, Gloria García, and Eduardo Torres-Cuevas, 471–73. Havana: Editorial Política, 1994.

——. "A propósito de la Escalera: El esclavo como sujeto político." *Boletín del Archivo Nacional* (Havana) 12 (2000): 1–13.

Garrigus, John D. "Catalyst or Catastrophe? Saint-Domingue's Free Men of Color and the Battle of Savannah, 1779–1782." *Revista-Review Interamericana* 22, no. 1–2 (1992): 109–25.

Gaspar, David Barry. *Bondmen and Rebels: A Study of Master-Slave Relations in Antigua: With Implications for Colonial British America.* Baltimore: Johns Hopkins University Press, 1985.

Gaspar, David Barry, and David Patrick Geggus, eds. *A Turbulent Time: The French Revolution and the Greater Caribbean.* Bloomington: Indiana University Press, 1997.

Gates, Henry Louis, Jr. *Figures in Black: Words, Signs, and the 'Racial' Self.* New York: Oxford University Press, 1987.

Gates, Henry Louis, Jr., ed. *The Classic Slave Narratives.* New York: Mentor, 1987.

Geggus, David Patrick. "The Causation of Slave Rebellions: An Overview." *Indian Historical Review* 15, no. 1–2 (1988–89): 116–29.

——. "The Enigma of Jamaica in the 1790s: New Light on the Causes of Slave Rebellions." *William and Mary Quarterly* 64, no. 2 (April 1987): 274–99.

——. "The French and Haitian Revolutions and Resistance to Slavery in the Americas: An Overview." *Revue française d'histoire d'outre mer* 76, no. 1 (1989): 107–24.

——. "The Haitian Revolution." In *The Modern Caribbean,* edited by Franklin W. Knight and Colin A. Palmer, 21–50. Chapel Hill: University of North Carolina Press, 1989.

——. *Haitian Revolutionary Studies.* Bloomington: Indiana University Press, 2002.

——. "Slave Resistance in the Spanish Caribbean in the Mid-1790s." In *A Turbulent Time: The French Revolution and the Greater Caribbean,* edited by David Barry Gaspar and David Patrick Geggus, 131–55. Bloomington: Indiana University Press, 1997.

——. "Slave Resistance Studies and the Saint Domingue Slave Revolt: Some Preliminary Considerations." Occasional Paper Series, Florida International University Latin American and Caribbean Center, Winter 1983.

——. "Slavery, War, and Revolution in the Greater Caribbean, 1789–1815." In *A Turbulent Time: The French Revolution and the Greater Caribbean,* edited by David Barry Gaspar and David Patrick Geggus, 1–50. Bloomington: Indiana University Press, 1997.

——. *Slavery, War, and Revolution: The British Occupation of Saint Domingue 1793–1798.* Oxford: Oxford University Press, 1982.

——. "The Slaves and Free Coloreds of Martinique during the Age of the French and Haitian Revolutions: Three Moments of Resistance." In *The Lesser Antilles in the Age of European Expansion,* edited by Robert L. Paquette and Stanley L. Engerman, 280–301. Gainesville: University Press of Florida, 1996.

——, ed. *The Impact of the Haitian Revolution in the Atlantic World.* Columbia: University of South Carolina Press, 2001.

Genovese, Eugene D. *From Rebellion to Revolution: Afro-American Slave Revolts in the Making of the Modern World.* Baton Rouge: Louisiana State University Press, 1979.

——. *Roll, Jordan, Roll: The World the Slaves Made.* New York: Vintage, 1974.

——. *The World the Slaveholders Made: Two Essays in Interpretation.* Rev. ed. Middletown, Conn.: Wesleyan University Press, 1988.

Gilroy, Paul. *The Black Atlantic: Modernity and Double Consciousness.* Cambridge, Mass.: Harvard University Press, 1993.

Ginzburg, Carlo. *The Cheese and the Worms: The Cosmos of a Sixteenth-Century Miller.* Translated by John Tedeschi and Anne Tedeschi. Baltimore: Johns Hopkins University Press, 1989.

——. *Clues, Myths, and the Historical Method.* Translated by John Tedeschi and Anne Tedeschi. Baltimore: Johns Hopkins University Press, 1989.

Gómez, Michael A. "African Identity and Slavery in the Americas." *Radical History Review* 75 (1999): 111–20.

——. *Exchanging Our Country Marks: The Transformation of African Identities in the Colonial and Antebellum South.* Chapel Hill: University of North Carolina Press, 1998.

Góngora, Mario. *Studies in the Colonial History of Spanish America.* Translated by Richard Southern. Cambridge: Cambridge University Press, 1975.

González-Ripoll Navarro, María Dolores. *Cuba, la isla de los ensayos: Cultura y sociedad (1790–1815).* Madrid: Consejo Superior de Investigaciones Científicas, 1999.

Goody, Jack. "Writing, Religion, and Revolt in Bahia." *Visible Language* 20 (1986): 318–43.

Gramsci, Antonio. *Antonio Gramsci, Letters from Prison.* Edited by Lynne Lawner. New York: Noonday, 1973.

Grandío Moráguez, Oscar. "The African Origins of Slaves Arriving in Cuba, 1789–1867." In *Transatlantic Connections: The Repeopling of the Americas and the New Slave Trade Database,* edited by David Eltis and David Richardson. Cambridge: Cambridge University Press, forthcoming.

Gutiérrez, Ramón A. *When Jesus Came, the Corn Mothers Went Away: Marriage, Sexuality, and Power in New Mexico, 1500–1846.* Stanford, Calif.: Stanford University Press, 1991.

Hall, Gwendolyn Midlo. *Africans in Colonial Louisiana: The Development of Afro-Creole Culture in the Eighteenth Century.* Baton Rouge: Louisiana State University Press, 1992.

——. *Social Control in Slave Plantation Societies: A Comparison of St. Domingue and Cuba.* Baltimore: Johns Hopkins University Press, 1971.

Halttunen, Karen. "Cultural History and the Challenge of Narrativity." In *Beyond the Cultural Turn: New Directions in the Study of Society and Culture,* edited by Victoria E. Bonnell and Lynn Hunt, 165–181. Berkeley: University of California Press, 1999.

Hamnett, Brian R. "Process and Pattern: A Re-examination of the Ibero-American Independence Movements, 1808–1826." *Journal of Latin American Studies* 29, no. 2 (May 1997): 279–328.

Hanger, Kimberly S. *Bounded Lives, Bounded Places: Free Black Society in Colonial New Orleans, 1769–1803.* Durham, N.C.: Duke University Press, 1997.

Harris, Robert L. "Dilemmas in Teaching African American History." *Perspectives* 36, no. 8 (Nov. 1998): 33–35.

Helg, Aline. "The Limits of Equality: Free People of Colour and Slaves during the First Independence of Cartagena, Colombia, 1810–1815." *Slavery and Abolition* 20, no. 2 (Aug. 1999): 1–30.

——. *Our Rightful Share: The Afro-Cuban Struggle for Equality, 1886–1912.* Chapel Hill: University of North Carolina Press, 1995.

Hensel, Silke. "Was There an Age of Revolution in Latin America? New Literature on Latin American Independence." *Latin American Research Review* 38, no. 3 (2003): 237–49.

Hevia Lanier, Oilda. *El directorio central de las sociedades negras de Cuba, 1886–1894.* Habana: Editorial de Ciencias Sociales, 1996.

Heywood, Linda M. "The Angolan-Afro-Brazilian Cultural Connections." *Slavery and Abolition* 20, no. 1 (April 1999): 9–23.

——. "Introduction." In *Central Africans and Cultural Transformations in the American*

*Diaspora*, edited by Linda M. Heywood, 1–18. Cambridge: Cambridge University Press, 2002.

Hilton, Sylvia L. "U.S. Intervention and Monroeism: Spanish Perspectives on the American Role in the Colonial Crisis of 1895–98." In *Whose America? The War of 1898 and the Battles to Define the Nation*, edited by Virginia M. Bouvier, 37–59. Westport, Conn.: Praeger, 2001.

Hobsbawm, E. J. *The Age of Revolution, 1789–1848*. Cleveland: World, 1962.

——. "Introduction: Inventing Traditions." In *The Invention of Tradition*, edited by Eric J. Hobsbawm and Terence Ranger, 1–14. Cambridge: Cambridge University Press, 1983.

Hochshild, Adam. *Bury the Chains: Prophets and Rebels in the Fight to Free an Empire's Slaves*. Boston: Houghton Mifflin, 2005.

Holt, Thomas C. "Marking: Race, Race-making and the Writing of History." *American Historical Review* 100, no. 1 (Feb. 1995): 1–20.

Houdaille, Jacques. "Negros Franceses en América Central a fines del siglo xviii." *Antropología e historia de Guatemala* 6, no. 1 (1954): 65–67.

Howard, Philip A. *Changing History: Afro-Cuban Cabildos and Societies of Color in the Nineteenth Century*. Baton Rouge: Louisiana State University Press, 1998.

Hünefeldt, Christine. *Paying the Price of Freedom: Family and Labor among Lima's Slaves, 1800–1854*. Translated by Alexandra Stern. Berkeley: University of California Press, 1994.

Inglis, Gordon Doug. "Historical Demography of Colonial Cuba, 1492–1870." Ph.D. diss., Texas Christian University, 1979.

James, C. L. R. *The Black Jacobins: Toussaint L'Ouverture and the San Domingo Revolution*. 2nd ed. New York: Vintage, 1963.

Jennings, Evelyn Powell. "State Enslavement in Colonial Havana, 1763–1790." In *Slavery without Sugar: Diversity in Caribbean Economy and Society since the 17th Century*, edited by Verene A. Shepherd, 152–182. Gainesville: University Press of Florida, 2002.

Jensen, Larry R. *Children of Colonial Despotism: Press, Politics, and Culture in Cuba, 1790–1840*. Tampa: University of South Florida Press, 1988.

Johnson, Michael P. "Denmark Vesey and His Co-Conspirators." *William and Mary Quarterly* 58, no. 4 (October 2001): 915–76.

Johnson, Sherry. " 'La Guerra Contra los Habitantes de los Arrabales': Changing Patterns of Land Use and Land Tenancy In and Around Havana, 1763–1800." *Hispanic American Historical Review* 77, no. 2 (May 1997): 181–209.

——. " 'Honor Is Life': Military Reform and the Transformation of Cuban Society: 1753–1796." Ph.D. diss., University of Florida, 1995.

——. "The Rise and Fall of Creole Participation in the Cuban Slave Trade, 1789–1796." *Cuban Studies* 30 (1999): 52–75.

——. *The Social Transformation of Eighteenth-Century Cuba*. Gainesville: University Press of Florida, 2001.

Johnson, Walter. "On Agency." *Journal of Social History* 37, no. 1 (Fall 2003): 113–24.

Johnson, Whittington B. *Race Relations in the Bahamas, 1784–1834: The Nonviolent Transformation from a Slave to a Free Society*. Fayetteville: University of Arkansas Press, 2000.

Jordan, Winthrop D. *Tumult and Silence at Second Creek: An Inquiry into a Civil War Slave Conspiracy*. Rev. ed. Baton Rouge: Louisiana State University Press, 1995.

Kapcia, Antoni. *Cuba: Island of Dreams*. Oxford: Berg, 2000.

Karasch, Mary C. *Slave Life in Rio de Janeiro, 1808–1850*. Princeton, N.J.: Princeton University Press, 1987.

Kent, Raymond K. "African Revolt in Bahia." *Journal of Social History* 3, no. 4 (Summer 1970): 334–56.

Kiddy, Elizabeth W. "Ethnic and Racial Identity in the Brotherhoods of the Rosary of Minas Gerais, 1700–1830." *Americas* 56, no. 2 (Oct. 1999): 221–52.

King, James F. "The Colored Castes and American Representation in the Cortes of Cádiz." *Hispanic American Historical Review* 33, no. 1 (Feb. 1953): 33–64.

Kinsbruner, Jay. *Not of Pure Blood: The Free People of Color and Racial Prejudice in Nineteenth-Century Puerto Rico.* Durham, N.C.: Duke University Press, 1996.

Kiple, Kenneth F. *Blacks in Colonial Cuba, 1774–1899.* Gainesville: University Presses of Florida, 1976.

Klein, Herbert S. *African Slavery in Latin America and the Caribbean.* Oxford: Oxford University Press, 1986.

——. *The Atlantic Slave Trade.* Cambridge: Cambridge University Press, 1999.

——. "The Colored Militia of Cuba: 1568–1868." *Caribbean Studies* 6, no. 2 (July 1966): 17–27.

——. *The Middle Passage: Comparative Studies in the Atlantic Slave Trade.* Princeton, N.J.: Princeton University Press, 1978.

——. *Slavery in the Americas: A Comparative Study of Virginia and Cuba.* Chicago: University of Chicago Press, 1967.

Knight, Alan. "Subalterns, Signifiers and Statistics: Perspectives on Mexican Historiography." *Latin American Research Review* 37, no. 2 (2002): 136–58.

Knight, Franklin W. "Cuba." In *Neither Slave nor Free: The Freedman of African Descent in the Slave Societies of the New World,* edited by David W. Cohen and Jack P. Greene, 278–308. Baltimore: Johns Hopkins University Press, 1972.

——. "The Free Colored Population in Cuba during the Nineteenth Century." In *Slavery without Sugar: Diversity in Caribbean Economy and Society since the 17th Century,* edited by Verene A. Shepherd, 224–47. Gainesville: University Press of Florida, 2002.

——. "The Haitian Revolution." *American Historical Review* 105, no. 1 (Feb. 2000): 103–16.

——. "Origins of Wealth and the Sugar Revolution in Cuba, 1750–1850." *Hispanic American Historical Review* 57, no. 2 (May 1977): 231–53.

——. *Slave Society in Cuba During the Nineteenth Century.* Madison: University of Wisconsin Press, 1970.

Kolchin, Peter. "American Historians and Antebellum Southern Slavery, 1959–1984." In *A Master's Due: Essays in Honor of David Herbert Donald,* edited by William J. Cooper Jr., Michael F. Holt, and John McCardell, 87–111. Baton Rouge: Louisiana State University Press, 1985.

Kuethe, Allan J. *Cuba, 1753–1815: Crown, Military, and Society.* Knoxville: University of Tennessee Press, 1986.

——. "La fidelidad cubana durante la edad de las revoluciones." *Anuario de Estudios Americanos* 55, no. 1 (Jan.–June 1998): 209–20.

——. "The Status of the Free Pardo in the Disciplined Militia of New Granada." *Journal of Negro History* 56, no. 2 (Apr. 1971): 105–17.

Kutzinski, Vera M. *Sugar's Secrets: Race and the Erotics of Cuban Nationalism.* Charlottesville: University Press of Virginia, 1993.

Kuznesof, Elizabeth Anne. "Ethnic and Gender Influences on 'Spanish' Creole Society in Colonial Spanish America." *Colonial Latin American Review* 4, no. 1 (1995): 153–76.

——. "More Conversation on Race, Class, and Gender." *Colonial Latin American Review* 5, no. 1 (1996): 129–33.

Labrador-Rodríguez, Sonia. " 'El miedo al negro': El debate de lo racial en el discurso revolucionario cubano." *Historia y Sociedad* (Puerto Rico) 9 (1997): 111–28.

Lachance, Paul. "Repercussion of the Haitian Revolution in Louisiana." In *The Impact of the Haitian Revolution in the Atlantic World*, edited by David P. Geggus, 209–30. Columbia: University of South Carolina Press, 2001.

Lampros, Peter James. "Merchant-Planter Cooperation and Conflict: The Havana Consulado, 1794–1832." Ph.D. diss., Tulane University, 1980.

Landers, Jane G. *Black Society in Spanish Florida*. Foreword by Peter H. Wood. Urbana: University of Illinois Press, 1999.

———. "Rebellion and Royalism in Spanish Florida: The French Revolution on Spain's Northern Colonial Frontier." In *A Turbulent Time: The French Revolution and the Greater Caribbean*, edited by David Barry Gaspar and David Patrick Geggus, 156–77. Bloomington: Indiana University Press, 1997.

Langley, Lester D. *The Americas in the Age of Revolution 1750–1850*. New Haven, Conn.: Yale University Press, 1996.

Lanier, Clément. "Cuba et la conspiration d'Apunte [*sic*] en 1812." *Revue de la société hatiienne d'histoire, de géographie et de géologie* 23, no. 86 (July 1952): 21–30.

La Rosa Corzo, Gabino. *Los cimarrones de Cuba*. Havana: Editorial de Ciencias Sociales, 1988.

———. *Runaway Slave Settlements in Cuba: Resistance and Repression*. Translated by Mary Todd. Chapel Hill: University of North Carolina Press, 2003.

———. "Sobre marcas de esclavos en Cuba." *Boletín del Museo del Hombre Dominicano* (Santo Domingo) 15, no. 21 (1988): 59–69.

Law, Robin. "Ethnicity and the Slave Trade: 'Lucumi' and 'Nago' as Ethnonyms in West Africa." *History in Africa* 24 (1997): 205–19.

———. *The Oyo Empire, c. 1600–c. 1836: A West African Imperialism in the Era of the Atlantic Slave Trade*. Oxford: Clarendon, 1977.

Le Riverend, Julio. "Homenaje a José Luciano Franco." *Revista Santiago* 44 (Dec. 1981): 115–25.

———. "José Luciano Franco: Pasión historiográfica." *Boletín del Archivo Nacional* (Havana) 4 (1990): 79–81.

Le Riverend, Julio, et al. *Historia de Cuba*. Havana: Editorial Pueblo y Educación, 1977.

Le Roy Laudrie, Emmanuel. *Montaillou: The Promised Land of Error*. Translated by Barbara Bray. New York: Vintage, 1979.

Lewis, Laura A. *Hall of Mirrors: Power, Witchcraft, and Caste in Colonial Mexico*. Durham, N.C.: Duke University Press, 2003.

Linebaugh, Peter, and Marcus Rediker. *The Many-Headed Hydra: Sailors, Slaves, Commoners, and the Hidden History of the Revolutionary Atlantic*. Boston: Beacon, 2000.

Lockhart, James. *Nahuas and Spaniards: Postconquest Central Mexican History and Philology*. Stanford, Calif.: Stanford University Press, 1991.

Lovejoy, Paul E. "Background to Rebellion: The Origins of Muslim Slaves in Bahia." *Slavery and Abolition* 15, no. 2 (1994): 151–80.

———. "Identifying Enslaved Africans in the African Diaspora." In *Identity in the Shadow of Slavery*, edited by Paul E. Lovejoy, 1–29. London: Continuum, 2000.

———. "*Murgu*: The Wages of Slavery in the Sokoto Caliphate." *Slavery and Abolition* 14, no. 1 (1993): 168–85.

———. *Transformations in Slavery: A History of Slavery in Africa*. Cambridge: Cambridge University Press, 1983.

——. "The Yoruba Factor in the Trans-Atlantic Slave Trade." In *The Yoruba Diaspora in the Atlantic World*, edited by Toyin Falola and Matt D. Childs, 40–55. Bloomington: Indiana University Press, 2004.

Lovejoy, Paul E., and David Richardson. "Trust, Pawnship, and Atlantic History: The Institutional Foundations of the Old Calabar Slave Trade." *American Historical Review* 104, no. 2 (April 1999): 333–55.

Lucena Salmoral, Manuel. *Los codigos negros de la America Española*. Madrid: Ediciones UNESCO, 1996.

——. "El derecho de coartación del esclavo en la América Española." *Revista de Indias* 59, no. 216 (May–Aug. 1999): 357–74.

Lux, William R. "French Colonization in Cuba, 1791–1809." *Americas* 29, no. 1 (1972): 57–61.

Lynch, John. *The Spanish American Revolutions, 1808–1826*. 2nd ed. New York: Norton, 1986.

Machado, Bruno Javier. *Casa Blanca: Hallé su oscura luz*. Havana: n.p., 1987.

"The Making of a Slave Conspiracy." Pts. 1 and 2. *William and Mary Quarterly*. 3rd Ser., vol. 58, no. 4 (Oct. 2001): 913–76; vol. 59, no. 1 (Jan. 2002): 135–202.

Mann, Kristin. "Shifting Paradigms in the Study of the African Diaspora and of Atlantic History and Culture." *Slavery and Abolition* 22, no. 1 (April 2001): 3–21.

Marchena Fernández, Juan. *Ejército y milicias en el mundo colonial americano*. Madrid: Editorial Mapfre, 1992.

Márquez, José de Jesús. "Conspiración de Aponte." *Revista Cubana* 19 (1894): 441–54.

Marrero, Levi. *Cuba: Economía y sociedad, azúcar, ilustración y conciencia (1763–1868)*. 15 vols. Madrid: Editorial Playor, 1972–92.

Martínez Heredia, Fernando. "Introducción." In *Espacios, silencios y los sentidos de la libertad: Cuba entre 1878 y 1912*, edited by Fernando Martínez Heredia, Rebecca J. Scott, and Orlando F. García Martínez, 13–19. Havana: Ediciones UNION, 2001.

Martínez-Vergne, Teresita. *Shaping the Discourse on Space: Charity and Its Wards in Nineteenth-Century San Juan, Puerto Rico*. Austin: University of Texas Press, 1999.

McAlister, Lyle N. *The "Fuero Militar" in New Spain, 1764–1800*. Gainesville: University of Florida Press, 1957.

McCaa, Robert, Stuart B. Schwartz, and Arturo Grubessich. "Race and Class in Colonial Latin America: A Critique." *Comparative Studies in Society and History*. 21, no. 3 (1979): 421–33.

McLeod, Marc C. "Undesirable Aliens: Race, Ethnicity, and Nationalism in the Comparison of Haitian and British West Indian Immigrant Workers in Cuba, 1912–1939." *Journal of Social History* 31, no. 3 (1998): 599–623.

Mellafe, Rolando. *Negro Slavery in Latin America*. Translated by J. W. S. Judge. Berkeley: University of California Press, 1975.

Méndez Capote, Renée. *4 conspiraciones*. Havana: Instituto Cubano del libro, 1972.

Miller, Joseph, C. "History and Africa / Africa and History." *American Historical Review* 104, no. 1 (Feb. 1999): 1–32.

Mintz, Sidney W. "The Caribbean as a Socio-Cultural Area." *Cahiers d'Histoire Mondiale* 9, no. 4 (1966): 912–37.

——. "The Caribbean Region." *Daedalus* 103, no. 2 (Spring 1974): 45–72.

——. "Slave Life on Caribbean Sugar Plantations: Some Unanswered Questions." In *Slave Cultures and the Culture of Slavery*, edited by Stephan Palmié, 8–28. Knoxville: University of Tennessee Press, 1995.

——. *Sweetness and Power: The Place of Sugar in Modern History*. New York: Viking, 1985.

Mintz, Sidney W., and Richard Price. *The Birth of African-American Culture: An Anthropological Perspective*. Boston: Beacon, 1992.

Mintz, Steven. "Models of Emancipation during the Age of Revolution." *Slavery and Abolition* 17, no. 2 (Aug. 1996):1–21.

Moliner Castañeda, Israel. *Los Cabildos Afrocubanos en Matanzas*. Matanzas: Ediciones Matanzas, 2002.

Montejo-Arrechea, Carmen Victoria. *Sociedades de instrucción y recreo de pardos y morenos que existieron en Cuba colonial: 1878–1898*. Veracruz: Instituto Veracruzano de Cultura, 1993.

Moore, Barrington, Jr. *Injustice: The Social Bases of Obedience and Revolt*. New York: M. E. Sharpe, 1978.

Morales Padrón, Fransico. "Conspiraciones y masonería en Cuba (1810–1826)." *Anuario de estudios americanos*, 29 (1972): 343–77.

Moreno Fraginals, Manuel. *La historia como arma y otros estudios sobre esclavos, ingenios y plantaciones*. Barcelona: Editorial Critica, 1983.

———. *El Ingenio: Complejo económico social cubano del azúcar*. 3 vols. Havana: Editorial de Ciencias Sociales, 1978.

Morgan, Philip D. "The Cultural Implications of the Atlantic Slave Trade: African Regional Origins, American Destinations and New World Developments." *Slavery and Abolition* 18, no. 1 (April 1997): 122–45.

Mörner, Magnus. *Race Mixture in the History of Latin America*. Boston: Little, Brown, 1967.

Morton-Williams, Peter. "The Yoruba Ogboni Cult in Oyo." *Africa* 30 (1960): 362–74.

Mott, Luiz. "A revolução dos negros do Haití e o Brasil." *Mensario do Arquivo Nacional* 13, no. 1 (1982): 3–11.

Mullin, Gerald W. *Flight and Rebellion: Slave Resistance in Eighteenth-Century Virginia*. Oxford: Oxford University Press, 1972.

Mullin, Michael. *Africa in America: Slave Acculturation and Resistance in the American South and British Caribbean, 1763–1831*. Urbana: University of Illinois Press, 1992.

Mulvey, Patricia A. "Slave Confraternities in Brazil: Their Role in Colonial Society." *Americas* 39, no. 1 (July 1982): 39–68.

Murray, David. "Capitalism and Slavery in Cuba." *Slavery and Abolition* 17, no. 3 (Dec. 1996): 223–37.

———. *Odious Commerce: Britain, Spain and the Abolition of the Cuban Slave Trade*. Cambridge: Cambridge University Press, 1980.

———. "The Slave Trade, Slavery and Cuban Independence." *Slavery and Abolition* 20, no. 3 (Dec. 1999): 106–26.

Nishida, Mieko. "Manumission and Ethnicity in Urban Slavery: Salvador, Brazil, 1808–1888." *Hispanic American Historical Review* 73, no. 3 (Aug. 1993): 361–91.

Novoa, José. "Los esclavos en Holguín (1720–1867): Estudio socio demográfico." Unpublished manuscript, 1998.

Nuñez, Benjamin. *Dictionary of Afro-Latin American Civilization*. Westport, Conn.: Greenwood, 1980.

Núnez Jiménez, Antonio. *Los esclavos negros*. Cuba: Fundación de la Naturaleza y el Hombre, 1998.

Okihiro, Gary Y., ed. *In Resistance: Studies in African, Caribbean, and Afro-American History*. Amherst: University of Massachusetts, 1986.

Oquendo, Leyda. "Las rebeldías de los esclavos en Cuba, 1790–1830." In *Temas acerca de la esclavitud*, 49–70. Havana: Editorial de Ciencias Sociales, 1988.

Bibliography

Ortiz, Fernando. *Los cabildos y la fiesta afrocubanos del Día de Reyes*. 1921. Reprint, Havana: Editorial de Ciencias Sociales, 1992.

———. *Cuban Counterpoint: Tobacco and Sugar*. Translated by Harriet de Onís. Introduction by Bronislaw Malinowski. Prologue by Herminio Portell Vilá. 1947. Reprinted with new introduction by Fernando Coronil. Durham, N.C.: Duke University Press, 1995.

———. *El engaño de las razas*. 1946. Reprint, Havana: Editorial de Ciencias Sociales, 1975.

———. *Los negros brujos*. 1906. Reprint, Havana: Editorial de Ciencias Sociales, 1995.

———. *Los negros curros*. 1909. Reprint, Havana: Editorial de Ciencias Sociales, 1986.

———. *Los negros esclavos*. 1916. Reprint, Havana: Editorial de Ciencias Sociales, 1975.

Ortiz, Pedro. *Carta al Rey*. Havana: UNEAC, 1990.

Pagden, Anthony. *Lords of All the World: Ideologies of Empire in Spain, Britain and France c.1500–c.1800*. New Haven, Conn.: Yale University Press, 1995.

Palmer, Colin. *Human Cargoes: The British Slave Trade to Spanish America, 1700–1739*. Urbana: University of Illinois Press, 1981.

Palmer, R. R. *The Age of the Democratic Revolution: A Political History of Europe and America, 1760–1800*. Princeton, N.J.: Princeton University Press, 1959.

Palmié, Stephan. "Ethnogenesis Processes and Cultural Transfer in Afro-American Slave Populations." In *Slavery in the Americas*, edited by Wolfgang Binder, 337–63. Würzburg: Könighausen und Neumann, 1993.

———. *Wizards and Scientists: Explorations in Afro-Cuban Modernity and Tradition*. Durham, N.C.: Duke University Press, 2002.

Paquette, Robert L. "From Rebellion to Revisionism: The Continuing Debate about the Denmark Vesey Affair." *Journal of the Historical Society* 4, no. 3 (Fall 2004): 291–334.

———. "Social History Update: Slave Resistance and Social History." *Journal of Social History* 24, no. 3 (Spring 1991): 681–85.

———. *Sugar Is Made with Blood: The Conspiracy of La Escalera and the Conflict between Empires over Slavery in Cuba*. Middletown, Conn.: Wesleyan University Press, 1988.

Paquette, Robert L., and Douglas R. Egerton. "Of Facts and Fables: New Light on the Denmark Vesey Affair." *South Carolina Historical Magazine* 105, no. 1 (January 2004): 8–48.

Paquette, Robert L., and Stanley L. Engerman, eds. *The Lesser Antilles in the Age of European Expansion*. Gainesville: University Press of Florida, 1996.

Parcero Torre, Celia María. *La pérdida de la Habana y las reformas borbónicas en Cuba, 1760–1773*. Valladolid: Junta de Castilla y León, Consejería de Educación y Cultura, 1998.

Pares, Richard. *War and Trade in the West Indies, 1739–1763*. London: Frank Cass, 1963.

Patterson, Orlando. "Slavery and Slave Revolts: A Sociohistorical Analysis of the First Maroon War, 1665–1740." In *Maroon Societies*, edited by Richard Price, 246–92. Garden City, N.Y.: Anchor Books, 1973.

———. *Slavery and Social Death: A Comparative Study*. Cambridge, Mass.: Harvard University Press, 1982.

Pérez, Louis A., Jr. *Essays on Cuban History: Historiography and Research*. Gainesville: University Press of Florida, 1995.

———. *On Becoming Cuban: Identity, Nationality, and Culture*. New York: HarperCollins, 1999.

———. *To Die in Cuba: Suicide and Society*. Chapel Hill: University of North Carolina Press, 2005.

Pérez-Cisneros, Enrique. *La abolición de la esclavitud en Cuba*. Prologue by Gaston Baquero. San José: Litografía e Imprenta LIL, 1987.

Pérez de la Riva, Juan. *El Barracón y otros ensayos*. Havana: Editorial de Ciencias Sociales, 1975.

———. *El Monto de la Inmigración Forzada en el siglo xix*. Havana: Editorial de Ciencias Sociales, 1979.

Pérez Guzmán, Francisco. *Bolívar y la independencia de Cuba*. Havana: Editorial Letras Cubanas, 1988.

Pérotin-Dumon, Anne. "Free Colored and Slaves in Revolutionary Guadeloupe: Politics and Political Consciousness." In *The Lesser Antilles in the Age of European Expansion*, edited by Robert L. Paquette and Stanley L. Engerman, 259–79. Gainesville: University Press of Florida, 1996.

Pierson, William Whatley, Jr. "Institutional History of the Intendencia." *James Sprunt Historical Studies* 19 (1927): 74–133.

Pike, Ruth. "Sevillan Society in the Sixteenth Century: Slaves and Freedmen." *Hispanic American Historical Review* 47, no. 3 (Aug. 1967): 344–59.

Poot-Herrera, Sara. "Los criollos: nota sobre su identidad y cultura." *Colonial Latin American Review*, 4:1 (1995): 177–83.

Portuondo, María M. "Plantation Factories: Science and Technology in Late-Eighteenth-Century Cuba." *Technology and Culture* 44, no. 2 (April 2003): 231–57.

Powell Jennings, Evelyn. "Forced Labor and Freedom in Havana's Public Works, 1763–1840." Paper presented at From Slavery to Freedom: Manumission in the Atlantic World, Charleston, S.C., Oct. 2000.

———. "In the Eye of the Storm: The Spanish Colonial State and African Enslavement in Havana." *Historical Reflections* 29, no. 1 (2003): 145–62.

———. "State Enslavement in Colonial Havana, 1763–1790." In *Slavery without Sugar: Diversity in Caribbean Economy and Society since the 17th Century*. Edited by Verene A. Shepherd, 152–82. Gainesville: University Press of Florida, 2002.

Queirós Mattoso, Kátia M. de. "A propósito de cartas de alforria na Bahia, 1779–1850." *Anais de historia* 4 (1972): 23–55.

Ramos, Donald. "Community, Control and Acculturation: A Case Study of Slavery in Eighteenth-Century Brazil." *Americas* 42, no. 4 (1986): 419–51.

Reid, Michele Bernita. "Negotiating a Slave Regime: Free People of Color in Cuba, 1800–1844." Master's report, University of Texas at Austin, 2000.

Reis, João José. "Différences et résistances: Les noirs à Bahia sous l'esclavage." *Cahiers d'études africaines* 32, no. 1 (1992): 15–34.

———. *Rebelião escrava no Brasil: A história do levante dos malês em 1835*. Rev. ed. São Paulo: Companhia das Letras, 2003.

———. " 'The Revolution of the Ganhadores': Urban Labour, Ethnicity and the African Strike of 1857 in Bahia, Brazil." *Journal of Latin American Studies* 29, no. 2 (May 1997): 355–93.

———. *Slave Rebellion in Brazil: The Muslim Uprising of 1835 in Bahia*. Translated by Arthur Brakel. Baltimore: Johns Hopkins University Press, 1993.

———. "Slave Resistance in Brazil: Bahia, 1807–1835." *Luso-Brazilian Review* 25, no. 1 (1988): 111–44.

Reis, João José, and Beatriz Gallotti Mamigonian. "Nagô and Mina: The Yoruba Diaspora in Brazil." In *The Yoruba Diaspora in the Atlantic World*, edited by Toyin Falola and Matt D. Childs, 77–110. Bloomington: Indiana University Press, 2004.

Rey, Nicolas. "Les Garifunas: Entre <mémoire de la résistance> aux Antilles et transmission des terres en Amérique centrale." *Cahiers d'études Africaines* 177 (2005): 131–63.

Rodríguez O., Jaime E. *The Independence of Spanish America.* Cambridge: Cambridge University Press, 1998.

Rodríguez Ochoa, Yoel. "Situación socioeconómica de la población libre de color en Santiago de Cuba: 1844–1865." Trabajo de Diploma en Licenciado, Universidad de Oriente, 1998.

Rout, Leslie B., Jr. *The African Experience in Spanish America, 1502 to the Present Day.* Cambridge: Cambridge University Press, 1976.

Rushing, Fannie Theresa. "Afro-Cuban Social Organization and Identity in a Colonial Slave Society, 1800–1888." *Colonial Latin American Historical Review* 11, no. 2 (Spring 2002): 177–201.

Russell-Wood, A. J. R. "Black and Mulatto Brotherhoods in Colonial Brazil." *Hispanic American Historical Review* 54, no. 4 (Nov. 1974): 567–602.

Saco, José Antonio. *Colección de papeles científicos, históricos, políticos, y de otros ramos sobre la isla de Cuba ya publicados, ya inéditos.* 2 vols. Paris: Imprenta de d'Aubusson y Kugelmann, 1858.

———. *Historia de la esclavitud: Desde los tiempos mas remotos hasta nuestros días.* 6 vols. 1879. Reprint, Havana: Editorial "Alfa," 1937.

Sánchez, Joseph P. "African Freedmen and the Fuero Militar: A Historical Overview of Pardo and Moreno Militiamen in the Late Spanish Empire." *Colonial Latin American Historical Review* 3, no. 2 (Spring 1994): 165–84.

Savelle, Max. *Empires to Nations: Expansion in America, 1713–1824.* Minneapolis: University of Minnesota Press, 1974.

Schmidt-Nowara, Christopher. *Empire and Antislavery: Spain, Cuba, and Puerto Rico, 1833–1874.* Pittsburgh: University of Pittsburgh Press, 1999.

———. "The End of Slavery and the End of Empire: Slave Emancipation in Cuba and Puerto Rico." *Slavery and Abolition* 21, no. 2 (Aug. 2000): 188–207.

———. "Still Continents (and an Island) with Two Histories?" *Law and History Review* 22, no. 2 (Summer 2004): 377–82.

Schwartz, Stuart B. "Colonial Identities and the Sociedad de Castas." *Colonial Latin American Review* 4, no. 1 (1995): 184–201.

———. "The Manumission of Slaves in Colonial Brazil: Bahia, 1684–1745." *Hispanic American Historical Review* 54, no. 4 (Nov. 1974): 603–35.

———. *Sugar Plantations in the Formation of Brazilian Society: Bahia, 1550–1835.* Cambridge: Cambridge University Press, 1985.

———, ed. *Tropical Babylons: Sugar and the Making of the Atlantic World.* Chapel Hill: University of North Carolina Press, 2004.

Scott, James C. *Domination and the Arts of Resistance: Hidden Transcripts.* New Haven, Conn.: Yale University Press, 1990.

———. *The Moral Economy of the Peasant: Rebellion and Subsistence in Southeast Asia.* New Haven, Conn.: Yale University Press, 1976.

———. *Seeing like a State: How Certain Schemes to Improve the Human Condition Have Failed.* New Haven, Conn.: Yale University Press, 1998.

———. *Weapons of the Weak: Everyday Forms of Peasant Resistance.* New Haven, Conn.: Yale University Press, 1985.

Scott, Julius S. "The Common Wind: Currents of Afro-American Communication in the Era of the Haitian Revolution." Ph.D. diss., Duke University, 1986.

——. "Crisscrossing Empires: Ships, Sailors, and Resistance in the Lesser Antilles in the Eighteenth Century." In *The Lesser Antilles in the Age of European Expansion*, edited by Robert L. Paquette and Stanley L. Engerman, 128–43. Gainesville: University Press of Florida, 1996.

Scott, Rebecca J. *Slave Emancipation in Cuba: The Transition to Free Labor, 1860–1899.* Princeton, N.J.: Princeton University Press, 1985.

Seed, Patricia. *Ceremonies of Possession in Europe's Conquest of the New World, 1492–1640.* Cambridge: Cambridge University Press, 1995.

Sewell, William H., Jr. "The Concept(s) of Culture." In *Beyond the Cultural Turn: New Directions in the Study of Society and Culture*, edited by Victoria E. Bonnell and Lynn Hunt, 35–61. Berkeley: University of California Press, 1999.

Shafer, R. J. *The Economic Societies in the Spanish World (1763–1821).* Syracuse, N.Y.: Syracuse University Press, 1958.

Sheridan, Richard B. "The Jamaican Slave Insurrection Scare of 1776 and the American Revolution." *Journal of Negro History* 61, no. 3 (July 1976): 290–308.

Sidbury, James. *Ploughshares into Swords: Race, Rebellion, and Identity in Gabriel's Virginia, 1730–1810.* Cambridge: Cambridge University Press, 1997.

——. "Saint Domingue in Virginia: Ideology, Local Meanings, and Resistance to Slavery, 1790–1800." *Journal of Southern History* 63, no. 3 (Aug. 1997): 531–52.

Skocpol, Theda. *States and Social Revolutions: A Comparative Analysis of France, Russia and China.* Cambridge: Cambridge University Press, 1979.

Slenes, Robert Wayne. "The Demography and Economics of Brazilian Slavery, 1850–1888." Ph.D. diss., Stanford University, 1975.

Smith, C. "Candlemas." In *New Catholic Encyclopedia.* 12 vols. New York: McGraw-Hill, 1967.

Smith, Mark M. "Remembering Mary, Shaping Revolt: Reconsidering the Stono Rebellion." *Journal of Southern History* 67, no. 3 (Aug. 2001): 513–34.

Sparks, Randy J. *The Two Princes of Calabar: An Eighteenth-Century Atlantic Odyssey.* Cambridge, Mass.: Harvard University Press, 2004.

Stinchombe, Arthur L. *Sugar Island Slavery in the Age of the Enlightenment: The Political Economy of the Caribbean World.* Princeton, N.J.: Princeton University Press, 1995.

Stolcke, Verena. *Marriage, Class and Colour in Nineteenth-Century Cuba: A Study of Racial Attitudes and Sexual Values in a Slave Society.* 2nd ed. Ann Arbor: University of Michigan Press, 1989.

Stubbs, Jean. *Tobacco on the Periphery: A Case Study in Cuban Labour History, 1860–1958.* Cambridge: Cambridge University Press, 1985.

Tannenbaum, Frank. *Slave and Citizen: The Negro in the Americas.* New York: Vintage, 1946.

Taylor, William B. *Magistrates of the Sacred: Priests and Parishioners in Eighteenth-Century Mexico.* Stanford: Stanford University Press, 1996.

Thomas, Hugh. "Cuba from the Middle of the Eighteenth Century to c. 1870." In *The Cambridge History of Latin America*, edited by Leslie Bethell, 3:277–96. Cambridge: Cambridge University Press, 1985.

——. *Cuba: The Pursuit of Freedom.* New York: Harper and Row, 1971.

——. *The Slave Trade: The Story of the Atlantic Slave Trade, 1440–1870.* New York: Simon and Schuster, 1997.

Thompson, E. P. *The Making of the English Working Class.* New York: Vintage, 1963.

——. "The Moral Economy of the English Crowd in the Eighteenth Century." *Past and Present* 50 (Feb. 1971): 76–136.

——. "Eighteenth-Century English Society: Class Struggle without Class." *Social History* 3, no. 2 (May 1978): 133–65.

Thornton, John K. *Africa and Africans in the Making of the Atlantic World, 1400–1800.* 2nd ed. Cambridge: Cambridge University Press, 1998.

——. "African Dimensions of the Stono Rebellion." *American Historical Review* 96, no. 4 (1991): 1101–13.

——. "African Soldiers in the Haitian Revolution." *Journal of Caribbean History* 25, no. 1–2 (1991): 58–80.

——. "The Coromantees: An African Cultural Group in Colonial North America and the Caribbean." *Journal of Caribbean History* 32, no. 1–2 (1998): 161–78.

——. " 'I Am the Subject of the King of Congo': African Political Ideology and the Haitian Revolution." *Journal of World History* 4, no. 2 (Fall 1993): 181–214.

——. *The Kingdom of Congo: Civil War and Transition, 1641–1718.* Madison: University of Wisconsin Press, 1983.

Tornero Tinajero, Pablo. *Crecimiento económico y transformaciones sociales: Esclavos, hacendados y comerciantes en la Cuba colonial, (1760–1840).* Madrid: Ministerio de Trabajo y Seguridad Social, 1996.

Torres-Cuevas, Eduardo. "De la ilustración reformista al reformismo liberal." In *Historia de Cuba: La colonia, evolución socioeconómica y formación nacional de los origines hasta 1867,* edited by María del Carmen Barcia, Gloria García, and Eduardo Torres-Cuevas, 314–59. Havana: Editorial Política, 1994.

Torres-Cuevas, Eduardo, and Eusebio Reyes. *Esclavitud y Sociedad: Notas y documentos para la historia de la esclavitud negra en Cuba.* Havana: Editorial de Ciencias Sociales, 1986.

Torres Lasqueti, Juan. *Colección de datos históricos-geográficos y estadísticas de Puerto Príncipe y su jurisdicción.* Havana: Imprenta "El Retiro," 1888.

Trouillot, Michel-Rolph. *Silencing the Past: Power and the Production of History.* Boston: Beacon, 1995.

Van Young, Eric. "Conclusion—Was There an Age of Revolution in Spanish America?" In *State and Society in Spanish America during the Age of Revolution,* edited by Victor M. Uribe-Uran, 219–46. Wilmington, Del.: Scholarly Resources, 2001.

——. "The Cuautla Lazarus: Double Subjectives in Reading Texts on Popular Collective Action." *Colonial Latin American Review* 2, no. 1–2 (1993): 3–26.

——. "Millennium on the Northern Marches: The Mad Messiah of Durango and Popular Rebellion in Mexico, 1800–1850." *Comparative Studies in Society and History* 28, no. 3 (1986): 385–413.

——. *The Other Rebellion: Popular Violence, Ideology, and the Mexican Struggle for Independence, 1810–1821.* Stanford, Calif.: Stanford University Press, 2001.

Victoria Ojeda, Jorge. "Jean François: De la revolución haitiana a su exilio en España." *Secuencia,* 58 (2004): 26–48.

Vinson, Ben, III. *Bearing Arms for His Majesty: The Free-Colored Militia in Colonial Mexico.* Stanford, Calif.: Stanford University Press, 2001.

——. "Race and Badge: Free-Colored Soldiers in the Colonial Mexican Militia." *Americas* 56, no. 4 (Apr. 2000): 471–96.

Vinson, Ben, III, and Stewart King, eds. " 'New' African Diasporic Military History in Latin America." Special issue, *Journal of Colonialsim and Colonial History* 5, no. 2 (Fall 2004), <http://muse.jhu.edu/journals/journal_of_colonialism_and_colonial_history/toc/cch5.2.html>. 19 May 2005.

Viotti da Costa, Emília. *Crowns of Glory, Tears of Blood: The Demerara Slave Rebellion of 1823.* New York: Oxford University Press, 1994.

Voelz, Peter M. *Slave and Soldier: The Military Impact of Blacks in the Colonial Americas.* New York: Garland, 1993.

Walker, Daniel E. "Colony versus Crown: Raising Black Troops for the British Seige on Havana, 1762." *Journal of Caribbean History* 33, no. 1–2 (1999): 74–83.

——. *No More, No More: Slavery and Cultural Resistance in Havana and New Orleans.* Minneapolis: University of Minnesota Press, 2004.

Williams, Eric. "The Negro Slave Trade in Anglo-Spanish Relations." *Caribbean Historical Review* 1 (Dec. 1950): 22–45.

Yacou, Alain. "La conspiración de Aponte (1812)." *Historia y Sociedad* (Puerto Rico) 1 (1988): 39–58.

——. "Esclaves et libres français a Cuba au lendemain de la revolution Saint-Domingue." *Jahrbuch für Geschichte vont Staat, Wirtschaft und Gesellschaft Lateinamerikas,* 28 (1991): 163–98.

——. "La Insurgencia Negra en la Isla de Cuba en la primera mitad del siglo XIX." *Revista de Indias* 53, no. 197 (1993): 23–51.

——. "La présence française dans la parte occidentale de l'île de Cuba au lendemain de la Revolution de Saint-Domingue." *Revue française d'histoire d'outre-mer* 74, no. 2 (1987): 149–88.

Zanetti, Oscar. "Realidades y urgencias de la historiografía social en Cuba." *Temas* 1 ( Jun.– Mar. 1995): 119–28.

Zanetti, Oscar, and Alejandro García. *Sugar and Railroads: A Cuban History, 1837–1959.* Translated by Franklin W. Knight and Mary Todd. Chapel Hill: University of North Carolina Press, 1998.

Zaragoza, Justo. *Las insurrecciones en Cuba: Apuntes para la historia política de esta isla en el presente siglo.* 2 vols. Madrid: Imprenta de Manuel G. Hernández, 1872–73.

Zeuske, Michael. "The Cimarrón in the Archives: A Re-Reading of Miguel Barnet's Biography of Esteban Montejo." *New West Indian Guide* 71, no. 3–4 (1997): 265–79.

# Index

Barrera y Domingo, Francisco, 54–55, 58

Barreto, Candelaria (slave), 129

Barreto, María Teresa (master), 129

Barreto, Teresa (free black), 108, 113, 114, 115

Barriaga, Maria Francisca (slave), 128

Barriaga, Miguel (master), 128

Bauer, Alice and Raymond, 15

Bavo (slave), 44

Bayamo, 44, 57, 65, 88, 94, 127, 149–50, 157–58, 165

Bayamo conspiracy, 2, 127–33; involvement of English slaves in, 45, 131–32; links to Puerto Príncipe rebellion, 128–29, 130–31, 148; and denouncement of rebellion, 128–29, 175; meetings to plan, 128–31, 133; and *cabildos de nación*, 130–31; execution and punishment for, 132; links to Holguín conspiracy, 148; and freedom offered to slaves for denouncing rebellion, 175. *See also* Aponte Rebellion

Belaguer, Joaquín (free black), 124, 127

Belen, María (slave), 56

Bell, David, 96

Benito (slave), 56

Bergad, Laird, 65

Betancourt, Juan René, 11–12

Biassou, Georges, 93, 164–65

Bight of Benin, 49–50

Bight of Biafra, 102, 237–38 (n. 141)

Blackness, 71–74, 99–100, 118, 188. *See also* Race

Blacks, 66, 72–73; interactions with whites, 74–75. *See also* Race; Slaves

Blanco, Manuel (free black), 82, 110, 112–13

Bolívar, Simón, 31

Borrego, José Ramón (slave), 132–33

Borrego, Pilar (free black), 145, 153, 176–77

Bourbon Reforms, 26–27, 48–49, 80, 82, 215 (n. 34)

*Bozales*, 39, 51–53, 99–100, 104, 108, 190, 259 (n. 3)

Bravo, José María, 75

Brazilian slavery, 33, 101, 104, 184–85, 186, 238 (n. 142)

Britain: rumored to aid Aponte Rebellion, 18, 122–23, 160–61; occupation of Havana by, 24–26, 41, 80–82, 145; antislavery actions of, 29–30, 37–38, 50–51, 160–61, 182–83; and Haitian Revolution, 40, 42

British Caribbean: slaves from, 43–45, 103, 129, 131–32, 160–61; connections to Cuba, 44–45, 221–22 (n. 158); compared to Cuba, 70, 129, 182–84; slave revolts in, 182–84

Brotherhoods, religious, 101–2, 117, 155

Buenos Aires, 32, 101

Bustamante, Antonio (master), 175

Caballero, Juan Domingo, 66

Cabaña, La (military fort and prison), 1, 4, 47, 95

*Cabildos de nación*, 18, 95–100, 103–19, 187–88; links to rebellion, 95, 108, 119, 123–24, 130–31, 144, 188; defined, 96–97, 236 (n. 119); functions of, 97, 111, 114–17; and slaves, 97–99, 108–9, 111; leadership of, 97–99, 108–15; and Creoles, 97–100, 104, 107–8, 110; dances and festivals of, 101–2, 106–9, 117–18; similarities with African societies, 102–3; growth of, 104–5, 110–11; as seen by whites, 105–6, 111–12, 117–18; and mulattos, 107; and free people of color militia, 107, 112–13; as surrogate for family, 107, 240 (n. 183); membership rights in, 107–8, 110, 113–14, 116–17; and *bozales*, 108; purchase of freedom for slaves by, 109, 116–17; as lending institutions, 109, 116–17; and members from different ethnicities, 109–10; and elections, 111–16; female participation in, 113–15; finances and savings of, 114–18; rural and urban members of, 115–16, 130

Cabrajal, Pedro (overseer), 123

Cabrera, Francisco (master), 89

Cabrera, Margarita (slave), 61

Cabrera, María Ramona (mulatta slave), 68–69

Cádiz, 32, 49, 93, 147, 158, 164, 166, 174

Calabar, Old, 102

Calcagno, Francisco, 10

Calderón, Domingo, 168

Calvo, Javier (free black), 86

Calvo, Nicolás, 58

Cameroon, 49–50

Canary Islands, 57, 225 (n. 53)

(n. 102). See also *Coartación*; *Código Negro Español*

*Libro de pinturas*, 3–4, 25–28, 53–54, 80–82, 91, 151, 156, 168–69, 210 (n. 28), 256 (n. 99)

Lima, Peru, 101

Lisundia, Juan Bautista (free black): role in rebellion, 61–63, 76–77, 78, 120–22, 139–43, 145–47, 163; execution of, 62, 120, 155; and Kongo nation, 108, 144

Literacy: role in Aponte Rebellion, 62, 84–85, 181–82, 184–85

London, 51, 133, 182

López, Benigno, 23

López, Pedro, 70

Louisiana, 82

Louverture, Toussaint, 3, 40–41, 47, 93, 164–65, 168; as coachman, 47

Lovejoy, Paul, 33, 53, 102

Luango *cabildo de nación*, 105

Lucumi, 96, 101, 104, 105, 162

Lucumi *cabildo de nación*, 104–5, 108, 110–11, 112, 117, 176

Lucumi Llane *cabildo de nación*, 108, 118

Luis (free black), 140

Lusado, María (master), 142–43

Machado, José Joaquín (slave), 22

Malagamba, Santiago (master), 158

Malê Rebellion (Brazil), 33, 184–85, 189

Mandinga, José María (slave), 175

Mandinga *cabildo de nación*, 105

Mandingas, 60, 101, 124, 140, 157, 162

Manumission, 63–65, 68, 89, 227 (n. 102)

Manzanillo, 132

Manzano, Juan Francisco (slave), 86, 138–39

Margarita (island), 82

María Antonia (slave), 66

María Belen (slave), 161

María Candelaria (slave), 159

Marino, Miguel (slave), 52

Maroons, 76, 87–88, 127

Maroon War, Second Jamaican, 42–43

Márquez, José de Jesús, 10

Márquez, Santiago, 135

Marriage, 106; interracial marriage, 71–73; between slaves and free people of color, 89

Martínez, Agustín (free black), 85, 88

Martínez Malo, Félix, 81

Martinique, 32, 162

Masters. *See* Slaveowners; Slavery

Matanzas, 58, 153

Mateo (slave), 106–7

Maximo (slave), 123

Mederos, José, 60

Medrano, Rafael (slave), 174

Meléndez (Puerto Rico governor), 163

Mellet, Julian, 59, 167

Mexico, 170–71; and free people of color militia, 82, 91, 233 (n. 55)

Middle Passage. *See* Slave trade

Militia, free people of color, 17–18, 52, 73–74, 78–95, 176, 187; Aponte's involvement in, 3; links to Aponte Rebellion, 3, 78–80, 94–95, 119, 140, 143–46, 155, 177; and Seven Years' War, 25–26; and American Revolution, 27–28, 216 (n. 42); guarding of slave ships by, 52, 87, 94; and racial identity, 73–74, 87–89, 91–92, 94, 233 (n. 38); deference to whites by, 80–81, 232 (n. 21); history of, 80–82; expansion of, 82–83, 85, 88; and *fuero* rights, 83–86, 91–92, 95, 97, 113, 146, 177; exercises, drills, and regulations of, 86, 91, 93–94; uniforms of, 86, 167–68; artisans in, 86–87; occupations and professions of, 86–87, 234 (n. 63); relationship with slaves, 87–90, 229 (n. 135); as slaveowners, 88–90, 94; as threat, 89–95; in Mexico, 91; treated like slaves, 91–92, 94; in Haitian Revolution, 93–94, 164–68, 180–81; and *cabildos de nación*, 107, 112–13, 119; and suppression of rebellion, 125, 234 (n. 75)

Miller, Joseph, 96

Minas, 96, 105, 128, 162

Mina and Mandinga *cabildo de nación* (Bayamo), 106, 107, 109, 130–31

Mina Guagni *cabildo de nación*, 95–99, 104, 107, 108–9, 113, 119, 144, 237 (n. 133)

Mintz, Sidney, 15, 61

Mobile, Alabama, 82

Monarchism, 18, 157–62, 169–71

Mondongo *cabildo de nación*, 105

Monroe, James, 133

Montalban (plantation), 1, 123

Montaño, Luisa (slave), 59–60

Montavlo, Luis (slave), 67

suses, 55–56, 69; indigenous population, 56

Portuonodo, Tomás (slave), 75

Poveda, Tomás (free black), 112

Puerto Príncipe, 66–67, 75, 77, 92, 122, 149–50, 157

Puerto Príncipe audiencia, 71–72, 122

Puerto Príncipe rebellion, 1–2, 122–27; meetings to plan, 122–24; and plantation revolts, 123; and *cabildos de nación*, 123–24; suppression of, 125; execution and punishment for, 125–27, 174–75; links to Bayamo conspiracy, 128–29, 130–31, 148; links to Holguín conspiracy, 135, 148; and freedom offered to slaves for denouncing rebellion, 174–75. *See also* Aponte Rebellion

Puerto Príncipe town council, 31–32, 45, 66, 75–76, 125, 127, 149, 173–74, 178

Puerto Rico, 82, 163, 176

Punishment: for rebellion, 2–4, 21, 46–47, 61–62, 78, 95, 120, 125–27, 132, 136–38, 146–47, 152, 155, 159–60, 173, 175–76, 189–90; of slaves, 36–37, 42, 52, 57–60, 106, 130–31, 138–39, 218 (n. 95); encoded by race, 57–58

Quakers, 29

Rabelo, Isabel (master), 123

Race: racial categories, 17, 48, 56–57, 68–71, 72–74, 96, 98–100, 104, 118–19, 186–87, 230 (n. 156); and *sociedad de castas*, 27; black population, 54–55; and labor stereotypes, 57, 224–25 (n. 52), 225 (n. 53); punishments specific to, 57–58; symbolism of, 57–58; free people of color population, 62–63, 68–71; interracial marriage, 71–73; and free people of color militia, 73–74, 79–82, 85, 87–89, 91–92, 94; and *cabildos de nación*, 97–100, 112–13, 115, 118–19

Rafaela (slave), 108

Recôncavo, 184

Reis, João José, 189

Rendón, Juan Ignacio: judicial investigation by, 1, 4–8, 25, 47, 147, 151–54, 155, 177

Revillagigedo (Mexican viceroy), 91

Reyes, Domingo (master), 67

Ribero, Antonio (free black), 108

Ribero, Daniel (free black), 87

Richardson, David, 102

Richmond, Virginia, 133, 181–82

Rigaud, André, 28, 41

Rio de Janeiro, 169

Rivafecha, María Gertrudis, 72

Roca, Luis (master), 67

Rochambeau (French general), 42

Rodríguez, Lazaro (free black), 113

Rodríguez, Rafael (free mulatto), 107

Rodríguez, Ramón, 75

Romay, Tomás, 35, 37–38, 53

Rosario (plantation), 3, 142–43

Royalism, 18, 157–62, 169–71. *See also* Monarchism

Ruan, José María, 77

Ruíz, Juan (free black), 107

Runaway slaves, 130, 132–33, 135, 149; and Spanish sanctuary policy, 43–44; urban runaway slaves, 66–67, 70, 76; and free people of color militia, 87–88

Rural society: connections to urban society, 46–48, 62, 75–77, 115–16, 138–39, 186, 190

Russia, 169–70

Saco, José Antonio, 11

Saenz, José María, 174

Saint Augustine, Florida, 2, 93, 126–27, 165

Saint Domingue, 21, 27–29, 30, 42–43, 131, 163, 170, 186; as seen by Cubans, 35, 37, 39–40, 70, 89–90, 106, 159; French émigrés to Cuba from, 39–40, 122, 150; slaves from, 51–52, 131–32. *See also* Haiti; Haitian Revolution

Salud (Havana neighborhood), 155

San Antonio Abad, 167

San Blas Chiquito festival (Bayamo), 128–30, 158

San Blas festival (Bayamo), 117, 128–30, 158

Sánchez, Esteban (free mulatto), 144

San José (plantation), 1, 123

San Juan de Uloa (military fort), 137

San Lazaro (Havana neighborhood), 52

Santa Ana (plantation), 3, 121, 140, 142–43

Santa Ana, José Manuel (free mulatto), 78

Santa Clara, 132

Santa Cruz, Agustín (free black), 84–85

people of color militia, 91–93; on *cabildos de nación*, 113; on rebellion, 122–23, 124, 132, 133, 138–40, 146, 151, 153–54, 160, 163, 166, 178

Spanish American wars for independence, 22, 31–32, 134; and emancipation, 31

Spanish king: rumored to be source of emancipation decree, 159, 170–71

Spanish sanctuary policy, 43–44

Stolcke, Verena, 72

Stono Revolt (South Carolina), 33, 43

Suangos *cabildo de nación*, 105

Sugar production: Cuban expansion of, 35, 48, 53–54, 61, 66, 68, 76, 104, 186

Suicide: by slaves, 60

Tamayo, Antonio (free black), 45

Tamayo, Blas (free black), 106–7, 130, 132

Tamayo, José María (free black), 2, 128, 130–33, 148

Tamayo, Juan (free black), 22, 132

Tamayo, Juan (master), 130

Ten Years' War, 10

Ternero, Salvador (free black): role in 1809 riot against French, 95; and free people of color militia, 95, 97, 113, 119, 144–46; and plans for rebellion, 95, 119, 143–47, 152, 165, 167, 168–69; execution of, 95, 120, 155; arrests prior to 1812, 95–96; and *cabildos de nación*, 95–99, 104, 105, 107–10, 113, 119, 144, 237 (n. 133); arrest in 1812, 146

Thomas, Hugh, 224–25 (n. 52)

Thomas, William (slave), 49–51, 61

Thompson, E. P., 16

Thornton, John, 33, 105, 162

Tinoco, Pablo Felix (master), 138

Tobago, 129

Torres, Esteban (free black), 113

Torture, 7–8, 36, 52, 57–58

Treaty of Paris (1763), 24

Treolar, Tomás, 101

Trinidad (plantation), 3, 46–47, 121, 142–43

Trinidad (slave), 67

Trinidad (town), 91

Trouillot, Michel-Rolph, 69

United States slavery, 33, 35, 37, 42, 68, 117

Uruguay, 82

Urban society: connections to rural society, 46–48, 62, 75–77, 115–16, 138–39, 186, 190; opportunities for freedom in, 64–69

Urbina (Santiago governor), 134–37, 149

Uribe, José (free black), 82

Vaillant, Juan Bautista (free black), 159

Vaillant, Antonio, 74

Valdés, Antonio, 9, 151

Valdés Melchor (master), 138, 158

Valdés, Tomás (master), 56

Valiente, Juan Baptista (free black), 34, 107

Van Young, Eric, 170–71

Varela, Felix, 11

Vásquez, Antonio José (slave), 128

Vásquez, Felipe (free mulatto), 89

Vásquez, Manuel (free black), 98–99, 107–8, 110

Vásquez Tamayo, Lorenzo (master), 2, 128

Velásquez, José Antonio, 73–74

Velásquez, Manuel José, 73–74

Venezuela, 31, 82

Vesey, Denmark, conspiracy (Charleston, S.C.), 41, 237–38 (n. 141)

Vicente (slave), 124

Villaverde, Cirilo, 9–10

Villegas, Juana (free black), 128

Virginia, 133

Washington, George, 3, 28, 214–15 (n. 20)

West Africa: as origin of slaves, 49–50, 52–53

Whiteness, 72–74, 112–13, 188. *See also* Blackness; Race

Whites: interactions with blacks, 74–75

Wilberforce, William, 29

Xavier, Francisco (Indian), 74

Xavier, Francisco (slave), 157–58

Yacou, Alain, 13

Yoruba, 32–33, 102–3, 104, 105, 144–45, 184, 240–41 (n. 206)

Zanetti, Oscar, 16

Zaragoza, Justo, 10

Zavedra, Francisco (slaveowner), 34, 37

Zorilla, Lucas (free mulatto), 83

# Envisioning Cuba

Matt D. Childs, *The 1812 Aponte Rebellion in Cuba and the Struggle against Atlantic Slavery* (2006).

Eduardo González, *Cuba and the Tempest: Literature and Cinema in the Time of Diaspora* (2006).

John Lawrence Tone, *War and Genocide in Cuba, 1895–1898* (2006).

Samuel Farber, *The Origins of the Cuban Revolution Reconsidered* (2006).

Lillian Guerra, *The Myth of José Martí: Conflicting Nationalisms in Early Twentieth-Century Cuba* (2005).

Rodrigo Lazo, *Writing to Cuba: Filibustering and Cuban Exiles in the United States* (2005).

Alejandra Bronfman, *Measures of Equality: Social Science, Citizenship, and Race in Cuba, 1902–1940* (2004).

Edna M. Rodríguez-Mangual, *Lydia Cabrera and the Construction of an Afro-Cuban Cultural Identity* (2004).

Gabino La Rosa Corzo, *Runaway Slave Settlements in Cuba: Resistance and Repression* (2003).

Piero Gleijeses, *Conflicting Missions: Havana, Washington, and Africa, 1959–1976* (2002).

Robert Whitney, *State and Revolution in Cuba: Mass Mobilization and Political Change, 1920–1940* (2001).

Alejandro de la Fuente, *A Nation for All: Race, Inequality, and Politics in Twentieth-Century Cuba* (2001).

CPSIA information can be obtained
at www.ICGtesting.com
Printed in the USA
LVOW08s2037271216
518858LV00003B/132/P

9 780807 857724